For Better and
For Worse

For Better and For Worse

Welfare Reform and the Well-Being of Children and Families

Greg J. Duncan

P. Lindsay Chase-Lansdale

Editors

Russell Sage Foundation ♦ New York

The Russell Sage Foundation

The Russell Sage Foundation, one of the oldest of America's general purpose foundations, was established in 1907 by Mrs. Margaret Olivia Sage for "the improvement of social and living conditions in the United States." The Foundation seeks to fulfill this mandate by fostering the development and dissemination of knowledge about the country's political, social, and economic problems. While the Foundation endeavors to assure the accuracy and objectivity of each book it publishes, the conclusions and interpretations in Russell Sage Foundation publications are those of the authors and not of the Foundation, its Trustees, or its staff. Publication by Russell Sage, therefore, does not imply Foundation endorsement.

Library of Congress Cataloging-in-Publication Data

For better and for worse : welfare reform and the well-being of children and families/ Greg J. Duncan, P. Lindsay Chase-Lansdale, editors.
        p. cm.
    Includes bibliographical references and index.
    ISBN 0-87154-245-5
  1. Child welfare—United States. 2. Family services—United States. 3. Public welfare—United States. I. Duncan, Greg J. II. Chase-Lansdale, P. Lindsay.
HV741.F66 2002
362.7'0973—dc21
                                         2001041785

The paper used in this publication meets the minimum requirements of American National Standard for Information Sciences—Permanence of Paper for Printed Library Materials. ANSI Z39.48-1992.

Text design by Suzanne Nichols

RUSSELL SAGE FOUNDATION
112 East 64th Street, New York, New York 10021
10 9 8 7 6 5 4 3 2 1

Contents

Contents

Contributors

P. Lindsay Chase-Lansdale is professor and chair of the doctoral program in human development and social policy in the School of Education and Social Policy and faculty fellow in the Institute for Policy Research at Northwestern University.

Greg J. Duncan is professor in the School of Education and Social Policy and a faculty associate in the Institute for Policy Research at Northwestern University. He is also director of the Northwestern University/University of Chicago Joint Center for Poverty Research.

David M. Casey is postdoctoral research fellow at the Elliot-Pearson Department of Child Development at Tufts University.

Danielle A. Crosby is research scientist in the Department of Human Ecology at the University of Texas at Austin.

Sandra K. Danziger is associate professor in the School of Social Work at the University of Michigan.

Kristina Daugirdas was research assistant at the Center on Budget and Policy Priorities.

Rachel E. Dunifon is assistant professor in the Department of Policy Analysis and Management at Cornell University.

Kathryn Edin is associate professor of sociology and faculty fellow at the Institute for Policy Research at Northwestern University.

Paula England is professor of sociology and research associate at the Institute for Policy Research at Northwestern University.

Nancy Folbre is professor of economics at the University of Massachusetts and cochair of the MacArthur Foundation Research Network on the Family and the Economy.

Thomas L. Gais is director of the Federalism Research Group at the Rockefeller Institute of Government, State University of New York.

Ron Haskins is a senior fellow at the Brookings Institution and a senior consultant at the Annie E. Casey Foundation.

Contributors

Ann E. Horvath-Rose is an economist at the Cornell Center for Policy Research in Washington, D.C.

Aletha C. Huston is Priscilla Pond Flawn Regents Professor of human development and family sciences at the University of Texas at Austin.

Cathy M. Johnson is associate professor of political science at Williams College.

Ariel Kalil is assistant professor in the Harris School of Public Policy at the University of Chicago.

Andrew S. London is associate professor of sociology at Kent State University.

Joan Maya Mazelis is doctoral candidate at the University of Pennsylvania.

Rashmita S. Mistry is postdoctoral research fellow at the Center for Developmental Science, University of North Carolina at Chapel Hill.

Kristin Anderson Moore is president and senior scholar at Child Trends in Washington, D.C.

H. Elizabeth Peters is professor of policy analysis and management at Cornell University.

Wendell Primus is director of income security at the Center on Budget and Policy Priorities.

Marika N. Ripke is a research scientist in the Department of Human Ecology at the University of Texas at Austin.

Jennifer L. Romich is doctoral candidate in human development and social policy at Northwestern University.

Ellen K. Scott is assistant professor of sociology at the University of Oregon.

Jack Tweedie is director of the Children and Families Program at the National Conference of State Legislatures in Denver.

Morgan B. Ward Doran is doctoral student in the Human Development and Social Policy program at Northwestern University.

Alan Weil is director of the Assessing the New Federalism project at the Urban Institute.

Thomas S. Weisner is professor of anthropology in the Departments of Psychiatry (Center for Culture and Health) and Anthropology at the University of California, Los Angeles.

W. Jean Yeung is research scientist and adjunct associate professor in the Department of Sociology at New York University.

Part I

Introduction and Policy Context

Chapter 1

For Better and For Worse: Welfare Reform and the Well-Being of Children and Families

Greg J. Duncan and P. Lindsay Chase-Lansdale

A new era in social welfare began when President Bill Clinton signed the Personal Responsibility and Work Opportunity Reconciliation Act (PRWORA) on August 22, 1996. Following six decades of guaranteed government aid for economically deprived children, the new bill eliminated the open-ended federal entitlement program, Aid to Families with Dependent Children (AFDC), provided block grants for states to impose strict work requirements and to set time limits on cash assistance, and made other sweeping changes affecting child care, the Food Stamp program, the Supplemental Security Income (SSI) program for children, and the Child Support Enforcement program. In addition, this legislation gives states numerous options, such as requiring employment of mothers with very young children, capping benefits so payments do not increase if recipients have additional children, and denying assistance to unmarried teen parents and their children.

The new state-designed welfare reforms appear to be stunningly effective. Caseloads fell by approximately half between 1993 and 2000, with many of the welfare exits accompanied by sustained involvement in the labor market. Politically, all sides seem to agree that the reforms have been successful, although there is disagreement on how best to focus future policy efforts, especially as reauthorization of PRWORA approaches in 2002.

Lost in the caseload counts and political rhetoric is the subject of our book: the effect of welfare reforms on children's well-being and development. Despite the professed child-based goals of the reform legislation, remarkably little attention has been paid to tracking and understanding its effect on family functioning and child well-being. Caseload declines have been dramatic, but caseload declines do not necessarily translate into enhanced family and child well-being.

To be sure, the debate surrounding welfare reform was filled with assumptions and predictions about those reforms and their effects on children. Conservative advocates argued that reform-induced transitions from welfare to work would benefit children by creating positive role models of their mothers, promoting maternal self-esteem and sense of control, introducing productive daily routines into family life, and eventually fostering career advancement and higher earnings for parents. Most prominently, conservatives argued that the reforms would eliminate our welfare "culture" by sending a powerful message to teens and young women that it is in their interest to postpone childbearing until they can support their children within the context of marriage. Opponents argued that the reforms would overwhelm severely stressed parents, deepen the poverty of many families, force young children into unsafe and unstimulating child care situations, and reduce parents' ability to monitor the behavior of their older children, leading to problems in child and adolescent functioning.

To sort through the conflicting theories and evidence regarding the effect of welfare reform on children, we organized two national conferences under the auspices of the Northwestern University/University of Chicago Joint Center for Poverty Research. The first, held in Chicago in May 1998, and less than a year after most states first implemented their reforms, featured papers with disciplinary perspectives on family process and child development as well as empirical papers on links among employment, family process, and child development, using data that predated the 1996 reforms. The second, held in Washington, D.C., in September 1999, featured papers that addressed, with more recent data, important research and policy questions concerning the initial effect of the reforms on low-income families. For this volume, we selected about half of the papers presented at the two conferences and asked authors to update them in light of recent developments.

We are very grateful to the Assistant Secretary for Planning and Evaluation, Department of Health and Human Services; the Annie E. Casey Foundation; and the John D. and Catherine T. MacArthur Foundation for generously supporting these conferences.

ORGANIZATION OF THE BOOK

The volume begins with a history of the 1996 reforms by Ron Haskins. Haskins provides a historical and political context for the volume by reviewing the development of the liberal welfare state between 1935 and 1972 and offering insightful analyses of social legislation during this period. His lively political history of the reforms shows how conservatives capitalized on both President Clinton's pledge to "end welfare as we know it" and public concerns over such social problems as out-of-wedlock childbearing and the surging welfare caseloads of the early 1990s, generating the broad political support needed for the radical reforms of 1996. Haskins was chief of staff for the Ways and Means Subcommittee on Human Resources in the U.S. House of Representatives and thus provides an insider's perspective on this history.

The rest of the volume is organized into three sections, "What States Are Thinking and Doing," "How Families and Children Are Faring," and "Policy Approaches and Options for the Future."

WHAT STATES ARE THINKING AND DOING

Given the striking change in welfare policy to decentralize authority from the federal government to the states, we designed this section to address key issues in state policymaking. Cathy M. Johnson and Thomas L. Gais set the stage, summarizing lessons drawn from the Rockefeller Institute of Government's State Capacity Study, an ambitious project that examines how nineteen states are implementing welfare reform. The authors present three theories of how state policies on welfare reform implementation may affect child well-being: family structure theory, resource theory, and environmental theory. Family structure theory argues that states' top priority is to promote marriage as the key factor in healthy child development. Resource theory and environmental theory emphasize employment as the way to improve child well-being, with the former focusing on policies that improve family income and the latter assuming that children benefit from employed parents because of the experiences of routine, order, and discipline. Johnson and Gais then analyze which theory is best reflected in state implementation of reforms and best illustrates states' decisions and policies.

Kristin Anderson Moore, president of Child Trends, describes her experiences working with state welfare officials to develop a data collection agenda for evaluating the effects on children and families of the many welfare waiver experiments of the early 1990s. She details the process of finding common ground between researchers and state policymakers to articulate how welfare reform might affect children and families in addition to how states might assess child and family outcomes. Moore demonstrates how such collaborations between child and family researchers and state welfare administrators are essential for understanding the effect of welfare reform within and across states.

Alan Weil is a leader of the Urban Institute's large-scale project, Assessing the New Federalism. His chapter focuses on devolution per se and asks the question, Does state flexibility in program design yield more effective welfare policies? Using data from the Urban Institute project, Weil explores why states have taken different approaches to implementing reforms and develops a typology of states based on the mixture of carrots and sticks they use. He demonstrates considerable diversity in states' approaches to caseload reduction, work supports, and work requirements and concludes that state flexibility in implementing welfare reform may be a contributing factor to current successes. He cautions, however, that it remains to be seen whether devolution leads to policies that are more effective in protecting children in poverty.

The final chapter in this section is by Jack Tweedie, director of the Children and Families Program at the National Conference of State Legislatures. Tweedie has worked closely with eight states in their efforts to track cohorts of welfare recipients, as many leave the welfare rolls because of sanctions and time limits. His chapter summarizes the mixed picture that emerges from these efforts, showing significant numbers of families leaving welfare both because of state sanction policies and because fewer families reach the time limits. Moreover, limited data from these eight states indicate that those who have left the welfare rolls because of sanctions or time limits have lower levels of employment and earnings than do other exiters. Tweedie focuses the spotlight on the dearth of information on sanction and time limit policies and how these may affect children.

HOW FAMILIES AND CHILDREN ARE FARING

This section consists of data-driven analyses of likely and actual changes in child well-being and family functioning brought about by the reforms. Greg J. Duncan, Rachel Dunifon, Morgan Ward Doran, and W. Jean Yeung use prereform data from two national longitudinal surveys to examine differences in family process, maternal mental health, and child well-being among families with different patterns of welfare, work, wages, and family structure. Arguing that differences between low-socioeconomic status (SES) welfare-reliant families and working families provide an upper-bound estimate of changes that might be expected from welfare reform, they find remarkably few differences between the two types of families but much larger differences between them and higher income and intact families.

The sociologists Ellen K. Scott, Kathryn Edin, Andrew S. London, and Joan Maya Mazelis summarize findings from a large-scale ethnographic study of how welfare reform is playing out in poor neighborhoods in Cleveland and Philadelphia. The surprise is the extent to which welfare-reliant mothers believe that current welfare policies have negative consequences for families and that reform-inspired jobs will help raise families' material standard of living. Less surprising are the many concerns these mothers have for minimizing the adverse effects of their increased work hours on their children's well-being.

One of the most ambitious studies tracking welfare leavers is the Women's Employment Study, directed by Sandra Danziger and Sheldon Danziger of the University of Michigan. Ariel Kalil, Rachel E. Dunifon, and Sandra K. Danziger summarize the results of two rounds of interviews with a representative sample of women who had been receiving welfare in the early stages of Michigan's ambitious reforms. Their chapter focuses on how children are affected by their mothers' transitions from welfare to work. They find no evidence that children are harmed by such transitions; if anything, their mothers report that their children are better behaved and have better mental health.

Although a number of family- and child-focused welfare reform experiments were in progress at the time of our conferences, only the Milwaukee New Hope project had completed its evaluation. The developmental psychologists Rashmita S. Mistry, Danielle A. Crosby, Aletha C. Huston, David M. Casey, and Marika Ripke summarize the strong, positive effects of the comprehensive set of work-conditioned supports on the achievement and behavior of boys in New Hope families. Their findings point to the importance of work supports for families, and their chapter suggests that parents use increased earnings from employment to enrich their children's experiences by means of child care, after-school, and extracurricular programs.

Experimental programs such as the New Hope program feature wage supplements in order to make work pay. Federal policy has moved in the direction of wage supplements through the expansion of the Earned Income Tax Credit (EITC) in the mid-1990s, and states can also provide such work supports by establishing or expanding their own EITC programs. Using results from intensive interviews with Milwaukee single mothers, Jennifer L. Romich and Thomas Weisner document the nearly universal salience of federal and state EITC programs in Wisconsin, explain why mothers prefer that it be paid in a single lump sum rather than monthly, and show how families use it.

One of the stated goals of the 1996 reforms was to reduce nonmarital childbearing, particularly among teenagers. The economists Ann Horvath-Rose and H. Elizabeth Peters use state differences in the timing and structure of welfare waiver provisions of the early 1990s to infer which provisions affect nonmarital childbearing. Their findings suggest that family cap waivers implemented by states are linked to reductions in nonmarital births.

POLICY APPROACHES AND OPTIONS FOR THE FUTURE

A clear message leading up to passage of PRWORA in 1996 is that the American public has all but abandoned the view that programs should provide a universal safety net in favor of what has been called an "employment-contingent social contract." The prevailing view is that every able-bodied family in the United States, regardless of income level or family responsibility, should seek employment before turning to the government for support. Rights of working families might include wage supplements, child care, health insurance, and other supports. As PRWORA is reauthorized in 2002, one focus will include debates over whether and how to strengthen work supports in the future. In addition, policymakers will address the fact that a number of families have not or will not successfully move into the labor force and thus risk losing cash benefits because of sanctions and time limits. Research and policy issues for these families are very different, including such matters as barriers to employment, the effect on children of living in deep poverty and residential instability, and the "carrying capacity" of kin networks.

The chapters in the final section provide differing perspectives on policy options for the future. Wendell Primus, former chief of staff for the Ways and Means Subcommittee on Human Resources and now at the Center for Budget and Policy Priorities, and coauthor Kristina Daugirdas highlight the fact that falling caseloads have not always led to increased family incomes, and they propose a set of additional reforms to reduce child poverty. The sociologist Paula England and the economist Nancy Folbre develop policy recommendations that recognize the value of mothers' formal labor market work as well as their informal, child-related work. Although celebrating the successes of the 1996 reforms, Ron Haskins provides his own set of recommendations for additional policy changes that would both improve our nation's work supports as well as its safety net.

In the book's final chapter, we pull together the most important lessons gleaned from these chapters. We find many grounds for optimism. Welfare reform, the expansion of the EITC, and booming economic conditions have combined to bring many mothers into the labor force, lift some children out of poverty, and perhaps even reduce the number of teens' nonmarital births. What is true for some families and children, however, does not hold for all, so our optimism is tempered. The most comprehensive data on positive child outcomes emerge from experimental antipoverty programs, and it remains to be seen whether most states will be as generous in their work support policies. Moreover, we know the least about the fortunes of families that are unable to leave the welfare rolls or that face the most barriers to securing permanent jobs that will lift their families from poverty.

The next few years will continue to be a remarkably favorable time for state experimentation with innovative approaches for assisting low-wage families in gaining a permanent foothold in the formal labor market. We emphasize the many ways in which state efforts can be directed toward an important—and forgotten—role of welfare reform: enhancing the well-being and life chances of poor children.

Chapter 2

Liberal and Conservative Influences on the Welfare Reform Legislation of 1996

Ron Haskins

B etween the Great Depression and the congressional elections of 1994, liberals had dominated the formation of American social policy. This dominance was so complete that even one of the two or three most important Republicans since the end of World War II, Richard Nixon, was a protoliberal in most matters of domestic policy. In neat Hegelian fashion, this liberal dominance produced a reaction against federal social programs, which culminated in substantial changes in social policy following the Republican sweep of Congress in 1994.

The reaction was prompted in part by the failure of many social programs to achieve their goals. As the noted program evaluator Peter Rossi (1987) would have it, if predictions are based on what is known from scientific evaluations, the expected net effect of any new social intervention is zero. The problems with American social policy, however, run much deeper than the mere failure of a few programs. The American people appear to have rejected some of the most fundamental tenets of liberal social policy, if indeed they ever agreed with them. Consider the following dichotomy. On one side are social programs that provide benefits to people who are not expected by the American public to work. The Social Security programs, which provide cash for the elderly and the disabled and their dependents, lead the list of these popular programs. On the other side are welfare programs for the able-bodied, such as the Aid to Families with Dependent Children (AFDC) program. These programs are suspect because American taxpayers expect able-bodied adults to support themselves and their families.

The welfare system as it existed on the eve of the Republican takeover of Congress in 1994 provided many benefits to many people, especially single mothers and their children. It also, however, violated the instincts and values of the American public by providing generous benefits to millions of able-bodied adults. My purpose in this chapter is to examine the arguments put forth by liberals and conservatives as they struggled to change a welfare system that all conservatives and many liberals regarded as deeply flawed. I review the emergence of the liberal welfare state between 1935 and 1972, examine several weaknesses in the programs that portended difficulty, assess the underlying factors that shaped the welfare debate of 1993 to 1996, and then examine the goals of liberals and conservatives as they shaped the reform legislation President Bill Clinton signed into law on August 22, 1996.

TAX, SPEND, ELECT: LIBERALS BUILD THE WELFARE STATE

My most fundamental argument is that liberals constructed the welfare state, especially after 1965, without heeding the distinction between welfare programs that were acceptable to Americans and those that were not. Eventually, most Americans came to believe that welfare programs encouraged nonwork and induced other behavioral problems among the able-bodied poor.

Insurance Programs Based on Work

Liberals began their long campaign to wrap all Americans in entitlement benefits by creating insurance programs designed to help people who were not expected to work or whose benefits were contingent on previous work. The centerpiece of this agenda, and indeed the centerpiece of American social policy, is the Social Security Act. Signed into law by President Franklin D. Roosevelt in 1935, Social Security firmly established the principle that the federal government would provide guaranteed benefits to various groups of qualified citizens. Many of the programs contained in the original act were justified—and are still widely understood—as insurance. In 1995, on the eve of the welfare debate, 37.4 million retired workers, wives and husbands of retired workers, widowed mothers and fathers, and various dependents received Social Security benefits of nearly $292 billion.

The Social Security legislation of 1935 also contained the Unemployment Compensation program, which provided entitlement benefits to qualified unemployed workers. The Unemployment Compensation program was also based primarily on insurance principles and, except during recessions, has been financed entirely by a flat percentage tax paid by employers on behalf of their employees. In 1995 almost 8 million workers received benefits, equaling $21 billion.

The Social Security Act is the greatest piece of social legislation ever enacted in America. It provided guaranteed benefits for the elderly, the unemployed, and many of their dependents. These programs were universal or nearly universal, were financed by taxes paid into reserved accounts, and were somewhat redistributive. They were built to be popular and, therefore, to last. So far, both goals have been achieved, and the popularity of the program has lasted for more than six decades.

So popular were these programs, in fact, that Congress significantly expanded them during the 1950s and 1960s. Specifically, a series of legislative actions beginning in 1956 created the Disability Insurance program, which provided cash to workers who became disabled and were no longer able to engage in gainful economic activity. By 1995 nearly 5.9 million disabled workers and their spouses and children received benefits, totaling close to $41 billion. In 1965 Congress created the Medicare program. This program, supported in part by a dedicated tax, provides health benefits to the qualified elderly and disabled. In 1995 Medicare provided health benefits worth $160 billion to more than 8 million beneficiaries.

Four universal programs with redistributive features, four programs with dedicated taxes and accompanying trust funds, four programs directly connected to work, four programs that continue to enjoy huge support from the American public—taken together, these four programs are the high-water mark of liberalism in America. Although Social Security and Medicare face uncertain futures because of financing problems, only a cynic or poor loser could doubt that the American public owes a great debt of gratitude to liberals for creating these four pillars of American social policy.

Welfare Programs

The insurance-based entitlements described were not the only items on the liberal social policy agenda. Since the Great Depression, and more particularly since the 1960s, liberals have tried to provide entitlement benefits to all Americans, not just to those who worked or who were in families with workers. Indeed, among the fondest goals of liberals was the redistribution of income. Few American liberals have adopted the socialist goal of redistributing the nation's wealth based strictly on individual or family need, but a major component of the liberal soul is a willingness to tax middle-class and wealthy Americans to provide benefits to poor and low-income Americans (and, as it has turned out, to resident noncitizens). As Martin Gilens (1999) shows, the American public is quite willing to help the poor, perhaps in part because of our tradition as a religious nation. Whatever the reason, for many Americans the very definition of fairness became the willingness to support income redistribution.

Thus nestled among the seedling Social Security programs in the Social Security Act of 1935 was the little welfare acorn called Aid to Dependent Children (later called Aid to Families with Dependent Children, or AFDC). This tiny and inconspicuous program grew into the towering oak that is the huge array of federal and federal-state social programs designed to provide benefits and services to the poor. Beginning with the Lyndon Johnson administration's War on Poverty during the mid-1960s, new social programs and spending on social programs grew dramatically. The three most important new programs—in addition to Medicare—were Medicaid, the Food Stamp program, and the Supplemental Security Income (SSI) program.

By the mid-1970s the broad outlines of American social policy were evident. The outline might be thought of as consisting of three tiers. On the top tier were the insurance programs providing universal benefits: Social Security, Medicare, Disability Insurance, and Unemployment Compensation. On the second tier were the means-tested entitlement programs: AFDC, Medicaid, food stamps, and SSI. The third tier consisted of a few hundred means-tested programs, most of them small, that competed with one another for annual appropriations.

This overview would not be complete without a numerical accounting of tiers two and three. At the beginning of the welfare debate in 1995, House Republicans asked the Congressional Research Service (CRS) to estimate the number of federal social programs. The CRS counted 336 social programs divided into eight domains; no domain contained fewer than 8 programs (cash welfare), and one domain (child care) had more than 150 programs. Spending, in constant dollars, on these means-tested programs rose consistently between 1950 and 1995, from less than $1 billion in 1950 to more than $375 billion in 1995 (Burke 1995; Rector and Lauber 1995), with a slight drop between 1981 and 1982. There was, in short, a blizzard of social programs and a flood of spending.

THE RUN-UP TO THE GREAT WELFARE REFORM DEBATE OF 1995 TO 1996

Between enactment of the SSI program in 1972 and enactment of welfare reform in 1996, there was a curious stability in American social policy. Existing programs were expanded and new ones were added, but they were small and of little conse-quence. Nixon's Family Assistance Plan (FAP), which failed in 1971, would have revolutionized American social policy by providing every family with a guaran-teed income. The FAP was the last attempt to significantly expand the second tier of the welfare state. As surprising as it now seems, the major leadership for the expansion was provided by a Republican president who was defeated in his efforts by liberals in the Senate who wanted a higher guaranteed benefit level (Moynihan 1973). There were attempts to reform welfare under President Jimmy Carter, but these attempts also came to naught (Lynn and Whitman 1981). President Ronald Reagan, too, began his presidency with a welfare reform agenda, much of which he actually managed to pass in the budget act of 1981 (U.S. House of Represen-tatives 1991, 656–57). However, these reforms did not change welfare programs in any permanent way. The most significant reform tightened the AFDC disre-gard rules so that many working recipients who were combining welfare bene-fits with income were forced to leave the rolls. The disregard rules were later eased so that even these modest Reagan reforms were watered down before the end of his presidency.

Despite these modest changes in welfare law, there were nonetheless porten-tous developments that set the stage for the big changes of 1996. The following is a selective examination of a partial set of the gathering forces.

Dependency

Throughout the period under discussion, one of the two or three welfare issues about which liberals and conservatives argued the most was whether welfare pro-grams induced dependency. This issue has a long and colorful history. One of the most arresting statements of the issue was made by Alexis de Tocqueville in his 1835 *Memoir on Pauperism* (see also Kristol 1995, 43–45). The most original and inter-esting part of Tocqueville's argument was the theory of human nature on which his conclusions were based. He held that there are two incentives to work: the desire to "improve the conditions of life" and the basic need to live. Every human has the second but not the first. Thus if public welfare provides enough on which to live, many will accept the welfare and abandon the desire to improve their conditions. As Tocqueville put it: "A law which gives all the poor a right to public aid, whatever the origin of their poverty, weakens or destroys the first stimulant and leaves only the second intact" (Drescher 1968, 14).

Tocqueville's views, of course, were based solely on observation and are, therefore, open to challenge. Not surprisingly, given the lack of systematic data, the debate about how public aid affects the motivation to work raged for centuries (Himmelfarb 1985). However, modern social science has produced strong and consistent evidence that public welfare does reduce work. A review of these studies (see Danziger, Haveman, and Plotnick 1981) indicates that AFDC reduces the hours of work by single mothers (see also Moffitt 1992).

The evidence on hours worked by welfare recipients, however, is only half of the story. The other half is the evidence on whether recipients use welfare as a temporary crutch to overcome a life crisis, such as divorce or sudden unemployment, or whether they adopt welfare as a way of life and remain on the rolls for long periods of time. This question was answered definitively by Mary Jo Bane and David Ellwood in 1983. Figure 2.1 shows the results of their work. Of the recipients on welfare at any given moment, 65 percent will eventually be on the rolls for eight years or more. At its peak in 1994, the AFDC caseload totaled about 5.1 million families. Thus, using Bane and Ellwood's results, in 1994, on the eve of the welfare debate, about 3.3 million adults were in the middle of spells that had already or would eventually exceed eight years.

Not surprisingly, figure 2.1 was a favorite among Republicans during the welfare debates of both 1987 to 1988 and 1995 to 1996. A table based on Bane and Ellwood's results was placed in the Committee on Ways and Means *Green Book* (U.S. House of Representatives 1996, 505), which is read avidly by congressional

FIGURE 2.1   /   Dependency of Welfare Recipients, in Years

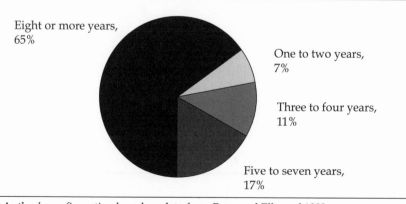

Eight or more years, 65%

One to two years, 7%

Three to four years, 11%

Five to seven years, 17%

Source: Author's configuration based on data from Bane and Ellwood 1983.

staff and other Washington policy wonks and even, it is rumored, by a few members of Congress. In addition, Republican members frequently used the figure in discussions with constituents at town meetings, and several members used charts similar to figure 2.1 on the House floor during the welfare debate of 1995 to 1996.

Caseload dynamics are not easy to grasp. This fact, combined with the fervid desire of partisans on both sides to make the data fit their view of reality, led to no end of mischief with caseload data. In the end, however, having watched the use of these numbers by politicians since the mid-1980s, I think Bane and Ellwood's (1983) finding that 65 percent of recipients are on welfare for eight years or more astounded almost everyone and was the clear winner in the battle for people's understanding of whether dependency was a serious problem. I would further argue that the Bane and Ellwood study is the single most influential piece of social science evidence used in a major congressional debate on social policy in the last decade or more. Ironically for university scholars, one of their most creative and definitive productions was used by Republicans to drive home the point that welfare dependency was real. More spirited members even argued that welfare dependency was a disease foisted on unsuspecting victims by the welfare state and that the science that confirmed the diagnosis was the data on caseload dynamics.

Illegitimacy

By 1995 the nation had been subjected to an avalanche of illegitimate births (see figure 2.2). Led by Charles Murray (1993) and many others, conservatives were intent

FIGURE 2.2 / Nonmarital Births and Percentage of All Births That Are Nonmarital, 1980 to 1995

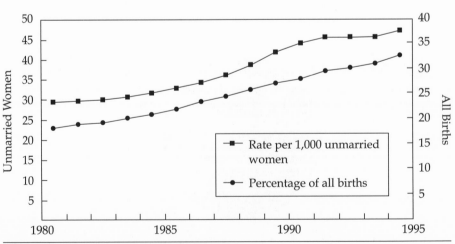

Source: Author's configuration based on data from Ventura and Bachrach 2000.

on making illegitimacy a central issue of the welfare debate. The essence of the conservative position was that the guarantee of welfare benefits—not only cash, but food stamps, Medicaid, and housing as well—led young men and women to a reduced state of vigilance in avoiding pregnancy before marriage. There is of course a substantial research literature on whether AFDC contributed to illegitimacy, but as might be expected, liberals (such as Ellwood and Bane 1985) interpreted the literature as supporting the position that welfare did not cause illegitimacy, while conservatives (Haskins 1996) interpreted the same evidence as demonstrating that AFDC was clearly related to increased rates of illegitimacy. In truth, because there are no experimental studies, the results and their interpretation are ambiguous. Of course, conservatives did not allow the lack of consensus in the social science literature to dull their claims about illegitimacy. The argument that guaranteed welfare benefits contributed to increased illegitimacy rates makes sense to most Americans. This fact, coupled with the widely known negative effects of illegitimacy on mothers and children (Roth 1994), was enough justification among conservatives for the emphasis on illegitimacy.

Once again, the value issue was central. Republicans, as well as important Democrats such as President Clinton, discovered that voters responded to the argument that AFDC directly violated the moral precept that only married adults who can provide for the economic and emotional needs of their children should have babies. The fact that traditional rules of marriage and sexuality were being challenged throughout the period under discussion does not vitiate the fact that the majority of Americans remained traditional in their judgments about illegitimacy, especially when they saw their tax dollars supporting a system that subverted their values.

There is little doubt that many Democrats also deplored illegitimacy. A classic claim by conservatives is that, beginning in the 1960s, liberals decided to allow everyone to create their own set of values, to do their own thing (Kristol 1995). Whatever the truth about this claim, it is certain that, by 1995, very few members of Congress thought illegitimacy was simply a matter of individual expression. On the contrary, both Democrats and Republicans were greatly concerned about the causes and consequences of illegitimacy. In fact Clinton was more outspoken than any other president about the tragedy of illegitimacy; he was even given to stating flatly that it was "wrong" for young people to have children they could not support outside of marriage.

Thus conservatives were successful in making illegitimacy a major part of the welfare reform debate, but at least part of their success was attributable to the fact that liberals were in substantial agreement that illegitimacy was a major problem and that the consequences were bad for both the mother and the child. Liberals, however, were less willing than conservatives to single out welfare programs as a major cause of illegitimacy, let alone to use illegitimacy as the rationale for major changes in welfare programs.

A minor problem in the conservative rhetoric about illegitimacy was that no one knew of any policies that had a good chance of increasing abstinence, reducing pregnancy, or promoting marriage (U.S. Department of Health and Human Services 1995). Even the studies on attempts to reduce second pregnancies were discouraging

(Maynard 1997). Undaunted, Republicans argued that the best approach was to do everything possible to attack the problem, especially by rewarding states that tried new approaches. So great was the problem, and so serious the consequences, that conservatives insisted on trying as many things as possible to reduce illegitimacy.

The Empirical Basis of Mandatory Work Programs

Charles Murray's revolutionary book *Losing Ground* (1984) caused a huge stir during this period, but his shocking recommendation to end welfare programs cold turkey was never pursued as a serious policy option even by very conservative Republicans. Nonetheless, Murray's book and the reaction to it left the impression among conservatives, and perhaps a number of moderates and liberals as well, that something was fundamentally wrong with welfare in general and with entitlement welfare in particular. Murray's work also had a stimulant effect on conservative, not to mention liberal, thinkers and activists. Murray's most important contribution may have been to bring renewed respectability to conservative thinking about the causes of poverty and the effects of welfare programs.

Although not as colorful as Murray's controversial book, Larry Mead's *Beyond Entitlement* (1986) proposed a partial solution to welfare dependency, which was to have immense influence. Mead argued that the poor needed authoritarian welfare programs to force them to adopt appropriate behaviors. The most important such behavior, of course, was work. Thus Mead argued that welfare-to-work programs with clearly stated requirements backed by tight administration and quick sanctions would help many recipients enter the workforce.

Work became the cannonball of the Republican welfare reform agenda. As other issues—time limits, block grants, illegitimacy—developed, work remained the central issue of the debate. Beginning as early as the 1960s, Republicans extolled the virtues of work as the antidote to welfare dependency. In doing so, Republicans were squarely within a tradition of welfare reform going back at least to Victorian England, in which conservatives held that work is redemptive. Work requires consistency, schedules, alarm clocks, routines, cooperation, self-discipline—all the traits, in short, that conservatives believed would rescue welfare recipients from the companions of sloth, booze, idleness, illicit sex, "hanging out" (Himmelfarb 1985). Moreover, in the modern American context, conservatives argued that work was easily available and would inevitably lift the poor out of poverty (Mead 1992).

This agenda was greatly strengthened by the high-quality research on welfare-to-work programs conducted by the Manpower Demonstration Research Corporation (MDRC) (Gueron and Pauly 1991) and others. In setting the standard for policy research, MDRC studies incorporated all of the hallmarks of scientific evaluations: random assignment, large sample sizes, experiments conducted under field conditions, multiple outcome measures, and benefit-cost analyses. The basic results were unequivocal: welfare-to-work programs that emphasized job search and that were tightly administered produced significant increases in earnings and decreases in welfare rolls. The effects may not have been huge, but they were consistent. Such programs were also generally cost beneficial.

Seldom has social science presented a clearer case to policymakers: aggressively conducted work programs clearly lessen both caseloads and spending. This consistent result gave a strong impetus to mandatory work programs. Beginning with the debate on the Family Support Act of 1988, conservatives adopted the mantra, "What works is work." Here was a message that resonated with both policymakers and the American public.

So successful was this message that, by the time the welfare reform debate began again in earnest during the presidential election of 1992, many liberals agreed that work programs must be a part of any welfare reform legislation. Conservatives, however, insisted on establishing a work program that was much more demanding and directive than most Democrats were willing to support. Specifically, conservatives argued that, given the indifferent results of previous welfare reform, it was imperative to send a clear message that this time recipients would actually be forced to work if necessary. Hence conservatives intended to end the entitlement to cash benefits, impose a time limit on the receipt of cash benefits, impose a requirement that states move a specific percentage of their caseloads into work programs, and impose stiff sanctions on both individuals and states that did not fulfill the numerical work requirements. Unlike previous welfare reform debates, then, after 1992 the debate was about the amount of work required, the specific conditions of work, and the consequences for individuals and states of not working—rather than on whether recipients should be required to work.

The Family Support Act of 1988

That these details of work programs were vital is amply demonstrated by the welfare reform debate of 1987 to 1988, which led to passage of the Family Support Act. Liberals were forced both by the MDRC research and, even more fundamentally, by the popularity of work with the American public to declare that they supported work. Conservatives believed, however, that the liberal commitment to work was paper-thin, as evident in the history of federal welfare reform legislation "requiring" work. The Work Incentive (WIN) program, established in 1967, was a typical example. The WIN program required all persons aged sixteen and older applying for or receiving AFDC to register for work. However, so many AFDC recipients were exempt and so few recipients were penalized for ignoring the requirement that most welfare offices continued the routine operation of determining eligibility and writing checks; the WIN program barely had an effect (Mead 1986). By 1987 WIN funding had declined to $110 million from its peak of $365 million in 1981.

Although conservatives attempted to make work the centerpiece of welfare reform in 1988, liberals were intent on continuing their campaign to expand welfare, particularly by requiring all states to provide AFDC coverage to two-parent families. After two years of rancorous debate, especially in the House, Congress settled on a compromise bill that conservatives believed leaned distinctly to the left.

More specifically, there were no work requirements imposed on parents in the regular AFDC caseload. Rather, the legislation established the Job Opportunities and Basic Skills (JOBS) training program, which provided states with around $1 billion per year to help adults leave welfare by joining the workforce. States were given mandatory participation standards, but participation was broadly defined to include education, training, and job search. To illustrate just how insignificant the work requirements were, by 1994, six years after enactment of the JOBS program, fewer than 25,000 of the 5 million adults on AFDC—about 0.5 percent of the caseload—were in work programs.

In the end, the Family Support Act did not provide a resounding victory for the principles being pursued by either liberals or conservatives. Because all of the major programs remained intact and were actually expanded somewhat, because about half of the AFDC caseload was exempted from any participation requirement, because virtually no one was required to work, and because day care and Medicaid were guaranteed for adults on AFDC who participated in jobs programs or who left the rolls, liberals should be accorded an edge on the partisan tally sheet. However, as is always the case with federal legislation, the importance of any particular piece of legislation is conditioned at least as much by subsequent legislation as by previous legislation. The next big reform bill was to advance all the small victories won by conservatives in the Family Support Act.

The New Consensus

In 1986, under the sponsorship of the Bradley and Olin foundations, Michael Novak and Doug Besharov of the American Enterprise Institute in Washington, D.C., organized a group of twenty policy intellectuals, including several with government experience, to examine welfare programs and make recommendations for reforming welfare. Called the Working Seminar (1987), the group was composed of both left-of-center public figures, such as Robert Reischauer, Alice Rivlin, Barbara Blum, and Franklin Raines, and right-of-center figures, such as John Cogan, Charles Murray, Larry Mead, and Glenn Loury. After approximately one year of meetings, commissioned background papers, and discussions, the seminar recommended very substantial, even radical, reform of welfare programs, especially the AFDC program. In fact, the recommendations are uncanny in their anticipation of several major provisions of the 1996 reform legislation.

The seminar's recommendations began by emphasizing the importance of welfare dependency and other behavioral dysfunctions. Although no government program could by itself solve these problems, the report argued, federal, state, and local governments have been assigned fundamental tasks that, although limited, are indispensable to the common good (100). Clearly, because some of the nation's leading conservatives were members, the seminar's endorsement of government's role in helping poor people find work and in supplementing their income showed that many conservatives recognized the important role government must play in welfare reform. In part, perhaps, conservatives agreed to this definitive statement because the report also emphasized the role that the private sector, including religious organizations, should play in emphasizing personal responsibility as an antidote to behavioral dysfunction. The report goes on to recommend mandatory work requirements, sanctions for not fulfilling work requirements, and time limits on cash welfare benefits, making cash aid transitional in nature. Although the report did not recommend that AFDC be allocated by block grant, it did strongly recommend that more authority and flexibility be shifted to the state and local levels and that states continue to experiment with innovative programs.

One of the most important and interesting sections of the report compared the seminar's approach and conclusions on welfare reform with the approach and conclusions taken by four other commissions that had issued reports during the previous year. These included reports from the American Public Welfare Association; the Project on the Welfare of Families cochaired by Governor Bruce Babbitt of Arizona and former Republican secretary of the Department of Health, Education, and Welfare, Arthur Flemming; the Task Force on Poverty and Welfare appointed by Governor Mario Cuomo of New York; and President Reagan's Low Income Opportunity Board (Working Seminar 1987, 74–82). Each of these reports focused on welfare dependency as a primary problem, stressed the connection between welfare benefits and reciprocal obligations by recipients, emphasized policies to strengthen personal responsibility and self-reliance, and examined ways to make AFDC temporary.

The report from the Working Seminar as well as the reports from other groups representing several points along the political spectrum show that the big issues, including mandatory work and time limits, were clearly on the table almost a decade before the welfare reform debate of 1995 to 1996. Moreover, a prestigious group of conservative and liberal policy intellectuals seemed to endorse the major policy proposals that were to create such havoc in Congress and between liberals and moderates within the Democratic Party nearly a decade later. Perhaps it is too much to claim, as the Working Seminar report did, that there was consensus on welfare reform provisions such as time-limited benefits, mandatory work with sanctions, major devolution to states of responsibility for designing welfare programs, and federal funding of small (including faith-based) organizations to address behavioral problems. It does seem fair, however, to conclude that both liberal and conservative policy intellectuals were convinced that welfare dependency and other behavioral problems were the major issues that had to be addressed by welfare reform. At the very least, there was a willingness to seriously consider radical reforms.

Liberal Influences

For those who doubt this formulation, consider four examples of liberals who were well aware of how far federal social policy had departed from American values and how radical the reforms might become. The first example is President Clinton—or rather, presidential candidate Clinton. Clinton saw clearly that several liberal policies were alienating voters. During the presidential campaign of 1992, Clinton put this knowledge to good use in developing campaign themes, particularly regarding welfare. Thus two of the most popular themes of his campaign were "ending welfare as we know it" and "two years and out." That a Democratic presidential candidate would use these themes is surprising; that he and his lieutenants would emphasize that these themes helped him in several close races during the primaries and the general election shows that at least some Democrats realized the political effectiveness of abandoning positions taken by liberals and even the advantages of attacking those same positions. For liberals who wanted to defend and even expand the means-tested aspects of the welfare state, these developments were exceedingly dangerous.

David Ellwood's ground-breaking book *Poor Support* (1989) is a second indication that many liberals were aware that the welfare state was flawed and needed reform. Although Ellwood would be pilloried by the Left for his scholarly work on welfare reform, as well as the leading role he played in the Clinton administration's welfare reform efforts (see Lynn 1993; Piven 1996), *Poor Support* was a serious and creative attempt to transform AFDC into a program that could provide benefits while simultaneously addressing the problem of dependency. Ellwood came under fire from the Left because he was one of the first liberals to recommend time limits on AFDC entitlement benefits. Of course, Ellwood also insisted that time limits would be appropriate only if accompanied by a federal guarantee of a job for recipients who reached the time limit. Another of the major items on the Ellwood agenda, subsequently adopted by President Clinton, was "making work pay." For Ellwood, the cornerstone of making work pay was significant expansion of the Earned Income Tax Credit (EITC). Unlike his liberal critics, Ellwood played a major role in providing the intellectual justification for an EITC increase and persuading President Clinton to propose, and members of Congress to support, the increase, which they did by passing a huge expansion of the EITC in 1993. Because he played such a vital role in this striking policy achievement, Ellwood must be given a major share of the credit for putting the tidy sum of an additional $15 billion in cash (compared with pre-1993 EITC law) into the pockets of poor and low-income working Americans each year. Let anyone with a greater policy achievement continue throwing stones.

A third example is provided by Christopher Jencks, one of the most widely respected of the liberal scholars who study social policy. As early as 1992, Jencks would write that, "until liberals transform AFDC, so that it reinforces rather than subverts American ideals about work and marriage, our efforts to build a humane welfare state will never succeed" (Jencks 1992, 13). Jencks went on to argue that an important part of the solution to welfare was to make work pay, a proposition that came to play an important role in the welfare debate. As usual, Jencks's writing about the cultural contradictions of AFDC cut right to the heart of the matter: AFDC was un-American. In this understanding, Jencks was eventually joined by a host of state and federal liberal policymakers. When the moment of truth arrived in 1995, AFDC had few defenders.

The fourth liberal influence on the growing perception that AFDC was a failure was Mickey Kaus's seminal book *The End of Equality* (1992). The subject matter of the Kaus book was considerably more than welfare, but his welfare chapters (7, 8, and 9) touch on and accept, at least in part, nearly all the claims about welfare that were standard fare for conservatives. In particular, Kaus grants that welfare has played an important, though by no means exclusive, role in the breakdown of the family and the rise of illegitimacy, in the creation of the "ghetto underclass," and in the decline of work in the underclass.

Kaus's radical solution is to recommend that most welfare benefits, not just AFDC but food stamps as well, be conditioned on work. Under Kaus's system, all able-bodied adults would work or they would lose most of their welfare benefits. The larger issue addressed by Kaus was that of social inequality and its growth in America. Because he viewed the growth of social inequality as the most important issue of our times, Kaus's book is a search for the policies that would promote social equality. Work is one of the experiences that all classes in society share. Moreover, Americans place a very high value on adults who work hard to support themselves and their children. As a result, any group that becomes known for nonwork is, by definition, unequal to the working classes. Government support for nonwork exacerbates the problem of social inequality both because it encourages nonwork and because productive citizens resent being forced to support those who so conspicuously flout the value Americans place on work and self-support. Promoting work by welfare-dependent adults would, in Kaus's view, strike a major blow against social inequality.

Kaus's was perhaps the most radical welfare reform idea put forth by any major figure since Murray. It would have ended much more than merely AFDC and would have greatly expanded government. Liberals immediately attacked the proposal because it in effect ended the entitlement to both AFDC and food stamps and virtually ended welfare for anyone who refused to work. Conservatives cited the proposal incessantly because they were only too happy to argue that "even liberals" admitted that AFDC must be abandoned and that mandatory work was the best replacement. Because most conservatives rejected the idea of big government guaranteeing jobs, they were reluctant to fully support Kaus's proposal.

Besides adding speed to the momentum for reform, Kaus's break with the traditional liberal agenda of expanding welfare benefits without requiring work—as outlined both in his book and in a previous (1986) article in the *New Republic*—represented an important symbolic victory for the reform movement. Kaus had served as a senior writer for the *New Republic,* the leading intellectual and cultural journal of the Left for most of this century. Indeed, one of its founders was Herbert Croly, a dominant liberal thinker during the Progressive Era and the author of *The Promise of American Life,* a prime document of American liberalism. Despite this background, the editors of the *New Republic* supported Kaus and endorsed his radical proposal. Later, in July 1996, as the crucial welfare votes in Congress approached, the *New Republic* urged both Congress and President Clinton to support the Republican welfare reform legislation. It would be impossible to think of a more striking piece of evidence that important elements of the American Left recognized the serious problems of AFDC and the need for a change in the entitlement mentality that had been almost the sine qua non of American liberalism.

PREPARATION BY HOUSE REPUBLICANS

Between the enactment of the Family Support Act of 1988 and the Republican takeover of Congress in 1994, Republicans on the Committee on Ways and Means in the U.S. House of Representatives developed most of the specific legislative proposals, the arguments on which these proposals were based, and the expertise among members of Congress that provided the basis for the initial reform legislation that worked its way through various committees and onto the House floor by March 1995. Because the final reform legislation grew from this initial bill, the history of this determined group of Republicans is worthy of attention.

In October 1991 the Wednesday Group, a band of about forty moderate House Republicans, published a paper entitled "Moving Ahead: Initiatives for Expanding Opportunity in America" (Wednesday Group 1991). The paper was the final product of a year-long task force led by moderate Bill Gradison and conservative Vin Weber, both widely respected members of the House. Gradison and Weber initiated an aggressive press strategy to bring attention to their report, which resulted in substantial press coverage, including a supportive article by the syndicated and highly regarded David Broder, which appeared in the editorial pages of newspapers across the nation.

The report provided extensive evidence to counter the conventional wisdom that federal social spending had been cut during the 1980s and that the tax code had become less progressive under the Reagan-Bush tax policy. The report went on to argue that, despite increased social spending and more progressivity in the tax code, many of the nation's leading social problems—poverty, crime, drug dependency, welfare dependency, school dropout—had increased dramatically since the 1960s.

Several recommendations from the Gradison-Weber report are central to the concerns of this chapter and show that some of the essential components of the 1996 welfare reform law were being supported by moderate Republicans as early as 1991. These include mandatory work and time-limited AFDC. Because these reforms were untested, the report recommended large-scale demonstrations to explore the effect of these and other welfare reforms.

In the spring of 1992 Clay Shaw, the senior Republican on the welfare subcommittee of the House Committee on Ways and Means and an influential member of the Wednesday Group, along with Nancy Johnson and Fred Grandy, who had worked with Shaw on the Wednesday Group report and were Shaw's colleagues on the Ways and Means welfare subcommittee, wrote and circulated a background paper entitled "Moving Ahead: How America Can Reduce Poverty Through Work" (Shaw, Johnson, and Grandy 1992). This paper, a detailed follow-up to the 1991 Wednesday Group paper on poverty, presented the rationale and specific proposals that Shaw and his colleagues thought could receive bipartisan support.

The report opens with an extensive analysis of the financial prospects of mothers who attempt to leave welfare. The analysis examines EITC, child care, health insurance, and child support. In many of its particulars, the analysis is similar to that in Ellwood's *Poor Support* and to that of Jencks in chapter 6 of *Rethinking Social Policy*. Indeed, the Shaw report's declaration that the "major goal of Republican welfare policy is to insure that families willing to work will be better off financially once they leave welfare and to achieve this goal, not by cutting welfare benefits, but by subsidizing work" (4) could have been taken directly from either Ellwood or Jencks or, for that matter, from the 1992 Clinton campaign. Thus by the early 1990s making work pay was a major item on the welfare reform agenda of both leading liberals and conservatives.

The Shaw report went on to propose legislative strategies to address several domains of social policy, three of which are especially pertinent to welfare reform. First, Shaw and his colleagues strongly endorsed the waiver process by which states were being allowed to ignore certain provisions of welfare law in order to conduct experiments. Initiated during the Reagan administration and coordinated by the Low-Income Opportunity Working Group (1986) headed by Chuck Hobbs, a special assistant to President Reagan, the process of recruiting states to engage in demonstrations was a major tenet of the Reagan approach to welfare reform. The underlying logic of the approach was that the Social Security Act permitted exemptions from specified provisions of welfare law for the purpose of experimentation that would never have been approved by Democrats in Congress. Allowing states to experiment and to develop unique programs would have the desirable political effect of showing that they were capable of actually thinking up innovative policies and implementing them.

Thus a consistent part of the Republican welfare reform agenda was expanding state control over welfare programs. Shaw and his colleagues proposed to formalize the process by creating an Office of Welfare Reform Demonstrations with an annual budget of $1 billion. The office would recruit states to conduct three specific demonstrations: time-limited AFDC, mandatory work and public jobs, and child support assurance. The first two of these policies, minus the public jobs, remained on the Republican agenda throughout the welfare reform debate.

The Shaw report was issued in the midst of the 1992 presidential election, which featured extensive rhetoric about welfare reform. Ironically, President George Bush did not make welfare reform a central feature of his campaign, but his opponent, Bill Clinton, did. Liberals must certainly have been of two minds on the major role that candidate Clinton was playing in the welfare reform debate. They must have been as surprised as conservatives by the amazing spectacle of a Democrat presidential candidate carrying the fight to a Republican candidate on welfare reform. On the other hand, many liberals must have worried that the whole process might get out of hand. After all, welfare intellectuals, including respected liberals such as Jencks, Reischauer, Kaus, and Ellwood, were supporting rather remarkable changes in welfare, including mandatory work and time limits. Further, influential Republicans in the House had written legislation that embodied many of these proposals. At the very least, Clinton was aiding and abetting radical changes in welfare that were already very much under consideration. As long as Democrats controlled the Congress, the odds of serious reform breaking out were minimal. But what if Republicans did the impossible and seized control of Congress?

Of course, Clinton won the presidency in 1992 and Democrats strengthened their hold on the Senate and maintained a margin of more than eighty votes in the House. However, rather than proceed with a relatively moderate version of welfare reform, in which the entitlement to AFDC would be retained and time limits would be imposed only if (as Ellwood, Kaus, and others had recommended) a job— and child care, medical insurance, and other benefits—were guaranteed, President Clinton made the fateful decision to delay welfare reform and move ahead with health care reform.

This decision left the field open to Republicans. Seizing this opportunity, Shaw and Rick Santorum, who had just joined the Ways and Means Committee and who, because of a quirk in committee rules, became the leading Republican on the welfare subcommittee, joined Ways and Means chairman Bill Archer in convincing the House Republican leadership to appoint a welfare reform task force. The task force was to build on the recommendations of the two Republican reports and on legislation previously written by Shaw and his Ways and Means colleagues and develop a legislative proposal that all House Republicans could support. This the leadership readily agreed to do, putting Santorum and Tom DeLay, a member of the Republican leadership, in charge and appointing several members representing four House committees in addition to the Ways and Means Committee. The organization of the task force was loose, and as many as thirty members participated in one or more of the task force's half-dozen meetings. Equally important, the members were represented by their staff at some of the ten or more staff meetings, during which the issues were discussed in detail and specific recommendations were formulated for the members to consider.

While the Clinton administration focused on health reform and the task force assigned by the president to write the administration's welfare reform bill held its semipublic slugfests, House Republicans were quietly developing detailed legislative proposals that almost all Republicans would support. In fact when the task force was finished in the fall of 1993, its legislative proposal (H.R. 3500) was endorsed by nearly every House Republican.

Following H.R. 3500, Newt Gingrich, then the second-ranking Republican in the House, asked Ways and Means Republicans and Republicans on the Education and Labor Committee to work with conservative interest groups, such as the Heritage Foundation, the Family Research Council, the Christian Coalition, and others, to formulate a welfare reform proposal that would unite members, as H.R. 3500 had done, but that would also appeal to the conservative activist base of the Republican Party. The product of this work, based on H.R. 3500, was H.R. 4. This bill was one of the ten bills that composed the Contract with America and on which Republicans across the nation campaigned during the fateful 1994 congressional elections. It was also the bill, somewhat modified, that was introduced as the chairman's bill for consideration by the Committee on Ways and Means in January 1995 and that, after many modifications, was signed into law by President Clinton in August 1996.

THE FINAL WELFARE REFORM LEGISLATION

The final law, the Personal Responsibility and Work Opportunity Reconciliation Act, ended the entitlement to cash assistance and replaced AFDC with Temporary Assistance for Needy Families (TANF), transferred decision-making authority for welfare programs to states, instituted a block grant funding scheme, imposed a five-year (cumulative) lifetime limit on receipt of cash assistance, and required recipients to work at least thirty hours a week by the year 2000 in exchange for benefits. States were also required to move a certain portion of their caseload into the workforce by various deadlines. Many in the media and the scholarly world, especially those on the Left, believe the final legislation is harsh (Edelman 1997). Moreover, these critics seem to believe that the legislation is harsh because conservatives had the votes and implemented their own agenda without making accommodations for the concerns raised by liberals. This sentiment is misleading. The final bill was highly bipartisan and is now, at least temporarily, very popular among elected officials and the American public. Even the media, including the news reporting (not the editorial writing) in the *New York Times* and the *Washington Post,* seem to offer at least grudging acceptance of the legislation's timeliness, popularity, and most surprising of all, early success.

Table 2.1 shows the provisions of several of the most important bills that were considered during the congressional debate. The provisions selected for the table capture both the major policies contained in the final bill and the issues that caused the most partisan fighting during the course of the debate.

Replacing AFDC by Temporary Assistance for Needy Families (TANF)

AFDC provided entitlement benefits to individuals who did not work and who had children, often outside marriage, whom they could not support. Although the classic liberal defense of AFDC was that it was a crucial part of the safety net that protected all Americans, conservatives argued that the safety net was really a hammock and that as long as adults were entitled to benefits, all too many would, as Tocqueville predicted, take the benefits and become mired in the culture of welfare. By the time House Republicans introduced their bill in January 1995, the sides were clear and the arguments well known and well rehearsed. Most of the arguments were replays from the Family Support Act of 1988 and earlier debates. In 1995 and 1996, however, the debate took place in a political environment that differed in three fundamental ways from that of previous debates.

First, Republicans controlled both houses of Congress. As a result, not only could they call the press conferences and organize the hearings that would ensure that their proposals and arguments were presented in the most favorable light but also they could write the bills that would be considered for legislative action. The most basic proposition of democratic government is that the majority can work

TABLE 2.1 / Major Provisions, Selected Welfare Reform Bills

Provision	H.R. 3500	H.R. 4	Shaw Mark	Deal	Clinton I	Clinton II	Final Bill
Temporary Assistance for Needy Families (TANF)							
Mandatory job	No	No	No	Yes	Yes	Yes	No
End	Yes	Yes	Yes	No	No[a]	No[a]	Yes
Entitlement							
Block grant	No[b]	Partial	Yes	No	No	No	Yes
Time limit	Yes	Yes	Yes	Yes	Yes	Yes	Yes
Work	Yes	Yes	Yes	Yes	Yes	Yes	Yes
Definition							
Percentage standards	Yes	Yes	Yes	Yes	Yes[c]	Yes[d]	Yes
Sanctions, state	Yes	Yes	Yes	Yes[e]	Yes[f]	Yes[e]	Yes
Sanctions, individual	Yes	Yes	Yes	Yes	Yes	Yes	Yes
Child care block grant	No	No	Yes	Yes[g]	No	Yes	Yes
Child support	Yes	No	Yes	Yes	Yes	Yes	Yes
Illegitimacy	Yes	Yes	Yes	Yes	Yes	Yes	Yes
SSI for addicts	No	Yes	Yes	Yes	No	Yes	Yes
SSI for children	No	No	Yes	Yes	No	Yes	Yes
Noncitizens' benefits	Yes	Yes	Yes	Partial[h]	Partial[h]	Partial[h]	Yes

Source: Author's compilation.

[a] Both Clinton bills continued the entitlement of states to unlimited cash benefit matching funds and the entitlement of (eligible) individuals to benefits and required states to pay benefits to all persons eligible under state standards.

[b] H.R. 3500 would have given states the option to convert AFDC into a block grant.

[c] Clinton's 1994 bill retained work participation percentage requirements for two-parent AFDC-UP (unemployed parent) families and, after the first two years of benefits, imposed participation standards for all families in the program that required work.

[d] Clinton's 1996 bill imposed work percentage requirements for all families, although some families were exempt from the requirement.

[e] For second consecutive failure, the secretary of Health and Human Services was authorized to cut the federal matching rate for cash benefits (AFDC in Deal bill, temporary employment assistance in Clinton's 1996 bill) by up to 5 percent.

[f] Reduction in AFDC matching rate for some AFDC benefits.

[g] Deal repealed the child care and development block grant and all AFDC-related child care, putting child care funding into a new section of the title 20 block grant. However, it retained the entitlement of individual families to child care.

[h] Deal and both Clinton bills deemed a sponsor's income and resources as available to a qualified noncitizen until naturalization, thereby reducing the chances the noncitizen would qualify for welfare benefits.

its will. On welfare, Republicans maintained their majority on almost all major issues through numerous votes in several committees and on the floor of both houses of Congress.

Second, thirty states had Republican governors, up from seventeen in 1993, a few of whom had been pursuing welfare reform for many years and who had developed substantial knowledge of welfare programs and ways to reform them. These governors, especially Tommy Thompson of Wisconsin and John Engler of Michigan, presented forceful testimony before congressional committees endorsing the Republican reforms. In hearings before the Committee on Ways and Means in the House and the Finance Committee in the Senate, the Republican governors (often joined by Democratic Governor Tom Carper of Delaware) put up a colorful and vigorous defense of Republican policies as well as an attack on central features of current welfare programs, such as federal control, entitlements, and barriers to work. In addition, in the winter of 1996 when welfare reform seemed to be on the critical list following two Clinton vetoes, the governors breathed life back into the process.

Third, Republicans who wanted to reform welfare were blessed with a Democratic president who was sympathetic with their views. When Clinton ran on a platform of "ending welfare as we know it" and "two years and out" during the presidential election of 1992, many Republicans doubted his sincerity. Their distrust deepened when he replaced welfare reform with health at the top of his agenda in 1993 and 1994. In 1995 and 1996, however, Republicans could set the agenda. The president could no longer say he was for serious welfare reform without acting. Republicans could and did force him to act.

The heart of the Republican agenda was a three-part policy to replace AFDC. First, the individual entitlement to cash welfare would end. Although Democrats fought to save the entitlement, Republicans doubted that it would be possible to achieve serious reform unless the strongest possible message was sent to the public, to state and local governments, to welfare agencies, and to recipients themselves.

As shown in table 2.1, both of the president's bills, as well as the Nathan Deal bill offered by House Democrats, were strikingly similar to the Republican bills on most provisions and in addition were far more conservative than any previous welfare reform bill supported by a majority of Democrats. Yet the Democratic bills maintained the entitlement. This suggests that welfare entitlement was a feature of their system of public benefits on which liberals placed the highest value. Liberals wanted all Americans to be protected against adversity. Conservatives regarded this goal as too sentimental. Risk is at the center of the capitalist enterprise. Yes, risk must be tempered by some types of insurance, but it often seemed to conservatives that the goal of liberals was to drain life of all risk, thereby causing people, as Toqueville foresaw, to lose the discipline imposed on human behavior by the knowledge that personal decisions about work and family have major effects on life prospects. Conservatives wanted to reimpose serious consequences for choices about education, work, sex, and marriage. The issue was where the line between risk and entitlement should be drawn; conservatives were determined to move the line in the direction of more personal responsibility and accountability.

A five-year lifetime limit on receiving cash assistance was the second important feature of the Republican strategy to replace AFDC. Republicans believed that ending the entitlement was a meaningless gesture if individuals could retain their cash benefit indefinitely. If a specific time limit could be placed on benefits, the signal that welfare was temporary would be unmistakable. Equally important, from the first day of benefit receipt, adults would know that they had a fixed period of time to achieve their independence from welfare. Although to many liberals and social critics the time limit was the harshest part of the conservative agenda, Republicans in both the House and Senate strongly supported it, and the time limit was a major feature of every Republican bill. Surprisingly, and perhaps a sign that the time limit became almost synonymous with serious reform, the major Democratic bills also contained some version of time limits.

The insistence on mandatory work was the third vital feature of the AFDC replacement strategy. Because of all the past failures to establish serious work programs, and because they distrusted the pro-work rhetoric of Democrats, Republicans insisted that the work program be based on three characteristics: a definition of work that excluded most educational activities, a participation standard that stipulated the percentage of each state's caseload that must be involved in work programs, and sanctions on both states and program participants. These characteristics were all far more conservative and daring than anything contemplated in the 1988 Family Support Act.

Two other provisions in the debate should be mentioned. First, it will be recalled that Ellwood, Kaus, and many other liberals wanted to provide a government guarantee of a job. This requirement was fulfilled by both the Deal bill and the Clinton bill. Democrats argued, with considerable justice, that guaranteeing work was a reasonable compromise between the desire of liberals to protect individuals from adversity and the desire of conservatives to ensure that able-bodied adults would not be allowed to live on welfare without trying to achieve independence. Even so, conservatives were solidly opposed to government-run job programs, both because past experience suggested that these programs would be inefficient and ineffective and because they would contribute substantially to the growth of government. Conservatives wanted less, not more, government. In the end, no public jobs were created in the federal legislation, although states could provide them on their own, using federal funds.

The second provision that must be mentioned is the block grant. It would be possible to create each of the features of AFDC reform described here, which would have the effect of converting welfare to a job program, without creating a block grant (a fixed sum of money given to states to achieve specific, usually broad, goals). The 1996 welfare reform legislation would have been only a little less radical if a block grant had not been created. Republicans, however, were intent on a block grant to control spending, to move major responsibility for conducting welfare programs to the state and local levels, and to reduce the size and power of the federal government.

The trifecta of terminating the entitlement, imposing time limits, and requiring a strong work program was the major Republican achievement in the 1996 welfare reform legislation. At the symbolic level, the repeal of a major New Deal program was a first and may signal that the nation is on the path to major changes in its conception of welfare. Even those who now believe that these reforms were too harsh may come to change their minds in time. Republicans were attempting to shock a system that, from their perspective as well as the perspective of a majority of Americans and many elected Democrats, was trapping people in poverty and dependence. By defining the specific reforms needed to change the system and sticking doggedly to them throughout the two years of debate, Republicans convinced a majority of Democrats and a Democratic president to adopt their conception of what it meant to "end welfare as we know it."

Illegitimacy

The emphasis on illegitimacy by conservatives pushed Republicans into positions that were widely viewed as extreme. As the Santorum-DeLay task force was in the final stage of writing H.R. 3500, Empower America, a conservative think tank headed by William Bennett, Jack Kemp, and Vin Weber, issued a public denunciation of the task force's recommendations. Their major criticism was that illegitimacy, not mandatory work, should head the Republican charge on welfare reform. There were a host of policies under discussion that, taken together, could form a broad attack on illegitimacy, but few of them were supported by evidence that they could produce significant effects. Moreover, many were controversial and their inclusion in a bill designed to show Republican unanimity on welfare reform could drive away Republican moderates.

More than any other issue of the welfare debate, the battle over illegitimacy was more a fight among Republicans than between Republicans and Democrats. This issue continually threatened to break apart the Republican coalition because conservatives, especially those outside Congress, threatened to publicly oppose the Republican bill unless stronger anti-illegitimacy measures were adopted.

The most radical policy considered by Republicans was to end all or most welfare support for illegitimate births. Charles Murray, Robert Rector, and others strongly supported this policy, but few elected Republicans were willing to publicly support cutting children born outside marriage from welfare benefits for the duration of their childhood. However, a less draconian version of this policy emerged and attracted considerable support among conservative Republicans. In the spring and summer of 1994, as Republicans from several House committees worked with the conservative profamily groups on the bill that would become H.R. 4, there was serious internal conflict among Republicans in the House and between House Republicans and the family groups outside Congress. The conflict was caused by the desire of some members and the family groups to permanently end both AFDC and food stamps for illegitimate children born to teen mothers. After a protracted struggle, all sides agreed on two policies.

First, states would be prohibited from increasing the cash welfare benefit if a mother receiving welfare gave birth to another child. This policy, which came to be known as the family cap, eventually became very popular in the states. Second, states would be prohibited from providing cash benefits to unwed teen mothers. Both of these policies were included in H.R. 4, in the original Shaw markup bill considered by the Human Resources Subcommittee in February 1995, and in the bill passed by the House of Representatives in March 1995. The provisions then became a matter of lively debate on the floor of the Senate, and both were defeated in separate votes. Subsequently, House Republicans attempted to include the family cap in the final bill, but the Senate, aided by a parliamentary rule that applied to the final bill, refused to go along, and the provision was dropped.

Despite the defeat of both the family cap and the prohibition on cash welfare for minor, unwed mothers, Republicans were able to include in the final bill a host of provisions designed to reduce illegitimacy, many of which were supported by Democrats. Several comments about these provisions are in order. The block grant structure of TANF gives states much more flexibility to try innovative policies than did previous law. Thus states are now free to implement policies such as the family cap and limits on cash benefits for teen mothers, which would have been difficult or impossible under AFDC. In fact more than twenty states have already implemented the family cap; in the future, states may well try other ways to reduce illegitimacy because of two provisions in the new law that reward them for reducing their illegitimacy rates.

The first provision is the $200-million-per-year performance bonus fund. States that excel in achieving the goals of the TANF program, which include increasing the proportion of children in two-parent families, promoting marriage, and reducing illegitimate births, are given cash bonuses. Second, up to five states that reduce their illegitimacy rate are eligible for an annual payment of up to $20 million, provided the state's rate of pregnancy terminations is less than the rate in 1995.

Another approach to illegitimacy taken by Republicans was to provide $50 million per year for five years in entitlement funding for abstinence education. This provision was the target of some controversy in the Senate and during the House-Senate conference during the fall of 1995 because Democrats, responding to lobbying by Eunice Shriver and others, tried to broaden the definition of abstinence to include the use of birth control. The statute contains a detailed definition of abstinence education, which pointedly does not allow advocacy of birth control. Indeed, a legal interpretation of the statute (Haskins and Bevan 1997) indicates that no program that advocates the use of birth control, or "safe sex," can receive funds.

Illegitimacy is the nation's gravest social problem. In the eyes of many researchers and policymakers, illegitimacy is a root cause of welfare, violence, crime, and a host of other problems. Although Murray (1993) believes that the only way to stop illegitimacy is to end welfare payments for illegitimate children, the welfare debate of 1996 shows that there is very little support for such a radical approach. Even the scaled-back version contained in the House welfare bill of March 1995 was defeated on the Senate floor in September by a resounding vote of seventy-six to twenty-four, with a majority of Republicans in opposition. Thus we must hope that the milder policies adopted in 1996, and the financial incentives for states to develop innovative approaches, will have an effect in the years ahead. If not, the nation will continue to be afflicted by illegitimacy and its consequences.

CONCLUSION

In his message to Congress in 1935, the year he signed the Social Security Act, President Roosevelt (1938) stated flatly that welfare was a "narcotic" and "a subtle destroyer of the human spirit" that "induces a spiritual and moral disintegration fundamentally destructive to the national fibre." The nation, he said, "must and shall quit this business of relief." Simply put, Roosevelt knew that welfare created the moral hazards that accompany nonwork. What he probably did not know was that something very much like a culture would grow up around lives based on permanent welfare and fatherless families. For more than half a century, American policy for helping the poor ignored Roosevelt's injunction to quit the business of relief. Indeed, the nation did quite the opposite, building a large means-tested welfare state. Worse, until very recently, the nation's welfare programs required almost nothing from their beneficiaries except continued destitution.

By 1996 most Americans, nearly all elected Republicans, and a majority of elected Democrats came to believe that Roosevelt's fears and predictions had proved correct. As a result, the Congress and the president took a giant step in the direction of forcing parents of dependent children to behave more responsibly by making welfare contingent on preparing for, seeking, and actually entering employment. National policymakers also put the force of the federal government behind a movement to encourage more responsible sexual behavior and sent a much clearer message than in the past that it was wrong to have children outside marriage whom single parents could support neither emotionally nor financially.

Why did the nation ignore Roosevelt's warning for so many years and why did the nation take a U-turn in 1996? That the nation had created a massive welfare state that provided trillions of dollars in benefits to millions of poor and low-income Americans, often on an entitlement basis, is beyond dispute. That the nation was spending more and more money on these programs without obvious compensating benefits is equally certain. Although the programs had, over the years, helped millions of Americans survive a personal crisis and even in many cases get back on their feet following unfortunate life events, the programs also reduced work among young parents, subsidized a shocking increase in the number of illegitimate births, led to intergenerational dependency on welfare, contributed to the rearing of a huge and growing proportion of the nation's children in fatherless families, and stifled the development of children growing up in welfare-dependent and fatherless families.

Liberals created these programs in the name of compassion for the unfortunate. To some extent, liberals gained politically from being the party of welfare, but the rewards for being the party of social insurance were even greater. Many liberals, particularly in the academic world, defended the expansive welfare system up to and even after the turning point of 1996. This record suggests that liberals were motivated primarily by the desire to protect people, especially children, from the ravages of poverty—even if the poverty was of their own making.

Moreover, it seems highly likely that chance played an important role in the history that we have traced. In 1935 Roosevelt may have been one of the few people who believed that "relief" posed a moral hazard. The typical ADC beneficiary at the time was a widow, and the incipient ADC program was small, but two demographic events left the growing program exposed as a cultural outlier. First, the years after 1960 produced a relentless increase in the number of mothers entering the workforce. That working mothers, millions of them single, should work to pay taxes so that other single mothers could stay home with their children made for a highly unstable political situation. Second, every uptick in the number of mothers entering the workforce was matched by an increase in the number of illegitimate births. For many Americans, that mothers who failed to work were also violating fundamental American values about responsible sex and responsible parenting further jeopardized programs widely perceived to support both nonwork and irresponsible parenthood.

These trends inevitably produced a moment of reckoning. Why this moment came in 1996 is impossible to fully explain, but the coincidence of four conditions must play an important role in any reasonable account. The first was a Democratic president who supported serious reform and indeed was among the most effective politicians of his time in publicizing both the problems of welfare and the potential solutions. Second, just as this president was giving credibility to traditional conservative claims about the defects of welfare and proposing solutions that no national Democrat had proposed before, Republicans seized control of both chambers of Congress for the first time in forty years. Third, members on the most important committees of jurisdiction in the House of Representatives had a comprehensive welfare reform bill ready to introduce, and a group of Republican members had both the expertise and the determination to push the bill through the legislative process. Fourth, Republican control of Congress was matched by Republican control of the nation's governorships. Several of these Republican governors were devoted to and experienced in welfare reform and worked tirelessly to support the Republican bill in Congress. These conditions ensured that the president would have the opportunity to sign a major reform bill.

As it turned out, he had three opportunities, the last one of which he grabbed. The days of tireless tinkering with welfare were over; the nation was set on a course of deep reform, the results of which are now being determined.

REFERENCES

Bane, Mary J., and David T. Ellwood. 1983. "Slipping into and out of Poverty: The Dynamics of Spells." Working Paper 1199. Cambridge, Mass.: National Bureau of Economic Research (September).

Burke, Vee. 1995. "Cash and Noncash Benefits for Persons with Limited Income: Eligibility, Rules, Recipient and Expenditure Data, FY1992–FY1994." 96-159 EPW. Washington, D.C.: Congressional Research Service.

Danziger, Sheldon, Robert Haveman, and Robert Plotnick. 1981. "How Income Transfers Affect Work, Savings, and the Income Distribution: A Critical Review." *Journal of Economic Literature* 19(3): 975–1028.

Drescher, Seymour. 1968. *Tocqueville and Beaumont on Social Reform*. New York: Harper and Row.

Edelman, Peter. 1997. "The Worst Thing Bill Clinton Has Done." *Atlantic Monthly* 279(3): 43–58.

Ellwood, David. 1989. *Poor Support: Poverty in the American Family*. New York: Basic Books.

Ellwood, David T., and Mary J. Bane. 1985. "The Impact of AFDC on Family Structure and Living Arrangements." In *Research in Labor Economics,* edited by R. G. Ehrenberg. Vol. 7. Greenwich, Conn.: JAI Press.

Gilens, Martin. 1999. *Why Americans Hate Welfare: Race, Media, and the Politics of Antipoverty Policy*. Chicago: University of Chicago Press.

Gueron, Judith M., and Edward Pauly. 1991. *From Welfare to Work*. New York: Russell Sage Foundation.

Haskins, Ron. 1996. "Does Welfare Encourage Illegitimacy?" *American Enterprise* 7(4): 48–49.

Haskins, Ron, and Carol S. Bevan. 1997. "Abstinence Education Under Welfare Reform." *Children and Youth Services Review* 19(5-6): 465–84.

Himmelfarb, Gertrude. 1985. *The Idea of Poverty*. New York: Random House.

Jencks, Christopher. 1992. *Rethinking Social Policy: Race, Poverty, and the Underclass*. Cambridge, Mass.: Harvard University Press.

Kaus, Mickey. 1986. "The Work Ethic State." *New Republic,* July 7, 1986, 22–33.

———. 1992. *The End of Equality*. New York: Basic Books.

Kristol, Irving. 1995. *Neoconservatism: The Autobiography of an Idea*. New York: Free Press.

Low-Income Opportunity Working Group. 1986. *Up from Dependency: A New National Public Assistance Strategy*. Washington: Office of the President.

Lynn, Laurence E., Jr. 1993. "Ending Welfare Reform as We Know It." *American Prospect* 4(15): 83–92.

Lynn, Laurence E., Jr., and Whitman, David. 1981. *The President as Policymaker: Jimmy Carter and Welfare Reform*. Philadelphia: Temple University Press.

Maynard, Rebecca. 1997. "Paternalism, Teenage Pregnancy Prevention, and Teenage Parent Services." In *The New Paternalism: Supervisory Approaches to Poverty,* edited by L. M. Mead. Washington, D.C.: Brookings.

Mead, Lawrence M. 1986. *Beyond Entitlement: The Social Obligations of Citizenship*. New York: Free Press.

———. 1992. *The New Politics of Poverty: The Nonworking Poor in America*. New York: Basic Books.

Moffitt, Robert. 1992. "Incentive Effects of the U.S. Welfare System: A Review." *Journal of Economic Literature* 30: 1–61.

Moynihan, Daniel P. 1973. *The Politics of a Guaranteed Income: The Nixon Administration and the Family Assistance Plan*. New York: Vintage.

Murray, Charles. 1984. *Losing Ground: American Social Policy, 1950–1980*. New York: Basic Books.

———. 1993. "The Coming White Underclass." *Wall Street Journal,* October 29, 1993.

Piven, Frances F. 1996. "Was Welfare Reform Worthwhile?" *American Prospect* 7(27): 14–15.

Rector, Robert, and William F. Lauber. 1995. *America's Failed $5.4 Trillion War on Poverty*. Washington, D.C.: Heritage Foundation.

Roosevelt, Franklin D. 1938. "Annual Message to the Congress (January 4, 1935)." In *The Public Papers and Addresses of Franklin D. Roosevelt with a Special Introduction and Explanatory Notes by President Roosevelt*. Vol. 4. New York: Random House.

Rossi, Peter. 1987. "The Iron Law of Evaluation and Other Metallic Rules." *Research in Social Problems and Public Policy* 4: 3–20.

Roth, Byron M. 1994. *Prescription for Failure*. New Brunswick, N.J.: Transaction.

Shaw, E. C., Nancy L. Johnson, and Fred Grandy. June 1992. "Moving Ahead: How America Can Reduce Poverty Through Work." Washington: House Committee on Ways and Means.

U.S. Department of Health and Human Services. 1995. Report to Congress on Out-of-Wedlock Childbearing. PHS 95-1257. Hyattsville, Md.: National Center for Health Statistics.

U.S. House of Representatives. 1991. *1991 Green Book: Background Material and Data on Programs within the Jurisdiction of the Committee on Ways and Means*. Washington: U.S. Government Printing Office.

———. 1996. *1996 Green Book: Background Material and Data on Programs within the Jurisdiction of the Committee on Ways and Means*. Washington: U.S. Government Printing Office.

Ventura, Stephanie J., and Christine A. Bachrach. 2000. "Nonmarital Childbearing in the United States, 1940–1999." *National Vital Statistics Reports* 48(16). Hyattsville, Md.: National Center for Health Statistics.

Wednesday Group. 1991. "Moving Ahead: Initiatives for Expanding Opportunity in America." Washington: House of Representatives (October).

Working Seminar. 1987. *A Community of Self-reliance: The New Consensus on Family and Welfare*. Washington, D.C: American Enterprise Institute.

Part II

What States Are Thinking and Doing

Chapter 3

Welfare Reform, Management Systems, and Policy Theories of Child Well-Being

Cathy M. Johnson and Thomas L. Gais

C hildren's interests were frequently invoked during the congressional debate surrounding the 1996 Personal Responsibility and Work Opportunity Reconciliation Act (PRWORA). Supporters surely brought other values and beliefs to bear when developing and assessing the legislation: some thought the act would cap federal spending on welfare or increase the supply of labor to American businesses. However, the act encompassed mainly programs for which only families with children were eligible, and much of the debate centered on how best to end dependency, illegitimacy, and even poverty in families with children, including presumed generational cycles involving children not yet born.

As Congress deliberated, those who supported the act, those who wanted to amend it, and those who opposed it all argued that they were the ones who knew what was best for children. Behind these claims rested different ideas about what children needed and how public policy could improve children's lives. The act failed to resolve these competing visions, not an unusual outcome in American politics, and it reflects several distinct ideas about what is best for children.

What happens to these different approaches to children's well-being depends on what the states do as they develop their own programs and implement the requirements of the Personal Responsibility Act. This chapter, therefore, asks the question, How have states addressed the interests of children in their welfare reforms—not just in their formal policies but also in the ways in which they implement those policies in their management or administrative systems? The chapter draws on field research conducted by nineteen research teams, one for each state included in the State Capacity Study, for the Rockefeller Institute of Government of the State University of New York. The teams collected data according to a common report at the state level as well as through visits to two local welfare offices in each state. The information collected spanned the ways in which states have organized or reorganized their management systems, often encompassing a vast number and variety of public and private institutions, to carry out their welfare programs.

This research can reveal the policy theories that are being enacted in the day-to-day operations of state and local welfare systems. By policy theories, we mean the explicit—and implicit—postulated causal connections between policies and desired outcomes. We consider what kinds of services are provided, in what sequence, to which persons, and to what apparent ends, and we determine what agency missions, types of expertise, and data management capacities are brought to bear on the tasks of running welfare programs. By examining state and local institutions and processes, we can begin to discern what these new welfare systems are organized to do—and by the same token, what they do not seem to be doing.

PRWORA contains three major approaches to children's well-being, three policy theories that relate program activities to the interests of children. The family structure theory contends that children benefit from being born to families that are able to care for them, specifically, not to unmarried couples or teens. The resource theory holds that children benefit from increased resources as caregivers enter and progress in the workforce. The environment theory maintains that children reap psychological and sociological benefits from being part of a family in which the head of the household works. Although PRWORA includes elements of all three of these policy theories, our research finds that states are creating welfare systems most consistent with the environment theory. States have written laws, constructed management systems, and allocated resources around the task of moving parents into the workforce, but they have done much less to ensure that working parents have higher family incomes. Indeed, many states have management systems and policies that hinder families from combining work, cash assistance, and in-kind benefits. With the emphasis on work rather than on increasing family resources, state programs are most consistent with the idea that the simple fact that a parent works creates a more structured, better functioning environment for children.

FAMILY STRUCTURE THEORY

The family structure theory is highlighted in the preamble to the Personal Responsibility and Work Opportunity Reconciliation Act of 1996 (Public Law 104-93, 110 Stat. 215, Title 1, Sec. 101), which opens with a congressional finding that "marriage is the foundation of a successful society." Marriage is an "essential institution" for promoting children's interests, and children require "responsible fatherhood and motherhood" for a successful upbringing. These statements underscore the belief that children's well-being is protected and advanced most when children are reared in two-parent families. Indeed, Congress continued the preamble with a detailed account of the problems encountered by children reared in single-parent homes: they are more likely to receive public assistance and for longer periods of time; they are more likely to have problems in school and low educational achievement; they are more likely to be involved with the juvenile justice system and live in neighborhoods with higher crime rates; and they are more likely to grow up to be adults who are poor, do not marry, and receive welfare.

The preamble reflects the fact that, for many legislators, the key to improving children's lives is to alter the structure of families by reducing out-of-wedlock births and promoting marriage. Representative James Talent (R-Mo.) professed that "the growth in illegitimacy is the single most important change in our country in the last generation. It is a fact so powerful that it annihilates all other facts" (U.S. House of Representatives 1996, 4). Representative Clay Shaw (R-Fla.) explained that the best way to fight poverty was to encourage marriage and discourage out-of-wedlock births. Representative Tim Hutchinson (R-Ark.) echoed this thought with, "It may take a village, but it sure takes a father" to rear children successfully (12). For these legislators, the problem is single-parent families, not poverty, welfare receipt, school failure, or juvenile delinquency. These are secondary problems that would wane if all children were born and reared within the institution of marriage.

Advocates of the family structure theory argue that "you get what you pay for" and that Aid to Families with Dependent Children (AFDC) paid for and promoted single motherhood.[1] They believe that withdrawing public assistance from single mothers—or making assistance less attractive—will hinder the formation of single-parent families by encouraging women to forgo childbearing or to get married before or when they become pregnant. Congressional adherents of this view pushed for federal provisions requiring states to impose family caps and to deny aid to unwed teen mothers and their children (Katz 1995). They were unsuccessful in imposing such federal mandates, but they were able to include in the act provisions allowing states to adopt these measures. The act also requires states to demand that teen mothers live at home and attend school in order to receive public assistance.

The act also allows states to pursue policy tools aimed at promoting marriage. These include granting aid to two-parent families, based on the idea that aid provided only to single-parent families encourages families to break apart, and implementing employment and training programs for men, based on the idea that men will not marry if they do not have adequate jobs.[2] Such proposals received little attention in congressional discussions about welfare reform, although the block grant provisions gave states the latitude to experiment with these alternatives.

However, as the debate moved out of the Congress and states began to implement the act, an important change occurred in the focus of the reforms. By and large, states have rejected the family structure theory. They have placed less emphasis on encouraging marriage and reducing out-of-wedlock births, particularly in relation to their strong focus on promoting work.

Some states have created new disincentives for teens or unmarried women (and to a lesser extent, men) to have additional children. Family caps, in a strict sense, exist in eighteen states: sixteen states deny all support to children born or presumably conceived while receiving welfare, and two states offer only flat grants that do not adjust to family size. An additional five states reduce grants to additional children or require the grants to be provided to third parties or in the form of vouchers (Stark and Levin-Epstein 1999). That family caps are found mainly in the South and the West, however, reduces their potential effect; benefit levels tend to be low in these regions, and thus the financial disincentives are small. In Mississippi each child adds only twenty-four dollars per month to a household's cash benefits (U.S. House of Representatives 1998).

In short, other than complying with the federal requirement that teen parents live with an adult if they want to receive benefits for themselves and their children, states have done little to target teen births. States have not emphasized services or programs explicitly designed to reduce teen birth rates through their welfare program, and no state has adopted a major initiative of the House to deny aid outright to unwed teen mothers.

States also have done relatively little to promote marriage. The use of financial incentives to encourage marriage has not spread across the states, and few other policy suggestions have emerged. Fatherhood programs tend to be spotty and small in scope, and because early evaluations, such as a recent assessment by the Manpower Demonstration Research Corporation (Doolittle et al. 1998), show little promise of effectiveness, states may be reluctant to expand them. States are required by federal law to establish paternity and to tighten up child support enforcement, but these activities are aimed at requiring financial contributions from noncustodial parents and not at promoting joint parenting among mothers and fathers. In fact some analysts believe that these requirements will further separate children from their fathers (Sorensen and Lerman 1998).

Aside from family caps, which are relatively easy to administer and save rather than cost states money, states have done little to change marital or reproductive behavior. Although there may be consensus on the wisdom and desirability of preventing pregnancies among teens and unmarried couples, there is no political consensus on how to do it. A common response to this uncertainty is to create fairly unspecific, poorly funded programs and to devolve the controversial decisions to local governments and agencies (Nathan, Gentry, and Lawrence 1999). In some states, various proposals with the express purpose of controlling reproductive behavior were debated by legislators. These were, however, extremely controversial, and legislators found it easier to turn away from them and instead to build coalitions around policies focused on work.

RESOURCE THEORY AND ENVIRONMENT THEORY

Although the preamble to the Personal Responsibility Act highlights marriage and the reduction of out-of-wedlock births, the stipulations of the act itself focus on moving welfare recipients into the workplace and off the welfare rolls. Through time limits and work requirements, the act emphasizes paid employment by single mothers. Republicans, as well as many Democrats, lauded the replacement of AFDC, a program adopted to enable mothers to stay home with their children, with Temporary Assistance for Needy Families (TANF), a program that provides only temporary aid with the expectation that mothers will come to support their families with earnings (Bryner 1998). When President Bill Clinton signed the Personal Responsibility Act, he praised it for being "tough on work" and for correcting deficiencies in earlier versions of the legislation, which he characterized as "soft on work."[3]

In contrast to their focus on family formation, states have put enormous emphasis on employment goals. Although state welfare reforms are diverse, most states share a strong focus on employment, with an emphasis on a "work-first" model, which seeks to create an immediate attachment to the workforce, rather than focusing on education and other development of human capital (Nathan and Gais 1999). One of the more surprising changes in the aftermath of PRWORA, as well as in the more comprehensive waiver programs, has been the widespread and often bipartisan political support for this new emphasis on work. Although partisan fights erupted in some states and on some issues, those divisions were more the exception than the rule. The political allure of the work-first approach was strong and showed some promise of establishing a widely accepted mission, which AFDC had long lacked.

Although the act distinctly demands greater emphasis on paid employment, it does not present any one particular reason for moving women on welfare into the workforce. There can be many justifications for an increased emphasis on paid employment, and one argument linking these policy changes to children's interests was that employed parents—typically mothers—would promote child well-being. Policymakers have been somewhat vague about the particular aspects of child well-being they thought would improve if parents moved from welfare to work, but generally their expectations fall in two categories, either the resource theory or the environment theory.

Proponents of the resource theory argue that working parents improve children's material well-being: employment brings higher incomes, which could be used to purchase the things children need. The idea that paid employment should make one better-off than receiving public assistance is the principle behind the Clinton administration's phrase "make work pay" (Bane and Ellwood 1994). Clinton reiterated this sentiment when he signed the act, explaining that "the best antipoverty program is still a job."[4] Republican members of Congress "also argued that even low wage jobs would provide families with more money than welfare" (Haskins 2001). This approach to child well-being requires not only that mothers get jobs that pay at least as much as they might receive in cash assistance and food stamps but that they also receive adequate support services, such as child care and transportation assistance, to make up for the increased costs of going to work. Some advocates of this theory also emphasize the need for education and training so that women can obtain higher-paying jobs (Dukakis and Kanter 1988; Bentsen 1990), and others suggest various forms of wage supplements (Burtless 1997), assuming that adults with little work experience and few skills are unlikely to acquire such positions.

This resources model, however, was not the only argument in favor of work-based reforms. Policymakers rarely rely only on material wealth to champion work, given that a host of studies document the difficulty of substantially raising the incomes of poor men and women through employment alone (Bane and Ellwood 1994; Blank 1997; Edin and Lein 1997; Gueron and Pauly 1991). Downplaying increased income as a central goal of work, many policy advocates instead see work as an activity that changes people for the better. When this view of work is applied to child well-being, it forms the crux of the third theory, the environment theory.

Adherents of the environment theory emphasize a desire to improve the nature of children's upbringing, and they present work as the key to this transformation. An employed parent is a better parent, they argue, one who, by working, transmits to her children the psychological benefits she realizes from being a worker: structure, self-esteem, self-confidence, self-discipline. During the congressional debate on welfare reform, for example, Representative John Ensign (R-Nev.) proclaimed, "I grew up with a single mom.... And I watched my mom get up every day and go to work....

What we need in this country is to have children watching their parents go to work on a daily basis" (Congressional Record 1995, H3363). Parents who worked would be more responsible, disciplined, and structured, and they would expose their children to the world of work and the characteristics needed to survive in it. Work would "give children of this country an opportunity and incentive to enjoy the American dream, to get off the welfare system, to know what the free enterprise system is about."

The increased earnings obtained through employment are a good but not a necessary aspect of the environment theory. Work is salutary even if it does not lead to upward mobility because of the effect it has on the behavior and attitudes of mothers and their children (Mead 1996). Consequently, this theory places little emphasis on education and training or on the various ways of supplementing the earnings of low-income workers. What is important is that women receiving welfare go to work and get off the rolls; how much they earn or their prospects of advancement are unimportant.

One support service that is critical to the environment theory, however, is child care. At least implicit in the theory is the idea that poor mothers receiving welfare may not be very good mothers and that their children will be better off if the mothers go to work and the children receive alternative care (Johnson 1998). Some adherents of this theory believe so passionately in the transformative value of work that they place much less importance on the quality of care received by these children; others emphasize the need for quality care that provides better developmental opportunities for poor children.

WORK NOT WELFARE: INSTITUTIONAL CHANGE AND INCREASING COMPLEXITY

In the early stages of the implementation of the Personal Responsibility Act, states translated work requirements in the federal act into major changes in the institutions of welfare. States assigned employment bureaucracies greater control over the design and operation of welfare programs. The procedures that families face when applying for and receiving TANF communicate the expectation that women will work, that they will move into the labor force as quickly as they can, and that states will apply sanctions to enforce compliance (Nathan and Gais 1999). The basic character of the benefits has changed enormously. Although state spending on cash assistance has declined dramatically, states have greatly increased their spending on child care and employment services (Ellwood and Boyd 2000). Finally, states are devolving greater responsibilities in conducting and designing programs to local governments, contractors, and local offices of state agencies.

Thus most state welfare systems are more complex, devolved, and work oriented than they were just a few years ago. The question is, Do they implement either of the two work-based theories (resource theory and environment theory) found in the Personal Responsibility Act? The answer is yes, to an extent, and to the extent that any theory has been implemented, it is the environment theory, not the resource theory, that has been implemented. The initial conditions of the environment theory require only that states succeed in promoting work, and those conditions seem to have been met. A complete implementation of the environment theory, of course, requires monitoring or detection of the environments facing children, and it is true that states and localities are not doing that. However, the resource theory is even less fully implemented. The particular character of reform programs—and the institutional changes that help to create that character—encourages work but also appears to make it more difficult for families to combine earnings with other sources of support, including public assistance and in-kind entitlement benefits. Exceptions exist, but the tendency of most state and local systems is to promote either welfare or work, with higher costs imposed on those who want to mix the two.

The capacity to mix earnings and assistance (beyond direct work support services, such as child care and transportation) is critical because it is increasingly clear that, even in good economic times, earnings and child care assistance (and other assistance in paying for the direct costs of working) are typically insufficient to increase family incomes, much less lift families out of poverty. This premise is hardly new. Recent evaluations of the New Hope project in Milwaukee and Florida's Family Transition program underline the point. These projects were widely interpreted as successful, in part because of their moderate impact on earnings, especially for families that were not initially employed. Yet the estimated increase in earnings would not have compensated for the loss of income if the families had lost their food stamps or cash assistance. Thus any increase in overall income depended on the continued receipt of all assistance for which the families were eligible (Bos et al. 1999; Bloom et al. 1999).

If welfare systems were designed to increase overall family resources, they would consequently accept, and even encourage, families to combine earnings with various forms of assistance. This would be translated into a strong emphasis on work participation rates for persons on welfare, with less emphasis placed on caseload reduction. These systems would limit diversion activities to providing job search assistance and helping with short-term emergencies, but they would not create unnecessary barriers to program entry. States would also design and implement eligibility systems to ensure that families qualifying for food stamps, Medicaid, the Earned Income Tax Credit (EITC), and other entitlements would, in fact, receive those benefits if the families wanted them. States would also pass through to the families the child support, or at least a large part of it, collected from noncustodial parents. Such systems would also have fairly generous income and asset disregards, thereby minimizing the implicit tax on earnings in terms of cash assistance or other benefits. The welfare system would be well integrated with the state or district's workforce development system. Rather than merely offering job placement, job-readiness training, and other services designed to get people into any job fast, it would make available to parents the whole panoply of work services, including skills training, that could enable parents to acquire higher paying jobs. Recertifications would be relatively infrequent, and data on earnings—not just caseloads, work participation rates, or duration of employment—would be tracked and treated as significant measures of performance.

This, of course, is a tall order, and no state has all of these characteristics. Most states are less accommodating to combining earnings and welfare; instead, they stress either work or welfare. This emphasis is not always explicit or obvious, but several institutional and policy factors discourage families from combining earnings and cash or other forms of assistance for extended periods of time.

For example, the new welfare processes are much more complex and burdensome for families that want to get and keep assistance, and the effect is to discourage families that can avoid welfare from relying on it. This is, of course, precisely the signal that many states and localities want to give: welfare should be a last, not a first, resort. A caregiver who enters a welfare office may now be expected to search for work before her application can be approved or even before she applies for assistance. States and localities may offer short-term diversion assistance, often a small grant that precludes continuing assistance in the near future. Applicants may be immediately required to cooperate in securing child support from a noncustodial parent. Some local welfare offices are expected to know about and to refer families to local charitable and other private service organizations. Caregivers may be expected to attend general orientation meetings, job clubs, or parenting training. Although states and localities treat personal responsibility agreements, self-sufficiency contracts, and other such instruments in a variety of ways—from guiding the basic relations between caseworkers and clients to simply seeing them as another document to sign—they can demand frequent meetings and fairly intrusive questions and activities, including home visits. In sum, the new goals of nondependency, engagement, and employment are often expressed in more intense processes, which many clients may be more than happy to avoid.

A second policy factor that discourages families from combining earnings and cash assistance is the fact that the new employment and welfare processes have not replaced, but have been added onto, the older "quality control" processes meant to minimize eligibility errors (what Bane and Ellwood call the compliance-eligibility culture of AFDC offices). Even though PRWORA repealed AFDC quality control, most of the states in our research sample had not relaxed their efforts as of early 1998, and some actually stepped up their antifraud activities. In addition, many of the states in our study reported that they still felt pressure from the federal government to minimize eligibility errors in the Food Stamp program, which in some cases is still handled by the same personnel who review clients for TANF assistance. Thus families are facing not only new, complicated, and sometimes intrusive processes surrounding work preparation, personal responsibility agreements, orientations, and sometimes separate visits to a workforce development agency but also the extensive documentation and review processes that have long characterized AFDC application and recertification procedures.

Finally, state policies concerning child support make it harder or less attractive for families to mix earnings and cash assistance. States are putting greater emphasis on securing child support orders for families on welfare rolls and on securing support from noncustodial parents. However, nearly all states keep a portion of the child support payments to offset the costs of providing cash assistance (Gallagher et al. 1998). This policy encourages families with support to leave welfare, and it makes it difficult for families that remain on the rolls to increase their incomes by combining cash assistance, child support, and earnings.

Thus complex work-first processes along with persisting and even enhanced antifraud and quality control measures increase the hassle of getting and staying on welfare and of mixing earnings and cash assistance. The inability to receive child support while receiving cash assistance may make it even less worthwhile for working parents to supplement their earnings with cash assistance. Families that can find work and low-cost day care with relatives may consider it to be neither feasible nor desirable to stay on the welfare rolls, even though the extra assistance would help them increase their overall incomes. The result is that despite the many new services available to TANF families, as well as the increased generosity of state income and asset disregards (Acs et al. 1998), the administration of the laws tends to discourage many working families from enjoying these benefits.

ACCESS TO FOOD STAMPS AND MEDICAID

Although several factors may inhibit families from combining earnings and cash assistance, other factors may make it more difficult for families to augment their earnings with in-kind benefits, such as food stamps and Medicaid. Enrollment in both programs has declined. Between 1996 and 1997, Medicaid enrollment for nondisabled children—who are likely to be in the poor families served by TANF—declined by 3.3 percent, from an estimated 20.5 million to 19.9 million (Thompson and Nathan 1999). The decline is surprising, in part because Medicaid eligibility has expanded in recent years as the number of children in low-income families without medical insurance has continued to grow.

Enrollment in the Food Stamp program declined from a peak in March 1994, when 28 million people participated in the program, to 18.7 million in September 1998. Household participation has seen similar change, falling from 11.3 million households in March 1994 to 7.8 million in September 1998. These declines are not totally unexpected. Declines in Food Stamp program enrollment are common during periods of economic growth, such as the middle and late 1990s, given that eligibility depends primarily on family income and assets. The declines, in light of recent policy changes, are also hardly anomalous. Federal legislation in 1996 eliminated these benefits to legal aliens and imposed new work requirements on able-bodied individuals without dependent children.

Yet the scope, pattern, and timing of these changes suggest that more than economic factors and changes in eligibility rules are at work. Most of the decline in enrollment in the Food Stamp program is not among legal aliens and able-bodied individuals without dependents but rather among poor families with dependent children. Between 1994 and 1997, 61 percent of the program's enrollment decline was because of a drop in the number of families receiving cash assistance (U.S. Department of Agriculture 1999), even though many families remain eligible for food stamps after leaving cash assistance. Of course, this decline in participation by families may be the result of the economy, as more poor families find jobs. In a time-series analysis of Food Stamp program caseloads, however, caseload declines at the state level were found to be significantly related to a simple measure of the implementation of state welfare reforms, after controlling for changes in unemployment, typically the strongest economic variable in models of welfare enrollment (Wallace and Blank 2000). There is also indirect survey evidence that participation in state welfare programs may affect participation in the Food Stamp program; a 1997 national survey found that departures from the Food Stamp program were higher (62 percent) among families that left welfare in the previous year than among families that had not been receiving cash assistance (of whom only 46 percent left the program [Zedlewski and Brauner 1999]). The decline is not only found in the Food Stamp program. In an analysis of early welfare reforms in California and Florida, one study found that work-first programs had a significant and depressive effect on Medicaid participation (Ellwood and Lewis 1999).

These studies are not conclusive. Yet even if the precise effects are unknown, the implementation of state and local welfare reforms poses several problems, even fundamental dilemmas, regarding participation in safety net programs, and these problems have the potential of limiting the income gains of low-income families. Many of the ways in which states are changing institutional roles to create a stronger emphasis on work may concurrently be creating new problems of access to food stamps and Medicaid. By assigning greater responsibilities to employment bureaucracies, states are giving greater control over the treatment of welfare families to agencies and contractors whose traditional missions have placed little or no emphasis on ensuring access to safety net benefits. Also, in a few states and localities, private organizations have been given major roles in administering TANF programs—even, in a few locations, to the point of handling eligibility functions. Yet privatizing TANF creates an institutional separation between cash assistance and safety net programs, given that food stamps and Medicaid are still handled by public employees. This institutional separation might be bridged by sharing offices, sharing information systems, and encouraging close working relations, but those bridges are difficult to build and maintain.

In addition, the more complex processes used to promote work may also make it difficult to ensure full access to entitlements. By front loading welfare intake processes with new requirements and activities, there is some risk of discouraging clients from applying for safety net benefits. Potential TANF applicants may not learn about the availability of food stamps or Medicaid, even though they may qualify for them, if they accept a diversion payment in lieu of an application, if they find a job during an initial job search but the expected earnings are insufficient to lift the family out of poverty, or if they refuse to comply with initial work search or other TANF-related program requirements and fail to return to the social services office, under the impression that they cannot access other benefits. At the back end of the process, TANF families appear to be leaving the program at greater rates and under more diverse circumstances, as they get jobs, receive sanctions, increase earnings, or choose to leave to stop the time-limit clock. A higher departure rate, in turn, means more opportunities for families to drop out of safety net programs because of misunderstandings by frontline workers about policies, wrong actions by welfare information systems (Maxwell 1999), failures to inform caregivers about their options, or a myriad of other reasons.

Another potentially limiting factor is the administration of safety net programs, which may be better adapted to a dependent, than to a working, population. Remaining in these programs may impose transaction costs, which many working families are unwilling or unable to pay. In most states, the Food Stamp program requires quarterly and in-person recertification; states are reluctant to relax these requirements because the U.S. Department of Agriculture still imposes substantial penalties for errors. The problem is less acute for Medicaid, because small changes in income are less likely to require changes in benefits and because the federal government places less emphasis on quality control and much greater emphasis on outreach (Thompson and Gais 2000). Nonetheless, Medicaid remains an extraordinarily complicated program with an enormous number of eligibility categories (Ellwood 1999), and that complexity alone makes it difficult to keep families fully informed of their options, particularly when working families in secondary labor markets are undergoing frequent changes in their financial circumstances.

The more general problem is administering a coherent social services system with very mixed messages. Time limits, self-sufficiency plans, diversion benefits, work requirements, and other mechanisms are designed in part to minimize reliance on TANF, especially cash assistance. On the other hand, federal signals seem to press for maximizing outreach and enrollment for Medicaid and the State Children's Health Insurance Program (SCHIP) and, under the Food Stamp program, minimizing eligibility errors. Particularly in states and localities in which all of these programs are administered by the same offices and the same people, a consistent bureaucratic message is not easy to convey to frontline workers and their supervisors, much less to clients. Breaking up these administrative structures so that each of these missions can be stressed may make sense from a bureaucratic perspective, but that institutional separation may create fragmented systems that are difficult for clients to understand and access. Thus it is no small administrative challenge to maintain the basic safety net programs, including their missions and coverage, while creating another and very different system that focuses on jobs: to do so may require strong connections among agencies and a frank acceptance of their differing goals and of the resulting tension between these agencies.

In sum, our argument suggests that, in most instances, families are unlikely to see significant increases in their overall income because of important features and issues in state and local implementation. Sometimes families may be on the welfare rolls and sometimes they may be working, but combining sources of support from both systems may become increasingly uncommon. We do not yet know this outcome to be true, but although work participation rates of welfare recipients have increased significantly in most states, those increases are generally much smaller in magnitude than are the declines in caseloads, and many of those who are counted in those rates are not receiving any earnings. As a result, the absolute number of families with earnings and income support has probably fallen in recent years; and as we would expect, overall income levels have dropped among the lowest income, single-parent families—despite strong increases in earnings, especially when food stamps are included as income (and before EITC is considered, which is not affected as much by these implementation issues as are cash assistance and food stamps).[5]

Of course, it is also possible that working, even without short-run increases in income, may eventually lead to higher incomes. Some of the welfare "leaver" studies that track families over many quarters through administrative records show slight increases in earnings over time (Born 1999), yet these effects are neither strong nor easy to interpret at the level of individual families, and it is unclear whether these increases produce overall increases in income. It is not unreasonable to say, then, that most states have not yet implemented the resources theory.

RELYING ON A THEORY OF HOME ENVIRONMENT

Although the Personal Responsibility Act encompasses three major theories of how children could benefit from welfare reform, only one of these theories is widely implemented—and that perhaps more by default than by design. States do relatively little to alter the structure of families in which children are reared, and they have not adopted policies or developed management systems that expedite combining wages with cash and in-kind assistance to increase family resources. They do, however, strongly promote and facilitate work and worklike activities, whether or not these result in increased overall income. Thus most of the effects on children must arise from the environment model, under the assumption that a working parent will improve children's well-being by altering the way in which children are reared.

The environment model, however, depends on several assumptions. It assumes that work by the head of the household leads to a more structured, orderly life at home rather than a chaotic or stressful one. It assumes that a working parent feels greater control over her life, greater independence, and a greater competence, which carries over into her family role. It assumes that children see and realize a relation between hard work and achievement rather than hard work that is unrecognized and unrewarded. It assumes that children are well cared for in reasonably safe and nurturing child care facilities rather than being supervised by an unreliable patch-work of caregivers. Moreover, once these hypotheses—that claim that, simply by working, a parent helps her children—are explicated, it becomes apparent that the model depends on other factors besides the employment of the mother, including the psychological health of the mother, the family's interactions with one another, and the availability of quality child care.

Whether this model is correct, it is nonetheless untested, and states are not collecting the information needed to examine even the simplest aspects of the model. Our study of welfare information systems and their capacities shows that states collect and report little information about children's environments or the factors that affect how well the environment theory works. States know very little about child care arrangements or needs among families on welfare. In the Rockefeller Institute's field research questionnaire, a number of questions important to the implementation of welfare reform were posed, yet the questions dealing with children were those that states were least able to answer (Nathan and Gais 1999). Welfare information systems were found to be adept at keeping track of the basic status of welfare cases—how many applications were filed, how many were approved, how many cases were active at a particular site, and to a lesser degree, how many were assigned to a work activity and how many were actually working. However, very few state information systems could report on whether families lacked child care (and were thus exempt from work requirements) or how long they had been waiting for child care services. Similarly, states fail to capture much information about children and their home environments in their "tracking studies," which constitute most of what passes as evaluation in the post-AFDC world: these studies focus on adult employment behavior and on the capacity of families to stay off the welfare rolls (General Accounting Office 1999).

Lacking even basic information about children and where they spend their days, states do not have the means to examine more complicated questions about work conditions, family dynamics, and child development, factors that are central to the environment theory of child well-being.[6] These problems are compounded by second-order devolution: the decentralization of programs within states to local welfare offices or systems. Although state-level data on child well-being and some of these intermediate conditions may be obtainable, though at substantial cost, collecting information on these connections in each locality is certainly a formidable problem.[7]

The environment model is implemented incompletely by the states because they do not examine the connection between a working parent and children's well-being. Implementing the other two models creates even more difficulties for the states. The continuing political struggles over sexuality, and especially teen sexuality, may make it complicated for many states to construct strong coalitions in favor of any concrete approach to reduce teen and out-of-wedlock births. Although the resource theory may have straightforward causal links between its proximate and ultimate objectives—that is, increasing families' material resources will improve child well-being—putting the theory into effect poses complex administrative problems in the context of the work-first approach. Finding ways to satisfy concerns about quality control without overburdening working parents may require enormous creativity. Most of all, however, the resource theory demands good management at the level of social service systems, not just at the TANF or program level. Increasing family resources in a significant way may require greater connectivity among three difficult-to-reconcile social program principles: work first, which is largely represented in state and local TANF systems; entitlements, which are still well represented in the Food Stamp and Medicaid programs; and human capital investment, which underlies most state workforce development systems (although this, too, is undergoing change as the federal Workforce Investment Act places new emphasis on core, work-first activities [see King and O'Shea 2001]). The tensions between the administration and operation of these basic principles are real, and they can easily lead to mutual disruption and even deterioration. The signaling and institutional realignments used to implement work-first programs may undermine access to entitlements, but given the kinds of jobs that most welfare recipients are moving into, we may be unable to expect major increases in family resources unless all three systems are reconciled, and most states still seem to be some distance from meeting these management challenges.

The political appeal of the environment theory as a way to connect welfare reform to children's interests may stem from the fact that the causal connection between a working parent and children's well-being can be assumed so easily. If policymakers presuppose that an employed head of household improves children's upbringing, they can concentrate on establishing systems that promote and enforce work, without concern about the consequences for children. Although even this is not easy and has required much effort by the states, it is less difficult than establishing a work program and monitoring, studying, and improving children's environment. Yet as a result, children will have to depend on the success of a policy theory—the environment theory—whose ultimate connections with child well-being are more assumed than observed—and that are probably not very well understood.

NOTES

1. This argument about AFDC has been made by many people in many places; see Murray (1984) and Popenoe (1996). To place current views of poverty and welfare in historical context, see Patterson (1994).

2. The argument that AFDC should be granted to two-parent families in order to prevent families from breaking up was made by President John F. Kennedy when he proposed AFDC-UP in 1961. See Kennedy (1961). The argument that two-parent families do not form because men lack adequate jobs was advanced by William Julius Wilson (1987).

3. White House Office of the Press Secretary, Statement by the President, August 22, 1996.

4. White House Office of the Press Secretary, Remarks by the President at the Signing of the Personal Responsibility and Work Opportunity Reconciliation Act, August 22, 1996.

5. For analyses of Current Population Survey data on family income in 1997 and before, see Primus (1999).

6. There are also obvious privacy questions about collecting these sorts of data. Child Trends' excellent publication (Child Trends 1999) suggests that states analyze these causal connections to child well-being using a variety of measures, including teacher surveys, in-home surveys and direct observations, and direct child assessments. That approach may address the "black box" character of the current way in which the environment theory is implemented, but it is also intrusive and certainly expensive.

7. Data on child poverty by state is often averaged over several years to obtain reasonably good estimates. See, for example, Bennett and Li (1998), which uses five-year averages to get good estimates of child poverty at the state level. The U.S. Census Bureau estimates county-level poverty rates for children or young people in its Small Area and Poverty Estimates program, but the latest data available in fall 1999 are for income in 1995, and the errors in the estimates are quite large.

REFERENCES

Acs, Gregory, Norma Coe, Keith Watson, and Robert Lerman. 1998. *Does Work Pay? An Analysis of the Work Incentives under TANF.* Washington, D.C.: Urban Institute.

Bane, Mary J., and David T. Ellwood. 1994. *Welfare Realities: From Rhetoric to Reform.* Cambridge, Mass.: Harvard University Press.

Bennett, Neil G., and Jiali Li. 1998. "Young Child Poverty in the States." Early Childhood Poverty Research Brief 1. New York: National Center for Children in Poverty.

Bentsen, Lloyd. October 1990. "Reforming the Welfare System: The Family Support Act of 1988." *Journal of Legislation* 16: 133–40.

Blank, Rebecca. 1997. *It Takes a Nation: A New Agenda for Fighting Poverty.* Princeton, N.J.: Princeton University Press.

Bloom, Dan, Mary Farrell, James J. Kemple, and Nandita Verma. 1999. *The Family Transition Program: Implementation and Three-year Impacts of Florida's Initial Time-Limited Welfare Program.* New York: Manpower Demonstration Research Corporation.

Born, Catherine. 1999. *Life After Welfare: Third Interim Report.* Baltimore: School of Social Work, University of Maryland.

Bos, Hans, Aletha Huston, Robert Granger, Greg Duncan, Tom Brock, and Vonnie McLoyd. 1999. *New Hope for People with Low Incomes: Two-Year Results of a Program to Reduce Poverty and Reform Welfare.* New York: Manpower Demonstration Research Corporation.

Bryner, Gary. 1998. *Politics and Morality: The Great American Welfare Reform Debate.* New York: W. W. Norton.

Burtless, Gary T. 1997. "Welfare Recipients' Job Skills and Employment Prospects." *The Future of Children* 7(1): 39–51.

Child Trends. 1999. *Children and Welfare Reform: A Guide to Evaluating the Effects of State Welfare Policies on Children.* Washington, D.C.: Child Trends.

Congressional Record. 1995. 104th Cong., 1st sess., H3363 (March).

Doolittle, Fred, Virginia Knox, Cynthia Miller, and Sharon Rowser. 1998. *Building Opportunities, Enforcing Obligations: Implementation and Interim Impacts of Parents' Fair Share.* New York: Manpower Demonstration Research Corporation.

Dukakis, Michael S., and Rosabeth M. Kanter. 1988. *Creating the Future: The Massachusetts Comeback and Its Promise for America.* New York: Summit Books.

Edin, Kathryn, and Laura Lein. 1997. *Making Ends Meet: How Single Mothers Survive Welfare.* New York: Russell Sage Foundation.

Ellwood, Deborah A., and Donald J. Boyd. 2000. *Changes in State Spending on Social Services Since the Implementation of Welfare Reform: A Preliminary Report.* Albany, N.Y.: Rockefeller Institute.

Ellwood, Marilyn R. 1999. *The Medicaid Eligibility Maze: Coverage Expands but Enrollment Problems Persist.* Washington, D.C.: Urban Institute.

Ellwood, Marilyn R., and Kimball Lewis. 1999. *On and off Medicaid: Enrollment Patterns for California and Florida in 1995.* Washington, D.C.: Urban Institute.

Gallagher, L. Jerome, Megan Gallagher, Kevin Perese, Susan Schreiber, and Keith Watson. 1998. *One Year After Federal Welfare Reform: A Description of State Temporary Assistance for Needy Families (TANF) Decisions as of October 1997.* Washington, D.C.: Urban Institute.

General Accounting Office. 1999. *Welfare Reform: Information on Former Recipients' Status.* GAO/HEHS-99-48. Washington: U.S. Government Printing Office.

Gueron, Judith M., and Edward Pauly. 1991. *From Welfare to Work.* New York: Russell Sage Foundation.

Haskins, Ron. 2001. "The Second Most Important Issue: Effects of Welfare Reform on Family Income and Poverty." In *The New World of Welfare: Shaping a Post-TANF Agenda for Policy,* edited by Rebecca Blank and Ron Haskins. Washington, D.C.: Brookings.

Johnson, Cathy M. 1998. "Welfare and Work: What Happened to Feminist Perspectives?" Paper presented at the annual meeting of the Midwest Political Science Association, Chicago (April 23–25, 1998).

Katz, Jeffrey L. 1995. "House GOP Welfare Plan Shifts Focus from Work to Teen Mothers." *Congressional Quarterly Weekly Report* (January): 160–61.

Kennedy, John F. 1961. "Presidential Address: Program for Economic Recovery and Growth." In *Congressional Quarterly Almanac 1961*. Washington: Congressional Quarterly.

King, Christopher, and Daniel O'Shea. 2001. "The Workforce Investment Act of 1998: Restructuring Workforce Development in States and Localities." Report. Rockefeller Institute, Albany, N.Y.

Maxwell, Terrance. 1999. *Information Federalism: History of Welfare Information Systems*. Working paper. Albany, N.Y.: Rockefeller Institute.

Mead, Lawrence. 1996. "Welfare Reform at Work." *Society* 33(5): 37–40.

Murray, Charles. 1984. *Losing Ground: American Social Policy, 1950–1980*. New York: Basic Books.

Nathan, Richard P., and Thomas L. Gais. 1999. *Implementing the Personal Responsibility Act of 1996: A First Look*. Albany, N.Y.: Rockefeller Institute.

Nathan, Richard P., Paola Gentry, and Catherine K. Lawrence. 1999. "Is There a Link Between Welfare Reform and Teen Pregnancy?" Rockefeller Report. Albany, N.Y.: Rockefeller Institute.

Patterson, James T. 1994. *America's Struggle Against Poverty 1900–1994*. Cambridge, Mass.: Harvard University Press.

Popenoe, David. 1996. "Family Caps." *Society* 33(5): 25–27.

Primus, Wendell. 1999. *The Initial Impacts of Welfare Reform on the Incomes of Single-Mother Families*. Washington, D.C.: Center on Budget and Policy Priorities.

Sorensen, Elaine, and Robert Lerman. 1998. "Welfare Reform and Low-Income Noncustodial Fathers." *Challenge* 41(4): 101–16.

Stark, Shelley, and Jodie Levin-Epstein. 1999. *Excluded Children: Family Caps in a New Era*. Washington, D.C.: Center for Law and Social Policy.

Thompson, Frank J., and Thomas L. Gais. 2000. "Federalism and the Safety Net: Delinkage and Participation Rates." Unpublished manuscript. Rockefeller Institute, Albany, N.Y.

Thompson, Frank J., and Richard P. Nathan. 1999. "The Relationship Between Welfare Reform and Medicaid: A Preliminary View." Paper presented to the National Health Policy Forum. Washington, D.C. (February 26, 1999).

U.S. Department of Agriculture. 1999. "Who Is Leaving the Food Stamp Program? An Analysis of Caseload Changes from 1994 to 1997." Food and Nutrition Service. Available at: *www.fns.usda.gov/fns/menu/Published/fsp/FILES/CRD.html*.

U.S. House of Representatives. 1996. *Causes of Poverty, with a Focus on Out-of-Wedlock Births: Hearing Before the Subcommittee on Human Resources of the House Ways and Means Committee*. Washington: U.S. Government Printing Office.

U.S. House of Representatives. 1998. *1998 Green Book: Background Material and Data on Programs Within the Jurisdiction of the Committee on Ways and Means*. Washington: U.S. Government Printing Office.

Wallace, Geoffrey, and Rebecca M. Blank. 2000. "What Goes Up Must Come Down? Explaining Recent Changes in Public Assistance Caseloads." In *Economic Conditions and Welfare Reform*, edited by S. Danziger. Kalamazoo, Mich.: W. E. Upjohn Institute.

Wilson, William Julius. 1987. *The Truly Disadvantaged*. Chicago: University of Chicago Press.

Zedlewski, Sheila R., and Sarah Brauner. 1999. *Declines in Food Stamp and Welfare Participation: Is There a Connection?* Washington, D.C.: Urban Institute.

Chapter 4

How Do State Policymakers Think About Family Processes and Child Development in Low-Income Families?

Kristin Anderson Moore

Welfare reform has been an ongoing process for decades, but until recently little attention was paid to the implications of welfare reform for children in welfare families. After the Family Support Act was passed in 1988, an evaluation of the impact of the Job Opportunities and Basic Skills (JOBS) training program on children was initiated by the U.S. Department of Health and Human Services (DHHS). Even before the 1996 legislation again reformed the welfare system, however, many states had begun to request waivers to experiment with modifying their welfare systems. States obtained waivers to try various time limits, family caps, earning supplements, and work requirements. Almost all states that received waivers were required by the federal government to conduct experimental–control group studies of primarily economic, labor force, and welfare outcomes, often based on data from their administrative records systems. Eventually forty-three states obtained waivers, and the importance of learning about the implications for children of these new state-level experiments became an imperative.

The National Institute of Child Health and Human Development (NICHD) Family and Child Well-being Network was also initiated in the early 1990s with the goal of bringing basic social and demographic science to bear on policy issues. The usefulness of a long-term working relation between network members and administrators who wanted to study child outcomes under their state waivers became clear. Toward that end, the Administration for Children and Families (ACF) and the Office of the Assistant Secretary for Planning and Evaluation (ASPE) at DHHS launched an integrated effort to add child outcome components to ongoing state evaluation efforts. The ASPE provided funding to NICHD network members to work with states to develop evaluation designs and to develop state-level indicators of child well-being. The ACF, meanwhile, opened a competition among states interested in participating in a planning process that would culminate in funding for evaluations of the impact of state waiver policies on children. In September 1996, twelve states were funded by the government to participate in this one-year planning process: California, Connecticut, Florida, Illinois, Indiana, Iowa, Ohio,

/ 53

Oregon, Michigan, Minnesota, Vermont, and Virginia. Members of the NICHD network began working with them in October 1996. The Department of Health and Human Services wanted to transfer knowledge and methods from the Job Opportunities and Basic Skills (JOBS) program and the National Evaluation of Welfare-to-Work Strategies (NEWWS), as appropriate. Under subcontract to Manpower Demonstration Research Corporation (MDRC), Child Trends had designed and conducted a longitudinal study of children ages three through five years for the JOBS evaluation. Accordingly, given their experience with the Child Outcomes Study, Child Trends staff took the lead on this project. A series of meetings was held in Washington, D.C., and continued at the state level. The observations described here derive from these meetings and other correspondence. Of course, the state welfare administrators were not researchers, and the researchers were not policymakers. Therefore, to carry out this project it was necessary for participants to work closely with, and to listen carefully to, one another.

More than half of the state representatives had already selected an evaluation firm to conduct their state-level waiver evaluation (either MDRC, Mathematica, or Abt). These evaluators had considerable experience with evaluation design, although they varied in their familiarity with studies of child development and family processes. They also committed themselves to working with staff from other evaluation firms and the Network/Child Trends technical assistance team to agree on common study designs and constructs. The degree of cooperation in the service of a larger goal was very impressive and made this project possible. (See Child Trends 1999 for additional details about the project, constructs, and measures.)

PROJECT ON STATE-LEVEL CHILD OUTCOMES

At the first meeting, in November 1996, the research team introduced a set of categories useful for distinguishing types of information about children. A fourth category was added during the meeting to account for the survey-based studies that do not play a major role in the Project on State-Level Child Outcomes but that represent a major component of all work on families, poverty, and welfare. These came to be referred to as the four I's:

- Impact studies: experimental-control group studies in which participants are randomly assigned to either the experimental or the control group. If the study is well-designed and implemented, causal implications can be drawn for the population in the study.

- Intervening mechanisms: the ways in which welfare programs may affect children. Intervening mechanisms are first affected by a policy or program; they, in turn, affect children's development and well-being. Intervening mechanisms can be examined within impact or inferential studies.

- Indicators: a measure of a behavior or a condition or status that can be tracked over time, across people, and across geographic units (Moore 1997).

- Inferential studies: studies that fall between indicator and impact studies; they go beyond indicator studies in that they attempt to assess causality but they cannot provide definitive evidence regarding causality. Causality is inferred through statistical analyses rather than by virtue of the design, as with impact analyses.

One goal in delineating these categories was to distinguish among evaluation approaches. Some approaches make it possible to address causality, while others do not. Another goal was to encourage state policymakers to distinguish between measures of child well-being and intervening mechanisms. This proved to be a crucial distinction. Another goal was simply to have a common language to use throughout the project.

The importance of these distinctions was illustrated during the initial meeting. Participants broke into subgroups to discuss child outcomes of interest to states and intervening mechanisms through which states might affect child well-being. A central point of agreement among the states was that poverty and health insurance are the primary indicators of child well-being. However, researchers who study children and families do not define poverty and health insurance as measures of child well-being. Income is a family- or household-level variable, while health insurance is a measure of service availability. They may be important inputs to child well-being, but they are not measures of child well-being. In the language of the four I's, they are intervening mechanisms. Therefore, although respecting the importance placed on poverty and health insurance by the state representatives, the researchers wanted to identify elements of child well-being that might be affected by welfare waivers, for example, measures of child health and safety, behavior problems, socioemotional well-being, and academic success.

Intervening Mechanisms

A separate task was to identify the intervening mechanisms that policymakers and citizens in the states believed would produce these child outcomes. Although state-level policymakers initially tended to view receipt of services (such as health insurance) and indicators of family well-being (such as poverty) as measures of child well-being, they came to define these as intervening mechanisms that might be affected by welfare reform and that, in turn, might affect children's outcomes, including child health and safety, behavior, socioemotional well-being, and academic attainment.

An especially clear example of this process occurred during a gathering of the Welfare Peer Assistance Network (WELPAN). This group was composed of the heads of the welfare agencies in the upper Midwest and was organized by Tom Corbett of the University of Wisconsin and Theodora Ooms, then head of the Family Impact Seminar. They planned to discuss the Project on State-Level Child Outcomes, given that six of these states had been selected to be among the twelve states in the project. Time for discussion was limited, and it became apparent that words were not communicating well, so we worked through a diagram describing a model of the change process for which welfare administrators are responsible (see figure 4.1, top panel). (See also Zaslow et al. 1995 and Child Trends 1999 for a discussion and literature review.) The central question for welfare administrators has been whether welfare reform affects the employment, income, and welfare dependency of adults. However, if a person is interested in the children in welfare families, the model must be expanded (figure 4.1, middle panel).

Moreover, to understand child well-being, one must add new constructs to the model. However, welfare reform is not focused directly on children, as is, for example, Head Start. Therefore, it is not immediately obvious why adult employment and welfare dependency would affect children. Yet research on children's development has uncovered a number of parental and family factors—maternal depression, for example—that affect children's well-being. Traditionally, welfare administrators have not viewed their responsibilities as extending to mothers' depression. However, a concern about children's well-being pushes us to add this new factor to the model (figure 4.1, bottom panel). Although welfare administrators had not originally thought about welfare reform as a process with complex implications for family dynamics, parent psychological well-being, and child development, once they were asked to think about it that way, it made sense to them.

To articulate this process, the larger group developed a model over a period of months that described the factors that determine child well-being. State policymakers weighed the evidence on intervening mechanisms and children's outcomes in considering a model. The model began with welfare reform laws, moved to parent labor force behavior and family income and services, then on to parent-child interaction and child care, and from there to child well-being. To build and flesh out the model, researchers asked state representatives to, in the words of Bob Lovell of Michigan, "tell stories" that progressed through the various steps in the process, from the reform of laws and policies to changes in adult outcomes, to changes in family processes, and then to changes in child well-being.

The final model evolved over time. In the model shown in table 4.1, intervening mechanisms are distinguished from outcomes. Income and health insurance, the indicators initially considered by policymakers to represent child well-being, describe parent and family outcomes. State representatives remained interested, of course, in services and family-level outcomes; however, they came to see them (at least for the purposes of this project) as intervening mechanisms that affect children's development and well-being, which are represented (in the far-right column of the table) by measures of child health and safety, education, and social and emotional adjustment.

FIGURE 4.1 / Evolution of a Model for Welfare Reform and Children

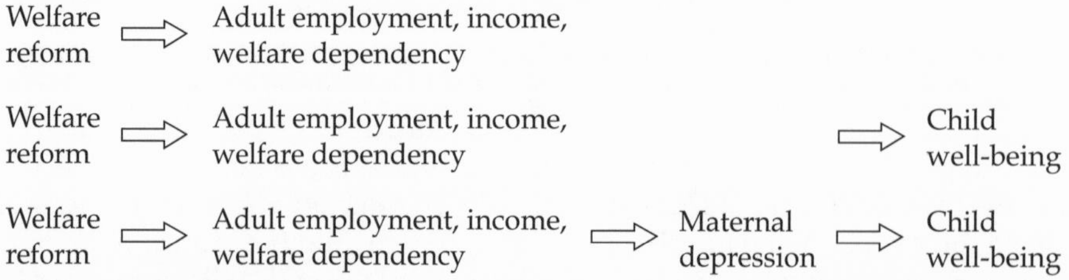

Source: Author's configuration.

TABLE 4.1 / Core Constructs Through Which Welfare Reform Affects Families

	Intervening Mechanisms		
Targets of Policy	Other Variables	Affected Areas of Child's Environment	Child Outcomes

• Family income
  Total income
  Sources of income (mother's earnings, father's earnings, child support, welfare, food stamps, SSI, foster care–adoption)
  Stability of income
  Financial strain or material hardship
• Parental employment
  Any versus none
  Health benefits through employment
  Wages (hourly)
  Hours of employment
  Stability of employment
  Education–licenses
  Job skills (hard)
  Multiple jobs concurrently
  Barriers to employment (harassment, violence)[a]
• Family formation
  Nonmarital birth–marital birth
  Child-family living arrangements
  Marital status (whether married to biological or nonbiological father)
	• Psychological well-being
	  Depression
	• Stability
	  Foster care
	  Child care
	  Income
	  Residence
	  Marital status or cohabitation
	  Child living or not living with family
	• Absent parent involvement
	  Child support
	  Paternity establishment
	  Contact with child
	• Use of health and human services
	  Food stamps
	  Medicaid (awareness, use, eligibility)
	  Child care subsidy (awareness, use, eligibility)
	  Access to medical care
	• Consumption
	  Income spent on child care and rent
		• Child care
		  Type
		  Extent
		  Quality (group size, ratio, licensing, parent perception)
		  Stability
		  Child care calendar for last several years[a]
		• Home environment and parenting practices
		  Child abuse or neglect (administrative data)
		  Domestic violence or abusive relationships
		  Family routines
		  Aggravation or stress in parenting
		• HOME (emotional support and cognitive stimulation scales)[a]
			• Education
			  Engagement in school (ages six to twelve)
			  School attendance[b]
			  School performance[b]
			  Suspended or expelled[b]
			  Grades (ages six to twelve)
			• Health and safety
			  Hunger–nutrition (ages five to twelve)
			  Rating of child's health (ages five to twelve)
			  Regular source of care (ages five to twelve)
			  Teen childbearing (ages fourteen to seventeen)[b]
			  Accidents and injuries[b]
			• Social and emotional adjustment
			  Behavior problems index (ages five to twelve)
			  Arrests[b]
			  Positive behaviors–social competence scale (ages five to twelve)

Source: Child Trends 1999.
[a]From in-home survey.
[b]From all-child module.

It is important to note that most of the state representatives were generally quite positive about welfare reform. Indeed, several reported that their state was so positive about reforming welfare that they thought it would be difficult to maintain a control group receiving the standard Aid to Families with Dependent Children (AFDC) "treatment." They tended to see welfare as a problematic or ineffective system in need of change. Carol Baron of Virginia emphasized the need to list constructs in positive, not just negative, words. Thus their story lines included positive as well as negative components from the very start. Bob Lovell articulated two competing hypotheses for Michigan. One hypothesis was that the role of the parent is essential and that children benefit from the security of having a parent at home, which argues in favor of traditional AFDC policies. The second hypothesis was that children learn respect for work and also that they benefit from the regular household schedule that results from parents working, which argues in favor of welfare reform.

Participants were clear about the changes that were intended by their states. A primary goal was to change the source of family income, that is, to move families to self-sufficiency and away from dependency on public support. Although they believed it was important that families not fall deeper into poverty, several specifically noted that it was not necessarily their responsibility to raise people out of poverty. Their job, as they saw it, was to alter the source of family income from public to private. They speculated that such a change in the source of family income might have implications for children. Although the type and nature of the effects on children were less clear, participants hypothesized a number of potential pathways.

How Might Having a Working Parent Affect Children?

A primary goal of welfare reform, as noted, is to change the source of family income from public to private sources, and in the view of state welfare administrators, the primary source of that private income—and the focus of welfare reform—is work. State representatives weighed their experiences and the research evidence and suggested an extensive range of changes that might be activated by welfare reform policies.

ROLE MODEL OF A WORKING PARENT   The benefit of having a role model who is employed was mentioned by a number of state representatives. Indeed, some noted that a role model would be more important for older than for younger children. In their discussions of role models, state representatives also mentioned the importance of family routines, hypothesizing that changes in welfare policy might produce families with more structured family routines and that this might improve child outcomes. Others suggested that subsidized work, although it would not alter the source of family income, might in the short run affect children positively by establishing family routines. Effects might vary for different subgroups of recipients (by age of the child, family type, or disability status), and thus a particular policy might be a disaster for some and a success for others.

PARENT PSYCHOLOGICAL WELL-BEING   Welfare administrators anticipated a number of other changes induced by work, including a decrease in parental isolation. WELPAN administrators posited a reduction in parental stress and improvements in parent-child interactions, although conversations with lower-level state administrators generally indicated more mixed expectations. Joel Rabb of Ohio suggested that welfare recipients who are successful in moving into work may adopt better routines and improve parental self-esteem, while recipients who are unsuccessful in obtaining steady work may experience stress. Parents' psychological well-being was discussed primarily in its relation to stress. Self-esteem was believed to be important, although state administrators were clear that measuring such a subjective element as self-esteem might cause political problems. Some nominated work orientation instead.

TURBULENCE   On the negative side, instability was raised as a possible consequence of reaching time limits on receipt of cash assistance imposed under welfare reform. Participants suggested that children may be passed around among family members when the custodial parent reaches the time limit. Instability in child care, education, income, and family structure were all noted. Even if the changes were ultimately for the better (a move to a better school, for example), the process of change was recognized as difficult for children.

COST OF POSSIBLE EFFECTS ON CHILDREN   One participant noted, and others echoed, the tendency of states to think first about effects that will cost states more money over time, such as increased referrals to child protective services and foster care, increased juvenile delinquency, more injuries, more accidents and emergency room visits, increased truancy, and greater use of food banks and shelters. Concern about costs often pushes states to focus on teenagers because it is during these years that children get into the kind of trouble that costs taxpayers money. In addition, issues tracked by the media, such as homelessness, child abuse, and foster care, were important, and policymakers saw a need for data to answer questions asked by reporters and elected officials. In short, child outcomes with implications for state spending and effects that could have political reverberations would be of particular concern.

FAMILY STRUCTURE   Other participants noted potential effects on family formation, family structure, and family stability. The role of fathers was discussed in this context, and it was noted that time limits may lead to family formation and to possible effects on child support. Some suggested that the presence of males can create obstacles to working for women. It was noted that marriage is an assumed good, but participants were skeptical that marriage is good for everyone under all circumstances. The possibility of conflict and violence was raised. State administrators wondered how the presence of males who may or may not be relatives or husbands affect children. Another concern about family structure was the possibility that the penalties embodied in welfare reform legislation would affect custodial arrangements and result in some children being moved into kinship care.

CHILD CARE   Child care was brought up by a number of state participants. Many worried about the availability of care when those relatives who had provided informal child care were now subject to work requirements. They also wondered whether children would be left to care for themselves, what types of care they would receive, and whether it would be quality care.

PARENTING Parenting issues received some attention although not as much as other intervening mechanisms. This may be because many states rely on administrative record data to evaluate their programs, and they are unaccustomed to the idea of visiting families and collecting data on parenting practices directly. Some participants worried that pressure on a mother to enter the workforce might lead to problems between the mother and the child and that this might be a further stress on already stressed families. State representatives also noted that supervision and unhurried time with the child might decrease.

THE SET OF CORE CONSTRUCTS

Much effort was expended to encourage state partners to list all the ways that welfare reform might affect families and children. The list eventually had to be winnowed because the cost and burden of examining all possible processes was too great. To augment their policy perspective, state representatives sought advice from researchers on which constructs mattered and which could or could not be measured well. To prioritize the list, state representatives voted on the measures that they wanted to remain in the final set of core constructs. In a few instances, the researchers encouraged state representatives to include some constructs, such as parenting, that might not otherwise be high priorities for the states.

As important as it was to consult with states about the mechanisms through which they expected welfare to affect children, the outcomes and intervening mechanisms considered to be lower priorities were also illuminating. States eliminated cognitive achievement as measured by tests because they believed the programs they were implementing were more likely to affect school attendance, tardiness, and engagement in learning than learning itself (especially in the time frame of their evaluations). States also dropped measures of attitudes in favor of other topics. Maternal depression was the one measure of parental psychological well-being that was retained in the core list. Parenting measures were of moderate interest and were retained primarily because of their importance to researchers on the technical assistance team as an intervening measure. The final set of core items is shown in figure 4.2.

CONCLUSION

Although child well-being was salient and important to state welfare officials, their initial tendency was to lump together measures of child well-being with measures of service receipt and family well-being. When asked to distinguish intervening mechanisms (such as services) from measures of child well-being, however, they were willing and able to do so. State welfare administrators generally focused on

FIGURE 4.2 / Conceptual Framework of Parent and Family Outcomes Following
State Discussions

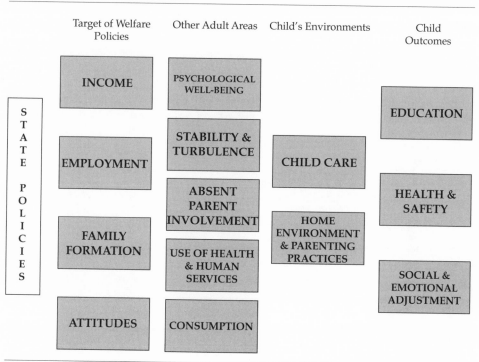

Source: Child Trends 1999.

adult outcomes, and their expectations for welfare reform ranged from mixed to
fairly positive. Their hypotheses for how welfare reform might affect children were
also mixed and included both positive and negative expectations. Welfare administrators were open to the possibility that effects might be complex and that they
might vary for different subgroups receiving welfare.

Over the course of numerous discussions, state welfare administrators suggested
a number of intervening mechanisms through which a reform effort designed to
focus on adults might nevertheless affect children. These mechanisms not only
included the expected factors of employment, income, and dependency but also
went beyond these to include family routines, parental stress, paternal involvement,
domestic violence, parental depression, other measures of parental psychological
well-being, the family's social support, its use of health and social services, parental
school involvement, child care, and mother-child interaction.

Thus state-level representatives, working with researchers from a number of dis-
ciplines, arrived at a variety of hypotheses regarding how welfare reform might affect
adults and families and, thus, children. A lengthy set of constructs was developed
and then winnowed. A subset of five states (Connecticut, Florida, Indiana, Iowa,
and Minnesota) subsequently received funding to move forward with experimental–

control group studies to examine these hypotheses. After defining the conceptual model and agreeing on constructs, as described here, the team moved on to develop common measurement and analysis strategies. The initial cooperation has continued, and reports informed by this project have started to be released (Bloom et al. 2000; Gennetian and Miller 2000).

This ongoing collaboration is essential to supporting analyses that look not only within states but also across states to examine how welfare reform affects children. Participants in this invigorating and exhausting process hope that the thinking that went into this project will be useful to researchers and policymakers in other states as they consider how welfare reform may affect families and children.

REFERENCES

Bloom, D., J. J. Kemple, P. Morris, S. Scrivener, N. Verma, R. Hendra, with D. Adams-Ciardullo, D. Seith, and J. Walter. 2000. *The Family Transition Program: Final Report on Florida's Initial Time-Limited Welfare Program.* New York: Manpower Demonstration Research Corporation.

Child Trends. 1999. *Children and Welfare Reform: A Guide to Evaluating the Effects of State Welfare Policies on Children.* Washington, D.C.: Child Trends.

Gennetian, Lisa, and Cynthia Miller. 2000. *Reforming Welfare and Rewarding Work: Final Report on the Minnesota Family Investment Program.* Vol. 2, *Effects on Children.* St. Paul, Minn.: Department of Human Services.

Moore, Kristin A. 1997. "Criteria for Indicators of Child Well-being." In *Indicators of Children's Well-being*, edited by R. M. Hauser, B. V. Brown, and W. R. Prosser. New York: Russell Sage Foundation.

Zaslow, M. J., Kristin Moore, M. J. Coiro, and D. R. Morrison. 1995. "The Family Support Act and Children: Potential Pathways of Influence." *Children and Youth Services Review* 17: 231–49.

Chapter 5

Program Redesign by States in the Wake of Welfare Reform: Making Sense of the Effects of Devolution

Alan Weil

our purposes are stated in the portion of the Personal Responsibility and Work Opportunity Reconciliation Act (PRWORA) that establishes the new Temporary Assistance for Needy Families (TANF) block grant. Each of these purposes—assisting needy families, ending parental welfare dependence, reducing out-of-wedlock pregnancies, and encouraging two-parent families—has ramifications for the well-being of children. Yet before these four purposes are enumerated, the legislation states that its purpose is "to increase the flexibility of States in operating a program designed to" achieve these goals. The clear implication of the legislative language is that state flexibility increases the likelihood that these goals will be achieved and that the well-being of children will be enhanced.

States led the way toward many of the substantive provisions that appear in PRWORA. Through waivers from the federal government, states experimented with time limits, work requirements, restructured work incentives, and other program innovations. Yet one feature of the waiver regime was the requirement that program innovations be subject to rigorous evaluation. TANF, in contrast, offers states enhanced program flexibility without the need for waivers or formal evaluation.

Does state flexibility in program design yield more effective welfare policies, as Congress believed? Just as one seeks to know whether income disregards or sanctions are good policies from the perspective of children's well-being, one should want to know whether state flexibility yields better policies and outcomes. Devolution of authority over social programs creates a particular challenge for those attempting to assess the effects of this shift in the structure of American federalism (Bell 1999). Although diversity among state policies may provide a means for exploring the effects of individual policy interventions, that diversity does little to shed light on the broader question of the effects of devolution itself.

This chapter draws on data collected as part of the Assessing the New Federalism project being conducted by the Urban Institute (Kondratas, et al. 1998). I examine three reasons for state policy variation under devolution, describing how each of these sources of variation can be analyzed to describe the effects of devolution. I then present a typology of early state responses to welfare reform and discuss how that typology can help disentangle the effects of devolution. Finally, I consider the longer term possibilities for understanding devolution.

THE POTENTIAL OF DEVOLUTION

Debates over federalism began before the creation of the United States and continue to this day. In the great political debates surrounding the formation of the union, arguments for centralization of authority or dispersion of that authority fell loosely into two categories: philosophical and functional. Philosophical arguments derive from the question, What are the defining features of national citizenship? In a large and heterogeneous nation, people accept a significant degree of variability across states in economic and social conditions. Yet certain civil and political rights, such as voting and freedom of speech, are deemed so fundamental as to require a uniform, national policy. Some substantive policies, such as national defense and basic regulation of commerce, cannot be subject to the varying preferences of individual states.

Functional arguments over federalism derive from the question, What allocation of responsibility between the federal government and the states will lead to the best outcomes? These arguments look at matters such as efficiency, effectiveness, experimentation, and interjurisdictional competition. Advocates often draw on the lofty philosophical rhetoric of federalism even when their motivations are functional. That is, for the advocate the preferred option of whether leadership is centered federally or at the state level often depends on whether the federal government or the states are seen as more likely to achieve the substantive outcomes that the advocate desires.

This chapter examines one major component of the functional side of the federalism debate: what devolution—the transfer of authority from the federal government to the states—means for state policy choices. It is important to note that there are other functional issues relevant to any debate on federalism, such as the federal and state governments' relative administrative capacity, political accountability, and fiscal capacity and priorities. These are equally important issues and must be incorporated into an overall approach to assessing devolution, but the focus here is on how devolution affects policy choices.

DEVOLUTION AND POLICY

Why might public policies in a devolved program be different from those in a centralized program? This section explores various structures of federalism and discusses the bases for variation in state policies.

The structure of American federalism is established in the U.S. Constitution. Article 6 declares unambiguously that the laws of the federal government are supreme, implying that the federal government has the power to preempt state laws when it chooses to do so. The federal government is formally one of limited powers, although the scope of those powers (recent political and constitutional controversy notwithstanding) remains broad. By contrast, from the federal government's perspective, states, as the original sovereigns, have power that is not inherently limited. Where there is no specific bar to state action, the states' authority is not constrained by the federal government.

Thus the American political system can support a wide range of intergovernmental relations. At one extreme, the federal government can set policy and administer programs while barring states from acting. At the other extreme, the federal government can step fully out of the way and leave all policy and programmatic discretion to the states. Although the structure of federalism is fixed, the political process determines how specific policy choices are allocated between the states and the national government. Federalism becomes most interesting when the political process yields a design that falls somewhere between the extremes.

In recent decades it has been taken as a given that the federal government plays a significant role in defining social welfare policy. (A variety of recent perspectives on federalism in social welfare policy can be found in Donahue 1997; Peterson 1995; and Rivlin 1992.) Federal statutes define large programs that provide cash, medical, and food assistance. Federal programs pay for school lunches, home heating costs, early education, and nutritional assistance for many low-income families. Despite the fact that most of these programs trace their origins back to local or state programs, the federal role is now well established.

Recent debates center around the possibility of returning part or all of the authority for these programs to the states, a process termed *devolution*. The creation of waiver authority for Aid to Families with Dependent Children (AFDC) under Section 1115 of the Social Security Act in 1962 (and the inclusion of Medicaid under that section when it was enacted three years later) was an early form of devolution. It created an option for state innovation beyond the bounds of specific options that states already had under federal law. As the states' interest in receiving waivers and the federal government's willingness to grant them increased in the last decade, the power and limitations of waiver authority became clear. On the one hand, differences across states in program design grew significantly, and options that the federal government never explicitly countenanced—such as time limits and so-called family caps—became part of the welfare plans in a number of states. On the other hand, this taste of flexibility led states to want more and to chafe at what one governor called "going hat in hand to Washington" to seek permission to administer social programs as the state deemed appropriate.

The enactment of PRWORA represents an additional step in the process of devolution. The creation of the TANF block grant, the consolidation of child care funding streams, and the authority for states to shift a share of their funds from one program to another all reflect the increasingly devolved nature of social policy subsequent to PRWORA. Yet even here devolution is limited. The PRWORA statute imposes significant new federal policy requirements on states. Three notable examples are the rule (with some exceptions) against providing cash benefits for more than five years in an adult recipient's lifetime, the rule against providing assistance to a family for more than twenty-four consecutive months unless the adult is working, and child support enforcement actions that every state must adopt.

Complete devolution would go beyond the conversion of old programs into block grants with a new but relatively limited set of federal requirements. The federal government could return to the earlier practice (found in other countries) of general revenue sharing, in which funds are allocated without being tied to specific program requirements. Alternatively, the federal government could simply repeal programs and leave states with full authority to respond to social problems as they see fit. The fact that these options are not being seriously debated suggests that, as American politics stands now, devolution may be significant but will not be complete.

In the event that states were freed from all federal policy constraints, it would be interesting to see what policies they would adopt in their place. If they continued the policies in place before devolution, it would suggest that federal policy constraints are more imagined than real. If states all adopted the same new policy, it would imply that, even though the federal policy was contrary to state objectives, a single, national policy could have been consistent with state goals.

As the first few years after the enactment of PRWORA have shown, however, devolution does yield policies that vary significantly from state to state (Gallagher et al. 1998; Zedlewski et al. 1998). Of course, there was significant variation among state policies before PRWORA, especially in the level of benefits provided to eligible families. PRWORA has opened up a new set of issues, and state choices reflect a good deal of variation. Whether devolution is a good thing depends on why that variation exists and how it affects the well-being of families and children.

POLICY VARIATION AMONG STATES

The first step in understanding the effects of devolution is to explore why states select differing policies. In general, there are three reasons for policies to vary. First, when left to their own, states may pursue different policy objectives. If their objectives differ, it is natural that their policy choices will differ. Second, states may, even when attempting to achieve the same objectives, believe that the circumstances in their state differ from those in other states, thereby necessitating a different set of policies. Third, even when states seek the same ends and face the same circumstances, states may employ different policies because there is a lack of consensus among states on the best mechanism for reaching a common goal. I refer to these three reasons as *pursuing different goals, tailoring to different circumstances,* and *experimenting with different mechanisms.*

Pursuing Different Goals

When states have entered a policy area in advance of the federal government—as occurred, for example, with environmental regulation and workers' compensation programs—variation among states in their goals was not surprising. Some states emphasized limiting employer liability as a means for encouraging economic growth, while others were more concerned with employee (in the case of workers' compensation) or citizen (in the case of environmental regulation) concerns. Over time, in areas in which state policies have diverged, pressure has built for the federal government to step in and constrain state differences. In fact the major historical moves to centralize power in the United States have arisen from the belief that differing goals among states create chaos or inefficiency and that national enterprises and economic growth require predictability and uniformity.

In the social policy realm, the federal government has routinely used the power of the purse to entice states to adopt policies they otherwise might not have chosen. Grant programs, whether fully federally funded or matching, create strong incentives for states to participate in a national program with national objectives. Once the state accepts the federal funds, it must adhere to all federal rules associated with the program. Even when federal funds are involved, variation among states' goals can occur. A clear example arises in the child welfare system. States have oscillated between family preservation and child protection as their primary goal. These differing goals, both inherent in child welfare policy, yield highly variable policies.

When devolution occurs, the federal hand is withdrawn. With their newfound flexibility, states can focus on their own goals, and policies across states will diverge if the goals of political leaders vary across states. Even in this era of devolution, however, federal law continues to establish the goals of even relatively devolved programs. For example, although the new State Children's Health Insurance Program (SCHIP) is far more devolved than Medicaid, the legislation sets forth the unambiguous goal: to "expand the provision of child health assistance to uninsured, low-income children." Although state approaches to implementing SCHIP vary substantially, all state programs quite clearly share this goal.

The circumstances related to welfare reform are more complex. The PRWORA legislation sets forth a series of goals: aiding needy families with children, reducing dependence on government benefits, reducing out-of-wedlock pregnancies, and encouraging the formation of two-parent families. However, the statute also explicitly declares that the goal is increasing states' "flexibility . . . in operating" their programs. Although almost all state plans and legislative enactments speak of encouraging "personal responsibility" and "self-sufficiency," other goals appear only in some states: providing support for the working poor, reducing poverty, eliminating the stigma of poverty, and even promoting respect for state human services employees.

Even when states use the same words or phrases in their goal statements, their intentions may not be the same, since these stated goals are often vague. A phrase such as *self-sufficiency* means different things to different people. Reasonable people will disagree about whether a family is less dependent if it no longer receives cash assistance but now obtains a child care subsidy and an Earned Income Tax Credit (EITC) while retaining medical assistance and food stamps. Even when two states list the same goals, the relative importance they give to those goals may differ, leading to quite different policy approaches.

In addition, the translation from goal statements on paper to program adminis-tration is far from perfect and can introduce another level of variation in state poli-cies. How well program administrators' views are aligned with those of the political leaders writing the legislation and how much control central administrators exer-cise over frontline workers' behavior varies greatly and will have a tremendous effect on how closely stated goals correspond with actual practice.

In an area as complex as welfare policy, it is unlikely that a single, unambiguous goal statement will capture what a state is trying to accomplish. More likely, a state's various goals will compete with one another, and the relative weight of each will vary among states. These varying goals and constellations of goals will yield varying polices.

Tailoring to Different Circumstances

Governors often note that states differ and that their special circumstances call for specific solutions. There is no question that states vary and that this variation is a legitimate basis for states to choose alternative policies. States planning to employ welfare recipients should choose strategies that match the skill demands of their labor markets. Likewise, states aiding families with child care placement should tailor their efforts toward the forms of care most available in that state.

An example of policy variation based on local differences is Wisconsin's empha-sis on transportation assistance as part of welfare reform because of the state's large rural population and limited public transit. Families can exclude a relatively large value for their vehicles from the overall asset limit, welfare agencies are given some responsibility for identifying and facilitating transportation for their clients, and a direct appropriation has been made toward expanding transit service, supporting rural transportation, and encouraging employers to provide transportation. If shown to be effective, other states might adopt these strategies. However, the priority that Wisconsin gives to transit and the effects of its transit policy on welfare recipients reflects, in part, conditions particular to that state.

Of course, circumstances differ across states in so many ways that it would be possible to consider all state policy variations as owing to different circumstances. From an analytic perspective, however, it is important to exclude from this cate-gory those differences that are owing to states' attempts to achieve different goals and to include only those policy differences that would be sustained as long as the different circumstances continue to exist.

Experimenting with Different Mechanisms

The most vivid metaphor for state variation in policies was coined by Supreme Court justice Louis Brandeis, who, in a dissenting opinion, saw states serving as the laboratories of democracy (*New State Ice Company v. Liebmann* 1932). The image is of multiple states confronting the identical problem and each selecting a policy, with imperfect knowledge of whether it will or will not work. Over time, evidence emerges that one state is achieving better results, and from this experiment the nation as a whole gains a better understanding of the policy. The image is compelling because, if the federal government had set a single policy, the experiment would not have occurred. The nation would have no way of learning if its policy choice was the best one.

Examples of this sort of experimentation are easy to find in social policy. One current example is found in the new State Children's Health Insurance Program. All states confront the difficulty of finding and enrolling eligible children in this new program, which targets a newly eligible population. Evidence of what is likely to work is limited. States have adopted a variety of approaches, some working through the schools, others through health care providers, yet others through community organizations. Some states accept applications that are mailed in, some allow applications to be processed at a location other than the welfare office, while other states provide kiosks in public places or are set up to receive electronic applications. Over time, the most effective approaches should become apparent.

Another example is child support enforcement; states have experimented with a variety of approaches, including immediate wage withholding and denial of certain professional and recreational licenses from those who were behind in making payments. States—with the common goal of improving collections—learned from each other and began adopting successful policies even before similar requirements were imposed by the federal government.

DEVOLUTION AND THE IMPLICATION FOR RESEARCH

Separating these three sources of policy variation—pursuing different goals, facing different circumstances, and adopting different methods—helps frame the question of how devolution affects the policy choices states make. Devolution may lead states and the nation to the best approaches to addressing certain social problems, it may permit states to adopt approaches that better match their needs, and it may yield overall improvement in outcomes considered important. Here I explore how to determine whether these positive outcomes are occurring.

Pursuing Different Goals

In determining whether devolution leads to better policies, variation in goals and objectives across states poses a problem. If states adopt different policies because they have different goals, no single yardstick can measure the policies' relative effectiveness. The metaphor of experimentation is lost, and unlike variations in state characteristics, it is difficult or impossible to control for different goals. This suggests three kinds of analysis: national data applied to national objectives, state data applied to national objectives, and state data applied to state objectives.

NATIONAL DATA APPLIED TO NATIONAL OBJECTIVES   One approach to understanding devolution is to examine changes in national indicators that are relevant to the policy change states have made. For example, attitudes toward devolution will be shaped by information such as whether the nation's poverty rate or non-marital birth rate rises or falls in the aftermath of welfare reform. Yet setting aside the obvious but critical issue of how one would construct the counterfactual—What would have happened to these rates if welfare reform had not been enacted?—this sort of analysis has a particular limitation in an era of devolution.

The first limitation is that devolution has not been pure, so in most policy areas there have been federal as well as state-initiated policy changes. Under welfare reform, are changes in national indicators due to federal policies, such as the five-year benefit limit, or to state policies, such as diversion programs and immediate work requirements? National data cannot differentiate between these effects. Therefore, although national data can help clarify the effects of the overall policy, they say little about the role devolution has played.

The second limitation is that national data do not describe regional or state-level variation in the relevant indicator. If national data show that those who left welfare are more likely to be uninsured than the working poor, one might be concerned. Concern might grow, however, if in a few states the rates of the uninsured were particularly high. National data can point policymakers in the right direction, but they may also leave important questions unanswered. Thus although national data play a central role in monitoring changes in key indicators subsequent to policy changes, they have little to offer on the more complex question of whether devolution has yielded better or worse policy.

STATE DATA APPLIED TO NATIONAL OBJECTIVES   Where state-level data are available, the same exercise can be performed analyzing state-specific changes in certain indicators. This comparison serves the evaluation-oriented purpose of determining whether the nation as a whole, or individual states, are doing a better or worse job in an era of devolution. Setting data limitations aside, how can a policy's effectiveness be evaluated when states have different goals? One option is to impose a single, implicit objective on all states and to measure their performance in meeting this objective, whether the state shares it or not. For example, reducing nonmarital births may be a top priority in one state but a lower priority in another. Still, an analysis of change in this indicator by state can indicate something about the effects of devolution.

Two recent reports use state-level data to examine progress against national goals. Robert Rector and Sarah Youssef (1999) rank state welfare reform efforts from "highly successful" to "poor" based solely on the rate of caseload reduction. Measuring state caseload reduction is one way of understanding the effects of devolution and welfare reform. Examining how these rates vary relative to state policy choices, as the authors have done, is also helpful. The terms *highly successful* and *poor* would be more apposite if all states had a primary goal of caseload reduction. Yet this is not the case.

A somewhat different example is a report issued by the Center on Hunger and Poverty (1998). In this report, states are ranked based on the degree to which their policies reflect "moving toward the central goal of promoting economic well-being among poor families." States gain points for positive incentives and lose points for sanctions. Setting aside the question of whether the authors are correct that exclusive reliance on positive incentives is the best way to promote the economic well-being of poor families, the risk here is that this simply stated goal is not the only one driving public policy. Some state policies reflect this goal but perhaps place a stronger value on the goal of ensuring that the social contract for assistance requires that people experience sanctions for failure to meet their obligations.

These analyses show both the uses and the limitations of this approach. One use is that they describe, at a state-specific level, something about the progress that the nation is making toward a particular goal, and they do this in the context of devolution: looking at how individual states are setting policy. One limitation is that they presume states have a particular goal when, in fact, there may be little evidence to suggest that the goal set forth is shared by all states or is an equally high priority for all states. This problem may be overcome when there are unambiguous national objectives stated in legislation, such as reducing the incidence of out-of-wedlock pregnancies, but is harder when evaluating progress toward more fluid concepts, like self-sufficiency.

If state-level studies do not look closely at state goals, they conflate into one metric what really are two separate questions. The first question is, How often do states, when given flexibility, adopt a certain policy goal? The second question is, How effective are states at achieving the goal, given that some of them are trying to achieve it while others are not (and have a different goal in mind)? It is not surprising that, in both of the examples, the states that come out best are the states that share the goal as framed by the author. They reveal little about how good or bad a job states are doing when measured against the states' own goals.

Despite these limitations, a series of analyses of this sort would say a great deal about the effects of devolution. States can be tested against the goals of reducing welfare caseloads, reducing child poverty, increasing the employment of parents, reducing out-of-wedlock births, reducing parental stress, and the like. As long as one acknowledges that not every state has set out to achieve all of these goals, this series could add up to a robust picture of the effects of devolution. Advocates who believe that a particular goal is paramount will judge the success or failure of devolution by drawing attention to whether the nation has made progress toward that one goal.

STATE DATA APPLIED TO STATE OBJECTIVES   If states are grouped by their own goals, two other kinds of analysis become possible. First, returning to the laboratory metaphor, the policies adopted by different states that share the same goal can be compared. That is, when two states seek to accomplish the same end, the differences in policies and in outcomes can give evidence on the relative effectiveness of their approaches. Second, given that state-level data are limited, in some circumstances data for a group of states that share a goal can be combined and compared with the combined data for another group of states with a different goal. Each of these approaches presents challenges, but each also offers tools for understanding the effects of devolution that are not available if every state is treated as trying to accomplish the same ends.

Despite the data limitations and the difficulty of grouping states by their goals in a manner that will gain broad acceptance, these two analyses are critical to an understanding of devolution. They are essential because they directly address the question of whether the effects of devolution are distinct from the overall national effects of various policy changes. This effort suggests the use of a typology, which I offer subsequently.

Tailoring to Different Circumstances

Having states tailor their policies to meet the particular needs of their populations is a possible benefit of devolution. However, variation in and of itself does not mean that states select the best policies for their populations. Analysis of the characteristics of the states must occur in conjunction with analysis of particular policies to help determine the extent to which policy variation reflects tailoring as opposed to poor application of knowledge of what works.

Differences among states in their circumstances create a tremendous challenge for those seeking to use policy variation as the basis for learning about which policies work better than others. Some of the more important differences among states can be controlled in analysis, although the methodological challenges in doing so are significant. Where these methodological hurdles cannot be overcome, there is still value in describing the concordance between state policy choices and circumstances particular to the state. For example, without saying whether a state should emphasize basic skills training or training that leads to career advancement, research can document the education levels of those on welfare. If a state stands out as having a strategy tailored to one population, when in fact a different population dominates the caseload, that information can help the state consider whether it has the proper policy emphasis. Distinct from research designed to measure the effects of policies, this research sheds light on the question of whether, as a result of devolution, state policies better match the problems the state faces.

Experimenting with Different Mechanisms

The metaphor of variation for the sake of experimentation has positive connotations, especially to a research audience. Presumably, however, it should be seen as such only if three conditions are met. First, no state adopts a policy that is beyond the bounds of national acceptability, thereby fundamentally threatening the well-being of that state's population. Second, some type of experimental analysis actually takes place, creating the information necessary to judge which policies are succeeding and which are failing. Third, there is a feedback of the experimental results into the policymaking process, yielding better policies in the long run (Sparer and Brown 1996). The first condition describes a political constraint on the extent to which devolution can occur and will be judged in the political process. The second and third conditions speak to the ongoing importance of studies that use an experimental design to determine the effects of specific policy interventions.

Combining Methods

An understanding of the effects of devolution must draw on each of these methods. National data helps track the overall progress of the country toward certain goals. State-level data shows how that progress varies around the country. State-level data, combined with knowledge about how states' objectives vary, also shows how effective state policies are in achieving those goals. An understanding of how interstate variations in policy relate to variation in circumstance will reveal the degree to which national solutions to social problems are realistic. Continued analysis of specific policy experiments will improve understanding of what works and what does not in addressing particular needs. Together, these methods can inform the question of how devolution affects policy and the well-being of the people those policies affect.

A TYPOLOGY FOR EXAMINING DEVOLUTION

No single typology can possibly capture how states have responded to devolution, primarily because state policies vary along so many axes and there is only a modest correlation among the policy choices states have made on each axis. States are setting new policies in areas such as work requirements, cash assistance time limits, child care subsidies, and medical assistance eligibility. The large number of variables makes creating coherent groupings difficult.

An additional complication in designing a typology is that many state policy choices are not linear. Income disregards can be expressed in dollar or percentage terms. They can vary over time. They can be different for different family structures or, as in Mississippi, be calculated differently depending on how quickly the parent found a job after applying for assistance (Urban Institute 1999). In addition, where change has been incremental, the boundaries between groups of states with similar policies can be fairly arbitrary. How important, for example, is the difference between an eligibility level of 200 percent of the federal poverty level as opposed to 220 percent? Typologies connote a sense of coherence; dividing up states based on fairly marginal differences falls short.

Yet a typology helps make sense of the complex choices states have made, simply by helping to describe what the policy consequences of devolution have been. In addition, a typology can help with the analytical tasks of judging states' progress against their own goals and expanding the data available for analysis by grouping states together.

A Typology Built Around Cash Assistance

For people interested in the well-being of children, it would be useful to create a typology that captures variation across states in their policies toward children. However, despite the fact that the authors of welfare reform intended that children would benefit, almost all state and federal welfare policies are directed at the behavior of adults. Other authors in this volume explore three possible theories of how these policies could affect children (see chapter 3, this volume). With work being the common theme around which welfare policy is designed, a typology of state approaches must examine variation in policies toward work: how much is required and how much it pays, possibly in combination with other benefits.

Welfare reform has been characterized as a redefined social contract for those receiving public assistance (see chapter 2, this volume). What in the past had been possible—long periods of welfare receipt with minimal work on the part of the recipient—is no longer available. Federal law limits the receipt of benefits, and many states have adopted even stricter standards. At the same time, a series of policy changes now encourage work by supplementing the low-paying jobs that most adults leaving welfare find.

The typology presented here is built around the combination of barriers and incentives that a state uses. States are placed into one of three groups depending on the strength of the barriers they present to remaining on cash assistance without working. They are also placed into four categories based on how strong their work incentives are for families leaving welfare. The result is a twelve-cell grid (see table 5.1). The measures used to classify states are more complex than presented here.

Many barriers to welfare receipt are available to states. The ones included in the typology are time limits (the length of time one can receive benefits before working and the total amount of time one can receive benefits at all); sanctions (the degree to which benefits are reduced or eliminated for failure to follow program requirements); and work requirements (how broad the definition is of what counts as work and the age of children that permit the parent to be exempt). These policies vary significantly by state, and together they express a notion of how difficult it is to receive benefits without working.

I exclude other policies that can serve as significant barriers to receiving cash benefits. Diversion policies, both formal and informal, can serve as such a barrier. The degree to which recipients are exempt from work requirements based on circumstances such as domestic violence or disabilities all help describe how hard the state is pushing to move recipients into work. Policies such as family caps and behavioral requirements for children (such as attending school or obtaining immunizations) can affect the effort required of a person who wishes to receive assistance. I do not include these items either for the practical reason that uniform data are unavailable or because they tend to affect subgroups of the overall welfare population.

I divide the barriers to welfare receipt without work into three categories. Because some of the key barriers were established in the federal legislation, states that have generally adhered to the federal standards are denoted as having *basic* barriers. I hes-

TABLE 5.1 / States Grouped by Formal Policies That Limit Welfare Receipt and Provide Work Supports

Level of Support	Limitations on Welfare Receipt Without Work		
	Basic	Strict	Most Strict
Supports reach well above twentieth percentile families	California, Hawaii, New Jersey, New York, Maine, Rhode Island	Connecticut, District of Columbia, Louisiana, Massachusetts, Minnesota, Mississippi, New Mexico, Pennsylvania, Vermont, Washington	Wisconsin
Supports reach twentieth percentile families	Michigan, Montana, Texas	Georgia, Kansas, North Carolina, Nebraska, Nevada, Oklahoma, Oregon	Arkansas, Florida, Tennessee
Supports phase out but TANF remains	Alaska, New Hampshire	Iowa, Illinois, North Dakota, South Carolina, South Dakota	Ohio, Utah, Virginia
All supports phase out at very low income	Indiana, Missouri	Alabama, Arizona, Colorado, Kentucky, West Virginia	Delaware, Idaho, Maryland, Wyoming

Source: Author's compilation.
Note: Specific measures used, data sources, and computations available from author.

itate to call these *weak,* given that even states in this category have created barriers to ongoing welfare receipt that are significantly tighter than under the old AFDC program. States that have adopted tighter limits (for example, shorter time limits) are categorized as having *strict* barriers. States that stand out as having adopted a combination of barrier policies are defined as having the *most strict* barriers.

The incentive side is more complex. National policies, such as the expanded EITC, are making low-wage work financially more desirable than it was in the past (see chapter 14, this volume). As Gregory Acs and colleagues (1998) document, in all of the twelve states studied, moving from no work to half-time work at the minimum wage improves the financial resources available to the family if that family receives all benefits for which it is eligible. That same research shows that the incremental gain in financial resources falls quickly as that family moves into full-time and higher-wage work. Yet states vary in how strong these incentives are, how sizable the offered support is, and to whom the support is offered.

The typology looks at four kinds of assistance states offer families as they move to work. As families on welfare begin to work, they may be able to keep a portion of their cash benefits if the state has sizable income disregards. Medical assistance is guaranteed for almost all families leaving welfare, but state policies vary in how far up the income scale they provide this assistance. Although the federal guarantee of child care assistance for families leaving welfare was repealed in PRWORA, states offer assistance to low-income families to varying degrees. Finally, some states provide an EITC that supplements the federal credit for working families.[1]

The typology distinguishes among four approaches that states have taken to creating work incentives. The first group is those states that provide work supports reaching relatively far up the income distribution. States fall into this category based either on an absolute scale (their benefits reach above 200 percent of the federal poverty level) or a relative scale (their benefits reach significantly above the twentieth percentile of family income in that state).[2] These measures are designed to capture states that reach a broad portion of their population with these benefits. The second group is those states that reach the twentieth percentile of family income in that state but do not go significantly above that level. These two groupings reflect work supports designed to reach families with income far higher than the typical family leaving the welfare rolls.

The third group of states does not offer such significant work supports but continues to provide cash assistance to families receiving TANF even as the family goes to work. Specifically, states fall in this category if a one-adult, two-child family that moves from no job to a half-time job at minimum wage retains at least 50 percent of the value of its cash grant relative to what it was when there was no earned income.[3] In the final group of states, TANF benefits phase out more quickly; this working family loses more than half of its benefits.

The Uses and Limitations of the Typology

Returning to the structure presented earlier, the typology is one method for grouping states according to their hierarchy of goals for welfare reform. Broadly defined, the distribution of states across the cells reveals that states vary in the relative weight they give to three particular goals. First is the goal of caseload reduction. Second is the goal of supporting the financial well-being of working families without regard to whether the families are receiving cash assistance. Third is the goal of improving the financial well-being of families receiving welfare as they first move into the workforce. States in the right-hand column of the table have created stronger barriers to families remaining on welfare and are more likely to see their caseloads decline, all else being equal. States in the top two rows of the table are taking steps to broaden their work supports beyond the traditional welfare population. States in the bottom two rows have not taken those steps. Those in the last row provide very limited cash support as a welfare family first moves into the labor force.

Although I hesitate to draw conclusions from where individual states fall on the grid—small changes in definitions or policies will shift many states from one cell to another—some broad conclusions are possible. First, all cells are filled, suggesting that there is variation across states in each of the studied dimensions. Second, the upper right and lower left cells have the fewest entries. This suggests that there is some correlation between having looser welfare limitations and broader work supports. Third, with the exception of Florida, none of the country's largest states appear in the bottom row or the right column. This suggests that the politics of these states does not permit the strictest of work requirements or the most limited cash benefits. Finally, the top row includes a somewhat unlikely mixture of traditionally liberal and relatively high-income states and much poorer states. This certainly reflects the specific structure of the typology, but it suggests that when state benefits are measured against the income distribution in their own states, some relatively poor states may perform as well as some higher income states.

The typology has some significant limitations. First and most important, it is based on formal policies, not on how those policies are implemented. One value of using policies in forming a typology is that they express what the state describes as its own objectives. If the typology describes groupings of states with similar goals, stated policies are a reasonable source. On a more practical level, comparable state-level data that reflect actual program administration generally do not exist. In the future, more of these types of data will become available, but for now formal policies are often the only data available for all states.

Second, the typology is simple in that it leaves out many dimensions of the relevant policies. Yet even in this simplified form, there are twelve cells, all of which are occupied. Additional data elements would add information, but the added data would then be lost as states are grouped together. Other analysts would select different variables to create a typology, but in the end the typology inherently condenses a large amount of the data input to create groupings of similar states.

Third, the typology does not capture a number of important dimensions of state policy. It does not look at state efforts to assist harder-to-serve populations, such as those with mental illness or those experiencing domestic violence. It does not look at levels of benefits, per se. It is designed to provide a broad description of state approaches and does not attempt to describe any particular policy dimension in detail. For any given research question, a typology should be built around the appropriate measures. For example, a study of child care, or an examination of the effects of welfare sanction policies, would each require a rather different typology. The one presented here is designed to be broadly descriptive and is based on early data on state policies.

Finally, the typology says disappointingly little about how children are affected by states' welfare policies. Children may benefit from increased family resources from work and more socially engaged parents, or they may suffer from reductions in benefits and parents attempting to juggle work and parenting responsibilities. In either case, the effects on children flow from the parents and community. At this stage of reform, there is far less emphasis on the quality of child care or parenting or the provision of services directly to children than there is on a range of requirements on and services for parents. Therefore, the typology is built on rules with respect to parents, not children.

Despite its limitations, the typology offers a more nuanced view of states' objectives in welfare reform than the general phrases *reduced dependency* and *increased personal responsibility* can capture. With states grouped by what they are trying to achieve, it is possible to answer questions such as, Do states that offer work supports further up the income scale promote greater wage progression among those who leave welfare? Are incentives or barriers more effective in reducing welfare caseloads? Are states' policy objectives stable over time? Where data are limited—and in the area of welfare they are quite limited—the typology can help researchers combine data across states to find some of these answers.

DEVOLUTION OVER TIME

Examining whether variation in state policy is stable over time yields greater understanding of the effects of devolution. Evidence of experimentation shows a benefit of devolution. As noted, the first condition of experimentation—variation among states' policy choices—has begun to be met. More evidence will be needed, however. If true experimentation is taking place, a reduction in that variation will be observable, at least within groupings of states that have the same goals, as states learn what works and what does not. One possibility is that states will modify their policies as they learn more. An alternative is that the federal government will step in and place requirements or proscriptions on state policies. Although the latter approach may be less appealing to states, it could still be viewed as a positive result of devolution: learning what works and then applying it to the nation as a whole.

A second possible benefit of devolution is the tailoring of policies to meet the particular needs of each state. If this is taking place, different states with similar goals but different policies will each succeed in achieving some objective. In some respects, this is the most exciting prospect for devolution. If this occurs, it suggests a value of devolution that could never be replicated by adopting a single national policy.

The greatest controversies surrounding devolution are likely to be over how much variation among states' policies the nation should accept. As long as variation is a product of experimentation or of tailoring to local needs or values, its value is easy to understand. The evidence from the era of AFDC suggests that the political system will accept a great deal of variation across states in their welfare policies. Yet if variation grows beyond a certain point, to the point that some states pursue goals that differ fundamentally or significantly from national norms, federal pressure to limit states' policy choices will also grow. This is not to say that federal policy will necessarily be any better at achieving the policy objectives. It is simply to note that the political system may demand a federal response.

The politics of devolution become even more challenging in the context of federal funding. Although states are expected to set their own priorities when spending their own tax dollars, what is the rationale for federal funding when states use those funds to reach different ends? The track record of this sort of support is not good; federal willingness to appropriate funds wanes as the link between the federal dollar and the specific program is broken.

When states are given more flexibility, they can use that flexibility to design programs that are more effective at reaching national objectives, but they can also use it to focus more closely on their own objectives. This is particularly true of welfare reform, in which national goals are somewhat ambiguous. The present variation in state policy choices reflects the tension inherent in the American federal system. State variation has positive connotations when it reflects the very real heterogeneity of the country. It raises concerns when that same variation seems to conflict with national objectives, such as alleviating hardship among needy families and children.

Today there is little evidence that state variation is an impediment to any of the national goals embodied in welfare reform. In fact, with states exploring new policies, grappling with the problems facing their own populations, and adopting this issue as their own, state flexibility may be contributing to the early judgment by some that welfare reform is a success. Whether this will remain the case—permitting devolution to be sustained—is a political question. Whether devolution yields policies that are more effective at supporting children in needy families is an empirical one. The challenges for research in answering the latter question are great, but it is an effort that must be made if an understanding is to be reached on what different forms of federalism mean for the nation. A combination of data on key indicators at the state level, knowledge about state policies, and a set of typologies to structure an understanding of state choices can help answer this question.

NOTES

1. Broad unemployment insurance coverage can also provide a work incentive, but I was unable to define a measure of breadth that is consistent with the other features of the typology, so it is excluded.

2. States are measured on four items: maximum family income for eligibility for child care assistance, medical assistance for children, medical assistance for adults, and the existence of an Earned Income Tax Credit. The child care measure is the maximum family income that permits the family to receive a child care subsidy but does not take into consideration the existence of waiting lists, which have a significant effect on who actually receives benefits.

3. This approach does not look at the absolute level of cash benefits but at the proportion maintained as the family goes to work. Certainly it is easier for a state with a larger grant to meet this test. By looking at the share rather than the absolute value, the measure seeks to capture the structure of the benefits as well as their absolute level.

REFERENCES

Acs, Gregory, Norma Coe, Keith Watson, and Robert I. Lerman. 1998. *Does Work Pay? An Analysis of the Work Incentives under TANF.* Washington, D.C.: Urban Institute.

Bell, Steven. 1999. *New Federalism and Research: Rearranging Old Methods to Study New Social Policies in the States*. Washington, D.C.: Urban Institute.

Center on Hunger and Poverty. 1998. *Are States Improving the Lives of Poor Families? A Scale Measure of State Welfare Policies*. Boston: Tufts University.

Donahue, John D. 1997. *Disunited States*. New York: Basic Books.

Gallagher, L. Jerome, Megan Gallagher, Kevin Perese, Susan Schreiber, and Keith Watson. 1998. *One Year After Federal Welfare Reform: A Description of State Temporary Assistance for Needy Families (TANF) Decisions as of October 1997*. Washington, D.C.: Urban Institute.

Kondratas, Anna, Alan Weil, and Naomi Goldstein. 1998. "Assessing the New Federalism: An Introduction," *Health Affairs* 17 (May-June): 17–24.

New State Ice Company v. Liebmann. 1932. 285 U.S. 262, 311.

Peterson, Paul E. 1995. *The Price of Federalism*. Washington, D.C.: Brookings.

Rector, Robert E., and Sarah E. Youssef. 1999. *The Determinants of Welfare Caseload Decline*. Washington, D.C.: Heritage Center for Data Analysis.

Rivlin, Alice M. 1992. *Reviving the American Dream: The Economy, the States, and the Federal Government*. Washington, D.C.: Brookings.

Sparer, Michael S., and Laurence D. Brown. 1996. "States and the Health Care Crisis: The Limits and Lessons of Laboratory Federalism." In *Health Policy, Federalism, and the American States*, edited by Robert F. Rich and William D. White. Washington, D.C.: Urban Institute.

Urban Institute. 1999. *Welfare Rules Database Beta Version*. Washington, D.C.: Urban Institute.

Zedlewski, Sheila R., Pamela A. Holcomb, and Amy-Ellen Duke. 1998. *Cash Assistance in Transition: The Story of Thirteen States*. Washington, D.C.: Urban Institute.

Chapter 6

Sanctions and Exits: What States Know About Families That Leave Welfare Because of Sanctions and Time Limits

Jack Tweedie

The wave of welfare reform that occurred from the mid-1990s through the late 1990s presents a rich opportunity to develop a research agenda and, through it, a greater understanding of such critical questions as, How do welfare recipients move or not move into work? How does welfare receipt affect self-esteem and work behavior? How can human capital approaches improve future earnings and family life? Such an agenda requires careful design, substantial resources, and time.

SOCIAL SCIENCE RESEARCH AND POLICYMAKING

A vital, yet narrower, policy question still unanswered in the research is the effect on families and children of sanctions for noncompliance with welfare rules. How are these families faring without welfare? As this chapter shows, information is only now emerging on these families; future research will no doubt offer greater insights. In five or ten years, because of the coincidence of investment in social research and rapid, far-reaching change, social science researchers will have a much better understanding of the families facing sanctions and also of the broader policy questions surrounding welfare.

In the meantime, social policy—states' decisions about how to structure and change their welfare programs—is moving much faster than the research. For state welfare policymakers, the time is now—states have a historic opportunity to transform welfare programs: they have the flexibility, and they have the money. The stunning drop in welfare caseloads means that almost every state has resources available for new or expanded programs. State policymakers can continue their work-based reforms, expanding services to recipients who have been unable to leave welfare, offering child care and transportation assistance to working poor families, even if they have never been on welfare, and providing job training so that low-income workers can improve their jobs. States can also think about new and expanded programs to help poor families and children: expanded Head Start, economic and community development, job training, and parenting skills for non-custodial parents. States have an unprecedented set of choices on how to remake their welfare programs into programs that serve low-income families and children. This opportunity will last only as long as the economy stays strong, political interest in welfare reform remains high, and the federal investment in resources and commitment to state flexibility remains high.[1]

Because the pace of change is so rapid, policymakers often make decisions about programs and strategies with very little research-based understanding of those programs. States invest money in job retention programs and earnings progression strategies despite having little data on how they work. Rather, they make an effort to recognize the critical challenges and do the best they can to devise answers to those challenges.

Social science researchers can do more to help in this effort. Although there are exceptions, most current research is not focused on helping policymakers; in fact, many academics are somewhat uncomfortable about being in the middle of policy debates and political issues. They focus on research that will meet the standards of other academics, not on research that will improve policymakers' understanding.

One way to think about how research can be of use to policymakers is to reconsider significance tests. Social science researchers strive for high levels of significance in order to (nearly) rule out the probability that their results might be due to chance. This is how researchers build research understanding; peer-review journals enforce significance tests rigorously. If one wants to publish research, it had better reach a 95 percent level of significance or better.

Policymakers, on the other hand, do not look at these questions in the same way. It would be generous to suggest that the probability of certain ideas working is better than a coin flip—a fifty–fifty chance. Therefore, even preliminary research can add to the understanding of policymakers. Research that is far too rough for publication or even presentation can still inform policymaking. When a researcher is only 60 percent confident that the relationship is genuine, it is still better than the 50 percent often available to the policymaker. Especially with issues of welfare, the politics and myths on both sides skew policymakers' understanding of critical issues. One of the lessons we can take from the events of the past few years is a humility about how little is understood about how welfare works and what factors influence welfare clients' behavior. Researchers must improve their understanding of these issues so they can help policymakers understand them. This does not mean abandoning rigorous social science research; rather, researchers should simply devote more effort to drawing lessons from their research.

Making the best possible estimate and working with those estimates is better than either overqualifying what is known or deferring comment until more definitive answers are available. In the discussion on sanctions and time limits, I rely on the limited existing research to identify the key questions and to piece together answers to them. I recognize that this is not an ideal process and that if I went back to my social science academic days I would conclude that I was far from able to address these issues in a way other social science researchers would accept. On the other hand, the understanding of time limits and sanctions that I can draw from existing state studies is better and more solidly grounded than the understanding most policymakers have. Policymaking will be better for this understanding.

Social science research tries to identify and measure the critical variables in such a way that the results can be generalized beyond the specific arena in which the research is done. For example, whether up-front job searches result in high employment rates both four months and fifteen months after clients leave welfare should not be place-specific—yes in Arizona, no in Mississippi. Rather, social science researchers ask what it is about Arizona and Mississippi that results in this difference. Policymakers, however, have a particular interest in their own state, which differs from other states in ways no one perhaps understands. They need information about their particular state to identify its critical policy issues.

Recent studies on those who leave welfare have engaged policymakers, who are happy with findings that combine high caseload decline with high employment rates. With the credit for the outcome comes responsibility for its aftermath, however. Policymakers must be receptive to the next challenge—directing services to working recipients so that they keep their jobs and increase their earnings. When policymakers hear that 50 percent of former welfare recipients are finding jobs but that in the neighboring state 56 percent are finding jobs, they immediately focus on how their state can do better. Research into outcomes reinforces policymakers' concerns with outcomes and also reinforces their continuing interest and investment in welfare policy. Maintaining and building this interest requires state-specific studies, even if these studies do not increase overall understanding of the effects of welfare programs.

SANCTIONS, TIME LIMITS, AND EXITS

Welfare programs have imposed new work and program participation requirements on welfare recipients. Most analysts and policymakers expected significant numbers of recipients to drop off the rolls because of those requirements, either because recipients were unable to fulfill the requirements or because they preferred to work or do without cash assistance rather than meet those requirements. During the first stages of welfare reform, much concern focused on the fate of families that left welfare because of sanctions. Thousands of recipients lost benefits due to sanctions. A General Accounting Office report (2000) estimates that more than 35,000 recipient families lost benefits in each month during 1998. There does not appear to be a clear trend in the frequency of sanctions after that time.

Most of our current knowledge about the outcomes of welfare reform is about recipients who have left welfare. State research has focused on those who leave and, other than cataloguing the reasons that recipients or administrative data give, little further attention has been paid. Most states that base research on samples of case closures have not structured their samples to focus on sanctions or time limits. It is therefore difficult to draw specific conclusions about the outcomes of those who were sanctioned or who had reached their time limits. Because of the magnitude of case closures, policymakers want to know about all exits, but they will not be specifically concerned about sanction and time limit exits unless researchers demonstrate that these exits are significantly different from all exits. And clear data about that are not yet available.

In looking at recipients leaving welfare, policymakers focus on several questions, which provide the basis for evaluating the effects of sanctions:

- How many recipients are working?

- How much do former recipients earn from work? Do they earn more than the poverty level? And do they increase their earnings over time?

- In households in which no adult works, how do the families support themselves? And are these sources of support stable over time?

- Are recipients better or worse off after leaving welfare? Do they experience hardships or deprivation; that is, are unable to make rent payments, are late paying utility bills, are running out of money for food?

Using these questions as a framework, I examine the results of studies in eight states (Iowa, Tennessee, South Carolina, Arizona, and Maryland on sanctions; North Carolina, Massachusetts, and Utah on time limits) on how those who were sanctioned or who reached their time limit are faring. These studies highlight both what is known and what is not known about sanctions and their effects on families.

Iowa

Iowa implemented welfare reforms—the Family Investment program—in October 1993.[2] The new policies require recipients to participate in a variety of activities designed to move them toward self-sufficiency: education, job search, job readiness, and work. A recipient who is not disabled and who is not caring for an infant is required to negotiate and fulfill a Family Investment Agreement, which outlines a plan to move the recipient off welfare and into a job. Recipients who do not complete an agreement or who fail to carry out the responsibilities in their agreement are assigned to the Limited Benefit Plan. Under the plan, recipients continue to receive full benefits for three months and reduced benefits for three more. (The plan was changed after the period of this study to eliminate the initial three-month period.) If recipients have not corrected their noncompliance by that time, they receive no benefits for six months. Assignment into the plan and termination after six months do not affect the recipient's eligibility for the Food Stamp program or Medicaid.

Iowa had approximately 35,000 welfare cases during this period. In the six-month period beginning November 1994, 4,224 cases were assigned to the Limited Benefit Plan. Most of those assignments (97 percent) were recipients who did not sign a Family Investment Agreement, and most of these involved failure to make a required appointment (31 percent of all assignments) or failure to keep a required appointment (58 percent). Slightly more than half (53 percent) of all Limited Benefit Plan assignments were cancelled, and recipients were returned to regular Family Investment program status as a result of signing a Family Investment Agreement or, in about 10 percent of the cases, winning an appeal. Most cases (64 percent) that were not cancelled resulted in exits from the Limited Benefit Plan before the six months of benefits were complete. Only 36 percent of the cases completed the six-month limited benefits period. Therefore, of the 4,224 recipients initially assigned to the plan, 710 cases (17 percent) reached the six-month limit and had their benefits eliminated.

To study the effects of this policy, researchers conducted an evaluation based on a survey of recipients who had lost their benefits in month seven of the Limited Benefit Plan. Researchers sampled 172 cases that received benefits in month six and had not received benefits in month seven. Ten were excluded in survey screening because they said they did not fit this pattern and indicated that they received benefits in the current month. Of the 162 cases remaining in the sample, researchers completed 137 interviews, for a response rate of 85 percent. The Iowa Limited Benefit Plan study gives partial answers to the four questions listed.

WORK RATES   In answer to the question of how many recipients were working, researchers found that 53 percent of the respondents had worked at least some of the time since losing their benefits. (Most surveys were carried out three to five months after the elimination of benefits.) There was no information about whether the former recipients had worked during the previous month.

EARNINGS AND POVERTY   Mean earnings were $170 a week. Interviewers also asked about household income: income before taxes and deductions for all household members from all sources, including work, welfare benefits, and food stamps. Mean monthly household income was $749 (22 percent of the respondents reported household incomes over $1,000 in the most recent month). There was no information available on whether former recipients increased their earnings over time.

OTHER SUPPORTS   Recipients were supporting themselves in different ways: 64 percent received food stamps (a mean of $275), and 6 percent reported Supplemental Security Income (SSI) (a mean of $469). Child support was received by 19 percent (a mean of $167), and 30 percent reported receiving Women, Infant, and Children (WIC) benefits. Two-thirds were enrolled in Medicaid. Respondents also received financial support from parents, spouses or partners, and other relatives. Twenty-eight percent reported increased support after losing benefits, while 16 percent reported less support. Respondents also reported assistance from community organizations: food bank (24 percent), emergency shelter (4 percent), crisis center (3 percent), and a soup kitchen (2 percent).

FAMILY WELL-BEING   To the question of whether families were better or worse off after leaving welfare and how many families experienced hardships or deprivation, the researchers found that more respondents (49 percent) reported a decrease in household income after losing cash assistance than reported an increase (40 percent).

Income swings were substantial; the mean gain was $496 per month and the mean loss was $384.

Tennessee

Tennessee implemented its Families First program in 1995.[3] For recipients subject to work requirements, Families First includes a sanction policy "to provide a consequence for not complying with program requirements" and "to promote responsible behavior in personal, family, and program activities." Three categories of behavior result in a full family sanction leading to the closure of the case: failure to cooperate with work or work-related Personal Responsibility Plan components, voluntary termination of employment, and failure to help officials collect child support.

Tennessee had a welfare caseload of 74,820 in January 1997. Between January and April 1997, 3,041 cases were closed. Of these closures, 846 were because of sanctions. Based on surveys, 86 percent of the sanctions were due to a failure to follow work or work-related Personal Responsibility Plan components (almost 75 percent of these involved failing to show up for appointments), 10 percent were because of failure to cooperate with efforts to collect child support from the noncustodial parent, and 3 percent were because of voluntary termination of employment.

WORK RATES Thirty-nine percent of the sanctioned cases and 42 percent of those who did not sign the plan were working full- or part-time at the time of the survey. Of those who were not working, 65 percent of sanctioned and 70 percent of nonsigners were looking for work.

EARNINGS AND POVERTY The amount that sanctioned recipients earned from work was, on average, $5.50 an hour. The survey report did not indicate how many were working full- or part-time, nor is there any wage distribution that would enable analysts to identify how many former recipients were earning more than the poverty level. The survey did not provide any basis for assessing changes in earnings over time.

OTHER SUPPORTS In households in which no adult worked, former recipients supported themselves in various ways: 14 percent were supported by family members, 10 percent received other benefit checks (disability, SSI, AFDC, Pell grants), 4 percent got support from a husband or spouse, 4 percent received child support, and 15 percent listed other miscellaneous sources; 17 percent answered "nothing." Researchers also asked all respondents whether they had help paying their bills. About half (51 percent) said yes. Of those receiving help, 71 percent listed family as a source; 14 percent, a husband; 9 percent, a boyfriend; and 12 percent, other. Only 1 percent listed a church or community agency.

FAMILY WELL-BEING The majority of respondents could pay their rent (66 percent) and their utility bills (68 percent). Even more (88 percent) received TennCare, Tennessee's Medicaid program.

South Carolina

South Carolina enacted comprehensive welfare reforms in 1995. These reforms included work requirements, a full-family sanction for the first instance of non-cooperation, increased earnings disregards, and a twenty-four-month time limit. In January 1997 South Carolina had a caseload of 36,660 families. Between October 1996 and December 1997, 15,412 recipients left the cash assistance program; 28 percent left because of a sanction.[4]

WORK RATES Administrative data (unemployment insurance wage records gathered by the Urban Institute) show that about 39 percent of sanctioned recipients worked in the first quarter after leaving welfare, and 44 percent were working in the fifth quarter after leaving. About a quarter (24 percent) of the sanctioned cases worked in seven or eight of the eight quarters after they left welfare. According to the unemployment insurance records, 27 percent did not work at all.

About 58 percent of all other closures (excluding sanctions) worked in the first quarter after leaving, and about 58 percent worked in the fifth quarter. More than a third of all cases (39 percent) of the nonsanction closures worked at least seven quarters out of eight, and 20 percent had no wages.

OTHER SUPPORTS Three months after closure, 73 percent of sanctioned cases who had not returned to welfare were receiving food stamps. The proportion of sanctioned cases receiving food stamps declined to 58 percent by the twelfth month, and 55 percent by the twenty-fourth month. Food stamp receipt for nonsanctioned closures was 59 percent in the third month, 50 percent in the twelfth month, and 44 percent in the twenty-fourth month after cash assistance ended.

FAMILY WELL-BEING Sanctioned recipients faced a significantly greater number of hardships, such as having trouble buying food or getting behind on shelter costs, after leaving welfare than they did while they were receiving welfare (see table 6.1). However, the increase in hardships is roughly parallel to the increase experienced

TABLE 6.1 / South Carolina: Family and Child Well-Being Among Sanctioned and Other Welfare Recipients (Percentage)

Problem	Sanctioned Families		Other Families	
	While on Welfare	After Leaving Welfare	While on Welfare	After Leaving Welfare
Had problem buying food	9	19	10	17
Had problem paying for medical care	3	11	4	11
Fell behind on housing costs	17	24	21	28
Electricity turned off because unable to pay	9	12	10	11

Source: South Carolina Department of Social Services 1998.

by nonsanctioned recipients that left welfare. When asked whether "life was better when you were getting welfare," 35 percent of sanctioned respondents agreed, compared with 26 percent of nonsanctioned respondents. When asked whether they "hardly worry about money anymore," 25 percent agreed, compared with 26 percent of nonsanctioned respondents.

Arizona

Arizona implemented its welfare reforms—EMPOWER—in 1995.[5] The reforms include a time limit of twenty-four months on the adult portion of the grant. They also include several progressive sanctions related to program participation, immunization, and child support. In the first month after noncompliance, the grant is reduced by 25 percent. Recipients failing to correct their noncompliance lose half of the grant in the second month; the case is closed if the requirements are not met by the third month.

Arizona's Department of Economic Security is conducting a study of cases closed for at least one month during the first quarter of 1998. The state's caseload was 41,233 in January 1998. It closed 10,647 cases in the first three months of 1998; 2,155 (20 percent) of these cases were closed due to sanction. The remaining cases were closed due to employment (19 percent), increased resources (9 percent), failure to comply with procedures (37 percent), and other reasons (15 percent).

WORK RATES   When surveyed, 40 percent of sanctioned recipients reported earnings. Administrative data show that 36 percent reported wages in the first quarter after exit, a figure that increased to 42 percent one year later. In addition, 40 percent had corrected their noncompliance and returned to cash assistance in the first twelve months after leaving. (The number of recipients with reported wages may overlap with those returning to welfare.) The work rate reported in the survey for nonsanctioned closed cases was much higher (61 percent), but a significant number (33 percent) returned to welfare in the first twelve months. In the administrative data, the work rate for nonsanctioned leavers declined slightly in the first year, from 57 percent in the first quarter to 52 percent in the fifth quarter.

EARNINGS AND POVERTY   Earnings for employed sanctioned cases were low relative to those for nonsanctioned cases and relative to earnings reported for leavers in other states. Mean quarterly earnings during the first quarter after exit for sanctioned cases who were working were $1,368. Earnings did increase over time: by the fifth quarter after leaving welfare, average quarterly wages were $2,052 (an increase of 50 percent). When asked about total income, which can include a spouse's or partner's earnings as well as other income, sanctioned respondents reported an average monthly income of $1,281, enough to move most families out of poverty. For nonsanctioned cases, earnings were much higher. Mean earnings in the first quarter after exit were $2,036. Their earnings also increased over time, rising to $2,548 by the fifth quarter after exit (an increase of 25 percent). Average monthly income for nonsanctioned cases was $1,470.

OTHER SUPPORTS   Among all sanctioned recipients, 73 percent were enrolled in Medicaid during the first quarter after exit, and 59 percent received food stamps. By the third quarter after exit, Medicaid enrollment rates dropped to 55 percent, and food stamp receipt declined slightly, to 52 percent. In the survey, 26 percent reported that their children were uninsured. Fewer nonsanctioned leavers were enrolled in Medicaid and the Food Stamp program: 54 percent were enrolled in Medicaid in the first quarter after exit and 47 percent received food stamps. By the third quarter after exit, Medicaid enrollment rates dropped to 46 percent, and food stamp receipt declined to 42 percent; 26 percent reported that their children were uninsured.

FAMILY WELL-BEING   When asked, recipients reported significant hardships, but in most cases these occurred as often or less often than they had when the recipients were receiving welfare (see table 6.2), with the exception of access to medical care. Other than having their utilities turned off, sanctioned recipients did not suffer more hardships than nonsanctioned recipients. That nonsanctioned recipients were more often unable to get medical assistance probably reflects the higher rates of Medicaid enrollment among sanctioned cases. Most sanctioned recipients reported being better off after leaving welfare. Compared with recipients who left for other reasons,

TABLE 6.2   /   Arizona: Family and Child Well-Being Among Sanctioned and Other Welfare Recipients (Percentage)

Problem	Sanctioned Families		Other Families	
	While on Welfare	After Leaving Welfare	While on Welfare	After Leaving Welfare
Family-child well-being				
Did not have enough to eat at times	31	25	28	24
Fell behind on housing costs	35	36	43	37
Utilities turned off because unable to pay	26	16	16	11
Unable to get needed medical attention	12	17	15	25
Forced into homeless shelter	3	3	4	3
Self-assessed well-being since leaving TANF				
Much better off		19		33
Better off		36		38
About the same		23		15
Worse off		17		11
Much worse off		6		2

Source: Westra and Routley 2000.

sanctioned recipients more often reported being worse off and less frequently reported being much better off.

Maryland

Maryland implemented full sanctions in its welfare program—the Family Investment program—in October 1996. Recipients were subject to a full sanction for two principal reasons: failure to cooperate with a work requirement and failure to assign child support to the state or to provide the information needed to establish or enforce a child support order. Full sanctions were imposed for the first noncompliance with either the work or child support requirements after a thirty-day conciliation period, in which the recipient could correct the violation.

Over the eighteen months between October 1996 and April 1998, the program closed 56,411 cases, and its caseload dropped by about one-third (Born, Caudill, and Cordero 1999). Of these case closures, 3,864 (7 percent of the total) were closed due to sanctions. Most sanctions were imposed for noncompliance with work requirements (89 percent).The Family Investment program is administered by county offices, and the use of sanctions varied considerably among those offices, from 3 percent of all case closings in Baltimore City to more than 15 percent of all closings in three counties. The incidence of sanctions also increased over time, from 4 percent of all closings in the first six months to 8 percent and 9 percent in the following two six-month periods.

WORK RATES   Fewer than two-fifths (38 percent) of sanctioned recipients were working in the first quarter after leaving the program. Work rates were significantly higher (56 percent) for recipients who left for other reasons. Sanctioned cases were also much more likely to return to welfare. In the first three months, 35 percent of sanctioned recipients corrected their noncompliance and returned to welfare, compared with 18 percent of recipients who left for other reasons. In the first six months, 38 percent of sanctioned recipients returned, compared with 22 percent of other recipients.

EARNINGS AND POVERTY   Median quarterly wages for sanctioned recipients in the first quarter after exit were $1,337. Average wages were $1,649. Median wages in the first quarter after exit for recipients who left for other reasons were considerably higher: $2,240. Average wages were $2,457.

North Carolina

North Carolina is one of several states with a two-year time limit that resulted in lost benefits for many recipients.[6] North Carolina was the first state to carry out a focused study of time-limited cases; this study provides a glimpse of how these recipients fared after losing cash assistance.

North Carolina's Work First program took effect in July 1996. It included a twenty-four-month time limit for recipients, subject to work requirements. Several family categories were exempted: child-only, disabled parents, parents caring for a disabled child, persons over age sixty-five, and parents under age eighteen who were in school. Extensions were available if a recipient could show good faith efforts to cooperate in getting a job. In the first four months of the program, 12,724 recipients faced the time limit. Paralleling the experience in most other states with time limits, almost all recipients had left welfare, at least for a few months, before reaching the time limit. By December 1998, 538 recipients (4 percent of those originally subject to the limit) exhausted their two years of benefits. Of these, 83 requested extensions from county welfare administrators; 28 were granted.

WORK RATES Of the 241 recipients contacted, 129 (54 percent) were working for pay, and another 23 (10 percent) were self-employed. About half (54 percent) were employed at the time their benefits ceased. Over half of this group had found jobs within the prior three months. Approximately 20 percent had not held a job in the four months since losing their benefits.

EARNINGS AND POVERTY Median monthly earnings from work for employed adults were $947. Self-employed former recipients earned much less: $259. The highest self-employed monthly income was $649. Nineteen percent of employed adults earned more than $1,371 (the poverty threshold for a family of four), while none of the self-employed adults did. Despite low earnings, more self-employed former recipients worked more than thirty hours a week (78 percent) than did the employed former recipients (64 percent). Three self-employed adults who worked more than forty hours a week earned less than $297 dollars a month, the maximum Work First cash payment for a family of four. Earnings were strongly related to education level.

OTHER SUPPORTS The survey provides limited information on the income and resources of recipients who were not working. Of those not employed or self-employed, most continued to receive food stamps (87 percent) and Medicaid (91 percent). Slightly more than half received housing assistance; 24 percent received a rent subsidy, and 29 percent lived in public housing. About 17 percent received disability payments, and 44 percent received child support (median monthly child support payment was $142).

FAMILY WELL-BEING The survey asked respondents if they believed the combined income from all sources was adequate to meet their family's needs. Among employed recipients, 41 percent reported that their income was adequate, compared with 24 percent of the unemployed and 35 percent of the self-employed. There is no comparative data on how many families thought that the level of income was adequate while on welfare. Some respondents reported housing changes: 11 percent moved to a different apartment or home, 4 percent moved in with family or a friend, and 3 percent sent a child to live with family or a friend. No one reported having a child placed in foster care or becoming homeless (although it must be recognized that telephone surveys may not be the most effective way to identify homeless families). Most families reported at least some difficulty obtaining food for their families after they left welfare; 53 percent reported difficulty getting enough food or the kinds of food they wanted to eat. That number, however, is significantly lower than the 72 percent who reported such difficulty while receiving welfare. Not surprisingly, food difficulties were concentrated among recipients who were not employed.

Massachusetts

Massachusetts adopted comprehensive welfare reforms in 1995 (Massachusetts Department of Transitional Assistance 2000). They required adult welfare recipients to get work in sixty days unless they were exempted from work requirements because they were disabled, caring for a disabled family member, or had a child under the age of twelve months. Recipients subject to the work requirement were also subject to a twenty-four-month cumulative time limit. Recipients who hit the time limit could qualify for an extension if, after meeting agency requirements, they continued to face difficult barriers.

The time limit took effect in November 1996; the first recipients reached the time limit in December 1998. In the first three months (December 1998 through February 1999), 4,085 recipients reached the time limit; 2,268 requested extensions, of which about 7 percent had been granted or had not been decided by April 1999.

WORK RATES   When interviewed six to sixteen months after being cut off from welfare, almost three-quarters of time-limited recipients (73 percent) were currently employed. A further 18 percent had been employed at some point after leaving welfare. Those who left welfare for other reasons were employed 71 percent of the time.

EARNINGS AND POVERTY   Median hourly wages for time-limited recipients were $7.73 an hour. They worked a median of thirty-two hours a week and earned $240 a week. Recipients who left for other reasons had higher wages (median of $8.88 an hour), worked more hours (median of thirty-seven hours a week), and had greater earnings (median of $301 a week). Equal numbers of time-limited recipients reported having more money after leaving welfare (41 percent) and less money after leaving welfare (40 percent). More than half (51 percent) reported higher levels of expenses and only 8 percent lower expenses. Substantially more of the recipients who left for other reasons reported more income (61 percent) than less income (25 percent). Of these, 61 percent reported higher expenses, and only 5 percent reported lower expenses.

OTHER SUPPORTS   Time-limited former recipients reported a number of additional supports. Nine percent had a spouse or partner who was working (median weekly earnings of $520), including about 10 percent of those cases in which the former recipient was not working (raising the number of households with work earnings to 76 percent). Eight percent were again receiving welfare benefits by qualifying for an exemption or receiving an extension. Thirty-eight percent were receiving child support (median of $33 per week). Most time-limited recipients had Medicaid coverage: 84 percent of adults and 87 percent of children. About half (52 percent) were receiving food stamps, 56 percent received housing assistance, and 34 percent had received fuel assistance since leaving welfare. More recipients who left for other reasons (20 percent) had spouses or partners who worked (median weekly earnings, $422). This included a quarter of the respondents who were not working, so that 78 percent of recipients had work earnings. Eleven percent were receiving welfare when interviewed. Equal proportions of "other" leavers and time-limited recipients (38 percent) received child support (median, $46 a week). Slightly fewer were covered by Medicaid: 80 percent of adults and 81 percent of children. Only 29 percent received food stamps, 50 percent housing assistance, and 23 percent fuel assistance.

FAMILY WELL-BEING   The study had respondents compare their well-being during and after welfare. More time-limited recipients said their financial well-being was worse (39 percent) than better (34 percent). More pointed to improvements in their emotional well-being (38 percent better, 34 percent worse), their housing (20 percent better, 15 percent worse), and their child-rearing (29 percent better, 18 percent worse). One-third (34 percent) said their food situation was worse, and 20 percent said it was better. Measures of food insecurity were also higher after welfare: 24 percent experienced severe food insecurity, compared with 13 percent while receiving welfare. Recipients who left welfare for other reasons reported improvements by large margins in four dimensions of well-being: financial (53 percent better, 24 percent worse), emotional (52 percent better, 24 percent worse), housing (29 percent better, 14 percent worse), and child-rearing (44 percent better, 14 percent worse). Slightly more families thought their food situation had worsened (32 percent better, 34 percent worse). These families also experienced an increase in severe food insecurity (21 percent after leaving, 15 percent while receiving welfare).

Utah

Utah adopted new work requirements, a full-family sanction for not complying with the requirements, and a three-year time limit as part of its comprehensive reforms in 1996 (Taylor and Barusch 2000). The state also moved responsibility for cash assistance and work support to the Department of Workforce Services and established a broad range of services to help recipients overcome difficult challenges such as substance abuse, limited work experience, and learning disabilities. The three-year time limit started in December 1996; therefore, the first recipients lost benefits because of time limits in December 1999.

The Department of Workforce Services contracted with the Department of Social Work at the University of Utah to conduct a study of long-term recipients and how they were affected by Utah's three-year time limit. The researchers conducted in-person interviews with recipients who had left the welfare rolls after receiving benefits for more than three years. They divided case closures into three categories: cases closed because of increased income, cases closed because of time limits, and cases closed for other reasons, including sanctions. Even the cases closed for income and other reasons had received cash assistance for more than three years. Most of these recipients were subject to the time limit, but they left welfare under the time limit. In this discussion, the study's three categories are maintained, primarily because 40 percent of the "other" group cases were closed for nonparticipation and an additional 19 percent of that group's cases were closed for failure to submit necessary documentation (both reasons related to sanctions). The two other primary reasons for closure in this category were no eligible child in the home and request of the client.

WORK RATES   When interviewed three to six months after losing benefits, 43 percent of the time-limit cases were employed. Significantly more of the increased-
income cases were employed (77 percent), but about the same proportion of "other"
cases had jobs (42 percent).

EARNINGS AND POVERTY   Employed respondents whose cases were closed because
of time limits earned an average of $750 a month, compared with $1,092 a month
for the increased-earnings group and $814 for the "other" group. In the time-limit
group, 32 percent of all families were over the poverty threshold, and 32 percent
were in deep poverty (under 50 percent of the poverty line). Sixty-eight percent of
the increased-income group were living above the poverty line; 13 percent were
in deep poverty. In the "other" group, 39 percent were over the poverty line, and
34 percent were living in deep poverty.

OTHER SUPPORTS   Recipients who lost benefits owing to time limits usually remained
enrolled in noncash public assistance programs, such as Medicaid, Food Stamp,
and public housing. Enrollment rates for food stamps and housing assistance for
time-limited cases were substantially higher than those for increased income or
other leavers. Use of the child care subsidy was significantly lower for time-limit
and other cases, part of which might be explained by the much higher work rate
among those leaving because of increased income.

FAMILY WELL-BEING   The interviewers used a series of diagnostic questions to identify barriers that recipients faced. In most cases, time-limit and other cases had significantly higher rates of difficult barriers to employment. It is also worth noting the
high barriers for all groups in many categories (see table 6.3) and that almost half
(47 percent) of time-limited cases experienced all three major categories of barriers:
work-education, family, and health-mental health. Time-limited recipients also suffered several hardships more frequently than those who left for increased income,
although the families of those who left for other reasons (including sanctions) often
suffered even more hardship. About half (49 percent) of time-limited recipients
reported that their lives were worse since leaving the cash assistance program, and
only 21 percent reported that life was better, a reversal of the much more positive pattern among recipients who left because of increased income and more negative than
the responses of recipients who left for other reasons.

THE OUTCOMES OF SANCTIONS AND TIME LIMITS

It is only a slight exaggeration to say that the stories in these eight states capture
what is known about the effects of sanctions and time limits on families leaving
welfare. In other words, little is known.

Using the questions as a framework, I compare the outcomes in the studies of
recipients who were sanctioned or who reached time limits with those of studies
that examined "leavers" in general—those who left welfare for all reasons. Several
states have undertaken such studies, helping answer the question of what happened to these families (Tweedie et al. 2001). Such comparisons get to the issue of

TABLE 6.3 / Utah: Family and Child Well-Being Among Cases Closed, by Reason of
Leaving Welfare (Percentage)

Variable	Increased Income	Time Limit Reached	Other Reasons
Services used at time of interview			
Medicaid	83	80	60
Food stamps	56	85	62
Child care assistance-subsidy	34	13	11
Public-section 8 housing	41	55	40
Barriers to employment			
Depression	35	48	55
Learning disability	23	32	24
Limited education	23	45	40
Limited work experience	18	43	42
Physical health problems	35	42	42
Severe domestic violence in past twelve months	8	17	19
Drug abuse	20	30	30
Alcohol abuse	32	27	24
Family hardship			
Could not pay rent	31	53	53
Evicted	3	5	13
Electricity or heat turned off	7	6	17
Phone disconnected	16	23	31
Not enough money to buy food	13	21	21
Child protective services referral	47	49	54
Self-assessed well-being since leaving TANF			
Life is better	52	21	35
Life is the same	30	30	28
Life is worse	18	49	38

Source: Taylor and Barusch 2000.

whether those leaving welfare because of sanctions or reaching time limits are different from those leaving voluntarily and, consequently, whether policies should reflect those differences.

Number of Recipients Who Are Working

Work rates among sanctioned cases in the four states that used currently employed or administrative data are remarkably similar: between 38 and 40 percent of the adults were working. Sanctioned cases in Iowa reported a higher work rate, but they were asked if they had worked since leaving welfare, which is likely to be higher. The studies summarized here also provide strong evidence that adults in sanctioned cases work less often. In the three states that report comparison measures for recipients who left for reasons other than sanction, the gap between sanctioned and other families averaged almost 20 percent (see figure 6.1).

A comparison between work rates for sanctioned recipients and work rates for all recipients leaving welfare in other states reinforces the sense that sanctioned recipients do not work as often as other leavers. Surveys in fifteen states find that work rates for recipients leaving welfare range from 52 to 75 percent, well above the survey results in Tennessee and Arizona. Ten states use administrative data and find that work rates range from 50 to 70 percent, higher than the rates in South Carolina and Maryland.

The evidence is less clear on recipients who left because of time limits. In three states for which studies are available, work rates vary considerably: North Carolina (54 percent), Massachusetts (73 percent), Utah (43 percent). In Massachusetts there is no statistical difference between the work rates of time-limited recipients and those of recipients who left for other reasons. In Utah the difference is stark (43 percent for time-limited recipients and 62 percent for recipients who left for other reasons). This difference holds up even though the time-limited recipients are compared only with others who received benefits for at least three years, including a

FIGURE 6.1   /   Employment Rates: Sanctioned, Time-Limited, and Other Cases (Percentage)

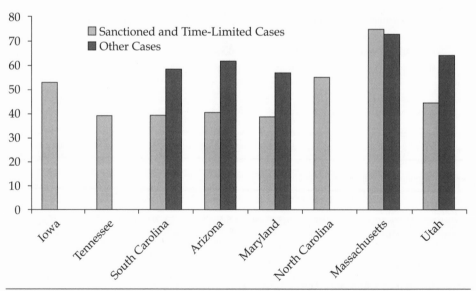

Source: Author's calculations based on data from Nixon et al. 1999; Bureau of Business and Economic Research, University of Memphis 1998; South Carolina Department of Social Services 1998; Westra and Routley 2000; Born et al. 1999; Maximus 1999; Massachusetts Department of Transitional Assistance 1999; and Taylor and Barusch 2000.

large number of sanctioned recipients, who also appear to do less well after they leave the cash assistance program.

Earnings from Work: Rising Above the Poverty Level

Studies of sanctioned recipients use very different measures of earnings and income, so it is difficult to compare results with results from studies in other states. The most straightforward comparisons are from Arizona and Maryland, which report data from both sanctioned and "other" families. In both cases, quarterly earnings of sanctioned recipients were substantially below those of recipients who left for other reasons (in Arizona, means of $1,368 for sanctioned recipients and $2,036 for "other"; in Maryland, medians of $1,337 and $2,240, respectively, for the two groups). In Arizona, the gap between sanctioned and other cases narrowed somewhat over time. By the fifth quarter after exit, wages for sanctioned recipients climbed to $2,052 (50 percent higher); those for recipients who left for other reasons, to $2,548 (25 percent higher).

The evidence from Arizona and Maryland is consistent with studies from other states. In the eight other states that report quarterly wages for all recipients leaving welfare, median wages ranged from $1,996 to $3,059, well above those of sanctioned recipients in Arizona and Maryland and consistent with the wages for "other" recipients.

Unlike employment rates, there was a consistent gap in earnings between those who left owing to time limits and those who left for other reasons. In Massachusetts median weekly earnings for "other" recipients were 25 percent higher than for time-limited recipients. In Utah mean earnings for non-time-limited recipients were 35 percent higher.

The low earnings and wages for sanctioned recipients suggest that there may be differences between these recipients and those who leave for other reasons. It makes some sense that those who are sanctioned for noncompliance may not be as successful in the workplace as those who leave for other reasons. Individuals who do not follow welfare rules, such as not showing up for a meeting (the primary reason for sanctions in Iowa) and not participating in required program activities (Tennessee), and who do not correct their noncompliance in three months (Arizona) are also possibly less likely to meet employers' expectations. Even this limited evidence suggests that states should consider providing job-readiness and job-coaching activities to help sanctioned former recipients overcome these difficulties.

How Families Support Themselves and the Stability of That Support

The studies of states employing sanctions and time limits provide a very limited picture of how families are supported if recipients are not working and are not receiving cash assistance. Some are supported by the mothers' spouses or boyfriends, some by their families, some by other benefit programs, and a few by child support. No survey breaks down these families to identify which have each form of support and which have no or few identifiable forms of support.

This lack of good family data is also true of the larger group of studies of families leaving welfare. Some reports look at household income as well as former recipients' earnings. For instance, an earlier study in Massachusetts reports that 58 percent of its former recipients were employed and that an additional 9 percent lived in households with a spouse or a significant other who worked (Massachusetts Department of Transitional Assistance 1999). In South Carolina 37 percent of former recipients did not work. Of that group, 11 percent lived in households in which a spouse or partner worked, and another 6 percent lived in a household in which another adult worked (South Carolina Department of Social Services 1998).

States also collect data on enrollment in the Food Stamp program and Medicaid. In cases of sanctions and time limits as well as other forms of exits, a large drop occurs in the number of recipients receiving food stamps and Medicaid. A significant number of recipients who appear to remain eligible leave the rolls. The number of families that leave Medicaid and the Food Stamp program increases rapidly over time. States that have recognized this as a problem and that have directed outreach and linking programs to retain families in these programs have seen significantly increased retention rates (Berkeley Policy Associates 2000). The states reporting here appear to focus attention on the relation between sanctioned and time-limited cases and the Food Stamp program and Medicaid. In the study states, enrollment in these programs was relatively high compared with national patterns. In the four states in which direct comparisons were made, sanctioned and time-limited recipients have significantly higher enrollment rates, much higher than would be expected from the differences in employment rates.

Are Families Better or Worse Off After Leaving Welfare?

Many state surveys asked questions about former recipients' sense of well-being or independence and are beginning to gain an understanding of how families fare after leaving welfare: their earnings tend to rise, but they experience slightly higher levels of deprivation after leaving welfare. There is also strong evidence that, although most families believe they are better off without welfare, they still struggle from day to day.

The national rates of hardship vary immensely, so it is difficult to compare the sanction and time-limit states on those measures. However, several state studies make direct comparisons. In those states, sanctioned recipients usually report rates of hardship that are similar to those of other families leaving welfare. In South Carolina and Arizona, both sanctioned recipients and "other" recipients report increased hardship compared with when they were receiving welfare, but there are only slight differences in the hardships reported between the groups. There are differences in former recipients' answers to more general questions about how they are doing. Sanctioned recipients in South Carolina more often said they were doing better when they were receiving welfare (35 percent, compared to 26 percent of "other" recipients), and sanctioned recipients in Arizona less often said they were much better off (19 percent, compared to 33 percent) and more often said they were worse off (23 percent, compared to 13 percent).

In Utah time-limited recipients reported being unable to pay the rent or to buy food more often than recipients who left for other reasons. They also said that their lives were worse since leaving welfare twice as often as they said that their lives were better. In Massachusetts time-limited recipients reported improvements on five dimensions (financial, emotional, child rearing, housing, and food security) much less often than "other" families and cited problems more often.

CONCLUSION

State studies are beginning to offer a picture of what is happening to families leaving welfare and the challenges that remain. The studies offer policymakers information about what issues remain in completing a remarkable transformation in their welfare systems. Many questions remain unanswered, however. Indeed, state studies generate even more questions. One set of questions about which there is little information involves those recipients who leave welfare because of sanctions or time limits. Most studies include these recipients as part of the larger group of recipients who leave welfare. There is strong evidence in the studies examined here that the difficulties of sanctioned recipients and, to a lesser extent, time-limited recipients are greater than those of recipients who leave for other reasons. More work is needed to extract the available information from existing studies. In addition, researchers must strive to design studies that will quickly provide a better understanding of these families and alert policymakers to potential problems in time to respond to those problems.

NOTES

1. For more information about state flexibility and available resources, see Tweedie, Reichert, and Steisel 1999.

2. This discussion of the Iowa welfare reforms and the Limited Benefit Plan is drawn from Nixon, Kauff, and Losby 1999.

3. This section is drawn from Bureau of Business and Economic Research, University of Memphis 1998.

4. Analysis is taken from relevant data tables given to the author by Marilyn Edelhoch, South Carolina Department of Social Services, in October 1999.

5. Information for this section was drawn from Westra and Routley 2000.

6. Information for this section was drawn from Maximus 1999.

REFERENCES

Berkeley Policy Associates. 2000. "Evaluation of the Colorado Works Program: Second Annual Report." Oakland, Calif.: Berkeley Policy Associates (November).

Born, Catherine, Pamela Caudill and Melinda Cordero. 1999. *Life After Welfare: A Look at Sanctioned Families*. Baltimore: School of Social Work, University of Maryland.

Bureau of Business and Economic Research, University of Memphis. 1998. "Summary of Surveys of Welfare Recipients Employed or Sanctioned for Noncompliance." Nashville: Tennessee Department of Human Services (March).

General Accounting Office. 2000. *Welfare Reform: State Sanction Policies and Number of Families Affected*. Washington: General Accounting Office.

Massachusetts Department of Transitional Assistance. 1999. *How Are They Doing? A Longitudinal Study of Households Leaving Welfare Under Massachusetts Reform*. Boston: Massachusetts Department of Transitional Assistance.

———. 2000. *After Time Limits: A Study of Households Leaving Welfare Between December 1998 and April 1999*. Boston: Massachusetts Department of Transitional Assistance.

Maximus. 1999. *Status of Families Leaving Work First After Reaching the Twenty-four-Month Time Limit*. Arlington, Va.: Maximus (May).

Nixon, Lucia A., Jacqueline F. Kauff, and Jan L. Losby. 1999. "Second Assignments to Iowa's Limited Benefit Plan." Washington, D.C.: Mathematica Policy Research (August).

South Carolina Department of Social Services. 1998. *Survey of Former Family Independence Program Clients: Cases Closed During July through September 1997*. Columbia, S.C.: Department of Social Services.

Taylor, Mary Jane, and Amanda Smith Barusch. 2000. *Multiple Impacts of Welfare Reform in Utah: Experiences of Former Long-term Welfare Recipients*. Salt Lake City: Department of Workforce Services (June).

Tweedie, Jack, Courtney Jarchow, and Andrea Wilkins. 2001. *Tracking Recipients After They Leave Welfare: Summaries of New State Tracking Studies*. Denver: National Conference of State Legislatures. Available at: *www.ncsl.org/statefed/welfare/weltrack.htm*.

Tweedie, Jack, Dana Reichert, and Sheri Steisel. 1999. *Challenges, Resources, and Flexibility: Using TANF Block Grant and State MOE Dollars*. Denver: National Conference of State Legislatures (September).

Westra, Karen, and John Routley. 2000. "Arizona Cash Assistance Exit Study: First Quarter 1998 Cohort: Final Report." Phoenix: Arizona Department of Economic Security (January).

Part III

How Families and Children Are Faring

How Different Are Welfare and Working Families? And Do These Differences Matter for Children's Achievement?

Greg J. Duncan, Rachel E. Dunifon, Morgan B. Ward Doran, and W. Jean Yeung

Welfare reform is upon us and many have already made the transition from welfare to work. There are good reasons to expect that these transitions will benefit many families and children; others, however, may not fare as well. Whether the changes help or hurt depends in large part on families' responses to welfare reform—the way they manage their time, effort, and division of family responsibilities; the effect on their self-esteem, stress levels, and other aspects of mental health; how their income changes; their connections to extrafamilial support networks; their strategies for seeking and keeping jobs; whether marriages, partnerships, divorces, or separations ensue; how fathers absent from the household alter their behavior; and how community-level resources and supports change in response to the new welfare regime.

The debate preceding the 1996 welfare reform legislation was filled with assertions about how welfare receipt harms family functioning and, depending on the politics of the speaker, how "ending welfare as we know it" either promotes or jeopardizes the well-being of the families and children involved. This debate, like many others, relied more on anecdote than analysis, but in this case for good reason: there is a dearth of systematic research on differences in family process and child well-being in welfare and working poor families.

SYNOPSIS

We investigate the extent to which families receiving Aid to Families with Dependent Children (AFDC) differ from other families in mental health and in the way they organize their time, manage their households, and spend their money. Our data were gathered before the 1996 reforms but still provide information on several useful comparison groups. Contrasts between welfare and middle-class families speak to popular stereotypes of welfare families. Contrasts between welfare and low-socioeconomic-status (SES) working families speak more to the possible consequences of welfare reform's welfare-to-work transitions.

Because welfare recipients and low-SES working families differ in ways often difficult to measure, our method of contrasting the characteristics of different subgroups of recipient and nonrecipient families may produce a biased picture of the likely effects of welfare-to-work transitions. However, we argue that these biases are likely to lead us to overstate the effects of reform. If so, our upper-bound estimates of the effects of welfare reform will be especially informative if they turn out to be small because bias from unmeasured characteristics is unlikely to be important in those cases.

Our data come from two nationally representative sources covering different historical periods. The first gathered its information in the early 1970s, the second in the early 1990s. The first of our data sets continued to follow family members, including children, until the mid-1990s. This allows us to investigate whether children growing up in families receiving welfare or having "bad" attitudes or family processes during the early 1970s showed lower achievements twenty years later, when the children had entered early adulthood.

We find large differences between welfare families and middle-class families in mental health, time use, and expenditures, even after statistical adjustments for differences in demographic characteristics, such as mothers' education and age. Occasionally, these differences "favored" welfare families, as with measures of parental alcohol consumption and how often the entire family ate meals together and got together with neighbors. Other times, there were no measurable differences between the two groups, such as parent-teacher involvement, parental willingness to leave teens alone unsupervised, housework done by children, and maternal self-esteem.

In most cases, however, the differences were substantial and favored middle-class families. Middle-class families had strikingly lower levels of maternal depression, lower subjective reports of family tension, and fewer hours spent watching television, as well as greater involvement in youth activities, higher (middle-class) interviewer ratings of the cleanliness of dwellings, and higher reported levels of fate control and precautionary behaviors.

Try as it may, welfare reform is unlikely to elevate welfare recipients into the middle class. Rather than asking how welfare-recipient families differ from middle-class families, it is more telling to examine differences between welfare families and low-SES working families, especially for single-parent working families.

When compared with welfare recipients, low-SES single working mothers reported closer, more loving, and less tense family relations, less housework, and in one of our data sets, less time spent watching television. By and large, however, welfare families differ very little from low-SES, single-mother, working families. When compared with welfare families, mothers in single-parent working families are just as depressed, hostile, and lacking in control of their fate. They spend no more time reading to their children, helping with their children's homework, or facilitating youth activities.

Suppose that welfare reform could somehow promote both work and marriage and, therefore, make welfare families resemble two-parent, low-SES families with children. Relative to welfare mothers, working but low-SES mothers in two-parent families report significantly less depression and hostility and feel more in control of their fates. As in many of our comparisons, causation here is ambiguous: marriage or partnering may indeed improve mental health, although it is also possible that better mental health improves one's chances of marriage.

Our comparisons provide fewer reasons to expect that parenting behaviors will improve as a result of welfare reform. Relative to low-SES, two-parent families, welfare families report eating together as a family and getting together with neighbors more frequently. On the other hand, levels of parent involvement in youth activities and the time children spent doing chores are higher in low-SES, working-mother, two-parent families relative to welfare families, and reported family tensions are less.

More often than not, mothers in low-SES, two-parent families are no different from mothers in single-parent welfare families. For example, they spend just as little time reading to their children and helping their children with homework and are no less willing to condone unsupervised time for their adolescent children as are mothers receiving welfare. Class, not welfare receipt, underlies many of these parenting differences.

Looking at the long-run correlates of some of our family process and mental health measures on the amount of schooling completed by children suggests that the social capital connections that parents make outside the family matter the most. But because these differ little across different groups of low-SES families, there is little reason to expect that welfare-to-work transitions will help children by promoting connections between family members and outside institutions.

More consistently important in our intergenerational models of children's schooling are a number of demographic characteristics, including the mother's own level of education, test scores, and age when her children were born. Strategies that focus on improving basic skills and delaying first births may well have a larger effect on children's success than policies directed at family process.

BACKGROUND

Christopher Jencks (1992) proposes four ways of identifying the individuals who compose the so-called "underclass" of American society. Two of his classification schemes—income level and income sources—deal directly with monetary measures of poverty. The other two, cultural skills and moral norms, speak to issues evoked by discussions and research on the lives of the poor—the extent to which low-income people do not "think, talk, and act like those who manage America's major institutions" (144). It is the perceived cultural and moral, rather than the financial, dimensions of poverty and welfare receipt that have fueled much of the debate over policies directed at the poor.

Recipients of the recently abolished cash income support program (AFDC) have received the most attention in this debate. Scholars and politicians alike have suggested that the women who received AFDC demonstrate attitudes and behaviors that differ from those of other women. It is often assumed that welfare receipt itself promotes behavior and attitudes that are at odds with middle-class values, harms the career prospects of mothers, and perhaps most important, prevents children from becoming productive adults.

The Culture of Poverty

Oscar Lewis (1966) was among the first researchers to identify and catalogue what he calls "the culture of poverty." In a study of Puerto Rican slums, he identifies a "strong feeling of fatalism, helplessness, dependence, and inferiority" (23) among the residents and concludes that psychiatric treatment may be the best way of addressing the misery he observes.

In *The Moynihan Report and the Politics of Controversy*, Lee Rainwater (1967) analyzes the passionate debate about potential cultural differences between the poor and the rest of society. The debate was sparked by Moynihan's report, which was published in the late 1960s and which examines trends of family deterioration among African Americans. In calling attention to increasing out-of-wedlock births, welfare use, and single-mother homes, Moynihan identifies the "pathology" of urban black families as a primary cause of these problems (75).

Moynihan links self-defeating attitudes among blacks to the deprivations imposed on them by whites through "three centuries of sometimes unimaginable mistreatment" (39).Thus in his view racial inequalities led to pathological cultural attitudes, which led to more poverty and family dysfunction. Others, however, interpret the causality of his argument differently, accusing Moynihan of "blaming the victim" by linking poverty to the attitudes of the poor (which is, in fact, only half of his argument).

Because of the ire directed at Moynihan after his report, researchers sympathetic to the plight of the poor hesitated to address issues of attitudinal and behavioral differences. Indeed, by the late-1970s the debate over the culture of poverty was judged to have vanished "without leaving significant intellectual residue" (Aaron 1978, 38). However, Charles Murray's *Losing Ground* (1984) quickly rekindled it during Ronald Reagan's presidency.

More recent ethnographic work on the poor provides rich descriptions of lives that seem strikingly foreign to middle-class readers and that imply vast cultural differences between classes. Elijah Anderson's *Streetwise* (1990) describes life in an urban neighborhood called Northton. In the chapter entitled "Sex Codes and Family Life among Northton's Youth," he describes how Northton's men play on women's desires for love and marriage in order to gain sexual favors, often leaving them alone and pregnant in the end. Anderson links these seemingly dysfunctional sexual attitudes to the dire economic situation of the area, calling the lack of sexual and parental responsibility among Northton men, "a mean adaptation to blocked opportunities . . . a grotesque form of coping" (113).

When describing the underclass, William Julius Wilson (1987) uses the term *social isolation*, rather than *the culture of poverty*. He does this deliberately so as to highlight the fact that the characteristics of the poor are responses to social and economic situations, not self-sustaining cultural traits. In Wilson's view, understanding the culture of the poor, which includes their attitudes and behaviors, is vital in understanding poverty itself.

Conservative commentators often draw an explicit connection between the attitudes and behaviors of the poor and dependent and their precarious economic position but attribute the former to the welfare programs themselves. Robert Rector (1993, 3) argues that the real cause of poverty is "a breakdown in the values and conduct that lead to the formation of healthy families and stable personalities, and promote self-sufficiency" among the poor. Based on his belief in such "behavioral poverty," he calls for large-scale reductions in social welfare spending.

Patterns of AFDC Use

Numerous studies show that spells (continuous periods of receipt) of AFDC are often quite short, typically lasting fewer than two years (Blank 1989; Fitzgerald 1991; Harris 1993; O'Neill et al. 1987; Pavetti 1993). However, most recipients have more than one spell of AFDC use, with nearly 60 percent of those who leave the program eventually returning for additional support (Harris 1996). When multiple spells are added together, the median length of total welfare receipt is roughly four years (Bane and Ellwood 1994; Pavetti 1995).

The characteristics of long-term recipients are identified in numerous studies, most notably in the work of Mary Bane and David Ellwood (1983, 1994), in a special report by Ellwood (1986), and more recently by LaDonna Pavetti (1995). Pavetti's estimates are typical in showing the likely problems of long-term recipients in making successful transitions to the labor force: 63 percent of long-term recipients (sixty or more total months of receipt) lack a high-school degree or a General Educational Development (GED) certificate when they first begin to receive welfare; 39 percent report no prior work experience; 53 percent are under age twenty-five; 58 percent were never married; and 52 percent had a child under the age of thirteen months. Nicholas Zill and colleagues (1991a) show that 56 percent of long-term AFDC recipients (and 44 percent of poor, nonrecipient mothers, and 10 percent of nonpoor mothers) score more than one standard deviation below the mean on a comprehensive achievement test.

The Psychological Characteristics of AFDC Recipients

Despite claims that the attitudes of welfare recipients differ from those of other women, it is unclear whether such differences exist and, even if they do, whether they result from time spent on welfare or whether they existed before and thus perhaps helped cause the welfare receipt. Zill and colleagues (1991a, 1991b) provide a statistical profile using national data on AFDC recipients and other mothers. They find substantially lower self-esteem for welfare recipients than nonpoor mothers but report no significant differences between welfare recipients and other poor mothers. A number of local studies of welfare recipients find strikingly higher levels of depressive symptoms among welfare mothers (1991a). However, Zill (1978) finds no significant differences in depression between low-income mothers who are married as opposed to never-married or divorced mothers.

Robert Plotnick, Marieka Klawitter, and Mark Edwards (1997) use data from the National Longitudinal Survey of Youth to predict young women's initial entry to welfare using psychological measures and a host of other factors. They find no evidence that prior levels of self-esteem or locus of control affect onset of welfare use. On the other hand, school-related attitudes, family background characteristics, and IQ scores do predict subsequent welfare use. Susan Popkin (1990) studied links between AFDC receipt and recipients' sense of efficacy. Through interviews with a sample of AFDC recipients from Chicago, she finds length of time on welfare to be the strongest negative predictor of efficacy (consisting of one measure of self-esteem and two measures of fate control). Low efficacy, in turn, affects respondents' beliefs about the difficulty of leaving welfare, with low-efficacy respondents less likely to view work as a viable option.

Elizabeth Oritz and Betty Bassoff (1987) studied fifty-three teenage welfare parents from California, examining their views about education, careers, and the future. On their measure of locus of control, the authors find welfare recipients to be less sure of the degree of control they have over their lives than nonrecipients. In addition, a much higher proportion of recipients than nonrecipients have no specific career goals and do not expect to graduate from high school.

AFDC and Children's Attainments

A key question is whether and how children's involvement in welfare programs affects their chances of becoming successful, independent adults. Undergirding much of the rhetoric of the War on Poverty is a simple income model, in which children's well-being and chances of success as adults depends on the level of their families' economic resources as well as on the amount of time parents "invest" in their children during childhood. Because income transfer programs such as AFDC augment the incomes of poor families and make it possible for mothers to spend time with their children rather than in the labor market, one might expect to observe better outcomes with an AFDC transfer system in place than without it.

Fears that welfare programs might harm rather than help children have several sources, the most prominent being that welfare receipt somehow breeds a harmful welfare "culture" in recipient families and neighborhoods. Concerning parents, Murray (1984) argues that the welfare system provides adults with a viable alternative to mainstream work and marriage. Through parental example and direct incentives, welfare may, in turn, encourage children to drop out of school, have their own children out of wedlock, and otherwise engage in behavior that will reduce their own chances of success as adults.

In her review of the literature on the intergenerational transmission of status, Mary Corcoran (1995) summarizes the arguments behind the welfare-culture model as follows:

When parents and neighbors rely heavily on welfare, the stigma associated with being on welfare disappears; parents and neighbors develop self-defeating work attitudes and poor work ethics; and these attitudes are passed on to their children. In addition, parental welfare recipiency provides children with poor role models for work and marriage. Girls raised in welfare-dependent homes and communities are more likely to drop out of high school, to have illegitimate births, and to go on welfare themselves. Boys raised in welfare-dependent homes and communities are more likely to grow up to father children out of wedlock, to drop out of high school, to hang out, engage in crime, and avoid regular work. Implicit in this welfare culture story is the assumption that welfare receipt changes parents', neighbors' and children's values, attitudes and behaviors. Parents, neighborhood residents and children eventually become "trapped" in poverty and dependency because of their deviant values and dysfunctional behaviors. (244)

One mechanism behind the welfare-culture model is that of role models. Life in a welfare-dependent home can provide a vivid example for children of the viability of a single-parent household with few connections to the formal labor market.

Another way in which welfare may harm children is by fostering weak labor-force attachments on the part of mothers. Weak attachment can create a number of problems for parents and children (Guo et al. 1996; Parcel and Menaghan 1994). First, for adolescents, parents unattached to the labor market may not be able to supply needed information and direct contacts to help the teenager in securing good jobs. A second and related point is that the more general set of "social capital" connections available to children of working parents may be greater than for children growing up in families with weak attachment to the labor force (Coleman 1988). Third, children in households in which parents do not work may fail to realize the strength of the links between schooling and a successful career and thus may be less motivated to finish high school or attend college (Guo et al. 1996). Fourth, for children of all ages, families in which adults do not work in the labor market may not provide the structure, stability, and predictability that children need (Parcel and Menaghan 1994). Finally, children growing up in families with working adults may benefit from the additional household responsibilities that they assume (Parcel and Menaghan 1994).

Empirical tests of beneficial or detrimental effects of welfare receipt on children are difficult to construct. Children from AFDC-dependent homes generally have few parental resources available to them, live in poor neighborhoods, go to low-quality schools, and so forth. A simple omitted-variables approach would view as crucial the need to adjust for the effects of these correlated conditions to assess the "true" effect of welfare receipt. Failure to do so will likely produce an overestimate of the apparent effect of parental AFDC receipt.

Proponents of a welfare-culture model might well view some of these correlated conditions as themselves products of parental welfare receipt. Suppose, for example, that welfare does indeed cause parents to eschew work, become single parents, and, as a result, have low incomes, live in poor neighborhoods, and send their children to low-quality schools. In that case, adjusting for the effects of the correlated conditions would cause the "true" effect of welfare to be understated because those correlated conditions represent the ways in which the detrimental effects of welfare operate. In this view, one should adjust only for differences in conditions that are not themselves the product of welfare-based incentives.

The extent to which income transfers actually influence the labor-market and demographic behaviors of adults is a matter of considerable debate. The most comprehensive and unbiased assessments (for example, Moffitt 1992) conclude that disincentive effects are indeed present, particularly for the labor supply of female household heads. Evidence of the effects of welfare incentives on demographic behavior is weaker and inconclusive.

Greg Duncan, Martha S. Hill, and Saul Hoffman (1988) present a revealing bivariate table using data on daughters whose parents' welfare receipt is observed while the daughters were between the ages of thirteen and fifteen and whose own welfare status is observed when they are between twenty-one and twenty-three years of age. They find that the majority of daughters from highly dependent parental families do not share the fate of their parents. At the same time, however, the fraction of daughters from highly dependent homes who themselves become highly dependent (20 percent) is much greater than the fraction of daughters from nonrecipient families who become highly dependent (only 3 percent). These suggestive associations are reinforced by sibling studies showing how much more likely a given woman is to receive welfare if her sister receives it also (Solon et al. 1988). An obvious problem in drawing conclusions about the intergenerational consequences of parental welfare receipt from bivariate associations is a lack of adjustment for other aspects of parental background and environment that may also affect a child's chance of subsequent success.

Analysts employ two strategies for uncovering the causal effect of parental welfare receipt. The first is to use multiple regression to adjust statistically for the effects of the correlated background and environmental conditions. Corcoran (1995) reviews many of the relevant studies; our discussion focuses on a subset of recent studies to convey the nature of the findings.

There is some indication that welfare receipt in the early or perhaps middle childhood years has more sustained and negative effects on outcomes than welfare receipt in later life phases. In the Baltimore Study of Teenage Motherhood, welfare receipt in early childhood is associated with low high school graduation rates, low literacy scores, and high grade failure rates, even after controlling for school readiness scores (Baydar et al. 1993; Brooks-Gunn et al. 1993; Guo et al. 1996). At the same time, welfare receipt in middle childhood also contributes to more negative outcomes in the adolescent years. Because readiness tests are given to the children at ages four or five, it is possible to chart how early welfare receipt contributes to diminished school readiness, which then sets children on a trajectory for later school problems. Other studies report that low readiness is associated with welfare receipt and with later school problems. At the same time, the timing of grade failure is associated with timing of welfare receipt, in that welfare receipt in middle childhood is associated with later grade failure, and welfare receipt in early childhood is associated with earlier grade failure (comparisons between grade failure in the early elementary school years and the later elementary school years). Thus welfare receipt has effects during both life phases, with somewhat different effects depending on the outcome of interest.

Most studies of welfare effects relate receipt during early adolescence to schooling and demographic behavior in late adolescence and early adulthood. For example, Peter Gottschalk (1992) uses young women in the National Longitudinal Survey of Youth sample to relate parent welfare receipt when the women were adolescents to these women's chances of having a child. After controlling for a long set of characteristics of the young women and their families, he finds substantial effects of parental participation in the AFDC program on childbearing for whites, blacks, and Hispanics. Observed AFDC-related birth rates by age eighteen are 50 percent higher for whites and more than 100 percent higher for blacks and Hispanics than simulated rates that assume no parental welfare receipt.

Duncan's (1994) analysis of the effects of parental welfare on completed schooling is noteworthy for its extensive controls for both family and neighborhood characteristics. He finds negative associations between parental welfare receipt and years of completed schooling for all four race-sex subgroups investigated, although the relevant coefficients are not statistically significant for white males. Gottschalk (1995) uses data on patterns of mother's welfare receipt after the daughter has left home to adjust for the effects of unobserved differences between families in which welfare is and is not received. After incorporating these adjustments, he finds for blacks, but not for whites, highly significant effects of parental welfare receipt on the chances that daughters will have AFDC-related births. Furthermore, the strongest effects are for parental receipt immediately before the daughter's possible fertility.

Duncan and W. Jean Yeung (1995) focus on the effects of welfare on the completed schooling of children. Like Gottschalk (1995), they include in some of their models measures of future welfare receipt of parents in an attempt to control for unmeasured sources of heterogeneity between parents who do and do not receive income from welfare. They find strong effects of parental welfare receipt, with both white and black children in recipient families completing roughly one year less schooling than children reared in families in which no welfare was received. Interestingly, Duncan and Yeung find different thresholds for the welfare effects across the two racial groups they studied. For both white males and females, it appears that any welfare receipt on the part of the parents is sufficient to produce the detrimental effect on completed schooling. On the other hand, black children reared in families in which welfare accounts for less than half of total family income complete as much schooling as black children reared in families in which no welfare is received. Detrimental effects of welfare receipt are observed only among black children reared in heavily dependent families.

Virtually all of the existing intergenerational studies are of a "black box" variety, in which parental welfare receipt is related to children's attainments but without measures of family process that would provide insight into the mechanisms at work. Explicit attention to such mechanisms is an important part of our own look at the intergenerational issues.

DATA

We draw our data from two longitudinal surveys, the National Survey of Families and Households (NSFH) and the Panel Study of Income Dynamics (PSID). Throughout our work we seek to maximize the comparability of samples and measures between the two data sources.

Our descriptive analyses of family process and mental health differences between welfare and nonwelfare families are based on two or three years of data on families with children drawn from very different historical periods: for the PSID the period is 1971 through 1972, a time of dramatic expansion in welfare, when relatively little stigma was attached to welfare receipt; for the NSFH the period is 1990 to 1994, also a time of dramatic caseload expansion but one coupled with a raging national debate about how to go about, in the words of then presidential candidate Bill Clinton, "ending welfare as we know it."

We formed the following groups in both data sets based on reports of work, welfare, and family structure over the three-year period before the NSFH interview and the two-year period before the 1972 PSID interview.[1]

- Welfare: families persistently headed by a low-SES (twelve or fewer years of completed schooling), single mother who works less than 250 hours a year and reports income from AFDC in all years. It constitutes the reference group in our analyses (the omitted group in the regressions). There are ninety-nine such cases in the NSFH and eighty-seven in the PSID.

- Low-SES, working, single mother: families persistently headed by a low-SES, single mother, but (at least over the three-year NSFH period and two-year PSID period) who never receives AFDC and works for 500 hours or more a year. There are 165 such cases in the NSFH and 103 in the PSID.

- Low-SES, two-parent, with a working mother: low-SES, two-parent families with a working (more than 500 hours a year) mother and no AFDC receipt. There are 410 such cases in the NSFH and 323 in the PSID.

- High-SES, working, single mother: families headed by high-SES (more than twelve years of completed schooling), single mothers who work for 500 hours or more a year and never receive AFDC. There are 154 such cases in the NSFH and 154 in the PSID.

- High-SES, two-parent, with nonworking mother: high-SES, two-parent families that never receive AFDC and in which the mother never reports working as many as 500 hours in any year. There are 136 such cases in the NSFH and 251 in the PSID.

- High-SES, two-parent, with working mother: the sixth group includes high-SES, two-parent families that never receive AFDC and have a mother who reports 500 hours of work in all (three in the NSFH, two in the PSID) years. There are 477 such cases in the NSFH and 251 in the PSID.

- Other: all other families are grouped in a residual "other" category. There are 1,641 such cases in the NSFH and 909 in the PSID.

The residual "other" category is large and extremely heterogeneous. It consists of families that change their structure, AFDC, or work over the two- or three-year periods used in the analyses. For example, many low-SES, single-parent families alternate between work and welfare from one year to the next or mix the two in the same year. These families fall into the residual group, as do the high-SES families that undergo a divorce or a change in maternal employment.

Family Process and Psychological Measures

Our two data sets provide a rich set of measures of family process, the networks and social capital connections that families established with others in the community, expenditures, as well as psychological characteristics.[2]
For the NSFH, we constructed measures of

- Family process and time use: the number of days a week that the family eats together; hours parents spend watching television with their children; hours of housework by mother; hours of housework by children; whether teenage children are left unsupervised; parental help with reading and homework; time spent by mother in youth-related activities; whether the family is reported to be loving and close; and family tensions.

- Family network and social capital: church attendance; parent-teacher association (PTA) attendance; visits to social clubs; frequency of getting together with neighbors; and number of friends outside the neighborhood.

- Psychological measures of the mother: CESD depression scale; Rosenberg self-esteem index; Pearlin mastery scale; and an index of hostility.

- Expenditure measures: mother's reported number of drinks of alcohol per day.

For the PSID, which treats husbands as heads of husband-wife families,[3] we constructed measures of

- Family process and time use: the number of days a week the family eats together; hours of television viewing; mother's housework hours; an interviewer rating of cleanliness of house; and frequency with which the household head reads a newspaper.

- Family network and social capital: church attendance; parent-teacher association (PTA) attendance; visits to social clubs; number of neighbors known to family; whether relatives live nearby.

- Psychological measures of the household head: personal control; future orientation; trust-hostility; orientation toward challenge versus affiliation; fear of failure; self-satisfaction; self-directed child; and an index of avoidance of unnecessary risks.

- Expenditure measures: alcohol expenditures; how often the head goes to bars; whether the family has medical insurance; cigarette expenditures; food expenditures per person; persons per room (a measure of the spaciousness of housing).

Our method for contrasting family process and psychological measures consists of estimating regression-adjusted differences between the welfare group and each of the other groups. Demographic controls used in all regressions include the head's race and years of completed schooling, the number of children, whether children under age five are present in the household, region, and city size. NSFH regressions also control for mother's age. PSID regressions control for age of mother at the birth of the child, disability status and sentence-completion test score of the household head, and the unemployment rate in the county of residence. We should note that some of these control variables—in particular mother's age, education, and family size—may lead to an understatement of the effects of welfare if welfare itself encourages more births, births at younger ages, and dropping out.

Our intergenerational analysis is based on a subset of the PSID sample. We track all children ages fourteen or younger in 1971, whose families were also interviewed in 1972, and track them in the data for as long as possible. If they were observed after age twenty and provide a report on their completed schooling, they are included in the intergenerational analysis. We use the most recent year of completed schooling data available to create the completed schooling measure. Our models of these children's schooling include as predictors the seven-category structure-work-welfare measure, demographic controls and the family process, social capital, expenditure, and psychological characteristics drawn from our analysis of the 1971 through 1972 data.

RESULTS

The differences show up in five areas: family process and time use, family networks and social capital, certain psychological measures, expenditures, and intergenerational consequences.

Family Process and Time Use

We begin with results on differences across groups in family process and time use (table 7.1). In all cases, the reference group consists of single mothers who persistently (two years in the PSID and three years in the NSFH) report AFDC receipt and virtually no work. The most interesting comparison group is the second, the low-SES, working, single-mother group, because welfare recipients who undergo successful welfare-to-work transitions would most resemble (at least demographically) this one.

Entries in the second column of the table show regression-adjusted differences between single-parent welfare and working families. All of the dependent variables in these regressions are standardized by division by the (whole-sample) standard deviation to facilitate comparisons across dependent variables.

The interpretation of the -0.76 entry in the first row of the third column may help to clarify the meaning of the numbers in the table. It means that, after adjusting for differences in the demographic characteristics listed at the bottom of the table, low-SES, married-couple-parent families in the NSFH data who work and do not

TABLE 7.1 / Family Process Differences Between Welfare Recipients, Single-Parent Working Families, and Other Groups

Family Process and Time Use Measures	Low Socioeconomic Status (Mother's Education ≤ Twelfth Grade)		High Socioeconomic Status (Mother's Education > Twelfth Grade)		
	Working, Single-Mother Family	Two-Parent Family, Working Mother	Working, Single-Mother Family	Two-Parent Family, Nonworking Mother	Two-Parent Family, Working Mother
Days a week family eats together					
NFSH	-.33	-.76**	-.24	-.62*	-.71**
	(.19)	(.16)	(.20)	(.18)	(.16)
PSID	-.61*	-.74**	-.51*	-.64**	-.67**
	(.22)	(.18)	(.23)	(.20)	(.19)
Television viewing Parents with children (NSFH)	-.07	-.33*	-.38*	-.50*	-.42*
	(.16)	(.14)	(.16)	(.17)	(.14)
Head of household (PSID)	-.83**	-.78**	-1.26**	-1.02**	-.98**
	(.21)	(.18)	(.23)	(.19)	(.19)
Housework hours of mother					
NSFH	-.44**	-.22	-.53**	-.19	-.51**
	(.16)	(.14)	(.17)	(.15)	(.14)
PSID	-.49*	-.36*	-.66**	.43*	-.24
	(.19)	(.16)	(.20)	(.17)	(.17)
Other NSFH measures					
Housework by children	.01	.28*	.01	-.10	-.05
	(.17)	(.14)	(.18)	(.16)	(.14)
Teens unsupervised	.15	.04	.07	.11	.09
	(.20)	(.17)	(.20)	(.18)	(.17)

(Table continues on p. 116.)

TABLE 7.1 / Continued

Family Process and Time Use Measures	Low Socioeconomic Status (Mother's Education ≤ Twelfth Grade)		High Socioeconomic Status (Mother's Education > Twelfth Grade)		
	Working, Single-Mother Family	Two-Parent Family, Working Mother	Working, Single-Mother Family	Two-Parent Family, Nonworking Mother	Two-Parent Family, Working Mother
Parent helps with reading and homework	.14 (.18)	−.08 (.15)	.20 (.18)	.32 (.16)	.23 (.15)
Hours of youth-related activities by mother	.32 (.21)	.35* (.18)	.40 (.21)	.35 (.19)	.33 (.18)
Family loving and close	.30 (.16)	.14 (.14)	.57** (.16)	.54** (.16)	.34* (.14)
Family tensions	−.67** (.20)	−.53** (.17)	−.70** (.20)	−.80** (.18)	−.62** (.17)
Other PSID measures					
Interviewer rating of cleanliness of house	.02 (.22)	.30 (.18)	.41 (.23)	.49* (.19)	.43* (.20)
Reads newspaper	−.08 (.21)	.17 (.18)	−.04 (.22)	.05 (.19)	.09 (.19)

Source: Authors' tabulation of data from the National Survey of Families and Households (NSFH), 1992–1994; Panel Study of Income Dynamics (PSID), 1970–1972.

Note: Low SES mothers on welfare is reference group. Standard errors in parentheses. NSFH data show that low-SES, two-parent, working-mother families are .76 of a standard deviation less likely to eat together than low-SES, AFDC-recipient families. This difference is significant at the .01 level. The corresponding difference in PSID data is −.74 of a standard deviation. All dependent variables are standardized by division by the whole-sample standard deviation. Coefficients for a heterogeneous group with other work and welfare characteristics are omitted. Control variables included in all regressions: mother's race and years of completed schooling; number of children; whether children under age five are present in the household; region; city size. NFSH regressions also control for mother's age. PSID regressions also control for age of mother at the birth of the child; disability status and sentence-completion test score of the household head; and the unemployment rate of the county of residence.

* $p < .05$. ** $p < .01$.

receive welfare are significantly (at the .01 level) less likely than single-parent welfare families to have meals together. The difference in frequency of eating together amounted to 0.76 standard deviations—more than two days a week. The corresponding entry in the row immediately below is −.74, which indicates a similar negative and significant difference in the PSID.

A more complete look at the entries in the second column shows that only five of fourteen family process measures differ significantly between the two groups of low-SES single mothers. PSID data from the 1970s (but not NSFH data from the 1990s) indicate that welfare-recipient mothers, as opposed to working single mothers, watch more television. Both surveys agree that welfare-recipient mothers report significantly more housework hours, although there is no significant difference in the PSID's interviewer ratings of how clean their apartments or houses are. Data from the NSFH reveal that welfare-recipient, single-mother households, as opposed to working, single-mother households, report significantly more family tensions.

The remaining columns of the table reveal many more family process differences between welfare recipients and both high-SES, single-parent families and high- and low-SES, two-parent families. Although a few of these differences (families eating together and housework) favor welfare recipients, most favor intact and high-SES families. Most consistent are differences indicating that welfare families report less loving and more tense family relations; and despite the greater housework, they are rated as having dirtier dwellings.

Contrary to stereotypes, there are no significant differences across the groups in the extent to which mothers report that they leave their teenagers unsupervised at various times during the day. Similarly, welfare recipients do not report reading newspapers any more or less than other families.

Family Networks and Social Capital

The two surveys provide a wealth of data on various kinds of connections that families might make with friends, relatives, and institutions such as churches, social clubs, and parent-teacher associations. A glance at the second column of table 7.2 reveals virtually no differences between welfare and working single mothers in making these kinds of connection. The only exception is getting together with neighbors, which occurs more frequently among welfare than working single-mother families. Thus if these comparisons provide upper-bound estimates of the effect of welfare-to-work transitions, it does not appear that such transitions will have any effect, either positive or negative, on the extrafamilial connections that families might establish. It is possible that work might lead to connections with co-workers that would not be captured in these measures.

As with the family process measures, there are more differences in extrafamilial connections between welfare families and high-SES and two-parent families. However, the differences are neither large nor very consistent across the two data sets. Compared with the welfare (and, as we have just seen, low-SES, single-parent

(*Text continues on p. 120.*)

TABLE 7.2 / Family Network and Social Capital Differences Between Welfare Recipients, Single-Parent Working Families, and Other Groups

Family Network and Social Capital	Low Socioeconomic Status (Mother's Education ≤ Twelfth Grade)		High Socioeconomic Status (Mother's Education > Twelfth Grade)		
	Working, Single-Mother Family	Two-Parent Family, Working Mother	Working, Single-Mother Family	Two-Parent Family, Nonworking Mother	Two-Parent Family, Working Mother
Church attendance					
NSFH	.31	.35*	.25	.34	.28
	(.20)	(.17)	(.20)	(.18)	(.17)
PSID	.32	.12	-.02	.34	-.01
	(.22)	(.18)	(.23)	(.19)	(.19)
PTA attendance					
NSFH	.16	-.01	.03	.11	-.07
	(.21)	(.18)	(.21)	(.19)	(.17)
PSID	-.01	.11	-.11	.27	.42*
	(.22)	(.19)	(.24)	(.20)	(.20)
Social clubs					
NSFH	.19	.21	.39*	.27	.45**
	(.17)	(.14)	(.18)	(.16)	(.14)
PSID	.04	.08	-.25	.17	.04
	(.22)	(.19)	(.23)	(.20)	(.20)

Other NFSH measures					
Socializing with neighbors	-.46**	-.52**	-.16	-.31*	-.51**
	(.17)	(.15)	(.18)	(.16)	(.15)
Number of friends outside of neighborhood	-.14	-.17	.07	-.08	-.15
	(.17)	(.14)	(.18)	(.16)	(.14)
Other PSID measures					
Knows neighbors	-.06	.24	-.17	.35*	.23
	(.21)	(.18)	(.22)	(.19)	(.19)
Relatives nearby	-.11	-.06	-.10	.01	-.07
	(.21)	(.18)	(.23)	(.19)	(.19)

Source: Authors' tabulation of data from the NSFH, 1992–1994; and PSID, 1970–1972.

Note: Low SES mothers on welfare is reference group. Standard errors are in parentheses. NSFH data show that low-SES, two-parent, working-mother families were .35 of a standard deviation more likely to attend church than low-SES, AFDC-recipient families. This difference is significant at the .05 level. All dependent variables are standardized by division by the whole-sample standard deviation. Coefficients for a heterogeneous group with other work and welfare characteristics are omitted. Control variables included in all regressions: mother's race and years of completed schooling; number of children; whether children under age five are present in the household; region; city size. NFSH regressions also control for age of mother at the birth of the child; disability status and sentence-completion test score of the household head; and the unemployment rate of the county of residence.

* *p* < .05. ** *p* < .01.

working) families, two-parent families report more frequent church and social club attendance but less frequent socializing with neighbors.

Psychological Measures

The literature contains many studies showing poorer-than-average mental health among welfare recipients. We argue that a more telling comparison is between welfare recipients and working single-parent households. The second column of table 7.3 shows no psychological differences between these two groups in any of the NSFH-based mental health assessments and very few differences in the PSID's psychological measures.

In contrast, and consistent with the literature, there are larger and much more consistent differences between the mental health of low-SES single mothers, both recipients and nonrecipients, and all other groups. In the NSFH, low-SES single mothers report significantly higher levels of depression and hostility and lower mastery than all other groups. There are no differences across any of the groups in reported self-esteem.

The mental health patterns in the PSID are not as consistent, perhaps because the PSID's measures usually consist of only one or two items rather than multi-item indexes. Most striking in the PSID are differences between two-parent and single-parent families, but this may stem largely from the use of fathers as respondents in two-parent families and mothers as respondents in the single-parent families.

The final entry in the list of PSID measures is a behavior-based index of avoiding of undue risks: fastening seat belts, having car or medical insurance, and having at least some reserve savings. Here welfare recipients have significantly lower scores than all other groups.

Expenditure Measures

Few stereotypes are as memorable as President Reagan's depiction of Cadillac-driving welfare mothers. Most of the expenditure measures available to us come from the PSID. There are virtually no significant differences in the pattern of expenditures of welfare and working single mothers (data not shown). The single exception is the higher levels of medical insurance reported by working mothers when these interviews were held in 1972. Given the increases in Medicaid coverage and the decline of employer-provided health insurance, it is unlikely that these differences persist today.

The higher incomes of the high-SES and two-parent, low-SES families enable them to spend more on both good and bad things. Relative to welfare families, high-SES families report drinking and smoking more but also spend more per person on food and enjoy more commodious housing. The results on alcohol consumption are surprising because other studies (for example, Zill et al. 1991a, table 12) find somewhat higher reports of alcohol-related problems among welfare mothers relative to other groups.

(*Text continues on p. 123.*)

(Table continues on p. 122.)

TABLE 7.3 / Psychological Differences Between Welfare Recipients, Single-Parent Working Families, and Other Groups

Psychological Measures	Low Socioeconomic Status (Mother's Education ≤ Twelfth Grade)		High Socioeconomic Status (Mother's Education > Twelfth Grade)		
	Working, Single-Mother Family	Two-Parent Family, Working Mother	Working, Single-Mother Family	Two-Parent Family, Nonworking Mother	Two-Parent Family, Working Mother
NSFH measures					
CESD depression scale	-.06	-.48**	-.47**	-.73**	-.49**
	(.16)	(.13)	(.17)	(.15)	(.13)
Rosenberg self-esteem index	-.09	-.09	-.06	-.12	-.06
	(.16)	(.14)	(.17)	(.15)	(.14)
Pearlin mastery scale	.12	.33*	.76**	.73**	.62**
	(.16)	(.14)	(.17)	(.15)	(.13)
Hostility index	-.17	-.24	-.30	-.45*	-.22
	(.16)	(.14)	(.17)	(.15)	(.13)
PSID measures					
Personal control	-.47*	.11	-.28	.26	.22
	(.21)	(18)	(.22)	(.19)	(.19)

TABLE 7.3 / *Continued*

Psychological Measures	Low Socioeconomic Status (Mother's Education ≤ Twelfth Grade)		High Socioeconomic Status (Mother's Education > Twelfth Grade)		
	Working, Single-Mother Family	Two-Parent Family, Working Mother	Working, Single-Mother Family	Two-Parent Family, Nonworking Mother	Two-Parent Family, Working Mother
Future orientation	.07	.15	−.10	.21	−.04
	(.22)	(.19)	(.23)	(.20)	(.20)
Trust-hostility	−.11	.16	.14	.07	.02
	(.21)	(.18)	(.22)	(.19)	(.19)
Challenge versus affiliation	−.30	.34	−.12	.40*	.45*
	(.22)	(.19)	(.23)	(.20)	(.20)
Fear of failure	−.18	.65**	−.20	.58**	.44*
	(.22)	(.19)	(.24)	(.20)	(.20)
Self-satisfaction	.08	.49**	.24	.56**	.44*
	(.22)	(.19)	(.23)	(.20)	(.20)
Self-directed child	−.10	−.22	.17	−.18	−.06
	(.22)	(.19)	(.23)	(.20)	(.20)
Undue risk avoidance	.42*	.86**	.55**	1.10**	1.06**
	(.19)	(.17)	(.21)	(.18)	(.18)

Source: Authors' tabulation of data from the NSFH, 1992–1994; and PSID, 1970–1972.

Note: Low SES mothers on welfare is reference group. Standard errors are in parentheses. NSFH data show that mothers in low-SES, two-parent, working-mother families scored .48 of a standard deviation lower on the depression scale than mothers in low-SES, AFDC-recipient families. This difference is significant at the .01 level. All dependent variables are standardized by division by the whole-sample standard deviation. Coefficients for a heterogeneous group with other work and welfare characteristics are omitted. Control variables included in all regressions: mother's race and years of completed schooling; number of children; whether children under age five are present in the household; region; city size. NFSH regressions also control for mother's age. PSID regressions also control for age of mother at the birth of the child; disability status and sentence-completion test score of the household head; and the unemployment rate of the county of residence.

* $p < .05$. ** $p < .01$.

Intergenerational Consequences of Welfare Receipt and Family Process

The PSID data provide a look at whether patterns of welfare receipt and family process observed in the early 1970s (when PSID children were ages zero through fourteen and living with their parents) have any long-run association with the school-related achievements of those children in their early adult years.

We began our exploration of this topic by comparing the average completed schooling levels of children reared in the seven groups of families defined by their family structure, welfare, and employment status (table 7.4). Using the welfare group as the reference and controlling for no other differences in demographic characteristics, we find that children growing up in welfare families complete significantly less schooling than children growing up in all other circumstances, including families with low-SES single working mothers (table 7.4, column 1). These unadjusted differences are striking and range between one and two years. Schooling differences between welfare and low-SES, working, single mothers average 0.97 of a year—a highly significant difference.

Controls for demographic characteristics of these reduce these differences substantially (table 7.4, column 2). In the case of welfare and low-SES, working, single mothers, the difference is cut by two-thirds, from 0.97 to 0.34 of a year, with the latter difference no longer statistically significant. Thus it appears that children's schooling differences are more a function of demography than welfare receipt itself, raising little hope that welfare-to-work transitions will have a large effect on achievements of children. Schooling differences between children reared in welfare and two-parent working families fall by nearly half, from 1.13 to 0.65 years, but remain significant in the presence of the demographic controls.

Our estimates of the intergenerational effects of parental welfare receipt are much cruder than those reported in the recent literature. One problem is that we use only a two-year (1971 through 1972) window for categorizing the work-welfare-family structure status of parental families, when in fact a whole-childhood window is much more appropriate. The contribution of our data is in gauging the role of family process variables.

Controls for the set of family process measures available in the PSID "account" for nearly one-third of the demographically adjusted differences in the completed schooling of children reared in welfare families and in working single-parent families (table 7.4, column 3). In fact, the collection of demographic and family process measures reduce the schooling difference between welfare families and all other groups to the point of statistical insignificance.

The apparent power of the family process measures to explain completed schooling suggests the utility of a closer look at the elements of family process that appear most influential. This is done in the first two columns of table 7.5, which report coefficients and standard errors on the PSID's family process measures from a regression that includes the welfare-family-work classification and demographic controls. To facilitate comparisons across measures, all independent variables are standardized

(Text continues on p. 126.)

TABLE 7.4 / Regression Coefficients on Work-Welfare-Family Structure, 1970 through 1972, from Models of Completed Schooling of Children, Without and With Control and Family Variables; Dependent Variables Years of Schooling Completed by Children

	Controls		
Family Group	None	Demographic[a]	Demographic[a] and Family Process
Working, poor, single-parent family	.97**	.34	.24
	(.34)	(.33)	(.32)
Low-socioeconomic status, two-parent family, working mother	1.13**	.65*	.30
	(.28)	(.28)	(.28)
High-socioeconomic status, single-parent family	1.55**	.66	.40
	(.39)	(.40)	(.39)
High-socioeconomic-status, two-parent family, nonworking mother	1.98**	1.16**	.43
	(.29)	(.32)	(.32)
High-socioeconomic-status, two-parent family, working mother	1.90**	1.01**	.48
	(.29)	(.32)	(.32)
Other	.93**	.45	.16
	(.27)	(.27)	(.26)

Source: Authors' tabulation of data from the PSID, 1970–1972.

Note: Low SES mothers on welfare is reference group. Standard errors are in parentheses. Without adjusting for any other differences, children growing up in low-SES, working, single-mother households completed .97 years more schooling than children growing up in low-SES welfare-receiving households.

[a] Demographic control variables are mother's race and years of completed schooling; number of children; whether children under age five are present in the household; region; city size; age of mother at the birth of the child; disability status and sentence-completion test score of the household head; and the unemployment rate of the county of residence.

* $p < .05$. ** $p < .01$.

TABLE 7.5 / Effects of Demographic and Family Process Measures on Completed Schooling of Children, 1971 and 1972

Measure	All Families		Low-Socioeconomic-Status Families	
	Coefficient	Standard Error	Coefficient	Standard Error
Family process and time use				
Days a week family eats together	.01	.05	−.02	.06
Television viewing	−.08	.05	.02	.06
Housework hours of mother	−.05	.05	−.07	.07
Interviewer rating of cleanliness of house	.16**	.05	.13	.07
Reads newspaper	.01	.004	.01	.01
Family network and social capital				
Church attendance	.15**	.05	.27**	.07
PTA attendance	.17**	.05	.07	.06
Social clubs	.20**	.05	.19**	.07
Knows neighbors	.11**	.04	.05	.06
Relatives nearby	.003	.05	.05	.06
Psychological				
Personal control	.07	.06	.05	.07
Future orientation	.03	.05	.11	.06
Trust-hostility	.04	.05	.07	.06
Challenge versus affiliation	.05	.05	.13	.06
Fear of failure	.05	.04	−.02	.06
Self-satisfaction	−.10	.05	−.05	.06
Self-directed child	.00	.05	−.04	.06
Undue risk avoidance	.26**	.07	.11	.08
Expenditures and other				
Alcohol expenditures	−.02	.06	−.04	.07
Goes to bars	−.02	.06	−.03	.08
Medical insurance	.00	.05	−.03	.07
Cigarette expenditures	−.13	.05	−.19*	.07
Food expenditures per person	.19	.06	.08	.09
Spaciousness of home (persons per room)	.12	.06	.06	.08
Statistically significant demographic controls				
Whether black	.11*	.04	.08	.05

(Table continues on p. 126.)

TABLE 7.5 / *Continued*

Measure	All Families		Low-Socioeconomic-Status Families	
	Coefficient	Standard Error	Coefficient	Standard Error
Whether child is female	.17*	.05	.18*	.06
Age at birth of child	.34**	.06	.28*	.08
Household head's word-test score	.14*	.05	.14*	.06
Age of household head	−.24*	.08	−.18	.09
Mother's education	.03	.06	.31*	.13

Source: Authors' tabulation of data from the PSID, 1971–1972.
Note: All independent variables are standardized by division by the whole-sample standard deviation. Work-welfare-family structure classification is included in the regression. Other demographic control variables are mother's race, and years of completed schooling; number of children; whether children under age five are present in the household; region; city size; age of mother at the birth of the child; disability status and sentence-completion test score of the household head; and the unemployment rate of the county of residence.
* $p < .05$. ** $p < .01$.

with division by whole-sample standard deviations. In the third and fourth columns of the table, we present results from the identical regression run on the subset of families in which the mother has no more than twelve years of schooling.

Interestingly, nearly all of the measures of social capital connections—church, parent-teacher association, and social club attendance; number of neighbors known to the family—have statistically significant, positive effects on children's completed schooling in the full sample. For the low-SES subsample, church and social club attendance are significant positive predictors of children's schooling. Notably, none of the family process measures is significant in the low-SES sample.

None of the family process and mental health measures is as powerful in explaining children's schooling success as demographic measures—maternal schooling, test scores, and age when her children were born. The power of mother's schooling in the low-income subsample is striking in light of the fact that that group of families is defined by a low level (twelve years or less) of mother's schooling, which limits the extent of variability in maternal schooling in the low-income subsample.

DISCUSSION

Two questions compose the title of our paper: How different are welfare and working families? Do those differences matter for children's achievement? We begin with summary answers to those questions and then discuss their implications for studies of welfare reform.

Our two data sets reveal vast differences between welfare families and middle-class families in mental health, organization of time, household management, and expenditures, even after statistical adjustments for differences in demographic characteristics such as mother's completed education, age, and in one of our data sets, a parent's test scores. Occasionally, as with measures of how often the entire family eats meals together or gets together with neighbors, parental alcohol and cigarette expenditures, and mother's housework hours, these differences "favor" welfare families. In some cases—most interestingly, parent-teacher association involvement, housework done by children, and maternal self-esteem—there are no measurable differences between the two groups.

In most cases, however, the differences are substantial and favor middle-class families. Compared with middle-class families, in welfare families we find strikingly higher levels of maternal depression, subjective reports of family tension, and hours spent watching television, as well as less time spent facilitating youth activities, lower fate control, and fewer precautionary behaviors.

As we state in the introduction, welfare reform is unlikely to elevate many welfare recipients into the middle class. Therefore, rather than asking how welfare-recipient families differ from middle-class families, it is more telling to examine differences between welfare families and low-income working families, especially single-parent working families. These differences may still overstate changes that we might expect in welfare families making successful transitions to work, but at least they provide a tighter set of upper-bound estimates of those possible changes.

By and large, welfare families differ very little from low-income working families. When compared with welfare families, mothers in single-parent, working families are just as depressed, hostile, and feeling out of control of their fate; and they spend no more time reading to their children, helping them with their homework, or promoting youth activities. Nor are there indications that either expenditures or the social capital connections of the two groups differ. In fact some of the differences favor welfare mothers, such as the number of meals eaten together, frequency of getting together with neighbors, and hours of housework. The only significant but certainly noteworthy differences favoring working single mothers are the subjective assessments of how loving and tranquil family relations are and their greater precautionary behavior.

Suppose that welfare reform could somehow promote both work and marriage. Relative to welfare mothers, working but low-income mothers in two-parent families report significantly less depression, hostility, and family tensions and feel more in control of their fates. Marriage or partnering may indeed improve mental health, an important benefit if true. An alternative interpretation of this correlation is that women with more positive mental health are more likely to marry or cohabit in the first place.

Our evidence provides fewer reasons to expect that parenting behaviors may change as a result of work and marriage. Relative to low-income, two-parent families, welfare families reported eating together as a family and getting together with neighbors more frequently. On the other hand, levels of parent involvement in youth activities and the time children spent doing chores are higher in low-income, working-mother, two-parent families relative to welfare families. More often than not, working mothers in two-parent families are no different from mothers in single-parent welfare families. For example, they spend just as little time reading to their children and helping their children with homework and are no less willing to condone unsupervised time for their adolescent children as mothers receiving welfare. Class, not welfare, underlies these parenting differences.

Our look at the long-run effects of our family process and mental health measures on the amount of schooling eventually completed by children is limited to the measures available in the PSID. The results suggest that it is not so much family process as the social capital connections parents make outside the family that matter the most for children's achievement. Church and social club attendance are significant positive predictors of children's completed schooling in low-income families. These two measures, plus PTA attendance and knowing neighbors, are important for the full set of families.

Will transitions to work because of welfare reform improve the social-capital connections of former welfare families and thus foster child development? Wilson's (1987) depiction of the underclass views their social isolation, particularly from middle-class and working families, as a key cause of their plight. Our measures of social connections are of a different sort, consisting of socializing with existing neighbors and attending church, PTA meetings, and the like. We find few differences in these connections between welfare and low-income, single-parent, working families. Thus there is little reason to expect that welfare-to-work transitions will help children by promoting connections between family members and their neighbors and institutions.

It is important to look beyond the at-best occasional importance of our collection of family process measures in accounting for children's achievement to the consistently important pattern of effects for the more mundane demographic characteristics, including the mother's own level of schooling, test scores, and age when her children are born. Improving basic skills and delaying first births have been promoted as strategies for improving the labor-market prospects of mothers. Our results suggest that these strategies may have a greater effect on children's success than policies directed at family processes themselves.

After lamenting the dangers of welfare mother stereotypes, we might be justifiably accused of generating our own set. Although we speak of our groups of welfare and working families as though they are distinct, it is important to end with an appeal to view welfare and working families as fluid and heterogeneous. Roughly half of the families in our two data sets did not fall neatly into our seven groups but instead mixed work and welfare, dropped in and out of the labor force, or underwent important family structure changes over the brief periods covered in our analyses. It is problematic to speak of welfare families, when families use welfare in so many different ways.

The heterogeneity also extends within our groups, particularly our comparison groups of welfare and low-income working families. For example, while the average level of depression is higher among single-parent than two-parent families, around 40 percent of welfare-recipients in the NSFH report depression scores that are healthier than average. There are many mentally healthy single parents and many depressed mothers in two-parent situations. Because it is apparent that welfare-to-work transitions are unlikely to produce large favorable changes in family process and child development, the essential task of welfare reform may be one of more selective supports for subsets of families whose welfare-to-work transitions will be the most difficult.

———

We are grateful to the Family and Child Well-being Research Network of the National Institute of Child Health and Human Development (U01 HD30947-06) for supporting Greg Duncan's research.

NOTES

1. For both data sets we imposed a three-year period over which family structure, welfare receipt, and work were relatively stable. This produced acceptable sample sizes for key single-parent groups in the NSFH but not in the PSID. Thus we opted for a three-year period in the NSFH and a two-year period in the PSID.

2. Details of the construction of these measures are found in a working paper with the same title as this chapter on the JCPR website, at *www.jcpr.org*

3. Following established survey procedure in the late 1960s, the PSID defined the husband as the head of two-parent households and conducted interviews with him. In the case of single-mother households, the mother herself is the head. Thus social-psychological measures in the PSID are taken from the head. In the case of the NSFH, these measures were always taken from the mother.

REFERENCES

Aaron, Henry J. 1978. *Politics and the Professors*. Washington, D.C.: Brookings.

Anderson, Elijah. 1990. *Streetwise*. Chicago: University of Chicago Press.

Bane, Mary J., and David T. Ellwood. 1983. "The Dynamics of Dependence and the Routes to Self-sufficiency." Final Report to the U.S. Department of Health and Human Services. Cambridge, Mass.: Kennedy School of Government, Harvard University.

———. 1994. *Welfare Realities: From Rhetoric to Reform*. Cambridge, Mass.: Harvard University Press.

Baydar, Nazli, Jeanne Brooks-Gunn, and Frank Furstenberg. 1993. "Early Warning Signs of Functional Illiteracy: Predictors in Childhood and Adolescence." *Child Development* 64(3): 815.

Blank, Rebecca M. 1989. "Analyzing the Length of Welfare Spells." *Journal of Public Economics* 39: 245–73.

Brooks-Gunn, Jeanne, Guang Guo, and Frank Furstenberg. 1993. "Who Drops out and Who Continues Beyond High School? A Twenty-Year Follow-up of Black Urban Youth." *Journal of Research on Adolescence* 3(3): 271–94.

Coleman, James S. 1988. "Social Capital in the Creation of Human Capital." *American Journal of Sociology* 94 (supplement): S95–S120.

Corcoran, Maria. 1995. "Rags to Rags: Poverty and Mobility in the United States." *Annual Review of Sociology* 21: 237–67.

Duncan, Greg J. 1994. "Families and Neighbors as Sources of Disadvantage in the Schooling Decisions of Black and White Adolescents." *American Journal of Education* 103(1): 20–53.

Duncan, Greg J., M. S. Hill, and Saul D. Hoffman. 1988. "Welfare Dependence Within and Across Generations." *Science* 239: 467–71.

Duncan, Greg J., and W. Jean Yeung. 1995. "Extent and Consequences of Welfare Dependence Among America's Children." *Children and Youth Services Review* 17(1/2): 1–26.

Ellwood, David. 1986. "Targeting 'Would-be' Long-term Recipients of AFDC." Report prepared for the Department of Health and Human Services. Princeton, N.J.: Mathematica Policy Research.

Fitzgerald, John. 1991. "Welfare Durations and the Marriage Market: Evidence from the Survey of Income and Program Participation." *Journal of Human Resources* 26: 545–61.

Gottschalk, Peter. 1992. "The Intergenerational Transmission of Welfare Participation: Facts and Possible Causes." *Journal of Policy Analysis and Management* 11(2): 254–72.

———. 1995. "Is the Correlation in Welfare Participation Across Generations Spurious?" Working Paper. Economics Department, Boston College.

Guo, Guang, Jeanne Brooks-Gunn, and Kathleen M. Harris. 1996. "Grade Retention and Persistent Economic Deprivation Among Urban Black Children." *Sociology of Education* 69(3): 217–36.

Harris, Kathleen M. 1993. "Work and Welfare Among Single Mothers in Poverty." *American Journal of Sociology* 99: 317–52.

———. 1996. "Life After Welfare: Women, Work, and Repeat Dependency." *American Sociological Review* 61: 407–26.

Jencks, Christopher. 1992. *Rethinking Social Policy*. New York: Harper/Perennial.

Lewis, Oscar. 1966. "The Culture of Poverty." *Scientific American* 215: 19–25.

Moffitt, Robert. 1992. "Incentive Effects of the U.S. Welfare System: A Review." *Journal of Economic Literature* 30: 1–61.

Murray, Charles. 1984. *Losing Ground: American Social Policy, 1950–1980*. New York: Basic Books.

O'Neill, June A., Laurie J. Bassi, and Douglas A. Wolf. 1987. "The Duration of Welfare Spells." *Review of Economics and Statistics* 69: 241–49.

Oritz, Elizabeth T., and Betty Z. Bassoff. 1987. "Adolescent Welfare Mothers: Lost Optimism and Lowered Expectations." *Social Casework: Journal of Contemporary Social Work* 68(7): 400–5.

Parcel, Toby L., and Elizabeth Menaghan. 1994. "Early Parental Work, Family Social Capital, and Early Childhood Outcomes." *American Journal of Sociology* 99(4): 972–1009.

Pavetti, LaDonna A. 1993. "The Dynamics of Welfare and Work: Exploring the Process by Which Young Women Work Their Way off Welfare." Ph.D. diss., Harvard University.

————. 1995. "Who Is Affected by Time Limits?" In *Welfare Reform: An Analysis of the Issues*, edited by Isabel V. Sawhill. Washington, D.C.: Urban Institute.

Plotnick, Robert, Marieka M. Klawitter, and M. Edwards. 1997. "Do Psychosocial Characteristics Affect Socioeconomic Outcomes? The Case of Welfare Use by Young Women." Unpublished manuscript.

Popkin, Susan J. 1990. "Welfare: Views from the Bottom." *Social Problems* 37: 64–79.

Rainwater, Lee. 1967. *The Moynihan Report and the Politics of Controversy*. Cambridge, Mass.: MIT Press.

Rector, Robert. 1993. "Why Expanding Welfare Will Not Help the Poor." Lecture Series. Heritage Foundation, Washington, D.C.

Solon, Gary, Maria Corcoran, Roger Gordon, and Deborah Laren. 1988. "Sibling and Intergenerational Correlations in Welfare Program Participation." *Journal of Human Resources* 23(3): 388–96.

Wilson, William J. 1987. *The Truly Disadvantaged*. Chicago: University of Chicago Press.

Zill, Nicholas. 1978. "Divorce, Marital Happiness, and the Mental Health of Children: Findings from the FCD National Survey of Children." Paper presented at the NIMH Workshop on Divorce and Children, Bethesda, Md.

Zill, Nicholas, Kristen Moore, Christine Nord, and Thomas Stief. 1991a. "Welfare Mothers as Potential Employees: A Statistical Profile Based on National Survey Data." Washington, D.C.: Child Trends.

————. 1991b. "The Life Circumstances and Development of Children in Welfare Families." Washington, D.C.: Child Trends.

Chapter 8

My Children Come First:
Welfare-Reliant Women's Post-TANF Views
of Work-Family Trade-Offs and Marriage

Ellen K. Scott, Kathryn Edin, Andrew S. London, and Joan Maya Mazelis

Moving into the workforce for welfare-reliant women, most of whom are single mothers of young children, entails a variety of trade-offs between work and family. These are the same trade-offs faced by more affluent Americans and adults in two-parent, dual-career families; however, single parents (mostly mothers) and the poor experience work-family conflicts very differently from married couples and the financially secure (Bianchi and Spain 1996; Cancian and Oliker 2000; Oliker 1995; Polakow 1993). Just as working women in dual-career households continue to do most of the child care and housework ("the second shift") (Cancian and Oliker 2000; Hochschild 1989), working women who have recently moved off welfare or are temporarily combining work and welfare must devise strategies for maintaining work and taking care of their children and households. Working single mothers face substantial (and underrecognized) conflicts between their worker and mother roles.

The effects of mothers' transitions from welfare to work on their children are likely to be complex (and possibly countervailing). If moving from welfare to work results in increased financial well-being, long-term growth in wages, and upward mobility, then women will likely be able to better provide for their children and move away from substandard housing and dangerous neighborhoods. In addition to financial gains, there are other potentially valuable benefits associated with work that might accrue to women and their families. These include enhanced self-esteem for the women, reduced stigma, and the ability to claim and model for their children values associated with self-sufficiency and work (see Iversen and Farber 1996). Although it is not yet possible to know if these outcomes will result from welfare reform, there is substantial reason to expect that the future will not be quite so bright for many women. If the benefits of work do not materialize, the potential costs associated with their welfare-to-work transition may be quite significant for their children.

There is considerable evidence that women who leave welfare for work are in worse shape than when they were on welfare and that many ultimately return to cash assistance (Edin and Lein 1997; Friedlander and Burtless 1995; Harris 1996;

Hershey and Pavetti 1997). Wages tend to be low and to grow slowly (Pavetti and Acs 1996). Recent evidence does not indicate a positive effect of welfare reform on income (Cancian et al. 1999; Primus et al. 1999). Results from the second wave of the Women's Employment Study suggest that women who accumulated labor market experience, even through intermittent employment, were better off financially and subjectively in their first two years after leaving Temporary Assistance for Needy Families (TANF) (Danziger et al. 2000). However, serious economic and subjective difficulties persisted: 37 percent of respondents who worked during at least 90 percent of the months (the fully employed) still received cash benefits; two-thirds received food stamps; and nearly 20 percent reported two or more hardships, such as being uninsured or having insufficient food for their children. Given that these outcomes were achieved in a strong economy, when jobs were abundant, there is reason to believe that financial gains may be lower in the future (assuming the economy will ultimately weaken) and that hardships may increase. If financial gains are low, or women are unable to continue working, their ability to improve the life circumstances of their children and families will be compromised.

The consensus is that children growing up in two-parent households fare better than those reared in single-parent families, although what accounts for these better outcomes remains less clear (Garfinkel and McLanahan 1986; Garfinkel et al. 1996; McLanahan and Sandefur 1994). If women marry (or otherwise partner) with men who are financially and otherwise stable, in addition to going to work or as an alternative to it, then marriage may offer welfare-reliant women a route out of poverty and a means to care for their children in circumstances that are better than those typical for women receiving welfare or for those working in low-wage jobs. Again, however, there is reason to question the likelihood of this outcome because there is little evidence that welfare receipt influences women's decisions about marriage (Moffitt 1998). If marital decisions have little to do with welfare, they are unlikely to change as a result of welfare reform.

In this chapter, we focus on how welfare-reliant mothers view work-family trade-offs and marriage in the age of welfare reform. We currently know little about how women who are facing work requirements and cash assistance time limits imposed by the Personal Responsibility and Work Opportunity Reconciliation Act (PRWORA) think about the potential costs and benefits of moving from welfare to work or of marrying. How will they resolve the various trade-offs that the choices they face entail? A report issued by the National Research Council (Maynard et al. 1998, 169) states:

Now more than ever, it is critical that trained social scientists conduct systematic, in-depth evaluations to further our understanding of the economic and social welfare of highly at-risk families; of the behavioral choices these families face and the decisions they make; and of the family, community, and social services they draw upon to meet the challenges faced by those living near or in poverty.

We concur with this view—that in-depth studies are critically needed now to help us better understand how welfare reform is playing out in the lives of welfare-reliant women. Such studies will yield invaluable data on both the intended and unintended consequences of devolution and welfare reform.

DATA AND METHODS

The data in this chapter come from the Project on Devolution and Urban Change, which is being conducted under the auspices of the Manpower Demonstration Research Corporation (see Quint et al. 1999 for additional details about the study). These data were drawn from baseline interviews conducted with approximately eighty welfare-reliant women in Cleveland and Philadelphia in 1997 and 1998, long before the implementation of time limits in either city and before substantial case-load declines. This sample reflects welfare recipients at the time that welfare reform was being implemented.

The women were recruited for participation in the study from six census tract clusters, or "neighborhoods" (three in each city), with moderate to high concentrations of poverty (at least 30 percent of families living in poverty) and welfare receipt (at least 20 percent of families receiving welfare). In each city, we selected two predominantly African American neighborhoods and one predominantly white neighborhood. The white neighborhood and one African American neighborhood in each city were termed *moderate poverty* (30 through 39 percent of the population lived below the poverty line in 1990). The additional African American neighborhood in each city was *high poverty* (40 percent or more of its population were officially poor in 1990).[1]

In each neighborhood, we recruited between ten and fifteen welfare-reliant women, using various strategies, including posting flyers, going door to door, and asking for referrals from community-based organizations and from women already enrolled in the study. We did not recruit through welfare agencies. We chose respondents with the aim of ensuring that each neighborhood sample included diversity along particular dimensions (age, education, work experience, length of welfare receipt, number and age of children). We purposefully did not recruit from housing projects, and we tried to minimize recruitment of women who received Section 8 or other forms of subsidized housing.[2]

The baseline interviews were often conducted over the course of several visits and added up to anywhere from three to eight hours. During these interviews we collected detailed life history data and asked women to tell us what they knew about welfare reform and how they thought it might influence their lives. We tape-recorded and transcribed each interview verbatim for coding and analysis. The themes discussed in this chapter emerged from an inductive analysis of the narrative data. All mentions of women's concerns about work, welfare, and their children's well-being were coded for analysis. These include innumerable spontaneous mentions about these issues throughout the lengthy interviews as well as some responses to specific questions. In qualitative analysis, spontaneous mentions are especially valuable because they signal the salience of particular issues for the respondents. Pseudonyms are used to protect the confidentiality of the women with whom we spoke.

THE COSTS AND BENEFITS FOR CHILDREN OF MOTHERS' WELFARE-TO-WORK TRANSITIONS

"My kids are my first concern." This sentiment was echoed repeatedly in the interviews that we conducted with welfare-reliant mothers in Cleveland and Philadelphia. In the face of mandatory work requirements and time limits, women expressed tremendous ambivalence about what they thought working outside the home would entail for their children and families. Although women saw work as potentially beneficial, in our baseline interviews they repeatedly discussed the tensions and dilemmas that working motherhood (mostly working single-parenthood) would pose in their lives. As they talked about various work-family trade-offs, the women consistently focused on what they thought working would mean for their children.

Benefits: Financial and Material Gain

National data collected during the 1980s indicate that mothers who leave welfare and go to work gain only a few cents an hour per year (Burtless 1995; Harris and Edin 1996; Spalter Roth et al. 1995). The low-wage jobs obtained by most who leave welfare provide very limited opportunities for upward mobility, at least in part because low-wage employers do not reward experience. More recent data suggest that this story has not changed much with the economic boom of the 1990s (Cancian et al. 1999; Primus et al. 1999).

Despite prior experience to the contrary and realistic expectations about the kinds of job they could likely obtain (see Scott et al. 2000, for a discussion of these women's job aspirations and expectations), the women anticipated that moving from welfare to work would result in considerable financial gains and improvements in material circumstances for themselves and their children.[3] Our respondents' expectations for future earnings were quite high, especially in the long run. In the short run, most mothers thought they would be at least a little better off financially once they started to work. This expectation was not entirely unreasonable, given that mothers who moved from welfare to a part-time job under TANF were allowed to keep a portion of their earnings and deduct a portion of their child care and transportation expenses from the amount that was "taxed" by welfare.[4] Although time limited, this was a much more generous set of supports than under the old system, and the women in this sample generally understood these new rules (Quint et al. 1999). However, these gains would be offset by the loss of income from unreported work in the informal economy, which would have to cease when women took full-time or nearly full-time jobs in the formal economy (see Edin and Lein 1997).

In discussing what they thought would happen after they were no longer eligible for welfare and no longer had the option of combining work and welfare, women said many different things.[5] Some women said they simply did not know what they would be doing or how life would be. Others expressed fear about losing Food Stamps and Medicaid but were generally optimistic about obtaining employment (Scott et al. 2000). Usually, however, there was ambivalence. Women often expressed concerns and uncertainties about the future while in the same interview expressing confidence that they would be better off financially. Perhaps one reason that women believed they would benefit materially from working is that they believed they now had no other choice.

In the short term, most women wanted to use the money that they expected to gain from working to pay bills and have enough to cover the "basics." They wanted to better provide for their children and get them what they needed and wanted without undue delay. Thinking about the future, when her child would be a little older, East Cleveland resident Jonetta, an African American mother of a seven-month-old child, told us:

> I think that working . . . will improve my family life. Because I'm sure my son will enjoy going shopping and getting a little candy money. And I'm sure that if [I work I will have that]. I'm on welfare and I'm always telling him "well, no, mommy doesn't have it. You have to wait. I don't have it. I can't do it right now." Whereas if I'm working, if I'm telling him to wait, he won't have to wait long. He won't have to wait a whole month. He'll probably only have to wait a couple days. And he can get a lot if I'm working. . . . If I'm working, I can give him more and I'm sure he'll like that.

Marcia, an African American resident of Philadelphia's Germantown section, hoped to see the end of the material deprivations that her children have been experiencing while she has been on welfare. She told us that going to work meant:

> A better way of living—bills paid. We [will] not worry about that heat being cut off, that electric being cut off. [My son] not wearing dogged-out shoes where his feet almost touching the ground. They can get that bigger coat because the coat they wearing is too tight. Oh girl, it is really deep.

Women often told us that their children suffered social repercussions, like teasing, as a consequence of the material deprivations. As a result, mothers hoped to be able to provide their children with better clothing and shoes as a means to buffer their children from the stigma of poverty and welfare receipt (see also Seccombe 1999).

In general, mothers wanted enough money to live an "average" life and provide the normal experiences that they believed every American child ought to have. They knew that welfare would not get them there, but they hoped that work would. Twenty-three-year-old Marcy, an African American respondent from Cleveland's Glenville neighborhood, had two children, a General Educational Development (GED) certificate, and was in her second year of community college. We asked her what she thought things would be like for her financially when she went to work. She said:

> Well, they would still be low because, you gonna want to catch up on your bills and stuff. . . . But I guess as time goes on, it'd be better. You would have . . . you would have money to be able to do something . . . go on family outings, you know. . . . Get yo' family and go out to eat, or something like that. Yeah. You save up enough vacation . . . and, you know you be able to travel—I mean you can do things that you wanna do. . . . We would be able to go to the movies, occasionally go out to eat, you know . . . go to the mall together as a family. You know, go out and just be out. . . . Don't gotta stay in the house or, stay in the neighborhood . . . go out! Be able to get out and be together as a family, and able to do something. Just go . . . even if you don't have enough money to buy a lot of things from the mall, we'd be able to go to the mall and [talking to her children] y'all would be together.

In the longer term, many women said they wanted to use the money to move from shared housing arrangements to their own apartments, from their economically and socially distressed neighborhoods to better neighborhoods in the city or suburbs, or from Philadelphia or Cleveland to other, less violent cities. Some hoped to send their children to private or parochial schools, where they would be safer and would be "pushed harder." As was the case when they talked about the short term, when they talked about improving their financial situation in the long term the central theme women voiced was how they would use additional money to make things better for their children.

Benefits: Respect

Beyond material gain, respondents also hoped to gain psychological and social benefits from working. They anticipated increased self-respect and confidence, gaining a sense of being part of the social mainstream, and increased respect from their children. We asked Kitina, a twenty-year-old white mother of one child, what things she thought she would gain by working. She responded, "My self-respect for one. I won't feel like all that I am is just a welfare recipient trying to collect. I'm going to be someone, no matter what anybody says. And then, in a couple years from now, I'll see where they're at and where I'm at."

Mothers often became enthusiastic when talking about how it would feel to be a worker. They imagined that work would energize and motivate them to take on new challenges. Denise, an African American resident of Philadelphia's North Central neighborhood, had a high-school degree and was learning word processing and data entry skills. She was from a stable, working-class background and had an extensive work history, although she had periodically relied on welfare between jobs. She said she was planning to start work again soon but worried about losing "time with my children." However, she also thought that by going to work again, she would gain self-esteem. Denise told the interviewer:

Well, that's a part of it. I gain more about myself, more self-respect, for me. It's just the energy to strive, to do more. You know, just that incentive, okay "well you can do this, take another step. You done did that, take another step." And that's what I gain by it. You know, I had a part-time job, "oh, well [Denise] take another step." And then I did it. And then something else, "go ahead, go for it."

Similarly, Jonetta from East Cleveland thought she would "gain a sense of responsibility, independence, and, like, more motivation. Because I know that I'm doing the right thing. That it's helping me build my career. It's helping me at home, save money. So I think working will be very beneficial."

We were surprised by how often mothers mentioned that their own children "disrespected" or "teased" them because they were on welfare. Women experienced the stigma associated with welfare in their relationships with their children and saw work as a means to improve their children's view of them as well as a means to increase their own self-esteem and confidence. We asked high-school graduate Lisa, an African American Germantown resident and thirty-one-year-old mother of six children, what she would gain from going to work. She said:

I think I will gain more respect from my children . . . and I will probably respect myself even more. I would probably have more confidence in myself because I would be a part of things, not just watching things. I would be a part of things. That is about it I guess.

Other respondents also believed that working would increase their children's respect for them and enhance the pride of the entire family. For example, East Cleveland resident Janelle said that working outside her home would improve her children's estimation of their mother:

Oh, what do I gain? A sense of self-worth, I get paid more money (laughs) money. You know, it's a funny thing, kids seem to respect you a little more when you're doing something. "Mommy's got to go to work. All right mom!" You know. You send them to school, and they know you've been here all day, you know, they kinda treat you differently. Well, "Mommy's been working." My oldest daughter, when I wasn't working, you know, she was, she come home from school, she didn't want to do nothing [to help around the house]. When I've been working, she don't mind. You know, I cook, and she'll do the dishes. You know, stuff like that, you can see. . . . So yeah, kids kinda respect you a little more. They won't be like, "she sit around the house all day, and when I come home she gonna want me to do something. She coulda did it herself, she was home all day."

Mothers generally thought their children would understand that the sacrifice of time with them was necessary for these financial and emotional gains. High school graduate Mary, a twenty-eight-year-old North Central Philadelphia resident and mother of three, had worked jobs in both the service sector and the illegal drug trade. We asked Mary: "What do you think your children might lose from you going back to work?" She said:

> I won't be home a lot, spendin' time with them, but they'll understand. "Mommy has to work and pay these bills and clothe y'all and feed y'all." My kids'll understand. [When people] ask them, "Where's your mom at?" "Oh she at work." They like to say that. To know that they mother's working. Ain't sitting home on her ass, watching TV and stuff like that. . . . They'd be proud of me. That I ain't sitting around. That I'm doing something with my life. In order to take care of them . . . financially.

Women often said they thought their children would welcome their employment because it would improve their status among friends. Even in neighborhoods of concentrated poverty, children have peers with parents who work, and these peers enjoy a clear social advantage over the children of nonworking parents because of the stigma associated with welfare receipt (Seccombe et al. 1998; Seccombe 1999). Germantown resident Lorraine, a thirty-three-year-old mother of three who has been living on welfare for nine years in a neighborhood that contains both workers and welfare recipients, said of her children:

> They will be happy. . . . Because this is what they want me to do. They don't like me on welfare. . . . I think I will gain more self-esteem because they get mad [at me for not working]. The other kids [are teasing them] . . . because the other kids are not [on welfare].

Janice, a white, divorced, thirty-two-year-old mother of five from Cleveland's Detroit-Shoreway neighborhood, is the daughter of factory workers. She has a ninth-grade education, has very little work history, and has been on welfare for nearly a decade. Janice reported:

> Well, you know, like when they start school or something, like that you know how the kids tease other children, they could say, "Not my mom, [she's not on welfare]." You know, they could have enough esteem to say, you know, "We don't worry about [money]." You know, things like that.

Benefits: Role Modeling

The women with whom we spoke thought not only that working would increase their own and their children's emotional well-being but also that working would allow them to model for their children important values. For many women, modeling these values was important because they thought they were relevant for their children's academic success, future employment, and upward mobility.

Mothers in our sample worried that their children would "make mistakes" or even "fail," as they believed they themselves had done. Many respondents believed that if they worked they would provide a positive role model, which would counteract the example that they had set while on welfare. Glenville resident Ophelia said:

> Each and every last one of my kids going to do something, because they're not going to be on no welfare. . . . Get you education, go to college, stay in school, get your good education, make them good grades, them B's and them A's, and get you a scholarship. . . . Don't make the mistake that I did, getting pregnant and then go jump on welfare. Uh-huh. I ain't going for that.

Janice, from Cleveland's Detroit-Shoreway neighborhood, told us about the advice she frequently gave her son:

> Like I told him, "Do you want to have to live the way I do?" And he said, "Mom, no, I don't want to have to be on welfare." I said, "Then you need to go through school, son. You need to get your education. I quit because I was stupid. I didn't know any better."

North Central resident Dorothy, a long-term welfare recipient with unusually successful children, told us that she had said to her children, "See, just because your mother failed doesn't mean that you have to fail. You can rise above your environment." She continued:

> I stress education. . . . I don't know how important it is to the next guy, but when I see children, I want you to strive, be the best—you do not have to be a product of the environment. You can overcome those obstacles. Because your mother failed doesn't mean that you have to fail.

Most respondents were convinced that they could model success through work. Wanda, from East Cleveland, was twenty-five years old and had one child and a GED. Wanda hoped that her children would "gain responsibility from it, learn how to go out and get a job away from welfare." Similarly, Rube, a twenty-three-year-old mother of three from Cleveland's Glenville neighborhood, said:

> It ain't nice [raising my kids on welfare]. That's how I feel. I don't want my kids to see me have to just getting a check without doing nothing. I want to be able to show my kids it ain't right. I don't think it's right. I really don't. I'm gonna try to do something about it. That's what I wanna do.

Tina, a mother of five from Germantown, was a second-generation welfare recipient with a tenth-grade education. She, too, wanted to model the day-to-day "structure" of going to work for her children. She believed that this experience would change their expectations about their own futures:

> In a sense, I hope that it brings about a change where my kids will see [the] structure of me going to work, having to be in a job and a certain amount of hours, not being here. . . . It just gives them something they get to look forward [to]. . . . "This is something that I will have to do when I get older. I am going to have to go out to work, I am going to have to be on time and prioritize myself and my bills."

Some mothers, such as North Central resident Denise, worried that if they and others like them did not go to work, their children simply would not know that work was the norm for most Americans. Denise had recently begun working when she told us that her work was already having a positive effect on her children and on others in the neighborhood. "It's . . . set an example for my children. It's set an example for . . . a lot of people to see, you know, people get up and go to work everyday, instead of just sitting around in front of the televisions or . . . on the corner, you know." She talked about how her work would create an incentive for her children. When Denise was asked what her children would gain from her working, she replied:

> The incentive to have that . . . to strive to do it too. [My children can say] "Oh, well she got up and she went out here, and she did what she had to do and . . . she's not out, hanging out, running the streets, you know, doing drugs and parties and all that. But she's out. . . ." Positive thoughts. Positive things.

In summary, many of our respondents expressed confidence that their entry into the labor force would enable them to be role models for their children, increase the family's sense of pride, as well as their own self-esteem, and give them material advantages. However, despite the financial and psychological benefits women hoped to gain from becoming employed, they also expressed considerable concern about the costs they imagined that working would present to their families. The women with whom we spoke were carefully weighing the advantages and disadvantages to entering the workforce, and they were not clear where the balance was. To them, the anticipated costs of work and the potential effects on their children of their increased absence were very worrisome and, to a large degree, uncertain.

Costs: Child Care and Supervision

Mothers in our sample knew that obtaining adequate child care would be one of the most critical obstacles they would face. This was of concern to them because they generally did not trust the professional child care services available to them, and they were uncertain how they would pay for them given that they would probably have no choice but to use them. Furthermore, and of greater concern, they believed that they would lose the ability to guide and supervise their children adequately. Women in our sample worried a great deal about the consequences of being less available to help their children get ready for school, to make sure they got to and from school safely, to supervise them with their play and homework, and to be certain that that they ate properly and went to bed on time.

Women's distrust of professional child care varied. At one extreme, Janice said that she would not take her children to a program because:

> You've got a lot of workers out here that confirm to be certified on and on like they're day care centers, a lot of children get hurt and molested and things like that. I'm not taking my children there. You know just like I told them before, if you recommend that you might as well stop my benefits cause I'm not taking my children there.

Many women expressed more moderate concerns about leaving their children with "strangers" for much of the day. However, in general, they acknowledged that this might become necessary, given the pace of reforms and the lack of family and friends available to care for their children.

The affordability of child care was a much-discussed issue during the baseline interviews because many mothers had not been told by their caseworkers that they were eligible for transitional child care benefits (see Quint et al. 1999). Mothers seldom had a relative or friend who could or would watch their children free of charge. Thus mothers with preschool children sometimes saw child care costs as a nearly insurmountable barrier to working or to even looking for work.

In addition to the cost of child care, women were worried about the logistics of combining work with child supervision. Most child care centers are not open at 6:30 or 7:00 in the morning, the time of day many respondents said they would need to drop their children off in order to travel to suburban jobs. Furthermore, neither we nor our respondents could find many child care centers offering care beyond 6 P.M. or on weekends. Because many mothers contemplated jobs that would require them to work afternoon or evening shifts, they saw lack of child care as a barrier to employment. Many women said that it would even be difficult to find a neighborhood babysitter to watch their children. This was particularly true in Philadelphia, where the relatively low reimbursement rate for home-based day care was an obstacle to securing this type of day care. Celena, a white Philadelphian from Kensington, had two children, ages two and eight. She said:

> Are they going to pay for my baby-sitter? Are they going to find me a baby-sitter? A good baby-sitter, no. They are going to pay your baby-sitter, yeah, $200 a month. There is not nobody out there that is going baby-sit no kid . . . for the times you have to have [to be away from] your kids, [for] that kind of money. No way. There is no way [they will watch my younger daughter all day] and then pick my [older] daughter up from school and take her [to school in the morning].

Respondents with children in elementary school described similar logistical difficulties with supervision. Janice, with five children, had just turned down a job because she would have had to be at work before her children's school bus arrived in the morning:

> There's no way I could [take a job] that early in the morning cause I have to get my kids on the school bus, you know, no one is here in the morning . . . if I get another barmaid job, it would have to be second shift when my kids get out of school and I know they're home.

Janelle, from East Cleveland, had trained as a home health aide but had a difficult time finding work that fit her children's school hours or allowed her to adequately supervise her five children:

> I can't work third shift. I don't want to work third shift. Cause I really don't want them here by themselves at night, and I can't work second shift, they're going to total my house up during the evening (laughter). I'll come home and I'll be running up every night, you know. And they're too young to even be here in the evening by themselves.

Janelle even worried about the logistical difficulties of working first shift:

> [My thirteen-year-old daughter] will have to pick up [the younger children] sometimes . . . if I'm working nine to five or eight to five or whatever, she'll be in charge for at least two hours . . . they know what they could and couldn't do. My phone will be [turned back] on, hopefully next week. So I'll be able to call home and give instructions. Ah, they will be latchkey people, but you know, so (laughs). . . . Even very, you know, well-off people, a lot of their children are latchkey. . . . I trust in the good Lord, to work it out, protect them.

Sunrise, from Germantown, who had been attending Job Search classes, had to depend on her middle school daughter to walk her elementary school daughter to school each day before she caught the bus to the middle school. The older child was late to school nearly every day. Although Job Search classes lasted only a few weeks, Sunrise worried what would happen if her job required her older daughter to be tardy on a daily basis.

Parents with children of all ages contemplated scenarios in which their children would be left unsupervised for various periods of time. They feared being stranded in the suburbs (where most job openings were) if bad weather disrupted public transportation. Mothers worried about missing work during a child's (or a child care provider's) illness and losing their job as a result. They also worried about handling school holidays and summers. Affordable after-school and summer programs that would cover all of the hours that mothers spent either at work or traveling to and from work were in very short supply. In short, the logistics of child supervision constituted a significant cost, which women had to weigh as they contemplated work.

Supervision and the cost of child care were not the mothers' only concerns. Mothers worried about not having adequate time at home to do all of the things that are needed to keep a family and household together. Mothers often described in great detail the time and energy it took to shop, cook, clean, do the laundry, visit the doctor, and otherwise maintain a household. Even more important than having time to get all of the day-to-day chores done, women wanted what they called "quality time" with their children. This involved such things as helping children with their homework, taking educational trips, reading stories, watching family videos, listening to the children's problems, and teaching them the right "values." "Quality time" was an often-repeated phrase in the baseline interviews.

Women in our sample had high aspirations for their children and saw success in schooling as their best route to upward mobility. Consequently, helping children with their homework was at the top of the list of concerns about lost "quality time." Dorothy, from Philadelphia, said that if she were to work her son would lose "coming home everyday, having his mom here, you know, and being there with his homework, and just helping him on the math, he would lose out in that area, because he's used to having his mom home every day." Similarly, Denise said her children would miss out due to "the fact that I can't be here with them, to help them do their homework, or if they have a problem or something, I can't be here, you know, for them." Most mothers worried that if they did not constantly monitor ("stay on" or "stay on top of") their children, they would not complete homework, would stop attending school, would quit "staying with the books," and would end up "rippin' and runnin' the streets." After all, this is what was happening to children all around them, according to the women in our sample. Furthermore, many expressed concern for their children's safety if they were left alone in dangerous neighborhoods. The mothers predicted that safety levels would decline further as a result of welfare reform. Their fears that neighborhood conditions would worsen exacerbated their concerns about not being adequately available to supervise their children.

Costs such as these were at the forefront of welfare recipients' minds as they evaluated their entry into the labor force. Although most mothers assumed that the costs would be compensated through material and psychological gains from working, the tensions women perceived between the costs and benefits of their full- or part-time work were acute. Although in many ways they looked forward to working, they worried that they were risking their children's futures. Women were concerned about the consequences of their absence from the home. How would the household continue to function smoothly? Who would mind the kids and ensure that their homework was done? Most critically, who would tend to their moral development and make sure that they were safe from harm?

Marriage and Children's Well-Being

Policymakers and others believe that marriage will allow some of the women who leave welfare to stay home with their children when they are no longer eligible for cash assistance. Increasing marriage is, in fact, an explicit goal of welfare reform.

When we talked with women about marriage, we found that some women said they would never marry for any reason, while others indicated that they had been or were already married (some unhappily). For many women in our sample, however, there was considerable ambivalence toward marriage; they thought they might marry or remarry in the future, under the right circumstances (for upward mobility) but were for the most part uncertain about when or to whom (even for those in long-term relationships). The most striking finding emerging from these baseline interviews was that many women put the material, physical, and emotional well-being of their children at the center of their considerations about future marriage. However, in contrast to the view that marriage will improve women's and children's well-being, many of the women with whom we talked rejected marriage because they said it would undermine their ability to take care of their children.

Reflecting dominant cultural values, the majority of women in our sample viewed marriage in idealized terms as a lifetime relationship to a near-perfect partner, who could provide a financially and otherwise stable life for the respondent and her children. In this vein, Denise told us, "I think . . . when you get married, your partner's supposed to be your best friend. You best friend, every . . . you know, the best in everything. You know, the best in communication, the best in trusting, the best in . . . the best!"

Although most of the women in our sample idealized marriage to some extent, we found that some women also rejected the possibility of future marriage because of bad experiences with former boyfriends and husbands. Many women identified problems with their partners' alcohol and drug use or inability to financially support the family as reasons for being skeptical about future marriage. Others identified domestic violence as the primary reason for their skepticism about future marriage. After failed marriages and relationships, many women seemed to have given up on men; they saw themselves as independent and were focused on making it as good as possible for themselves and their children. Some women believed that they themselves were no longer marriageable, at least in part because they had children. As Susan from Detroit-Shoreway in Cleveland put it: "It's like, nobody wants someone [with kids]. So, it's just me and my boys for now." Finally, a number of women expressed the concern that marriage would make it more difficult to separate from a man if things were not working out. Gayle from Detroit-Shoreway said of marriage in general:

It would have been nice then, you know, when I was younger and. . . . Now, it's no big thing. I mean, people are living together all the time. And it's easier to me. If it doesn't work out, you have no strings, no ties and you don't have to go through no legal bullshit, you know.

Yet in that conversation she also affirmed her ideals about marriage and her sense that she would marry under the right circumstances:

INTERVIEWER: Would you consider getting married or is it something that you've pretty much said, "I'm never gonna do that?"

GAYLE: Oh, I don't know. Maybe if the right guy came around and if things were different.

INTERVIEWER: What would a guy have to look like? Not look like, appearance, I mean, what would he be like?

GAYLE: Funny, have a job, just somebody that respected me and my daughter, you know, and didn't treat us like shit. I don't know.

Such ambivalence was typical in our conversations with women about marriage. Marriage was not generally a topic that arose spontaneously in the interviews, which suggests that it was not particularly salient for most women. Women tended to respond to direct questions about marriage, and about their aspirations and expectations regarding it, in ways that suggest that marriage was for them an abstract ideal more than a concrete goal.

When they did reflect on the possibility of marriage, one of the most prominent concerns they expressed was that it was not in their children's best interests. Although expressed in a variety of ways and for a variety of reasons, this ambivalence reflects the conflict they saw between their idealized aspiration to marry and their own past experiences with men. Given what they had experienced themselves, and what they had observed among their grandmothers, mothers, aunts, sisters, and women friends, many women understood that their standards for potential husbands excluded most, if not all, of the men with whom they came into contact. The men that our respondents knew were unable to provide the upward mobility desired by most women. Moreover, women said, these men were sometimes violent, cheated with other women, drank, used drugs, or posed a threat to their children.

Germantown resident April told us that the father of her younger three children used to "cheat" on her and "get into trouble." According to April, this relationship "stressed" her so much that she had to see a psychiatrist. Although April acknowledged that it was difficult to be a single parent, she did not think that having a man in her life was the solution:

> I ain't got time for nobody. I just got to focus on me and my kids. I ain't got time for that. Out of all the relationships that I have been in—I wasn't in that many but the ones I have been in—it wasn't worth it, so I got myself out of it. Too much crazy stuff involved; either they deranged, or you find out something wrong with them, [like] they on drugs or something . . . They just crazy, too much don't want to work. It is always something that you are going to find in a man that you just don't like. You might find one that want to argue too much, I ain't down with that. I ain't down with nobody hitting on me, I would have been done killed them and went to jail and I think that is worth it because I ain't going to let nobody hurt me.

Many women thought marriage would impede their ability to be good parents because they believed that men contributed little in terms of household help and competed with their children for their attention. Mothers sometimes reported that men (even those with whom they had had children) were jealous of their relationship with the children. Although some mothers did credit their children's fathers with "being there for them" and "helping out quite a bit," they did not seem to feel that marriage would enhance the bond between the father and his children. Virtually no mother we spoke with believed she ought to marry for the sake of her children. In fact, many women talked about marriage as something to think about for themselves "in the future," when their responsibilities as a parent were largely over.

Some women were concerned that men would threaten the safety of their children. Gayle, a white mother from Cleveland's Detroit-Shoreway neighborhood, had one child. She once lived with the father of her child but said he was an alcoholic and was abusive toward her. At the time of the interview, she did not let him come to her house because she was afraid of him. She said she has not entered into another relationship because she does not want her daughter to see her with a series of partners. She also said that she was afraid of what a man who was not her child's father might do to her child and reflected about future marriage as follows:

Maybe when [my daughter] gets a little older. Yeah, cause one of the reasons that I won't want to have a relationship is because I don't want to bring a whole bunch of men in front of her. 'Cause I don't want her to grow up thinking that's okay. It's not right. Plus you hear of all this stuff about boyfriends and the kids. I just, I wouldn't be able to sleep at night with a man in the house thinking that something was gonna happen to my kid.

Danielle from Kensington feared that men might mistreat children who were not their own or would fail to care for them: "I always thought I would get married. But I didn't though. Can't find the right person to marry me. If somebody's gonna be mean to my kids, my kids come before them." Denise, who plans to marry eventually but had no current partner at the time of the interview, said, "I would never get married to somebody else to help me raise my children. Because you can't really trust; you know, you can't never really trust nobody coming in your house like that."

Alice, a white respondent from Cleveland's Detroit-Shoreway neighborhood, also viewed marriage as an impediment to good parenting:

As I got older and started thinking about [my relationships with men], this is not the lifestyle that I want my children to be raised up 'cause I don't want my children out there doing the same thing we doing. So, I left [men] alone. . . . I never honestly was able to feel that way about a man. You know what I'm saying? That this is the man I plan to be with 'til I die . . . That's what it would take. But, I can never see myself being married, 'cause my children come first. And, by my children not being by no man that I'll marry, there would be a difference [in how he'd treat them], or you'd want me to have a child with you. You know what I'm saying? My children have to come first.[6]

Ophelia, whose own mother received welfare until she remarried and found work when Ophelia was ten years old, has never married. She is engaged to one of her children's fathers, who will soon be released from prison, but she is uncertain whether she wants him in her life again. She believes her children would resent the fact that this relationship would shift her attention away from them. Further, she spoke about the potential problems of bringing a man into her house:

> I don't know [whether welfare reform will make more people get married], but they got to make sure they know that man and if that man is going to keep a job. I ain't just going to jump up and get married—you know what I'm saying? Yeah, because they can mess around [with] crazy mens if they want to, and the kids get hurt. See, that's a lot of things I think about too, about having mens around when you got a bunch of girls.

She went on to say that she really did not know if she was ready to let the father back into her life, despite their engagement. She thought that the risks were too high.

For a variety of reasons, many women believed that marriage might not benefit their children and might even harm them. Thus marriage was sometimes seen as a selfish and irresponsible indulgence. The ambivalence expressed by these women reflects some degree of optimism about the prospect that these are marriage partners who can love and care for them and their current children; however, it also reflects reality-based concerns about the negative influence these men might have on their children and family life. Despite this ambivalence, it is clear that most women are putting the well-being of their current children first and thereby choosing to postpone or reject marriage.

DISCUSSION

In this chapter, we examine how welfare-reliant mothers view work-family trade-offs in the context of welfare reform. The women in our sample clearly understood that the rules for the receipt of welfare had changed and that they would soon be required to work or to find other means to support themselves and their children. They also knew that their eligibility for welfare was now time limited (see Quint et al. 1999 for additional details on what women in this sample knew about welfare reform).

As they contemplated the requirement that they move from welfare to work, they expressed both optimism and considerable concern about how they would balance work with parenting. The women in our sample believed that there were benefits for themselves and their children associated with moving from welfare to work. They assumed that their material circumstances would improve significantly when they worked for a paycheck. Even more striking, they appeared to have accepted the dominant ideology that welfare is bad and work is good. We find (consistent with the work of Iversen and Farber 1996) that our respondents believed that they and their children would be better off if the sole parent in the family were working. Only a working parent could give her children the impetus to "stay with the books" and "strive more" for a "brighter future" and a higher standard of living. Through work, mothers could model responsible behavior and engender improved self-esteem and self-confidence for themselves and their children.

In addition to the possible benefits of work, women also saw costs. Most women thought that it would be difficult, if not impossible, for them to find adequate and affordable child care or to properly supervise their children in all the ways full-time mothers can. They also expressed concern that they would lose the time necessary to keep their households functioning smoothly. Most important, however, our respondents indicated that working would mean that they would lose "quality time" with their children.

These work-family trade-offs posed a dilemma for women. They wanted the best for their children and saw both work and close supervision and maternal guidance as necessary. These women had high aspirations for their children and hoped their children would finish high school, go on to college, and escape the impoverished conditions of their childhood. Thus beyond women's fears for their children's safety and general well-being, the women with whom we spoke were concerned with the moral and intellectual development of their children in the absence of parental supervision. At the heart of this tension between how to be good workers and how to be good mothers was the question of how they could best assist their children in attaining upward mobility. At the core of their decisions about work was the desire to put their children first and do the right thing for them.

For current welfare recipients, welfare reform represents a fork in the road. If by going to work they attain the financial gains that they anticipate, improve their self-respect and confidence, and are able to move to better neighborhoods, the road looks good. However, if the financial gains do not materialize, they risk losing their ability to be good parents and to supervise their children in ways they see as essential. Thus one of the unanticipated effects of welfare reform could be the risk it poses to children. If single women who leave welfare for work do not realize economic improvement and lose the ability to adequately supervise their children, the real losers in the immediate future will be the children—and in the longer term, our entire society.

The well-being of their families was also the central concern for these women as they evaluated the possibility of marriage; however, their thinking about marriage seemed completely detached from welfare or welfare reform. Contrary to the popular assumption that marriage is a viable path out of welfare reliance and poverty, most of the women, for a host of reasons, did not consider marriage to be in their best interests or those of their children. Although marriage was held as an ideal by most of the women we interviewed, almost none had concrete plans to marry, and few could even imagine marrying at some point in the future. Tied up with dreams of social mobility and middle-class (or at least working-class) respectability, their ideal marriage was not attainable in the marriage market available to them. Moreover, many women saw marriage as a distinct threat to the well-being and safety of their children. Although policymakers make the assumption that marriage is inherently good for single parents, the women in our sample tended to see it differently. With marriage, they saw the potential for it to be more difficult to get rid of a male who was posing a threat. Finally, although the men in their lives made some financial and in-kind contributions to the families, by and large, they did not provide women relief from the double burden of financial and familial responsibilities.

Although women expressed little interest in marriage, the optimism they expressed about their futures in the world of the paid labor force should be a signal to policymakers that they now have a genuine opportunity to make a difference in the lives of poor women and children. Welfare recipients seem to believe that not only is work good for themselves but that it is good for their children. However, their work attitudes are predicated on the assumption that they will be considerably better off financially than they had been in past jobs and significantly better off than they would be if they continued to rely only on welfare. In short, mothers believe the benefits of going to work outweigh the costs primarily because they will end up with much more disposable income, which can be used to improve their children's lives.

Without significant employment supports, this expectation is not likely to be a reality for the majority of those still on the welfare rolls, even if labor markets remain as tight as they are currently. The true success of welfare reform will be if mothers' experiences in the labor market meet their basic expectation that work will give them significantly more disposable income (enough to outweigh the added expenses of working and the loss of health insurance, as well as to make up for the lost revenue from the income-generating activities they engaged in while on welfare). As more and more women with children move into work, policymakers might be willing (and states might be persuaded) to spend some of their welfare surplus on ensuring that the work-based safety net is strengthened substantially for all low-wage workers and their families. This can be accomplished by lowering the costs of work by providing long-term (not transitional) supports, such as sliding-scale child care and adult health care benefits, and increased housing and transportation assistance; and by supplementing mothers' incomes by increasing the minimum wage and pegging it to inflation or by further expanding the Earned Income Tax Credit.

This chapter reports on women's expectations at the time of the baseline interviews in 1997 and 1998. Since this baseline interview, we have reinterviewed the vast majority of these women several times. We continue to analyze the data to examine how work-family trade-offs play out in their lives, as they move from welfare to work and face time limits. The preliminary longitudinal analysis (London et al. 2000) suggests that the themes identified here continue to be salient in the lives of the women in our sample. Many of the women and their children have experienced both the costs and the benefits that they expected at baseline. The concerns they anticipated have influenced their decisions. The tensions between their obligations as workers and as mothers have presented considerable dilemmas for them as they responded to the mandates of welfare reform.

NOTES

1. Two studies define neighborhoods of concentrated poverty as those in which 20 percent or more of the residents live below the poverty threshold (Wilson 1987; Massey et al.

1994). The Project on Devolution and Urban Change chose a higher threshold of poverty strategically to target the most disadvantaged neighborhoods, where the effect of welfare reform is likely to be most evident.

2. Nationally, only about 20 percent of welfare recipients live in public or subsidized housing (U.S. House of Representatives 1998). We excluded persons living in public or subsidized housing because such housing was unevenly distributed in the selected neighborhoods. Additionally, the possible effects of welfare reform on housing stability and other aspects of family well-being might be mitigated by housing subsidies (see Edin and Lein 1997).

3. In addition to leveled job expectations (Scott et al. 2000), substantial unemployment in these counties may also impede their ability to sustain their optimism about employment and income growth. During a very strong economy, the unemployment rate in Cuyahoga County averaged 4.8 percent in 1997 and ranged between 3.9 and 4.9 percent in the first half of 1998. In Philadelphia County the unemployment rate averaged 6.8 percent in 1997 and ranged between 5.8 and 6.2 percent in 1998 (Quint et al. 1999).

4. In Cleveland the earned income disregard was $250 of income earned in a month, plus 50 percent of the remainder for eighteen months. In Philadelphia it was 50 percent of income earned in a month (Quint et al. 1999, table 3).

5. Time limits are different in Philadelphia and Cleveland. It is three years in Cleveland and five years in Philadelphia. In Cleveland, after two years off the welfare rolls, former recipients who had reached the three-year time limit would be eligible in particular (as yet unspecified) circumstances for two more years of cash assistance.

6. In the context of the interview, this quotation refers to the attitude she had always held toward men and marriage. However, ironically, she met a man who she did feel she could spend her life with, and they became engaged. Sadly, he was murdered shortly before this interview was conducted.

REFERENCES

Bianchi, Suzanne M, and Daphne Spain. 1996. *Balancing Act: Motherhood, Marriage, and Employment Among American Women*. New York: Russell Sage Foundation.

Burtless, Gary. 1995. "Employment Prospects of Welfare Recipients." In *The Work Alternative*, edited by D. S. Nightingale and R. H. Haveman. Washington, D.C.: Urban Institute.

Cancian, Francesca M., and Stacey J. Oliker. 2000. *Caring and Gender*. Thousand Oaks, Calif.: Pine Forge Press.

Cancian, Maria, Robert Haveman, Thomas Kaplan, Daniel Meyer, and Barbara Wolfe. 1999. "Work, Earnings, and Well-being after Welfare: What Do We Know?" Paper presented at the Welfare Reform and Macro-Economy Conference. Washington, D.C. (November 19–20).

Danziger, Sandra, Maria Corcoran, Sheldon Danziger, and Colleen Heflin. 2000. "Work, Income, and Material Hardship After Welfare Reform." *Journal of Consumer Affairs* 34(1): 6–30.

Edin, Kathryn, and Laura Lein. 1997. *Making Ends Meet: How Single Mothers Survive Welfare and Low-Wage Work*. New York: Russell Sage Foundation.

Friedlander, David, and Gary Burtless. 1995. *Five Years After: The Long-Term Effects of Welfare-to-Work Programs.* New York: Russell Sage Foundation.

Garfinkel, Irwin, Jennifer L. Hochschild, and Sara S. McLanahan, eds. 1996. *Social Policies for Children.* Washington, D.C.: Brookings.

Garfinkel, Irwin, and Sara S. McLanahan. 1986. *Single Mothers and Their Children: A New American Dilemma.* Washington, D.C.: Urban Institute.

Harris, Kathleen M. 1996. "Life After Welfare: Women, Work, and Repeat Dependency." *American Sociological Review* 61: 407–26.

Harris, Kathleen M., and Kathryn Edin. 1996. "From Welfare to Work and Back Again." Paper presented to the New School for Social Research, Conference on After AFDC: Reshaping the Anti-Poverty Agenda. New York (November 16).

Hershey, Alan M., and LaDonna Pavetti. 1997. "Turning Job Finders into Job Keepers: The Challenge of Sustaining Employment." *Future of Children* 7(1): 74–86.

Hochschild, Arlie. 1989. *The Second Shift: Working Parents and the Revolution at Home.* New York: Viking.

Iversen, Roberta R., and Naomi B. Farber. 1996. "Transmission of Family Values, Work, and Welfare Among Poor Urban Black Women." *Work and Occupations* 23(4): 437–60.

London, Andrew S., Ellen K. Scott, Kathryn Edin, and Vicki Hunter. 2000. "Ethnographic Perspectives on Welfare-to-Work Transitions, Work-Family Trade-offs, and Children's Well-being." Paper presented to Association for Public Policy Analysis and Management meetings. Seattle, Washington (November 2–4).

Massey, Douglas S., Andrew B. Gross, and Kumiko Shibuya. 1994. "Migration, Segregation, and the Geographic Concentration of Poverty." *American Sociological Review* 59: 425–45.

Maynard, Rebecca, Elisabeth Boehnen, Tom Corbett, and Gary Sandefur, with Jane Mosley. 1998. "Changing Family Formation Behavior Through Welfare Reform." In *Welfare, the Family, and Reproductive Behavior: Research Perspectives*, edited by Robert Moffitt. Washington, D.C.: National Academy Press.

McLanahan, Sara, and Gary Sandefur. 1994. *Growing Up with a Single Parent: What Hurts, What Helps.* Cambridge, Mass.: Harvard University Press.

Moffitt, Robert A. 1998. "The Effect of Welfare on Marriage and Fertility." In *Welfare, the Family, and Reproductive Behavior: Research Perspectives*, edited by Robert Moffitt. Washington, D.C.: National Academy Press.

Oliker, Stacey J. 1995. "The Proximate Contexts of Workfare and Work: A Framework for Studying Poor Women's Economic Choices." *Sociological Quarterly* 36: 251–72.

Pavetti, LaDonna, and Gregory Acs. 1996. *Moving Up, Moving Out, or Going Nowhere? A Study of the Employment Patterns of Young Women and the Implications for Welfare Reform.* Washington, D.C.: Urban Institute.

Polakow, Valerie. 1993. *Lives on the Edge: Single Mothers and Their Children in the Other America.* Chicago: University of Chicago Press.

Primus, Wendell, Lynette Rawlings, Kathy Larin, and Kathryn Porter. 1999. *The Initial Impact of Welfare Reform on the Incomes of Single-Mother Families.* Washington, D.C.: Center for Budget and Policy Priorities.

Quint, Janet, Kathryn Edin, Maria L. Buck, Barbara Fink, Yolanda C. Padilla, Olis Simmons-Hewitt, and Mary E. Valmont. 1999. *Big Cities and Welfare Reform: Early Implementation and Ethnographic Findings from the Project on Devolution and Urban Change.* New York: Manpower Demonstration Research Corporation.

Scott, Ellen K., Andrew S. London, and Kathryn Edin. 2000. "Looking to the Future: Welfare-Reliant Women Talk About Their Job Aspirations in the Context of Welfare Reform." *Journal of Social Issues* 56(4): 727–46.

Seccombe, Karen. 1999. *So You Think I Drive a Cadillac?: Welfare Recipients Perspectives on the System and Its Reforms.* Boston: Allyn and Bacon.

Seccombe, Karen, Delores James, and Kimberly B. Walters. 1998. "They Think You Ain't Much of Nothing: The Social Construction of the Welfare Mother." *Journal of Marriage and the Family* 60(November): 849–65.

Spalter Roth, Roberta, Beverly Burr, Heidi Hartmann, and Lois Shaw. 1995. *Welfare That Works: The Working Lives of AFDC Recipients.* Report to the Ford Foundation. Washington D.C.: Institute for Women's Policy Research.

U.S. House of Representatives. 1998. *1998 Green Book: Background Material and Data on Programs Within the Jurisdiction of the Committee on Ways and Means.* Washington: U.S. Government Printing Office.

Wilson, William J. 1987. *The Truly Disadvantaged.* Chicago: University of Chicago Press.

Chapter 9

Does Maternal Employment Mandated by Welfare Reform Affect Children's Behavior?

Ariel Kalil, Rachel E. Dunifon, and Sandra K. Danziger

A id to Families with Dependent Children (AFDC), legislated in the 1930s as an income maintenance program for widows and children, evolved over sixty years into a program that primarily served families headed by divorced, separated, or never-married mothers. The Personal Responsibility and Work Opportunity Reconciliation Act (PRWORA,) passed into law in August 1996, responded in part to concerns that AFDC encouraged joblessness (Mead 1992) and out-of-wedlock childbearing (Murray 1993); however, the driving force behind the legislation was the notion that cash assistance should be a temporary stop on the road toward employment (Bane and Ellwood 1994). Critics argued that the reforms might increase child poverty and that the stresses of low-wage, erratic employment could diminish maternal and child well-being (Duncan and Brooks-Gunn 1997; Primus 1999).

With the implementation of Temporary Assistance for Needy Families (TANF) in a robust economy, caseloads declined dramatically. Although there is likely to be considerable volatility in recipients' work trajectories, many former welfare recipients are finding jobs. However, only a minority have established long-term, full-time work patterns (Cancian et al. 1998). Potential barriers to employment, such as limited human capital, mental health problems, alcohol and substance abuse, and exposure to domestic violence are overrepresented among welfare recipients, and many of these factors are negatively associated with the ability to sustain part-time employment (that is, in compliance with the new welfare regulations) (Danziger et al., "Barriers," 2000).

Little information is currently available regarding the effects of PRWORA on child well-being. Children compose the majority of the poor population in the United States, and they represent two of every three people (9.3 of 13.6 million) who will be affected by welfare reform (U.S. Department of Health and Human Services 1999). Developmental theory suggests that increased employment for welfare mothers could improve their self-esteem, motivation, and sense of personal control. These improvements could lead to better parenting and concomitant improvements in the social, academic, or emotional adjustment of their children. Increased economic resources from earnings could also benefit children. On the other hand, welfare reform might increase psychological stresses or exposure to ecological stresses, which can be harmful to children. If employment is unstable or erratic, material hardships could ensue and family routines could be disrupted, thus diminishing child well-being.

In this chapter, we draw on new data from an ongoing longitudinal survey of current and former TANF mothers with young children to examine three potential pathways of influence of welfare reform on child outcomes: the extent of work participation among mothers who are in the process of leaving the welfare rolls, their transitions into and out of work over time, and the number of hours they are currently working. We test the association of these measures to children's positive and negative behaviors. We then investigate whether any work effects can be explained by families' experiences of economic and material hardship or by parenting stress and sense of efficacy.

Our analysis also employs an unusually rich array of characteristics typically unobserved in other studies. These include maternal and child demographic characteristics as well as psychiatric diagnoses of maternal depression, substance use, post-traumatic stress disorder, and exposure to domestic violence. Because these maternal characteristics are related to employment as well as child behavior, omitting them from the measurement model could bias estimates of the effect of mothers' work on children's behavior.

BACKGROUND

Recent studies address the issues of child development and adult behavior as it relates to welfare and welfare reform.

Child Development in Welfare Families

There are few significant or substantive differences in child developmental outcomes between welfare families and those that are poor but not welfare dependent (Kalil and Eccles 1998; Moore et al. 1995; Zill et al. 1991). Similarly, few differences exist between the two groups in the quality of the home environment and in parent mental health (see chapter 7, this volume; also see Klebanov et al. 1994). However, children in welfare families, relative to national samples, suffer from greater physical disabilities and more serious health conditions than their nonwelfare counterparts, and they have less positive outcomes on tests of cognitive development (Moore et al. 1995; Olson and Pavetti 1996). Among welfare families, negative child development outcomes are more pronounced when mothers report a low sense of personal efficacy and perceive multiple barriers to their own employment (Moore et al. 1995). However, recent studies using econometric methods find that most observed raw differences in child development related to welfare receipt disappear once unobserved family background characteristics are taken into account (Levine and Zimmerman 2000).

Welfare Reform and Adult Behavior

Studies of welfare mothers' work behaviors after August 1996 provide initial evidence of the consequences of welfare reform. These studies focus on mothers' work involvement and economic security, both of which have important implications for children's well-being. On two criteria, PRWORA is a success: caseloads are down and employment among welfare mothers is up. By March 1999 only 7.3 million recipients were enrolled in the AFDC program (U.S. Department of Health and Human Services, Administration for Children and Families 1999). Evidence regarding changes in income and economic well-being is less sanguine: the average disposable income of the poorest 20 percent of single mothers fell, on average, by $292 a year between 1995 and 1999, even though earnings rose by $2,300 a year per family, on average (see chapter 13, this volume). Given widespread evidence of the association between poverty—especially deep poverty—and negative child development outcomes (Duncan and Brooks-Gunn 1997), these early findings raise concerns for the implications of welfare reform on child well-being.

A handful of the new studies also examine adults' perceptions of their family's economic security. These psychological perceptions are relevant to children's well-being by virtue of their association with parents' mental health and parenting behavior. Two theoretical frameworks (see Conger et al. 1994; McLoyd 1990) posit that income loss results in "felt economic pressure" or "economic strain," a subjective perception of one's ability to make ends meet. According to the theory, mounting economic pressure increases psychological distress, erratic or punitive parenting behavior, and ultimately poor adjustment in children. This conceptual model is supported by empirical evidence from a number of studies. New evidence suggests that some families leaving welfare have difficulty making ends meet (Brauner and Loprest 1999). Unfortunately, it is not always clear from these studies whether and how families' economic well-being has changed as a result of having left welfare. In one study, former recipients were significantly more likely to report falling behind in house payments and not having enough money to buy food or to pay for child care, compared with their retrospective accounts of when they received cash assistance (Brauner and Loprest 1999). A concern has been raised that some families that are leaving or being diverted from welfare may not be receiving food stamps and Medicaid even though they continue to be eligible (Primus et al. 1999).

In contrast, a paper based on the Women's Employment Study finds that, on average, the women employed in more of the months during the study period (about twenty months) accumulated greater income and experienced less material hardship than those employed in fewer—or none—of the months (Danziger et al., "Work," 2000). The study assessed material hardships (for example, food insufficiency, a utility or phone shutoff, eviction, or going without medical care for oneself or one's children) and finds that, among those who worked in every month over the study period, 40 percent experienced at least one of the nine hardships examined. In contrast, 70 percent of those who had not worked experienced at least one of the hardships. This suggests that greater work involvement is associated with greater economic well-being among former and current welfare recipients.

WELFARE REFORM AND CHILDREN'S WELL-BEING

Almost no data are available on children's experiences in the new welfare programs. The work requirements of TANF are a major way through which welfare reform might affect children. A small set of studies that considers maternal employment in low-income families before welfare reform generally points to neutral or modestly better developmental outcomes for children whose mothers are employed, even when family income and maternal education are taken into account (Moore et al. 1995; Zaslow and Emig 1997). Maternal employment is associated with better maternal mental health (Hoffman and Youngblade 1999) and can benefit children in low-income families through additional income and the social and cognitive stimulation it provides the mother, which may lead to more positive interactions with children (Parcel and Menaghan 1990; Klebanov et al. 1994; Wilson et al. 1995). In national samples, more extensive maternal employment is linked to more positive outcomes for children in middle childhood (Menaghan et al. 1998). This may be because of the stability underlying continuous employment, the quality of jobs that tend to be long term, or the characteristics of mothers who are able to remain employed for extended lengths of time.

Other evidence points to some negative effects of maternal employment on children in low-income families. Parents employed in low-wage, repetitive, or unstimulating jobs provide less nurturing home environments than do parents with jobs that pay more or that offer more complexity and autonomy. Similarly, children of parents employed in low-wage jobs show less favorable outcomes than their counterparts in families with higher paying jobs (Menaghan and Parcel 1995; Moore and Driscoll 1997). One study of welfare recipients in the preform era finds that mothers who leave welfare for low-paying jobs and remain poor do not provide better home environments for their children compared with those who remain on welfare. If, however, the mother leaves welfare and escapes poverty, her children have higher achievement scores and fewer behavior problems (Wilson, et al. 1995).

Recent evidence from several experimental work-based demonstration programs sheds some light on how current welfare reform programs might affect children. Results from the National Evaluation of Welfare-to-Work Strategies (NEWWS), an experimental evaluation of the effect of the Family Support Act of 1988 (the welfare reform precursor to PRWORA), indicate that, for families with preschool children, the program yields some positive effects on cognitive development, unfavorable effects on physical health, and mixed effects on maternal-reported child behavior problems (Zaslow et al. 2000). Overall, however, the program has a minimal effect on children, and the effects are not widespread, suggesting that most children are not adversely affected by their mothers' participation in a welfare-to-work program.

In contrast, a different set of experimental evaluations identifies more consistently positive aspects of mandated work programs, particularly when the programs not only encourage work but also "make work pay." The Minnesota Family Investment Program (MFIP) finds that children of single-parent, long-term recipients have positive outcomes on measures of school performance and behavior problems compared to a control group enrolled in the traditional AFDC program (Knox et al. 2000). An important influence is the program's financial incentives, which leads to increased income and reduced poverty. Also important, MFIP has no negative effects on children of long-term recipients. Similarly, another experimental work-based income supplement program, New Hope, improves school performance and social behavior among school-age boys; in part this may be because of the children's increased participation in structured out-of-home activities (see chapter 11, this volume). Children in the experimental group increase their participation in such activities not only because parents spend more time at work but also because they have modestly more income to pay for such activities.

The overall effects of welfare reform on children's outcomes will depend on the confluence of state and local policies, family risk and protective factors, children's experiences inside and outside the home, and the patterns and quality of maternal work experiences (Zaslow et al. 1998). Welfare reform will likely bring about many changes in family life, and the ultimate effects on children will undoubtedly be a function of the interaction among, and the accumulation of, these changes and the particular outcome of interest. A comprehensive analysis of the pathways from welfare reform to children's developmental outcomes is beyond the scope of this chapter. Instead, we examine such aspects of mothers' employment as work involvement, work transitions, and work intensity. We also examine intervening variables such as the family's material hardships and income and parenting stress and efficacy. These variables, and their effects on children's behavioral adjustment, are examined in the context of relevant family characteristics.

Specifically, we pose the following questions:

- Are there differences in the levels of children's positive and negative behavior among families characterized by the extent of maternal work participation over a year, by the number of job transitions experienced by the mother, or by the number of hours the women are currently employed, controlling for basic demographic measures?

- If differences are found, do they persist after accounting for potential barriers to women's employment—that is, problems that could reduce mothers' work and affect child well-being, such as mothers' health, their mental health, and their exposure to domestic violence—or by intervening measures of family economic hardship, parenting stress, and efficacy?

THE SAMPLE

We used data from the Women's Employment Study (WES), a longitudinal study of a sample of women drawn from Michigan's TANF cash assistance rolls in February 1997 (after the state had begun to implement its TANF plans). The WES is being conducted at the University of Michigan under the auspices of the Poverty Research and Training Center at the School of Social Work. The first wave of WES interviews was completed between August and December 1997, with a random sample of 753 single mothers who were welfare recipients in an urban Michigan county in February 1997. The random sample was limited to recipients between the ages of eighteen and fifty-four, the average age being almost thirty (28 percent were under age twenty-five, 47 percent were between the ages of twenty-five and thirty-four, and 26 percent were thirty-five years or older). Almost nine out of ten lived in urban census tracts in the county.

Michigan's Family Independence Agency (FIA) provided names and addresses of all single-parent cases, and a stratified random sample was drawn; completed interviews represent an 86 percent response rate. The second wave of interviews was completed in the fall of 1998, with 693 respondents, representing a response rate of 92 percent. Information about the physical health, emotional well-being, and school performance of a focal child, as well as about maternal parenting practices and mother-child relationships, was collected if the mother had at least one child between the ages of two and ten years (designated the *focal child* at the first-wave interview). Of the mothers interviewed, 76 percent ($N = 575$) had a focal child.

For the present study, we used the sample of mothers with focal children.

Although the WES is not a typical welfare "leavers" study, many of the women in the sample were making the transition from welfare to work. Work participation increased substantially between the two waves of data collection: at the first-wave interview, 72 percent were receiving welfare and 65 percent were working; at the second-wave interview, 50 percent were receiving welfare and 75 percent were working. The data indicate that welfare receipt at the second-wave interview is significantly negatively associated with the percentage of months worked between waves and with the current number of hours worked. Thus these women decreased their welfare use and increased their employment over a one-year period. We seek to relate maternal work between the two waves to reports of children's behavioral adjustment at the second-wave interview.

THE MEASURES

The several measures we looked at are maternal work, demographic controls, barriers to employment, economic and parental well-being, and child behavior.

Maternal Work Measures

We related three measures of maternal work to children's behavioral outcomes. These are work involvement, work transitions, and work intensity.

WORK INVOLVEMENT   At the second-wave interview, work histories were collected for the months in which a woman reported any paid work between the two waves. We define *work involvement* as the proportion of months employed between the first wave (August through December 1997) and the second-wave interview, in the fall of 1998. There is a wide distribution of this measure: about 14 percent did not work in any of the months, but 46 percent worked in every month.

WORK TRANSITIONS   Because women who worked in some but not all of the months between the two waves experienced many types of work transitions, we included a measure of the number of work transitions a women experienced between waves. A work transition is defined as *movement from work to nonwork or from nonwork to work*. Of our sample, 60 percent experienced no transitions, 15 percent experienced one transition, 14 percent experienced two transitions, 6 percent experienced three transitions, 2 percent experienced four transitions, and about 2 percent experienced five or more transitions.

WORK INTENSITY   The third measure of employment is the number of hours the mothers had worked at the second-wave interview. This measure assesses employment at all jobs, although most mothers had only one job at the time of the interview. The measure of hours worked at all jobs was top-coded at seventy; the four women who reported more than seventy hours worked were assigned a value of seventy. This measure was then divided by forty to produce forty-hour-workweek increments.

The work transitions measure is correlated $-.28$ ($p < .01$) with the work involvement measure and $-.10$ with the work intensity measure ($p < .05$). The work intensity measure is correlated $.61$ ($p < .01$) with the work involvement measure.

Demographic Control Measures

To relate maternal work to children's behavior, we controlled for factors specific to the mother and her child. In our first set of analyses, we included a series of demographic controls measured at the second-wave interview: total years the mother received welfare since age eighteen, the age and race of the mother, the age and sex of the focal child, whether the mother had a high school degree, and whether a spouse or partner was living in the household. The means for these control measures are presented in table 9.1.

Barriers to Employment

Our next analyses added controls for a series of measures that represent potential barriers to employment. These measures are mothers' mental health, substance abuse,

TABLE 9.1 / Means for Analysis Sample

Measure[a]	Mean[a]	Standard Deviation	Minimum	Maximum
Anxious or depressed behavior, second wave	3.83	1.00	2.89	8.09
Antisocial behavior, second wave	3.53	0.99	2.34	7.02
Positive behavior, second wave	6.15	1.00	2.53	7.59
Change in anxious or depressed behavior between waves	−0.02	1.04	−3.85	3.65
Change in antisocial behavior between waves	−0.02	0.99	−3.41	3.18
Change in positive behavior between waves	−0.01	2.61	−9.00	9.00
Months worked between waves	0.67	0.38	0.00	1.00
Work week, second wave (fraction of forty hours)	0.61	0.48	0.00	1.75
Work transitions between waves (number)	0.84	1.26	0.00	6.00
Total years of welfare receipt	7.83	4.77	1.00	29.00
Age of mother (years)	30.17	6.47	19.00	55.00
Age of focal child (years)	5.71	2.39	2.00	12.00
Focal child is a girl[a]	0.51	0.50	0.00	1.00
Mother has no high school degree[a]	0.31	0.46	0.00	1.00
Mother is African American[a]	0.56	0.50	0.00	1.00
Spouse or partner lives in house, second wave[a]	0.32	0.47	0.00	1.00
Mental health diagnosis of mother, second wave[a]	0.24	0.43	0.00	1.00
Dependence diagnosis of mother, second wave[a]	0.03	0.18	0.00	1.00
Maternal health problem, second wave[a]	0.19	0.39	0.00	1.00
Child health problem, second wave[a]	0.18	0.39	0.00	1.00

(Table continues on p. 162.)

TABLE 9.1 / *Continued*

Measure[a]	Mean[a]	Standard Deviation	Minimum	Maximum
Severe domestic violence, second wave[a]	0.15	0.35	0.00	1.00
Mother was pregnant between waves[a]	0.18	0.39	0.00	1.00
Annual household income/total family size, second wave (dollars)	2,609.41	1,939.12	83.33	11,666.66
Hardships experienced, second wave[a]	0.60	0.49	0.00	1.00
Parenting stress, second wave	20.67	5.76	7.00	35.00
Mastery, second wave	22.46	3.35	13.00	28.00

Source: Authors' compilation.
Note: $N = 498$.
[a] Percentage, except where indicated.

physical health, experience of domestic violence, and pregnancy since the first-wave interview. The measures (see table 9.1 for the means) may be correlated both with maternal work patterns and with mothers' reports of their children's behavior.

MENTAL HEALTH AND SUBSTANCE ABUSE Mothers' mental health and substance dependence were assessed using diagnostic screening batteries for the twelve-month prevalence of psychiatric disorders as defined in the *Diagnostic and Statistical Manual,* revised, third edition (DSM-III-R): major depression, posttraumatic stress disorder (PTSD), alcohol dependence, and drug dependence. Questions are from the Composite International Diagnostic Interview (CIDI) used in the National Comorbidity Survey (NCS), the first nationally representative survey to administer a structured psychiatric interview (Kessler et al. 1994). All respondents who met the diagnostic screening criteria for a disorder were defined as having that disorder. We created two indicator variables, one for mothers who met the diagnostic criteria for any mental health measure (PTSD or depression) and another for those diagnosed with dependence on either drugs or alcohol.

PHYSICAL HEALTH The women were asked about physical limitations and to rate their general health using questions taken from the SF-36 Health Survey (Ware et al. 1993). Respondents who rated their general health as poor or fair and who scored in the lowest age-specific quartile (based on national norms) of the multiple-item physical functioning scale were defined as having a health problem. In addition, those who reported that at least one child in the family (not necessarily the focal child) had a physical, learning, or emotional problem that limited his or her activity were defined as having a child with a health problem. We included indicators for health problems of the mother and of any child.

DOMESTIC VIOLENCE   Domestic violence was measured by the Conflict Tactics Scale (CTS), a widely used measure of family violence (Strauss and Gelles 1986, 1990). A woman was coded as having experienced severe domestic violence if, during the past twelve months, she was hit with a fist or an object, beaten, choked, threatened with a weapon, or forced into sexual activity against her will. We included in our analyses an indicator for women who experienced severe domestic violence in the past year.

PREGNANCY   Finally, we controlled for whether the mother became pregnant between the first-wave interview and the second-wave interview. This measure could be associated both with mothers' work behavior and with their reports of their children's behavior problems.

Intervening Variables

We also looked for associations between maternal work and children's behavior that might be accounted for by measures of economic or parental well-being: material hardship, family income, mothers' mastery, and parenting stress.

MATERIAL HARDSHIP   The study explored the extent to which women experienced material hardships in the six months before the second-wave interview. We used this measure to test whether recent material hardship, as well as poverty level, accounted for any effect of employment on the child behavior outcomes. The material hardships assessed were food insufficiency, lack of health insurance for either the mother or children, instances in which the mother or her child did not receive needed medical care, and experiences of a utility shutoff, eviction or an episode of homelessness, and lack of a telephone.[1] We created an indicator of whether the mother reported any material hardships at the second-wave interview.

FAMILY INCOME   This measure was based on reported total household income in the year before the second-wave interview. This number was divided by household size to create a measure of income-family size. Four families reporting an annual income under $500 were assigned a value of $500; four families reporting incomes of greater than $35,000 were assigned a value of $35,000. (The minimum and maximum values for this measure in table 9.1 reflect these figures divided by family size.)

MOTHERS' MASTERY   Mothers' mastery was assessed with the Pearlin Mastery Scale (Pearlin et al. 1981), a seven-item summary scale (Cronbach's alpha = .79) that measures the extent to which mothers report feeling efficacious and in control of their lives. Representative items from the mastery scale include "I can do anything I set my mind to" and "What happens in the future depends on me." Items were scored on a four-point scale, in which a score of one indicates "strongly disagree" with a statement and a score of four indicates "strongly agree" with a statement. The theoretical range of the scale is seven through twenty-eight, higher scores indicating greater mastery.

PARENTING STRESS   The parenting stress scale is a seven-item index that measures the degree of stress or irritation mothers perceive in relation to their interactions with their children. This scale explores mothers' subjective sense of difficulty with regard to the parenting role and, in previous research, has been related to child maltreatment. Items for this scale were taken or adapted from Abidin's Parenting Stress Index (PSI) (Abidin 1990) and from the New Chance Study (Morrison et al. 1998). A sample item is, "I find that being a mother is much more work than pleasure." Items are measured on a five-point scale and are coded such that a score of one means "never" and a score of five means "almost always." The theoretical range of the scale is seven through thirty-five, higher scores indicating greater parenting stress. Cronbach's alpha for this scale is .81.[2]

Child Behavior

The dependent variables of interest in these analyses are measures of children's behavioral adjustment, assessed using maternal reports. The survey contained a subset of items from the Behavioral Problems Index (BPI) (Chase-Lansdale et al. 1991) and the Adaptive Social Behavior Index (ASBI) (Hogan et al. 1992). Identical or similar items have been used in other studies of low-income children (Hogan et al. 1992). Unfortunately, the survey did not include the entire twenty-eight-item BPI. The BPI used in the National Longitudinal Survey of Youth has separate subscales; in our study, complete subscales at the second-wave interview were available for the antisocial and anxious-depressed indicators.

The antisocial behavior measure (four items, alpha .61) includes items such as "bullies or is cruel or mean to others" and "breaks things deliberately," while the anxious-depressed measure (five items, alpha .63) focuses on sadness ("unhappy, sad"), fearfulness ("fearful"), and self-feelings ("feels worthless"). The third outcome, positive behavior, is measured with eight items (alpha .78) tapping the child's compliance. Anxious-depressed behavior is correlated (.46) with antisocial behavior and (– .38) with positive behavior. Antisocial behavior is correlated (– .57) with positive behavior. All three measures have been standardized by division by their standard deviation.

Some analyses controlled for a measure of children's behavior taken at the first-wave interview. For the positive behavior measure, assessments at the two interviews were identical. The behavior problems measures at the first wave differed slightly from the second-wave measures. To control for first-wave measures of behavior, some analyses included an index of negative behavior composed of eleven items measuring how often the child felt or complained that no one loved him or her and whether the child cheated or told lies, bullied others, was disobedient at home, was disobedient at school, did not seem sorry after misbehaving, felt worthless or inferior, was not liked by other children, was unhappy, was withdrawn, and felt that others were out to get him or her. The items were coded as one, not true, two sometimes true, or three, often true.

Finally, some analyses used the maternal work measures to predict changes in children's behavior between the two waves. Because the measures of negative behavior differed, comparable measures of first-wave and second-wave problem behavior were created. Specifically, the measures of behavior problems were rescaled to have a mean of 0 and a standard deviation of 1. With these standardized measures, the first-wave measure of behavior problems was subtracted from the second-wave measure, creating a measure of change.

THE RESULTS

Before performing our analyses, we examined how the sample of children in the WES compared with a national sample of children on some of our outcomes of interest. We compared the behavior problem scores of WES children with those of children in the Panel Study of Income Dynamics (PSID) Child Development Supplement. The PSID is an ongoing longitudinal survey of a representative sample of U.S. families. Started in 1968, the study collects data on employment, income, wealth, housing, food expenditures, transfer income, and marital and fertility behavior. The 1997 PSID Child Development Supplement is an addition to the PSID, providing nationally representative data on children and their families. Comparing children in the same age range (three through twelve years), we found that PSID and WES children did not differ on our measure of anxious-depressed behavior but that PSID children scored significantly lower ($t = 6.64$, $df = 2263$, $p < .01$) than WES children on the measure of antisocial behavior (PSID children with a score of 5.10 points; WES children with an unstandardized score of 6.03 points). Thus compared with a national sample, the economically disadvantaged children in the WES had higher levels of mother-reported antisocial behavior but did not differ on a measure of anxious-depressed behavior.

The average mother (see table 9.1) worked 67 percent of the months between the first and second waves and, at the second-wave interview, 61 percent of a forty-hour week (this includes mothers not working at all, who were assigned a 0 on this measure). The mothers experienced, on average, less than one job transition between waves (.84) and had almost eight years of welfare receipt during their adult years. A large minority of the mothers experienced mental health problems, health problems, recent pregnancy, and child health problems.

The relation between maternal employment measures and children's behavior are presented in tables 9.2, 9.3, and 9.4, using multivariate ordinary least squares (OLS) regressions. Dependent variables were standardized by division by their sample standard deviation. Therefore, the coefficients presented here reflect standard deviation changes in the child behavior measures.

The four models in the tables show the associations between mothers' work behavior and children's behavior, controlling for an increasing number of covariates. In the first model we controlled only for basic demographic control variables, measured at the second-wave interview. Including these controls allowed us to examine whether, controlling for important family characteristics, employment involvement over time, work transitions, and current work intensity were significantly associated with children's behavior.

In the second model we added controls for potential maternal barriers to employment because they represent additional ways in which children in families whose mothers work may differ from those in families whose mothers do not. We also included measures representing potential intervening variables between maternal employment and children's behavior, specifically, family income, material hardship, and parenting stress and efficacy. If these variables matter, including them should change the relation between children's behavior and mothers' work involvement, work transitions, and hours worked.

The third model includes a measure of children's behavior problems at the first wave. Including this measure allowed us to examine whether maternal work between the two waves is associated with any change in children's behavior. The fourth model uses the maternal work measures to predict a change in children's behavior between the two waves. This is an alternative means of controlling for children's behavior at the first wave.

Table 9.2 presents results predicting children's anxious-depressed behavior. An additional job transition is associated with an increase in anxious-depressed behavior of 12 percent of a standard deviation (first model). Neither work intensity nor the percentage of months worked between waves is significantly associated with children's anxious-depressed behavior. A one-point increase in the number of job transitions a mother experienced between waves is associated with an increase in children's anxious-depressed behavior of 9 percent of a standard deviation (second model), and including measures of family economic status, parenting stress, and maternal mastery did not reduce the associations between job transitions and increased child anxious-depressed behavior. However, parenting stress, mastery, and family income are all significant predictors of this outcome: mothers reporting more mastery and less parenting stress also report better behavior from their children on this measure; families with a higher income-family size report better behavior as well.

The third model in table 9.2 adds a control for children's negative behavior. Here, the job transitions variable is still positively and significantly associated with children's anxious-depressed behavior (coefficient of .07). In addition, income and maternal mastery are significant predictors of children's anxious-depressed behavior (the coefficient on parental stress loses significance in this model). Maternal mental health is a significant predictor of child behavior. Not surprisingly, child negative behavior at the first wave is significantly associated with anxious-depressed behavior at the second.

The fourth model in table 9.2 uses the maternal employment measures to predict changes in children's anxious-depressed behavior between the two waves. Here, none of the maternal employment measures is a significant predictor of anxious-depressed behavior. The only significant association is a link between mothers' having a diagnosis of a mental health problem and increased anxious-depressed behavior on the part of the children.

TABLE 9.2 / Maternal Employment and Children's Anxious-Depressed Behavior

| | Anxious or Depressed Behavior at Second Wave | | | | | | Change | |
| | Model 1 | | Model 2 | | Model 3 | | Model 4 | |
Measure	Coefficient	Standard Error	Coefficient	Standard Error	Coefficient	Standard Error	Coefficient	Standard Error
Months worked between waves	-.27	.15	-.14	.14	-.11	.13	-.05	.16
Additional forty-hour week, second wave	.09	.12	.00	.00	.08	.10	-.07	.13
Job transitions between waves	.12	.04**	.09	.04**	.07	.03*	.03	.04
Total years welfare receipt	-.01	.01	-.02	.01	-.01	.01	-.01	.01
Mental health problem, second wave[a]			.21	.11	.25	.10*	.29	.12*
Substance abuse diagnosis, second wave[a]			.40	.24	.32	.22	.19	.27
Health barrier, second wave[a]			.00	.11	.00	.10	-.02	.13
Child health barrier, second wave[a]			.16	.11	.10	.10	.02	.13
Severe domestic violence, second wave[a]			.14	.12	.04	.12	-.12	.14

(Table continues on p. 168.)

TABLE 9.2 / Continued

| | Anxious or Depressed Behavior at Second Wave | | | | | | Change | |
| | Model 1 | | Model 2 | | Model 3 | | Model 4 | |
Measure	Coefficient	Standard Error	Coefficient	Standard Error	Coefficient	Standard Error	Coefficient	Standard Error
Pregnant between waves[a]			.11	.11	.09	.10	.04	.13
Income/family size, second wave ($1,000)			-.05	.02*	-.05	.02*	-.05	.03
Hardships, second wave[a]			.08	.09	.04	.08	-.04	.10
Parenting stress, second wave			.02	.01**	.01	.01	-.02	.01
Mastery, second wave			-.04	.01**	-.03	.01*	-.01	.02
Negative behavior, first wave					.12	.01**		
N	498		498		496		496	
R-square	.10		.23		.33		.06	
Constant	3.35	.29	3.73	.50	2.23	.50	.71	.57

Source: Authors' compilation.
Note: All analyses control for age and race of mother; child age and sex; whether mother completed high school, and whether a spouse or partner was living in the household at second wave.
[a] Percentage, except where indicated.
* p < .05. ** p < .01.

Table 9.3 presents results predicting children's antisocial behavior. As in the previous table, in the first model an increase in the number of work transitions experienced by the mother is associated with worse behavior among children (coefficient of .09); however, an increase in the percentage of months worked by the mother between waves is associated with a decrease in children's antisocial behavior (coefficient of .31). In the second model, in which maternal barriers to employment and the potential intervening variables are included, no significant associations between the maternal work measures and antisocial behavior remain. Parenting stress is associated with children's antisocial behavior. In addition, an increase in the measure of income-family size is associated with a decrease in maternal reports of children's antisocial behavior.

In the third model a control for children's behavior is included. Again, no significant relation exists between maternal employment and children's antisocial behavior; the significant associations between family income, parenting stress, and antisocial behavior of the second model remain in this model. Children's behavior at the first wave is highly predictive of antisocial behavior at the second.

In the fourth model none of the maternal employment measures is a significant predictor of changes in antisocial behavior. Domestic violence at the second wave is associated with a decrease in antisocial behavior between waves. In addition, increased family income at the second wave is associated with a decrease in antisocial behavior between waves.

Table 9.4 presents results predicting children's positive behavior at the second wave. In the first model, none of the maternal work measures is associated with children's positive behavior. In the second model, parenting stress is a significant predictor of children's positive behavior; specifically, increased parenting stress is associated with less positive behavior by children. In addition, an increase in the measure of income-family size is associated with more positive child behavior. Finally, severe domestic violence is associated with less positive behavior. In the third model, a first wave measure of children's positive behavior is included. Again, none of the maternal employment measures is significantly associated with children's positive behavior; only parental stress and family income remain significant predictors. Not surprisingly, positive behavior at the first wave is a highly significant predictor of positive behavior at the second. The fourth model uses maternal employment measures to predict changes in positive behavior. Here, none of the variables of interest is a significant predictor of change.

DISCUSSION

In this investigation, we were primarily concerned with identifying the links between children's behavior and their mothers' employment. Does level of mothers' work participation affect the behavior problems of their children? Does the number of mothers' transitions between working and not working or their current number of hours worked a week affect these outcomes?

(Text continues on p. 174.)

TABLE 9.3 / Maternal Employment and Children's Antisocial Behavior

| | Antisocial Behavior at Second Wave | | | | | | Change | |
| | Model 1 | | Model 2 | | Model 3 | | Model 4 | |
Measure	Coefficient	Standard Error	Coefficient	Standard Error	Coefficient	Standard Error	Coefficient	Standard Error
Months worked between waves	-.31	.15*	-.21	.14	-.16	.13	-.11	.15
Additional forty-hour week, second wave	.18	.12	.00	.00	.08	.10	-.04	.12
Job transitions between waves	.09	.04*	.06	.04	.04	.03	.00	.04
Total years welfare receipt	.00	.01	-.01	.01	-.01	.01	.00	.01
Mental health problem, second wave			.05	.11	.09	.10	.13	.11
Substance abuse diagnosis, second wave			.35	.24	.25	.22	.14	.25
Health barrier, second wave			.09	.11	.07	.10	.06	.12
Child health barrier, second wave			-.09	.11	-.15	.10	-.23	.12

Severe domestic violence, second wave	−.08	.13	−.20	.11	−.33	.13*
Pregnant between waves	.10	.11	.07	.10	.03	.12
Income/family size, second wave ($1,000)	−.06	.02*	−.05	.02**	−.05	.02*
Hardships, second wave	.07	.09	.02	.08	−.05	.09
Parenting stress, second wave	.05	.01**	.03	.01**	.01	.01
Mastery, second wave	−.02	.01	.00	.01	.02	.01
Negative behavior, first wave			.16	.01**		
N	498	498	496	496	496	496
R-square	.06	.18	.35	.30	.09	.23
Constant	3.59	2.95	1.04	.51	0.49	.53

Source: Authors' compilation.
Note: All analyses control for age and race of mother; child age and sex; whether mother completed high school, and whether a spouse or partner was living in the household at second wave.
* $p < .05$. ** $p < .01$.

TABLE 9.4 / Maternal Employment and Children's Positive Behavior

| | Positive Behavior at Second Wave | | | | | | Change | |
| | Model 1 | | Model 2 | | Model 3 | | Model 4 | |
Measure	Coefficient	Standard Error	Coefficient	Standard Error	Coefficient	Standard Error	Coefficient	Standard Error
Months worked between waves	.25	.15	.15	.15	.03	.12	-.13	.42
Additional forty-hour week, second wave	-.14	.12	-.01	.00	-.04	.10	.17	.33
Job transitions between waves	-.07	.04	-.05	.04	.00	.03	.06	.11
Total years welfare receipt	.00	.01	.02	.01	.00	.01	-.01	.03
Mental health problem, second wave			.08	.11	.03	.09	.00	.31
Substance abuse diagnosis, second wave			-.01	.25	-.10	.20	-.45	.70
Health barrier, second wave			-.05	.11	-.04	.10	-.14	.33
Child health barrier, second wave			.01	.12	.08	.10	.42	.33

Severe domestic violence, second wave		-.30	.13*	-.14	.11	-.20	.37
Pregnant between waves		-.19	.12	-.09	.10	-.12	.33
Income/family size, second wave ($1,000)		.07	.02**	.04	.02*	.09	.07
Hardships, second wave		.13	.09	.10	.08	.18	.26
Parenting stress, second wave		-.04	.01**	-.02	.01**	-.02	.02
Mastery, second wave		.03	.01	.01	.01	-.02	.04
Positive behavior, first wave				.19	.01**		
N	498		498		484		484	
R-square	.08		.17		.45		.02	
Constant	6.04	.30	6.31	.52	2.70	0.49	1.34	1.48

Source: Authors' compilation.

Note: All analyses control for age and race of mother; child age and sex; whether mother completed high school; whether a spouse or partner was living in the household at second wave.

$* p < .05.$ $** p < .01.$

These questions were motivated by policy-relevant assumptions about the transition from welfare to work for low-income mothers. Many concerns expressed during the debates leading up to welfare reform centered on the potential effects of this transition. Hypotheses and some recent evidence suggest that mothers' working can produce economic instability among some families or increase their parenting stress now that they are required to balance work and child care. In contrast, welfare reform's promoters argue that, in the long-run, increased maternal employment could have a stabilizing effect on families, could improve mothers' self-image, and might instill better values and attitudes in their children. Given the relatively short time frame and the young age of the children in this sample, we were in a particularly good position to examine the hypothesis that mothers' working is associated with their children's behavior.

An important finding is the lack of significant, negative associations between extent of maternal work over time or current hours worked and child behavior. However, there is some suggestion that the number of transitions between work and nonwork is associated with more anxious-depressed behavior on the part of the children. Most of the mothers in our study experienced very few transitions, and the small effect size for the association is not of a magnitude deemed "policy relevant" (Zaslow et al. 2000). Nevertheless, significant and important negative effects could accrue to those families that experience a number of transitions.

Alternative specifications, such as using dummy categories representing patterns of work involvement, transitions, and work intensity, did not change the results. Thus these initial results provide little evidence that children are hurt by their mothers' increasing work participation. This study, however, does not measure the characteristics of the work that mothers engaged in, such as the wages earned, the work shift and schedule, the benefits, or the occupation. Measures such as these could be associated with child well-being and should be addressed in future work.

Some caution in interpreting the lack of effects of work intensity is also warranted in that it was mothers who reported their children's behavior problems as well as hours worked. Thus there is some concern that, for example, mothers in a more manageable work situation are more satisfied with their circumstances and are thus more likely to paint a rosy picture of their children's behavior. An important goal for future studies is to assess work intensity over time, similar to the way our longitudinal work involvement indicator was measured, in order to avoid the interpretation difficulties inherent in cross-sectional correlations.

In analyses not reported here, we explored the possibility that the pattern of results might depend on the child's sex; this hypothesis is not supported. We also examined "threshold" effects; that is, whether the employment measures are associated with being in the upper or lower quartile of the distributions of our child behavior measures. Again, we find no evidence for this hypothesis. We also tested for differences in the associations between our work measures and children's behavior for preschool and school-aged children separately but did not find any differences.

Our study does not address the issue of the welfare-to-work transition per se because some of the women were already working at the time of the first wave and some of the women who were working at the second wave continued to receive TANF benefits. Increasing levels of work participation over time among this sample, however, are associated with higher earnings, lower poverty rates, and decreased receipt of TANF (Danziger et al., "Work," 2000). In addition, the rate of welfare "leaving" in our sample is comparable to that reported at the national level. Thus this sample can be viewed as one that, on average, is "transitioning" from welfare into work. Our initial results do not support the claim that the work involvement aspects of welfare-to-work transitions among women drawn from the current TANF rolls are associated with either negative or positive outcomes for children.

Nevertheless, our study may not capture specific types of disruption in working or specific patterns of timing in combining work with welfare or in leaving welfare altogether. We counted the number of transitions between work and nonwork, but perhaps moving rapidly into employment and then quickly experiencing job loss could be detrimental to women and their families. Using a subsample of low-income families from the PSID child development supplement, one study (Hofferth et al. 2000) compares welfare "leavers" with "stayers" and low-income nonrecipients. Leavers consisted of two groups: those who formerly received welfare but left more than a year before and those who left welfare within the past year. Neither the children of current recipients nor the children of long-term leavers had behavior problems different from the children of low-income mothers who had never received welfare. In contrast, however, the children of "recent leavers" showed significantly higher levels of externalizing and internalizing behavior problems (controlling for background characteristics of the child and characteristics of the mother, including maternal IQ, depression, and parenting behavior). These results suggest that there may be some disruptions during actual transition periods that are associated negatively with children's behavioral adjustment. The present analysis, as mentioned, does not take into account the potential importance of subgroups in different transitional stages of leaving welfare.

In summary, this study indicates a relatively high prevalence of child antisocial behavior problems in a sample of TANF single mothers compared with a representative sample of U.S. families. Their children do not have a higher prevalence of anxious-depressed behavior. Increasing levels of maternal work participation over time and current work intensity do not significantly alter these dimensions of children's behavior or positive child behavior, on average. At the same time, we find some suggestion that increases in the number of transitions between work and nonwork are associated with increases in children's behavior problems.

The analysis presented here takes a short-term view of mothers' work participation and children's behavior. As we follow the respondents over a longer period of time, we may see that the women increase their work hours and intensity to the degree that they begin to face deeper work-family conflicts, which could affect how their children fare. On the other hand, as women work longer or move into higher quality and more stable jobs, we may observe greater improvements in child behavior. Answers to these questions await future research.

NOTES

1. Respondents were coded as being food insufficient if they reported that they sometimes or often did not have enough food to eat when asked, "Which of the following describes the amount of food in your household: enough, sometimes not enough, often not enough." This measure is also used in the Current Population Survey and the Third National Health and Nutrition Examination Survey (NHANES III). (See Alaimo et al. 1998 for a discussion of this measure.)

2. Although mastery and parenting stress were measured at both interviews, we examine only the second-wave measures in the present analyses. Our theory is that they are partially the consequences of work experiences; hence they may intervene in any association between work and the child behavior outcomes.

REFERENCES

Abidin, Richard R. 1990. *Index Short Form: Test Manual.* Charlottesville: University of Virginia. (Thirty-six-item version.)

Alaimo, Katherine, Ronette R. Briefel, Edward A. Frongillo, and C. M. Olson. 1998. "Food Insufficiency in the United States: Results from the Third National Health and Nutrition Examination Survey (NHANES III)." *American Journal of Public Health* 88: 419–26.

Bane, Mary J., and David T. Ellwood. 1994. *Welfare Realities: From Rhetoric to Reform.* Cambridge, Mass.: Harvard University Press.

Brauner, Sheila, and Pamela Loprest. 1999. *Where Are They Now? What States' Studies of People Who Left Welfare Tell Us.* Washington, D.C.: Urban Institute.

Cancian, Maria, Robert Haveman, Thomas Kaplan, Daniel Meyer, and Barbara Wolfe. 1998. "Work, Earnings, and Well-being After Welfare: What Do We Know?" Paper presented at the Joint Center for Poverty Research conference on Welfare Reform and the Macro-Economy. Washington, D.C., November 19.

Chase-Lansdale, P. Lindsay, Frank L. Mott, Jeanne Brooks-Gunn, and Deborah H. Phillips. 1991. "Children of the National Longitudinal Survey of Youth: A Unique Research Opportunity." *Developmental Psychology* 27: 918–31.

Conger, Rand G., Glen Elder, Frederick Lorenz, and Ronald Simons. 1994. "Economic Stress, Coercive Family Processes, and Developmental Problems of Adolescents." *Child Development* 65: 541–61.

Danziger, Sandra K., Mary Corcoran, Sheldon Danziger, and Colleen Heflin. 2000. "Work, Income, and Material Hardship After Welfare Reform." *Journal of Consumer Affairs* 6: 30.

Danziger, Sandra K., Mary Corcoran, Sheldon Danziger, Colleen Heflin, Ariel Kalil, Judith Levine, Daniel Rosen, Kristin Seefeldt, Kristine Siefert, and Richard Tolman. 2000. "Barriers to the Employment of Welfare Recipients." In *Prosperity for All? The Economic Boom and African Americans,* edited by R. Cherry and W. Rodgers. New York: Russell Sage Foundation.

Duncan, Greg J., and Jeanne Brooks-Gunn. 1997. *Consequences of Growing Up Poor.* New York: Russell Sage Foundation.

Hofferth, Sandra, Julia Smith, Vonnie McLoyd, and Jonathon Finklestein. 2000. "Achievement and Behavior Among Children of Welfare Recipients, Welfare Leavers, and Low-Income Single Mothers." *Journal of Social Issues* 56: 747–74.

Hoffman, Lois, and Lise Youngblade. 1999. *Mothers at Work*. Cambridge: Cambridge University Press.

Hogan, Anne, Keith Scott, and Charles Bauer. 1992. "The Adaptive Social Behavior Index (ASBI): A New Assessment of Social Competence in High-Risk Three-Year-Olds." *Journal of Psychoeducational Assessment* 10: 230–39.

Kalil, Ariel, and Jacquelynne Eccles. 1998. "Does Welfare Affect Family Processes and Adolescent Adjustment?" *Child Development* 69: 1597–1613.

Kessler, Ronald C., Katherine A. McGonagle, Shanyang Zhao, Christopher B. Nelson, Michael Hughes, Suzann Eshleman, Hans-Ulrich Wittchen, and Kenneth S. Kendler. 1994. "Lifetime and Twelve-month Prevalence of DSM-III-R Psychiatric Disorders in the United States: Results from the National Comorbidity Survey." *Archives of General Psychiatry* 51:8–19.

Klebanov, Pamela K., Jeanne Brooks-Gunn, and Greg J. Duncan. 1994. "Does Neighborhood and Family Poverty Affect Mothers' Parenting, Mental Health, and Social Support?" *Journal of Marriage and the Family* 56: 412–55.

Knox, Virginia, Cynthia Miller, and Lisa Gennetian. 2000. "Reforming Welfare and Rewarding Work: A Summary of the Final Report on the Minnesota Family Investment Program." Available at: *www.mdrc.org*.

Levine, Phillip B., and David J. Zimmerman. 2000. "Children's Welfare Exposure and Subsequent Development." Working paper 130. Chicago: Joint Center for Poverty Research. Available at: *www.jcpr.org*.

McLoyd, Vonnie C. 1990. "The Impact of Economic Hardship on Black Families and Children: Psychological Distress, Parenting, and Socioemotional Development." *Child Development* 61: 311–46.

Mead, Lawrence M. 1992. *The New Politics of Poverty*. New York: Basic Books.

Menaghan, Elizabeth, Susan Jekielek, Frank Mott, and Elizabeth Cooksey. 1998. "Work and Family Circumstances and Child Trajectories: When (and for What) Does AFDC Receipt Matter?" Paper presented at the Joint Center for Poverty Research Preconference on Family Process and Child Development in Low-Income Families, Chicago, May 8.

Menaghan, Elizabeth G., and Toby L. Parcel. 1995. "Social Sources of Change in Children's Home Environments: The Effects of Parental Occupational Experiences and Family Conditions." *Journal of Marriage and the Family* 57: 69–84.

Moore, Kristin A., and Amy Driscoll. 1997. "Low-Wage Maternal Employment and Outcomes for Children: A Study." *Future of Children* 7: 122–27.

Moore, Kristin A., Martha J. Zaslow, Mary J. Coiro, Suzanne M. Miller, and Ellen B. Magenheim. 1995. *The Jobs Evaluation: How Well Are They Faring? AFDC Families with Preschool-aged Children in Atlanta at the Outset of the Jobs Evaluation*. Washington: Office of the Assistant Secretary for Planning and Evaluation, U.S. Department of Health and Human Services.

Morrison, Donna, Martha Zaslow, and Robin Dion. 1998. "Completing the Portrayal of Parenting Behavior with Interview-Based Measures." In *Parenting Behavior in a Sample of Young Mothers*, edited by Martha Zaslow and Carolyn Eldred. New York: Manpower Demonstration Research Corporation.

Murray, Charles. 1993. "Welfare and the Family: The U.S. Experience." *Journal of Labor Economics* 11: S224–S262.

Olson, Krista, and LaDonna Pavetti. 1996. *Personal and Family Challenges to the Successful Transition from Welfare to Work.* Washington, D.C.: Urban Institute.

Parcel, Toby L., and Elizabeth G. Menaghan. 1990. "Maternal Working Conditions and Children's Verbal Facility: Studying the Intergenerational Transmission of Inequality from Mothers to Young Children." *Social Psychology Quarterly* 53: 132–47.

Pearlin, Leonard I., Melissa Lieberman, Elizabeth G. Menaghan, and Joseph T. Mullan. 1981. "The Stress Process." *Journal of Health and Social Behavior* 22: 337–56.

Primus, Wendell. 1999. Testimony. Subcommittee on Human Resources of the House Committee on Ways and Means. *Effects of Welfare Reform: Hearings Before the Subcommittee on Human Resources of the House Committee on Ways and Means.* 106th Congress.

Primus, Wendell, Lynette Rawlings, Kathy Larin, and Kathryn Porter. 1999. *The Initial Impact of Welfare Reform on the Incomes of Single-Mother Families.* Washington, D.C.: Center for Budget and Policy Priorities.

Straus, Murray A., and Richard J. Gelles. 1986. "Societal Change and Change in Family Violence from 1975 to 1985 as Revealed by Two National Surveys." *Journal of Marriage and the Family* 48: 465–79.

———, eds. 1990. *Physical Violence in American Families: Risk Factors and Adaptations to Violence in 8,145 Families.* New Brunswick, N.J.: Transaction Books.

U.S. Department of Health and Human Services, Administration for Children and Families. 1999. "Temporary Assistance for Needy Families (TANF), 1936–1999. U.S. Welfare Caseload Data." Available at: *www.acf.dhhs.gov/news/tables.htm.*

Ware, John E., Kristin K. Snow, Mark Kosinski, and Barbara Gardek. 1993. *SF-36 Health Survey: Manual and Interpretation Guide.* Boston: Health Institute, New England Medical Center.

Whipple, Ellen E., and Carolyn Webster-Stratton. 1991. "The Role of Parenting Stress in Physically Abusive Families." *Child Abuse and Neglect* 15: 279–91.

Wilson, Julie B., David T. Ellwood, and Jeanne Brooks-Gunn. 1995. "Welfare to Work Through the Eyes of Children: The Impact on Parenting of Movement from AFDC to Employment." In *Escape from Poverty: What Makes a Difference for Children?* edited by Lindsay Chase-Lansdale and Jeanne Brooks-Gunn. New York: Cambridge University Press.

Zaslow, Martha J., and Carol A. Emig. 1997. "When Low-Income Mothers Go to Work: Implications for Children." *Future of Children* 7: 110–15.

Zaslow, Martha J., Sharon McGroder, and Kristin Moore. 2000. "National Evaluation of Welfare to Work Strategies: Impacts on Young Children and Their Families Two Years After Enrollment: Findings from the Child Outcomes Study." Washington: Office of the Assistant Secretary for Planning and Evaluation, U.S. Department of Health and Human Services.

Zaslow, Martha J., Kathryn Tout, Carleen Botsko, and Kristin Moore. 1998. "Welfare Reform and Children: Potential Implications." Washington, D.C.: Urban Institute (June). Available at: *www.newfederalism.urban.org/html/anf23.html.*

Zill, Nicholas, Kristin A. Moore, E. W. Smith, Thomas Stief, and Mary J. Coiro. 1991. *The Life Circumstances and Development of Children in Welfare Families: A Profile Based on National Survey Data.* Washington, D.C.: Child Trends.

Chapter 10

Lessons from New Hope: The Impact on Children's Well-Being of a Work-Based Antipoverty Program for Parents

Rashmita S. Mistry, Danielle A. Crosby, Aletha C. Huston, David M. Casey, and Marika N. Ripke

B y current estimates, approximately one in five American children are poor, and children represent the largest segment (40 percent) of the poor population, even though they compose only one-fourth of the total population (Dalaker and Naifeh 1998). Social policies targeted toward poor parents represent one potential means for lowering the rates of childhood poverty. The 1990s witnessed a proliferation of research on the adverse consequences of poverty and low income on children's development (see Brooks-Gunn et al. 1997; Chase-Lansdale and Brooks-Gunn 1995; Huston et al. 1994; McLoyd 1998), and as a result, the links between poverty and child well-being are fairly well documented.

In contrast, the impact of welfare and antipoverty policies on families and children has been less well investigated, despite the fact that a majority of poor parents targeted by such policies are single mothers with young children (Kisker and Ross 1997). Most evaluations of policies aimed at poor parents focus on their effects on adult participants, primarily defining success as reductions in welfare use or costs and increases in employment and income. By changing parents' employment and income, however, these policies are also likely to have indirect effects on family life and, in turn, on children (Zaslow, Tout, et al. 1998).

In this chapter, we consider how poor children might be affected by welfare and employment policies aimed at their parents. Specifically, we evaluate the impacts of an employment-based, antipoverty program (New Hope) on children's well-being. Our goal in this study was twofold: to determine whether New Hope had an effect on children's development and, if so, why those effects occurred. A first step in considering these possible effects is to examine how antipoverty policies are structured and how they operate.

Two major policy streams affect poor families in the United States (see chapter 2, this volume). The first is generally called welfare and is centered around such cash assistance programs as Aid to Families with Dependent Children (AFDC) and its successor, Temporary Assistance for Needy Families (TANF). The latest version of the federal welfare policy, the Personal Responsibility and Work Opportunity Reconciliation Act of 1996 (PRWORA), is centered around a work-first philosophy, with the goal of moving adults from welfare to employment as quickly as possible. It signaled a departure from previous welfare legislation by requiring recipients (including mothers with young children) to seek paid employment, by imposing sanctions on recipients who fail to comply with requirements for job search and employment, and by placing a time limit on receipt of benefits.

A second policy stream, focused on income support, includes antipoverty strategies aimed at low-income, working parents. These policies are represented most clearly by the Earned Income Tax Credit (EITC), which was instituted as part of the federal income tax system in 1975 and which was greatly expanded in the 1990s. It has been estimated that the EITC reduced child poverty by 2.4 million children in 1996 (or one-seventh of the total number of poor children) (see Smeeding et al. 1999). Other income support policies, including health insurance (for example, through Medicaid and the Children's Health Insurance Program) and child care subsidies (for example, through the Child Care Development Fund), have also moved toward providing assistance to working families on the basis of family income rather than participation in the welfare system.

Both welfare and antipoverty strategies require parents to work, but income support policies represent an acknowledgment that employment alone is often insufficient to lift a family out of poverty. This is highlighted by recent estimates that indicate that about 5 million children live in families with incomes below the federal poverty threshold, despite the fact that at least one parent meets the work standard stipulated by PRWORA (Wertheimer 1999). In fact, extensive revisions to the package of income support policies currently available reflect growing recognition on the part of policymakers of a need to supplement the wages of low-income workers (see discussion in chapter 14, this volume).

New Hope represents an income support strategy based on the premise that work should be financially rewarding. New Hope was explicitly designed to reduce poverty and did not include time limits because it is assumed that an income support program should be available as long as parents are working and poor. The distinction between these two policy streams, in terms of their objectives and design, may be an important one when thinking about their potential effects on families and children.

HOW MIGHT PROGRAMS FOR PARENTS AFFECT CHILD WELL-BEING?

Although adults' employment and income are the direct targets of welfare and antipoverty policies, these policies probably affect children as well. There are two possible routes through which the policies can have an effect: by improving family resources (known as the family resource model) or through improved socialization (or family process) (Huston 1999; Mayer 1997).

Family Resources

Low family income, particularly during early and middle childhood, is associated with low performance in a number of areas, including school performance and behavior problems (Duncan and Brooks-Gunn 1997; Duncan et al. 1994; Duncan et al. 1998; Huston 1991; McLoyd 1998; Smith et al. 1997). According to the family resource model, the relation between income and child well-being is explained, in part, by the quantity and quality of goods that families consume as well as by the environments that children experience in and out of the home—sometimes called material, human, and social capital (Becker 1981; Coleman 1988; Haveman and Wolfe 1994). The quality of the home environment and, in particular, the level of cognitive stimulation (for example, a rich language environment, books and educational materials) appear to mediate the relation between income and child outcomes (Brooks-Gunn, Klebanov, and Liaw 1995; Watson et al. 1996). Increased income may allow parents to spend more on their children's skills, health, learning, and credentials, thereby contributing to their children's current achievement and future employability (Menaghan and Parcel 1991, 1995; Parcel and Menaghan 1990; Sewell and Hauser 1975).

Family income also influences parents' decisions about child care and out-of-school activities. Children's experiences in these environments play an important role in their academic achievement and social development. In general, formal, center-based child care provides more educational opportunities, and when quality is equivalent, it leads to more advanced cognitive and language development than informal child care does (Lamb 1997; NICHD Early Child Care Research Network 2000; Yoshikawa 1999). Mothers receiving welfare tend to rely on informal care arrangements (for example, relatives or friends) (Phillips 1995), but many low-income parents prefer center care and use it when it is made available (Phillips and Bridgman 1995; Quint et al. 1994). Policies that increase family resources may enable parents to use formal care arrangements that promote child well-being.

Environments outside the home are influential well beyond the preschool years. Participation in formal after-school programs that provide cognitive stimulation and positive adult interactions is associated with academic achievement among low-income children (Pierce et al. 1999; Posner and Vandell 1994, 1999). Increased income may also enable poor children to participate in organized extracurricular activities (for example, team sports or music lessons) that provide enriching experiences and supervision while parents are working. To the extent that they increase the use of high-quality child care and after-school programs, welfare and antipoverty policies can be expected to have positive effects on children's cognitive and social development.

Socialization Patterns

According to the socialization model, the link between child outcomes and parents' employment and income results from the parent's psychological well-being, parent-child relationships, and parental expectations and behavior. For low-income parents, such chronic stressors as single parenthood, life situations, financial worries, and the constant struggle to make ends meet can take a toll on well-being, which in turn diminishes their capacity to be sensitive and supportive parents (Conger et al. 1994; Conger et al. 1984; McLoyd 1990). Parents who experience economic hardship are pessimistic not only about their own lives, but also about the future of their children (Galambos and Silbereisen 1987). They are less likely to encourage college attendance and feel less competent in helping their children prepare for future work roles (Connie A. Flanagan 1988, as cited in McLoyd 1989).

On the one hand, paid employment often provides psychological benefits to low-income women, despite the many challenges and stressors that accompany it (D'Ercole 1988). In addition to increasing their financial security, employment often affords low-income, single mothers opportunities to lessen their social isolation and increase their self-esteem (Sears and Galambos 1993). On the other hand, dead-end, low-wage employment with few benefits may increase time pressure, work and family role strain, and hopelessness about the future; such employment may also have deleterious effects on parenting and child adjustment (Parcel and Menaghan 1997).

Both the resource and socialization models suggest that the effects of a social policy depend on whether family income increases, the circumstances and amount of parental employment, and the types of environment in which the child spends time when the parent is away from home. Fortunately, policymakers and researchers alike are becoming increasingly sensitive to the need to assess the impact of various social policy initiatives on child and family functioning. In fact, several recent large-scale evaluations of employment-based welfare and antipoverty programs have included measures of family and child well-being. To date, two "waves" of experimental studies of welfare and antipoverty initiatives include measures of child outcomes or parenting in an effort to understand possible influences on child development.

An early wave of studies sought to evaluate the impact of provisions contained in the 1988 Family Support Act. For example, the National Evaluation of Welfare-to-Work Strategies (NEWWS) tested the effects of mandatory employment and education activities under the federal Job Opportunities and Basic Skills (JOBS) training program (Freedman et al. 2000; Hamilton, Freedman, and McGroder 2000). Another study examined the effects of the New Chance program, which provided a variety of educational and personal development services as well as child care for young mothers (see Quint et al. 1997). Both evaluations found few and largely mixed effects on children. For example, New Chance led to increased educational attainment but did not have long-term effects on parent employment or family income. Although there were initially positive effects on parenting, there were negative effects on parents' perceptions of their child's behavior three-and-one-half years after random assignment to the program group or the control group. For school-age children, however, teachers rated boys in New Chance families more positively and girls more negatively than their counterparts in control families (Quint et al. 1997; Zaslow and Eldred 1998).

A second, more recent wave of studies evaluated the effect of key provisions of the 1996 welfare legislation. In the four years before PRWORA, many states used waivers to experiment with such policies as work-based earning supplements, mandatory employment, and time-limited welfare benefits. The Canadian Self-sufficiency Project (SSP) focuses on evaluating the effects of earning supplements (Michalopoulos et al. 2000; Morris and Michalopoulos 2000). The Minnesota Family Investment Program (MFIP) evaluates the combination of earning supplements and mandatory employment (Gennetian and Miller 2000; Knox et al. 2000). Finally, Florida's Family Transition Program (FTP) examines the combination of earning supplements and time limits (Bloom et al. 2000). Although a detailed discussion of individual studies is beyond the scope of this chapter, initial findings from these evaluations suggest that programs that increase parental employment and family resources can make a positive difference for children.

THE NEW HOPE EVALUATION

New Hope was a demonstration program representing an employment-based, income support strategy. It rested on fundamentally different assumptions than those of most welfare reform experiments. A group of community activists and experts on poverty policies founded New Hope during the late 1980s and early 1990s as an alternative to existing welfare programs. A major premise of the program was that adults who were willing to work full time should have the opportunity to do so and that regular employment should be financially rewarding (Bos et al. 1999). Rather than restricting participation to single parents or welfare recipients, the program targeted all of the working (or potentially working) poor. Individuals were eligible to apply for New Hope if they were aged eighteen or older with a family income at or below 150 percent of the federally defined poverty threshold; if they lived in one of two targeted service areas; and if they were willing to work.

The New Hope evaluation used a random assignment experimental design. Between August 1994 and December 1995, applicants living in two zip code areas of Milwaukee, Wisconsin, were randomly assigned to either a program group, which was eligible for New Hope benefits, or a control group, which was not. Both groups remained eligible for and subject to the requirements of other programs in the community. Most of the sample members had substantial experience in the program before full implementation of Wisconsin Works, the state welfare-to-work program, in 1997.

Participants in New Hope were eligible for the following benefits in any month that they worked thirty or more hours a week: a wage supplement that ensured that net income increased as they earned more; a child care subsidy for any child under the age of thirteen, which could be used for any state-licensed or county-certified child care provider, including preschool programs and extended day programs; and subsidized health insurance for the entire family. The child care and health care subsidies were commensurate with those available to some families through AFDC and Medicaid but were administered along with the wage supplements. The program also provided case management services to assist participants in job searches and other needs. If participants could not find unsubsidized employment, they were offered access to minimum-wage community service jobs, which counted toward the hours needed for New Hope benefits. (For a detailed description of the program's implementation, see Brock et al. 1997.) Although program participants were required to work full time to receive any of the benefits, the cafeteria-style system of support services allowed participants the flexibility to use the components of the program that matched their needs.

The Sample

Of 1,357 sample members, 745 (program group $N = 366$; control group $N = 379$) were identified for inclusion in a study of the program effects on families and children—the Child and Family Study (CFS)—because they had at least one child between the ages of one and ten years at baseline. Up to two focal children per family were selected. These children were between the ages of three and twelve at the time of the evaluation reported here, which was completed twenty-four months after random assignment.

CFS parents were overwhelmingly female (89.8 percent) and single heads of households (89.4 percent). A majority (55.1 percent) were African American, 29.2 percent were Hispanic, and 12.5 percent were non-Hispanic white. The ethnic background and family composition of the CFS sample were consistent with the populations particularly vulnerable to poverty. Single-mother households are much more likely to be poor than are two-parent families; and 14 percent of white children, 36 percent of African American children, and 34 percent of Hispanic children are poor (Chase-Lansdale and Brooks-Gunn 1995; Harper and Vandivere 1999; Wertheimer 1999).

At random assignment, CFS parents were, on average, twenty-nine years old. A majority (59.5 percent) had a high school education or a General Educational Development (GED) certificate, had worked full time at some point in their lives (82 percent), and were receiving some form of public assistance (80.7 percent). Slightly more than 30 percent reported no earnings in the twelve months before applying for the New Hope program, and of those with reported earnings, 88.9 percent had earned less than $10,000 (see Bos et al. 1999 for a detailed description of the sample demographic characteristics).

Data Sources

Data were compiled from parent reports, child interviews, teacher reports, and administrative data. A total of 578 parents (children, $N = 913$) were interviewed individually at home. Interviews were conducted with 230 children ages six through eight and 288 children ages nine through twelve. Teacher reports ($N = 420$) were obtained by questionnaires mailed to the child's school. Administrative data on employment, earnings, and receipt of public assistance were gathered for all 745 adults for the entire twenty-four-month period from State of Wisconsin records.

Benefit Use

A majority (80.9 percent) of CFS adults claimed at least one form of financial benefit. A total of 79.2 percent received an earnings supplement, for an average of 9.3 months; 39.9 percent used the New Hope health care subsidy, for an average of 11.6 months; 46.7 percent used the New Hope child care subsidy, for an average of 11.6 months; and 32 percent worked in at least one community service job. For people receiving benefits, the average monthly amounts were $126.18 for the earnings supplement, $281.12 for the New Hope health insurance subsidy, and $688.96 for the New Hope child care subsidy (Bos et al. 1999).

Analysis Procedures

We determined the effects of the New Hope program by comparing the program and control groups in ordinary least squares (OLS) regressions, while controlling for a number of individual and socioeconomic baseline characteristics (for example, parent's education, age, ethnic group, and gender; receipt of welfare in the prior year; earnings in the year before random assignment). We investigated whether the effects of the program differed depending on child's sex or age or parent's baseline employment status.

A statistically significant effect means that the program and control groups differed in ways that were unlikely to have occurred by chance. We also report effect sizes as one means of estimating the magnitude of the program's effects. An effect size is the difference between the program group and the control group on a particular outcome, expressed as a proportion of the standard deviation of the outcome for both groups combined (Cohen 1988). One general guideline for interpreting effect sizes is that 0.20 is small, 0.50 is medium, and 0.80 is large. It is not uncommon to observe small effect sizes in nonlaboratory research because of the many uncontrolled and unmeasured factors affecting the outcomes (Cohen 1988).

EFFECTS OF NEW HOPE ON CHILDREN'S WELL-BEING

New Hope led to increases in both employment and income for participants (see Bos et al. 1999 for details). Parents in the program group were employed for more quarters during the previous two years than were parents in the control group, and New Hope parents reported working significantly more hours than control parents. Parents in the program group also reported significantly higher average annual incomes than parents in the control group. The average annual incomes (including earnings, EITC, earnings supplement, AFDC, and food stamps) for two years were $14,050 for the program group and $12,948 for the control group.

The New Hope program had large and significant positive effects on two important aspects of children's development: their educational progress and aspirations and their social behavior. The effects occurred primarily for boys; that is, boys in the program group performed significantly better on several measures of academic and social behavior than did boys in the control group. The means are shown in table 10.1 (see Huston et al. 2001 for a detailed discussion of the effects of New Hope on the indicators of child well-being).

Teachers' assessments indicated that children in New Hope families were performing significantly better in school than were those in control families (see figure 10.1).[1] Teachers compared the children in the study with others in the same classroom on reading skill, math skill, intellectual functioning, motivation, oral communication, classroom behavior, and parental encouragement. Teachers also rated conformity to classroom rules and routines (such as "behaves so as not to disturb peers"), ability to work and complete tasks independently (such as "remains on task with minimal supervision"), and ability to make transitions without becoming distracted (such as "moves quickly to next activity"). Boys in the program group had significantly better classroom behavior than did boys in the control group (see figure 10.1, which indicates the amount by which the scores of children in the program group exceeded the scores of children in the control group). Teachers did not know the purposes of the study or that children and their families were involved in New Hope, so these ratings were not likely to have been influenced by teachers' conceptions about New Hope.

Children ages six through twelve were asked about their occupational aspirations (what job they would like to have) and expectations (what job they thought they would have) (Cook et al. 1996). Responses were coded for occupational prestige (Nakeo and Treas 1990). Educational expectations were assessed for children ages nine through twelve by asking how sure they were that they would finish high school, go to college, and finish college (Cook et al. 1996). Boys in New Hope families were more confident about finishing college, and expected to have jobs with higher levels of prestige, than boys in the control group families. The amount that the educational expectations and occupational aspirations of boys in the New Hope program exceeded those of boys in the control group is shown in figure 10.1.

New Hope also had positive effects on social behavior and behavior problems, primarily for boys (see figure 10.2). Teachers rated boys in New Hope families significantly higher than boys in control families on the Positive Behavior Scale, which measures compliance and self-control (for example, "thinks before he or she acts"), competence and sensitivity (for example, "gets along well with other children"), and autonomy (for example, "tries to do things for him- or herself") (Quint et al. 1997). Parents' ratings followed a similar pattern, although the difference between the program group and the control group was not statistically significant.

TABLE 10.1 / Children's Educational Progress and Social Behavior, New Hope Program

Outcome	Boys					Girls				
	Program Group	Control Group	Difference	Effect Size	N	Program Group	Control Group	Difference	Effect Size	N
Education and aspiration										
Teacher report										
SSRS academic subscale	3.27	2.95	0.32**	0.33	208	3.43	3.31	0.12	0.12	208
Classroom behavior	3.70	3.30	0.40**	0.38	208	4.10	4.10	0.00	-0.02	208
Child report										
Expects to attend college	4.33	3.76	0.57**	0.49	137	4.03	4.18	-0.15	-0.13	150
Expects to finish college	4.09	3.50	0.60**	0.46	137	3.94	3.93	0.01	0.01	150
Occupational aspirations	59.23	54.18	5.05**	0.29	241	56.42	57.87	-1.45	-0.08	251
Occupational expectations	58.23	54.09	4.14*	0.24	241	57.23	56.41	0.80	0.05	251
Positive social behavior										
Teacher report, total	3.62	3.29	0.33***	0.50	208	3.75	3.72	0.03	0.05	208
Parent report, total	3.95	3.87	0.08*	0.22	292	3.95	4.03	-0.08	-0.17	271
Problem behavior										
Teacher report, total	2.30	2.60	-0.30***	-0.48	208	2.22	2.10	0.13	0.21	208
Externalizing	2.07	2.50	-0.43***	-0.51	208	2.07	1.85	0.22**	0.27	208
Hyperactivity	2.64	2.95	-0.31**	-0.39	208	2.35	2.23	0.11	0.14	208
Discipline actions	2.87	3.30	-0.43**	-0.30	208	2.39	2.02	0.37**	0.26	208
Parent report, total for six-through-twelve-year-olds	4.57	4.84	-0.27	-0.22	164	4.76	4.52	0.23	0.19	161

Source: Huston et al. 2001.
* $p < .10$. ** $p < .05$. *** $p < .01$, two-tail.

FIGURE 10.1 / Teacher and Child Assessments of Child Outcomes, New Hope
Program (Percentage)

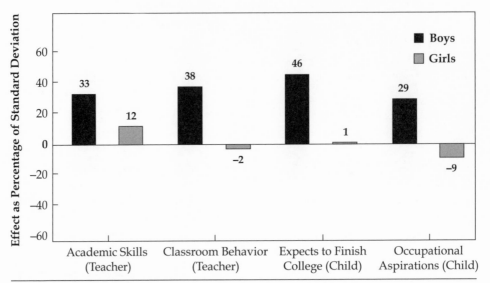

Source: Huston et al. 2001.
Note: Percentages are amount by which scores of children in the program group exceeded the
scores of children in the control group.

Teachers reported that boys in the program group had fewer "externalizing" problems (for example, "is aggressive toward people or objects," "has temper tantrums")
and less hyperactivity (for example, "is easily distracted," "acts impulsively") than
did control group boys.[2] Program group parents also reported that their boys had
fewer behavior problems than did control parents, but the difference was not significant. Teachers reported disciplining boys in the program group significantly less
often than boys in the control group (see table 10.1).

The picture for girls was more mixed. There were few effects of the program
on girls' social behavior, but those that did occur suggest that the program had
negative effects. Teachers rated girls in New Hope families as having more externalizing problems and reported disciplining them more frequently than they did
control group girls (see table 10.1). The differences in program effects between
boys and girls should be put in the context of overall gender differences. Girls
in both the program and control groups were generally doing better in school,
had better study skills, evidenced more positive social behavior, and displayed
fewer behavior problems than boys did. The New Hope program brought boys'
levels of academic performance and social behavior closer to the average levels
for girls in both groups.

In summary, two years after their families were randomly assigned to the New
Hope program, boys in New Hope families were making better academic progress,

FIGURE 10.2 / Teacher and Parent Assessments of Child Outcomes, New Hope
Program (Percentage)

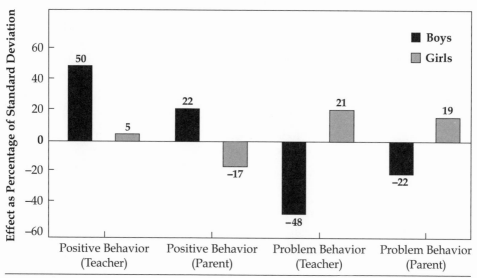

Source: Huston et al. 2001.
Note: Percentages are amount by which scores of children in the program group were higher or lower than the scores of children in the control group.

had better classroom behavior skills, had higher occupational aspirations and educational expectations, and displayed more positive social behavior in conjunction with fewer behavior problems than boys in control group families. The rigorous experimental design of the New Hope evaluation ensures that program and control groups did not differ systematically on important characteristics at the beginning of the study and that differences between the two groups can be attributed to the New Hope intervention.

These program effects are sufficiently large to have social significance as well as statistical significance. Using Jacob Cohen's (1988) criteria, many of the effects of the New Hope program were "small" to "medium." The largest effect sizes occurred for teacher ratings of boys' overall positive and problem behavior measures. Both had effect sizes of 0.50 or greater (see table 10.1), indicating that the average boy in the New Hope group scored above (for positive behavior) or below (for behavior problems) 69 percent of control group boys. For academic performance and aspirations, the effect sizes for boys fell between the small and medium levels. The average boy in a New Hope family scored above 62 percent of the control group boys on academic achievement and above approximately 69 percent of boys in the control group on their plans to attend college (Cohen 1988). These differences are sufficiently large to be socially important.

WHY DID NEW HOPE HAVE POSITIVE EFFECTS ON CHILDREN?

Earlier in this chapter, we describe two models for understanding the indirect effect of an antipoverty program on children's development: the family resource model and the socialization model. We collected several measures designed to test these two possible pathways of influence.

Family Resources

As mentioned, New Hope led to increases in employment and to modest increases in total family income. The figures for family income, however, do not include the New Hope child care subsidy, which added substantial resources for some families. In fact, program children spent more time in formal center-based child care for preschool and elementary school children, spent more time in extended day care for elementary school children, and were more likely to participate in such organized activities as sports, recreation and community centers, lessons, and clubs (see Bos et al. 1999 for details).

More specifically, children of parents in the program group spent almost twice as many months (6 months, as opposed to 3.2 months for the control group) in center-based care (including child care centers, preschools, and Head Start) and more than twice as many months (1.87, as opposed to 0.7 months) in school-based, extended day care than did children in control families. For both center-based and extended day care, the program-control group differences were statistically significant.

Although program families used center-based care more than control families for both boys and girls, the difference was significantly larger for girls. By contrast, program families used extended day care much more for boys than for girls.

Parents were asked how often their six-through-twelve-year-old children participated in five organized or structured activities involving adult supervision (such as sports, lessons, club and youth group activities). Children ages nine through twelve were also asked about participation in these activities. Parents in the program group reported significantly higher levels of participation in structured activities for their nine-through-twelve-year-old children than did parents in the control group. Program group parents also reported higher levels of participation in structured activities for their six-through-eight-year-old children than did control parents, but the difference was not significant. Among the nine-through-twelve-year-old children, those in the program group reported greater participation in clubs and youth groups than did control group children. These differences were somewhat larger for boys than for girls (see Huston et al. 2001).

In general, the data provide support for a family resources model. New Hope led to modest increases in parental employment and total family income and provided access to substantial child care and health care subsidies (see Bos et al. 1999). Children in New Hope program families spent more time in center-based and extended-day care, and they participated more frequently in structured out-of-school activities. It appears that greater economic resources, coupled with the availability of child care subsidies to New Hope participants, allowed parents to place their children in more formal, structured activities outside the home. These findings are consistent with other studies of welfare-to-work programs: when child care subsidies are available, parents use more formal child care arrangements (Zaslow, Oldman, et al. 1998).

Participation in formal after-school care programs that provide cognitive stimulation and positive adult interactions is associated with academic achievement and low levels of behavior problems, particularly among low-income children (Pierce et al. 1999; Posner and Vandell 1994, 1999). Conversely, early adolescent children without adult supervision during their out-of-school hours are at risk for behavior problems and poor adjustment, particularly if they live in low-income families or unsafe neighborhoods (Pettit et al. 1999; Marshall et al. 1997).

Socialization

To test the possibility that New Hope influenced children through specific socialization pathways, we included measures of parents' psychological well-being, parent-child relations, and parenting practices. Although New Hope had modest effects on some measures of parents' psychological well-being, it had little effect on parenting or parent-child relations.

To measure parents' psychological well-being, we included indicators of both enduring personality dispositions and characteristics likely to vary with situations and environmental contexts.[3] The results indicate mixed effects. Parents in the program group reported significantly greater hope of pursuing and meeting their goals, lower stress, and more social support than did parents in the control group, but they also reported significantly more time pressure. There were no program effects on worries about finances, depression, self-esteem, or locus of control (see Bos et al. 1999 for details).

Parents responded to questions that assessed parental warmth and control (Statistics Canada 1995), monitoring, and aspirations and expectations for their child's educational attainment (Medrich et al. 1982). Warmth (conveying positive feelings and praising the child) was also rated by observers in the home, using items from the HOME measure (Caldwell and Bradley 1984). Children ages six through twelve were asked about their positive relations (for example, "Your parent spends a lot of time talking with you") and negative relations (for example, "Your parent argues with you a lot") with their primary caregiver (McLoyd et al. 1994). There were virtually no overall effects of New Hope on parenting as perceived by the parent, the observer, or the child (see Bos et al. 1999 for details).

In short, there was little or no support for socialization processes as a pathway between adult participation in New Hope and child outcomes. Despite the fact that New Hope parents reported faring better than control group parents on some indexes of psychological well-being (greater hope and social support, along with a lower level of stress), these positive effects did not translate into measurable changes in parenting and parent-child relations. Socialization appeared to be less of an avenue for improvement in children's well-being than additional resources.

CONCLUSION AND POLICY IMPLICATIONS

Overall, the New Hope findings demonstrate that, for low-income families, a flexible and extensive package of supports designed to make work pay not only can increase adult employment and income but also can have positive effects on children's academic and social functioning. Parents' participation in New Hope had large and generally positive effects on their children's academic and social behavior in school and on the children's own aspirations for educational and occupational attainment. These findings support the idea that a work-based, income support program for parents that increases income as well as employment can have positive effects on children. Part of the appeal of New Hope is the flexibility of its design. It offered participants a package of services from which they could select the components that matched their needs. As welfare policies shift toward requiring all (or almost all) segments of the population to seek work, success will likely hinge on instituting policies that accommodate the needs of diverse groups of adults and families. The increased flexibility provided by PRWORA allows states to tailor programs for a wide range of families.

The potential importance of work and family supports for the well-being of children is highlighted when the effects of New Hope are considered within the context of emerging findings from the other experimental evaluations described earlier. The Next Generation study compares impacts on children and families across this set of programs (including New Hope), which have diverse policy features (Manpower Demonstration Research Corporation 2000). Although New Hope differed in several respects from most welfare reforms, it is noteworthy that other programs that encouraged employment by providing earning supplements (such as SSP and MFIP) had similar, positive effects on children's school achievement and social behavior. At the same time, programs that included mandatory employment services without mechanisms to increase family resources substantially (such as FTP and NEWWS) had few and mixed effects on children (see Morris et al. 2001). Taken together, these findings suggest that such policies as those contained in New Hope, which promote employment while increasing family resources, can have positive effects on child well-being. Future work from the Next Generation study will focus on identifying the specific mechanisms involved in program effects on children.

Although we cannot determine with certainty exactly why children reacted positively to the New Hope program, the findings point to child care and adult-supervised activities as one important pathway. When parents spend increased time working away from home, the activities and support systems for their children are likely to play an important role in determining the effects on children. New Hope provided the opportunity for parents to use formal, center-based child care, and many parents took advantage of that opportunity. Child care is critical to the way employment-based initiatives affect families and children. Approximately two-thirds of the children in families receiving welfare are younger than age six (Kisker and Ross 1997).

As more of these parents are ushered into the workforce, more young children are likely to be placed in nonparental care (Wertheimer 1999). Participation in formal, early child care and education programs can help to improve school readiness for children from families receiving welfare (Zaslow, Oldman, et al. 1998).

Child care and adult-supervised activities are important for school-age children as well as for preschoolers. Many New Hope parents used center-based child care during the after-school hours and during school vacations for their school-age children. Subsidies could also be used for other structured after-school programs. As children move through middle childhood, they begin to "age out" of child care, but they continue to profit from programs and activities that provide adult supervision, opportunities for positive peer contacts, and opportunities to learn new skills. These findings suggest that child care, extended day care, after-school activities, and other community programs for youth may significantly alter developmental trajectories for children in low-income families (Behrman 1999). Child care subsidies play a vital role in making affordable, high-quality child care and educationally enriched programs available to poor families (Cherlin 1995).

Legislation under PRWORA increases the availability of child care block grant funds and gives states more flexibility in designing child care assistance programs, yet it is still unclear how states are responding to these changes. Some states are not using all of their available funds. Because market rate surveys and reimbursement at the seventy-fifth percentile of child care rates are no longer required, states' efforts to cut costs and increase the availability of subsidies may result in compromises in the quality of care available (Zaslow, Oldman, et al. 1998).

Experimentally based research in this area can be used to inform states' efforts to reach certain segments of the poor population. In the New Hope evaluation, the differing effects on boys and girls highlight the importance of examining how pathways and impacts differ across subgroups. These effects may also vary by ethnic group, by kind of barrier to employment, by family composition, by age and marital status of the adults, and by certain child characteristics (such as special needs).

The positive effects of New Hope were much stronger for boys than for girls. In one respect, this is an encouraging finding because boys, on average, are at greater risk than girls for academic failure and problem behavior. One reason for the greater effect on boys was suggested in ethnographic interviews with a random sample of New Hope families and control group families (Weisner et al. 1999). Parents worried that their sons, more than their daughters, would become involved in delinquent activities. Acting on this worry, parents may have expended more effort and invested more resources in ensuring that boys had alternatives to hanging out with unsupervised peers after school. We know that boys were enrolled in extended day care more often than girls and that they spent more time in community and recreation centers. These supervised contexts may have been particularly effective because of boys' vulnerability when they are not supervised.

Boys and girls may have also responded differently to the role models provided by parents participating in New Hope. Overall, New Hope led boys and their parents to have higher aspirations for boys' futures, but for girls and their parents it had no effect or led to lowered aspirations. Children learn about the occupational world at home, and parental occupations influence children's occupational expectations (Furlong et al. 1996). Given that approximately 90 percent of the parents in our sample were women, girls may have used their participating parent as a role model more than boys did. In general, girls' aspirations are similar in status to the status of their mothers' occupations (Trice and Knapp 1992; Trice and Tillapaugh 1991). For the low-income families involved in New Hope, the realities of the low-wage employment world for women may have been apparent to New Hope daughters, whereas sons may not have considered their mothers' employment experiences as relevant to their own futures. The mothers, too, may have been influenced by this assumption. Thus their expectations for their sons' futures may have been higher than their expectations for their daughters' futures, given that most of the jobs held by the mothers were relatively low in status and wages.

The possibility that girls may relate their mothers' employment activities and experiences to their own lives may also explain the more frequent behavior and discipline problems at school for girls from New Hope families, compared to girls in the control group. The program girls may have been exhibiting increased assertiveness in response to their mothers' active work efforts. It is also possible that girls have responsibility for more household chores when mothers increase employment, but when we asked both parents and children about responsibilities for housework and sibling care, we found no differences between program and control children of either sex.

Although the findings presented here provide stronger support for a resource-based model of influence than for a socialization model, there is nonexperimental evidence that socialization processes within families mediated some of the effects of income and parental employment on children's well-being. In both program and control families, economic security predicted parents' psychological well-being and positive parenting, which in turn predicted children's positive social behavior and freedom from behavior problems (Mistry et al., forthcoming). Given these findings and pending replication in other data sets, the links among employment, economic hardship, and parenting have important implications for welfare reform. So much attention is focused on promoting transitions into the labor force that we often overlook the fact that many working poor families have multiple jobs and long commutes but still realize no substantial improvement in their economic well-being. New Hope offered supports that permitted parents to improve their economic well-being and to balance work with their family responsibilities.

Debates surrounding recent reforms of the welfare system have captured the national spotlight. The intense focus of current initiatives on enforcing workforce participation, reducing welfare rolls, and changing adults' behaviors signals a significant departure from antipoverty strategies and pre-PRWORA welfare programs. Discussions of these new reforms often contain little acknowledgement that employment per se does not ensure exemption from poverty (Burtless 1997). At the very least, we should be certain that new policies do not increase the considerable risks for health problems, academic failure, and behavior problems that children living in chronic poverty already face. However, "doing no harm" should not be sufficient. Income poverty does not occur in isolation; it is one example of a poverty cofactor that has consistently been shown to put children at a developmental disadvantage (Chase-Lansdale and Brooks-Gunn 1995; Rank 2000). Other examples include limited enrichment opportunities, either at home or at school, and restricted access to adequate child care and health care, including preventive care (Brooks-Gunn et al. 1999; McLoyd 1998). This suggests that to be most effective in enhancing the well-being of low-income children, policy initiatives should take a multilevel approach. That is, they should be designed to address the adverse consequences of socioeconomic disadvantage across several areas of influence in a child's life, including both the home environment and other environments to which the child is exposed (such as child care settings and schools). Both society and the individuals affected will reap benefits if such policies can make positive contributions to children's development. The New Hope evaluation indicates that an employment-based, income support policy can make some positive contributions to children's well-being. Although this program strongly encouraged work, it also provided support systems that many poor working families need to sustain themselves and their families.

NOTES

1. Teachers ranked children on predetermined scales of school performance, in this instance, the academic subscale of the Social Skills Rating System (Gresham and Elliott 1990) and the Classroom Behavior Scale (Wright and Huston 1995).

2. As measured in the Problem Behavior Scale of the Social Skills Rating System (Gresham and Elliott 1990).

3. Personality measures included self-esteem, measured by the Rosenberg Self-Esteem Scale (Rosenberg 1979), external locus of control, measured by the Pearlin Mastery Scale (Pearlin et al. 1981), and depressive symptoms, assessed with the CES-D (Center for Epidemiological Studies-Depression) scale (Radloff 1977). The remaining scales were designed to measure aspects of well-being that might be somewhat more responsive to changes in social context and economic circumstances. The State Hope Scale (Snyder et al. 1996) assesses hope about achieving goals (for example, "I am meeting the goals I set for myself"). Perceived social support was assessed by asking whether or not the person had received programmatic advice or assistance and whether or not the person had received emotional support or counseling in the previous two years. Time pressure was assessed by questions about how often the respondent felt rushed in general and how often he or she had extra time. Stress was assessed with an item asking how often during the past month the respondent had felt stressed "much or almost all of the time." Financial worry contained six questions about how much the respondent worried about paying bills, job security, having medical coverage, paying for food, affording adequate housing, and general financial health.

REFERENCES

Becker, Gary S. 1981. *A Treatise on the Family*. Cambridge, Mass: Harvard University Press.

Behrman, Richard E., ed. 1999. "When School Is Out." *Future of Children* 9(2): 1–7.

Bloom, Dan, James J. Kemple, Pamela Morris, Susan Scrivener, Nandita Verma, and Richard Hendra. 2000. *The Family Transition Program: Final Report on Florida's Initial Time-Limited Welfare Program*. New York: Manpower Demonstration Research Corporation.

Bos, Johannes M., Aletha C. Huston, Robert C. Granger, Greg J. Duncan, Thomas W. Brock, and Vonnie C. McLoyd. 1999. *New Hope for People with Low Incomes: Two-Year Results of a Program to Reduce Poverty and Reform Welfare.* New York: Manpower Demonstration Research Corporation.

Brock, Thomas W., Fred Doolittle, Veronica Fellerath, and Michael Wiseman. 1997. *Creating New Hope: Implementation of a Program to Reduce Poverty and Reform Welfare.* New York: Manpower Demonstration Research Corporation.

Brooks-Gunn, Jeanne, Pia Rebello Britto, and Christy Brady. 1999. "Struggling to Make Ends Meet: Poverty and Child Development." In *Parenting and Child Development in "Nontraditional" Families*, edited by M. E. Lamb. Mahwah, N.J.: Lawrence Erlbaum.

Brooks-Gunn, Jeanne, Greg J. Duncan, and Nancy Maritato. 1997. "Poor Families, Poor Outcomes: The Well-being of Children and Youth." In *Consequences of Growing Up Poor*, edited by G. J. Duncan and Jeanne Brooks-Gunn. New York: Russell Sage Foundation.

Brooks-Gunn, Jeanne, Pamela K. Klebanov, and Fong-ruey Liaw. 1995. "The Learning, Physical, and Emotional Environment of the Home in the Context of Poverty: The Infant Health and Development Program." *Child and Youth Services Review* 17: 251–76.

Burtless, Gary T. 1997. "Welfare Recipients' Job Skills and Employment Prospects." *Future of Children* 7(1): 39–51.

Caldwell, Bettye M., and Robert H. Bradley. 1984. *Home Observation for Measurement of the Environment.* Little Rock: University of Arkansas Press.

Chase-Lansdale, P. Lindsay, and Jeanne Brooks-Gunn, eds. 1995. *Escape from Poverty: What Makes a Difference for Children?* New York: Cambridge University Press.

Cherlin, Andrew J. 1995. "Policy Issues of Child Care." In *Escape from Poverty: What Makes a Difference for Children?* edited by P. Lindsay Chase-Lansdale and Jeanne Brooks-Gunn. New York: Cambridge University Press.

Cohen, Jacob. 1988. *Statistical Power Analysis for the Behavioral Sciences.* 2d ed. Hillsdale, N.J.: Lawrence Erlbaum.

Coleman, James S. 1988. "Social Capital in the Creation of Human Capital." *American Journal of Sociology* 94 (supplement): S95–S120.

Conger, Rand D., Glen H. Elder Jr., Frederick O. Lorenz, Ronald L. Simons, and Les B. Whitbeck. 1994. *Families in Troubled Times: Adapting to Change in Rural America.* New York: Aldine de Gruyter.

Conger, Rand D., John A. McCarty, Ronald K. Yang, B. Lahey, and J. P. Kropp. 1984. "Perception of Child, Child-rearing Values, and Emotional Distress as Mediating Links Between Environmental Stressors and Observed Maternal Behavior." *Child Development* 55: 2234–47.

Cook, Thomas D., Mary B. Church, Subira Ajanaku Jr., William R. Shadish, K. Jeong-Ran, and Robert Cohen. 1996. "The Development of Occupational Aspirations and Expectations Among Inner-city Boys." *Child Development* 67: 3368–85.

Dalaker, Joseph, and Mary Naifeh. 1998. *Poverty in the United States: 1997.* Current Population Reports, Series P60-201. Washington: U.S. Bureau of the Census.

D'Ercole, Ann. 1988. "Single Mothers: Stress, Coping, and Social Support." *Journal of Community Psychology* 16: 41–54.

Duncan, Greg J., and Jeanne Brooks-Gunn, eds. 1997. *Consequences of Growing Up Poor.* New York: Russell Sage Foundation.

Duncan, Greg J., Jeanne Brooks-Gunn, and Pamela K. Klebanov. 1994. "Economic Deprivation and Early Childhood Development." *Child Development* 65: 296–318.

Duncan, Greg J., W. Jean Yeung, Jeanne Brooks-Gunn, and Judith R. Smith. 1998. "How Much Does Childhood Poverty Affect the Life Chances of Children?" *American Sociological Review* 63: 406–23.

Freedman, Stephen J., Daniel Friedlander, Gayle Hamilton, Joann Rock, Marisa Mitchell, Jodi Nudelman, Amanda Schweder, and Laura Storto. 2000. *Evaluation of Alternative Welfare-to-Work Approaches: Two-year Impacts for Eleven Programs.* National Evaluation of Welfare-to-Work Strategies. Washington: U.S. Department of Health and Human Services.

Furlong, Andy, Andy Biggart, and Fred Cartmel. 1996. "Neighborhoods, Opportunity Structures, and Occupational Aspirations." *Sociology* 30: 551–65.

Galambos, Nancy L., and Rainer K. Silbereisen. 1987. "Income Change, Parental Life Outlook, and Adolescent Expectations for Job Success." *Journal of Marriage and the Family* 49: 141–49.

Gennetian, Lisa, and Cynthia Miller. 2000. *Reforming Welfare and Rewarding Work: Final Report on the Minnesota Family Investment Program.* New York: Manpower Demonstration Research Corporation.

Greenstein, Robert, and Isaac Shapiro. 1998. *New Findings on the Effects of the EITC.* Washington, D.C.: Center on Budget and Policy Priorities.

Gresham, Frank M., and Stephen N. Elliott. 1990. *Social Skills Rating System Manual.* Circle Pines, Minn.: American Guidance Service.

Hamilton, Gayle, Stephen Freedman, Sharon M. McGroder. 2000. *Do Mandatory Welfare-to-Work Programs Affect the Well-being of Children?* National Evaluation of Welfare-to-Work Strategies: A Synthesis of Child Research Conducted as Part of the National Evaluation of Welfare-to-Work Strategies. New York: Manpower Demonstration Research Corporation.

Harper, Michelle, and Sharon Vandivere. 1999. *Poverty, Welfare, and Children: A Summary of the Data.* Research brief. Washington, D.C.: Child Trends.

Haveman, Robert, and Barbara Wolfe. 1994. *Succeeding Generations: On the Effects of Investments in Children.* New York: Russell Sage Foundation.

Huston, Aletha C., ed. 1991. *Children in Poverty: Child Development and Public Policy.* New York: Cambridge University Press.

———. 1999. "Effect of Poverty on Children." In *Child Psychology: A Handbook of Contemporary Issues,* edited by C. Tamis-Lemonda and L. Balter. New York: Garland Press.

Huston, Aletha C., Greg J. Duncan, Robert Granger, Johannes Bos, Vonnie McLoyd, Rashmita Mistry, Danielle Crosby, Christina Gibson, Katherine Magnuson, Jennifer Romich, and A. Ventura. 2001. "Work-based Anti-Poverty Programs for Parents Can Enhance the School Performance and Social Behavior of Children." *Child Development* 72: 318–36.

Huston, Aletha C., Vonnie C. McLoyd, and Cynthia Garcia Coll. 1994. "Children and Poverty: Issues in Contemporary Research." *Child Development* 65: 275–82.

Kisker, Ellen E., and Christine M. Ross. 1997. "Arranging Child Care." *Future of Children* 7: 99–109.

Knox, Virginia, Cynthia Miller, and Lisa Gennetian. 2000. *Reforming Welfare and Rewarding Work: A Summary of the Final Report on the Minnesota Family Investment Program.* New York: Manpower Demonstration Research Corporation.

Lamb, Michael E. 1997. "Nonparental Child Care: Context, Quality, Correlates, and Consequences." In *Child Psychology in Practice*. Vol. 4, *Handbook of Child Psychology*, 5th ed., edited by W. Damon, I. Sigel, and K. A. Renninger. New York: John Wiley.

Manpower Demonstration Research Corporation. 2000. "The Next Generation Project: Analysis of the Effects of Welfare, Employment, and Anti-poverty Programs and Policies on Children and Families." Briefing materials. New York: MDRC (January 13).

Marshall, Nancy L., Cynthia Garcia Coll, Fern Marx, Kathleen McCartney, Nancy Keefe, and Jennifer Ruh. 1997. "After-school Time and Children's Behavioral Adjustment." *Merrill-Palmer Quarterly* 43(3): 497–514.

Mayer, Susan E. 1997. *What Money Can't Buy: Family Income and Children's Life Chances*. Cambridge Mass.: Harvard University Press.

McLoyd, Vonnie C. 1989. "Socialization and Development in a Changing Economy: The Effects of Paternal Job and Income Loss on Children." *American Psychologist* 44: 293–302.

———. 1990. "The Impact of Economic Hardship on Black Families and Children: Psychological Distress, Parenting, and Socioemotional Development." *Child Development* 61: 311–46.

———. 1998. "Socioeconomic Disadvantage and Child Development." *American Psychologist* 53: 185–204.

McLoyd, Vonnie C., Toby E. Jayaratne, Rosario Ceballo, and Julio Borquez. 1994. "Unemployment and Work Interruption Among African American Single Mothers: Effects on Parenting and Adolescent Socioemotional Functioning." *Child Development* 65: 562–89.

Medrich, Elliot A., Judith Roizen, Victor Rubin, and Stuart Buckley. 1982. *The Serious Business of Growing Up: A Study of Children's Lives Outside School*. Berkeley: University of California Press.

Menaghan, Elizabeth G., and Toby L. Parcel. 1991. "Determining Children's Home Environments: The Impact of Maternal Characteristics and Current Occupational and Family Conditions." *Journal of Marriage and the Family* 53: 417–31.

———. 1995. "Social Sources of Change in Children's Home Environments: The Effects of Parental Occupational Experiences and Family Conditions. *Journal of Marriage and the Family* 57: 69–84.

Michalopoulos, Charles, Dave Card, Lisa Gennetian, Kristine Harknett, and P. K. Robins. 2000. *The Self-sufficiency Project at Thirty-six Months: Effects of a Financial Work Incentive on Employment and Income*. New York: Manpower Demonstration Research Corporation.

Mistry, Rashmita S., Elizabeth A. Vandewater, Aletha C. Huston, and Vonnie C. McLoyd. Forthcoming. "Economic Well-being and Children's Social Adjustment: The Role of Family Process in an Ethnically Diverse Low-income Sample." *Child Development*.

Morris, Pamela A., Aletha C. Huston, Greg J. Duncan, Danielle A. Crosby, and Johannes M. Bos. 2001. *How Welfare and Work Policies Affect Children: A Synthesis of Research*. New York: Manpower Demonstration Research Corporation.

Morris, Pamela A., and Charles Michalopoulos. 2000. *The Self-sufficiency Project at Thirty-six Months: Effects on Children of a Program That Increased Employment and Income*. New York: Manpower Demonstration Research Corporation.

Nakeo, Keiko, and Judith Treas. 1990. *Computing 1989 Occupational Prestige Scores*. Methodological Report, General Social Survey 70. Irvine: Department of Sociology, University of California.

NICHD Early Child Care Research Network. 2000. "The Relation of Child Care to Cognitive and Language Development." *Child Development* 71: 960–80.

Parcel, Toby L., and Elizabeth G. Menaghan. 1990. "Maternal Working Conditions and Children's Verbal Facility: Studying the Intergenerational Transmission of Inequality from Mothers to Young Children." *Social Psychology Quarterly* 53: 132–47.

———. 1997. "Effects of Low-wage Employment on Family Well-being." *Future of Children* 7(1): 116–21.

Pearlin, Leonard I., Morton A. Lieberman, G. Elizabeth Menaghan, and Joseph T. Mullan. 1981. "The Stress Process." *Journal of Health and Social Behavior* 22(3): 337–56.

Pettit, Gregory S., John E. Bates, Kenneth A. Dodge, and David W. Meece. 1999. "The Impact of After-school Peer Contact on Early Adolescent Externalizing Problems Is Moderated by Parental Monitoring, Perceived Neighborhood Safety, and Prior Adjustment." *Child Development* 70: 768–78.

Phillips, Deborah A. 1995. *Child Care for Low-income Families: Summary of Two Workshops.* Washington, D.C.: National Academy Press.

Phillips, Deborah A., and Anne Bridgman, eds. 1995. *New Findings on Children, Families, and Economic Self-sufficiency.* Washington D.C.: National Academy Press.

Pierce, Kim M., Jill V. Hamm, and Deborah L. Vandell. 1999. "Experiences in After-school Programs and Children's Adjustment in First-grade Classrooms." *Child Development* 70: 756–67.

Posner, Jill K., and Deborah L. Vandell. 1994. "Low-income Children's After-school Care: Are There Beneficial Effects of After-school Programs?" *Child Development* 65: 440–56.

———. 1999. "After-school Activities and the Development of Low-income Urban Children: A Longitudinal Study." *Developmental Psychology* 35: 868–79.

Quint, Janet C., Johannes M. Bos, and Denise Polit. 1997. *New Chance: Final Report on a Comprehensive Program for Young Mothers in Poverty and Their Children.* New York: Manpower Demonstration Research Corporation.

Quint, Janet C., Denise F. Polit, Johannes M. Bos, and George Cave. 1994. *New Chance: Interim Findings on a Comprehensive Program for Disadvantaged Young Mothers and Their Children.* New York: Manpower Demonstration Research Corporation.

Radloff, Lenore. 1977. "The CES-D Scale: A Self-report Depression Scale for Research in the General Population." *Applied Psychological Measurement* 1(3): 385–401.

Rank, Mark R. 2000. Poverty and Economic Hardship in Families. In *Handbook of Family Diversity,* edited by D. H. Demo, K. R. Allen, and M. A. Fine. New York: Oxford University Press.

Rosenberg, Morris. 1979. *Rosenberg Self-esteem Scale.* New York: Basic Books.

Sears, Heather A., and Nancy L. Galambos. 1993. "The Employed Mother's Well-being." In *The Employed Mother and the Family Context,* edited by J. Frankel. Focus on Women Series, vol. 14. New York: Springer.

Sewell, William, and Robert Hauser. 1975. *Education, Occupation, and Earnings: Achievement in the Early Career.* New York: Academic Press.

Smeeding, Timothy M., Katherin E. Ross, and Michael O'Connor. 1999. *The Economic Impact of the Earned Income Tax Credit (EITC): Consumption, Savings, and Debt.* Working paper 13.

Syracuse, N.Y.: Center for Policy Research, Maxwell School of Citizenship and Public Affairs, Syracuse University.

Smith, Judith R., Jeanne Brooks-Gunn, and Pamela K. Klebanov. 1997. "Consequences of Living in Poverty for Young Children's Cognitive and Verbal Ability and Early School Achievement." In *Consequences of Growing Up Poor*, edited by Greg J. Duncan and Jeanne Brooks-Gunn. New York: Russell Sage Foundation.

Snyder, C. R., Susie C. Sympson, Florence C. Ybasco, Tyrone F. Borders, Michael A. Babyak, and Raymond L. Higgins. 1996. "Development and Validation of the State Hope Scale." *Journal of Personality and Social Psychology* 70: 321–35.

Statistics Canada. 1995. *Self-sufficiency Project: Self-complete Questionnaire, Parents.* Montreal: Statistics Canada.

Trice, Ashton D., and Linda Knapp. 1992. "Relationship of Children's Career Aspirations to Parents' Occupations." *Journal of Genetic Psychology* 153: 355–57.

Trice, Ashton D., and Paula Tillapaugh. 1991. "Children's Estimates of Their Parents' Job Satisfaction." *Psychological Reports* 69: 63–6.

Watson, Janine E., Russell Kirby, Kelly Kelleher, and Robert H. Bradley. 1996. "Effects of Poverty on Home Environment: An Analysis of Three-year Outcome Data for Low Birth Weight Premature Infants." *Journal of Pediatric Psychology* 21: 419–31.

Weisner, Thomas S., Lucinda Bernheimer, Victor Espinosa, Christina Gibson, Eboni Howard, Katherine Magnuson, Jennifer Romich, Devarati Syam, and Eli Lieber. 1999. "From the Living Rooms and Daily Routines of the Economically Poor: An Ethnographic Study of the New Hope Effects on Families and Children." Paper presented at the meeting of the Society for Research in Child Development. Albuquerque (April 1999).

Wertheimer, Richard F. 1999. *Working Poor Families with Children.* Summary report (February). Washington, D.C.: Child Trends.

Wright, John C., and Aletha C. Huston. 1995. *Effects of Educational TV Viewing of Lower Income Preschoolers on Academic Skills, School Readiness, and School Adjustment One to Three Years Later.* Lawrence, Kans.: Center for Research on the Influences of Television on Children.

Yoshikawa, Hirokazu. 1999. "Welfare Dynamics, Support Services, Mothers' Earnings, and Child Cognitive Development: Implications for Contemporary Welfare Reform." *Child Development* 70: 779–801.

Zaslow, Martha J., and Carolyn A. Eldred. 1998. *Parenting Behavior in a Sample of Young Mothers in Poverty: Results of the New Chance Observational Study.* New York: Manpower Demonstration Research Corporation.

Zaslow, Martha J., E. Oldman, Kristin A. Moore, and Ellen Magenheim. 1998. "Welfare Families' Use of Early Childhood Care and Education Programs and Implications for Their Children's Development." *Early Childhood Research Quarterly* 13: 535–63.

Zaslow, Martha J., Kathryn Tout, S. Smith, and Kristin A. Moore. 1998. "Implications of the 1996 Welfare Legislation for Children: A Research Perspective." *Social Policy Report: Society for Research in Child Development* 12(3): 1–34.

Chapter 11

How Families View and Use Lump-Sum Payments from the Earned Income Tax Credit

Jennifer L. Romich and Thomas S. Weisner

In 1990 and again in 1993, Congress approved significant expansions of the previously modest Earned Income Tax Credit (EITC). These increases targeted working families with children and transformed the EITC from a relatively obscure tax provision into our largest federal antipoverty transfer program and an important complement to other work-based elements of welfare reform. As the "heart of the work support system" (see chapter 14, this volume) that replaced Aid to Families with Dependent Children (AFDC), the EITC enjoys bipartisan support. Republicans like that it rewards work and addresses child poverty without imposing requirements on businesses that employ low-income workers. In an event publicizing his administration's role in the increases, President Bill Clinton lauded the expansions and celebrated a policy that made work its primary goal. The EITC, he said, is "not about more governmental or social workers, or more services. It's about more groceries and a car, more school clothes for the kids and more encouragement and hope to keep doing the right thing" (1998).

The extent to which these hopes for groceries, cars, school clothes, and more are realized is key to judging the effectiveness of the EITC as a primary aspect of welfare reform targeting families with children. Research on how the recent EITC expansions affect parents' work and family incomes is a start. A picture of the program's effect on labor supply and well-being is emerging. Most significantly, the EITC accounts for the largest share of the increase in formal work participation by single mothers over the past two decades (Meyer and Rosenbaum 2000). The tax credit also seems to have caused a slight decrease in labor force participation by secondary wage earners while having no empirically discernible effect on marriage decisions (Eissa and Hoynes 1998; Ellwood 2000). Furthermore, the program lifts more families with children out of poverty than any other government transfer program (Council of Economic Advisers 1998; Blank 1999; Greenstein and Shapiro 1998).

A next step is to understand how changing patterns in family income as a result of the EITC affect children's lives. Creating a link between the EITC and child well-being requires examining how families spend the credit. Are low-income families purchasing the projected groceries, cars, and school clothes? There is also a puzzle about when families choose to spend the credit. The vast majority receive it as a lump sum at the end of the tax year, even though they could get the bulk of their credit advanced in increments over the course of the year (General Accounting Office 1992).

Despite being almost universally chosen by EITC recipients, the lump-sum payment option may be politically vulnerable. In an attempt to balance the federal budget for fiscal year 2000, Congress debated changing the delivery mechanism of the EITC to a twelve-month pay out. This was proposed as a simple accounting trick, shifting three of the payments to the next fiscal year without affecting benefit levels and family well-being. House Majority whip Tom DeLay (R-Tex.) suggested that this change would actually aid families: "Working people don't need help with their annual budget. They need help with their monthly budget" (in Weiner 1999). The proposal ultimately died but not before prompting a small flurry of opposition, including negative statements from George W. Bush, then governor of Texas. However, the debate over the issue, and DeLay's comments in particular, illustrate an important point in analyzing antipoverty policy: policymakers' views of family budgets shape their decisions.

In this chapter, we draw on intensive qualitative data to provide a detailed description of how families view and spend their EITC. Drawing on economic theory, we examine ways to frame the lump sum versus advance payment trade-off, concluding that an augmented form of basic life-cycle consumption hypothesis best predicts the observed behavior.

BACKGROUND

The EITC began as a federal program but has been adopted by several states, among them Wisconsin. We describe these programs here, along with the program's underlying economic theory.

The Federal and the Wisconsin EITCs

The federal EITC is a refundable credit that targets low-income households with earned income. Administered through the Internal Revenue Service's federal income tax system, the credit supplements the earnings of single taxpayers and single- or dual-headed households with children. Unlike nonrefundable credits, the EITC can exceed the recipient's tax burden. A household that owes little or nothing in taxes still receives the credit—and a check.

The subsidy varies by income level and number of children, as the credit phases in, plateaus, and phases out with changes in the family's structure, which determines the lower and upper income levels for the maximum benefit as well as the point at which the credit phases out completely. Households with one child and 1999 earnings between $6,800 and $12,500 received the maximum benefit of $2,312.

Benefits for this household would phase out completely when earnings reached $26,450. The most generous benefit goes to families with two or more children. In the earnings range from $9,500 to $12,500, the subsidy is $3,816; complete phaseout occurs at $30,580 (Internal Revenue Service 1999c).

Since its inception in 1975, the federal EITC has grown in both size and scope. From 1986 to 1996, unadjusted outlays for the EITC expanded more than tenfold, from $1.4 to $19.2 billion. The IRS projected that in 1999, 18,954,000 families would claim credits, totaling just over $28 billion, or $1,516 per family (U.S. House of Representatives 1998, 872). The Congressional Budget Office expects outlays on the EITC to exceed the amount spent on family support transfers such as Temporary Assistance for Needy Families (TANF) and related programs.

Wisconsin is one of eleven states that offered an EITC for tax year 1999. Like most state EITCs, Wisconsin's is based on the federal qualifying restrictions. The Wisconsin EITC is available only to families with children and is prorated by number of children. Families with one qualifying child receive a credit equivalent to 4 percent of their federal amount; two qualifying children increases the credit to 14 percent. The federal credit is capped at two children, but the Wisconsin benefit is most generous to families with three or more qualifying children. Such families receive a refundable credit equal to 43 percent of their federal amount. A family with three children and earnings in the maximum credit range receives a $1,600 Wisconsin credit and a total of more than $5,000 from state and federal EITCs combined (Wisconsin Department of Revenue 1998a).

In 1979 the federal government initiated an advance payment option through which workers can receive a portion of their projected EITC credit in every paycheck. Only workers with children are eligible. The advance amount is based on projected income and cannot exceed 60 percent of the projected total credit for a one-child family. This cap applies to families of any size, essentially limiting families with two or more children to a hybrid payment structure, combining an advance payment and a lump sum-payment. In 1999 eligible workers could be paid up to $1,387 with their paychecks, providing they took the initiative to file a form W-5, the EITC advance payment certificate, with their employer (Internal Revenue Service 1999a, 1999b). At the state level, Wisconsin offers an option, the Working Family Tax Credit, that serves as an advance equal to the nonrefundable portion of the credit (Wisconsin Department of Revenue 1998b).

There is some concern that the federal advance payment form is underused. More than 98 percent of families receive the entire credit as a lump sum along with their income tax refund (McCubbin 2000). In the 1993 Omnibus Budget Reconciliation Act, congressional attention focused on the low use of the advance. A report commissioned by Congress recommended increasing public awareness of the advance option. This call has been echoed by not-for-profit organizations (General Accounting Office 1992; Center on Budget and Policy Priorities 1998). Whether a wage earner claims the advance credit or not makes a difference in household income flow. For a person with two children and earning $15,000 in 1998, receiving the EITC in one lump sum of $3,174 rather than $115 advanced per month, with the balance of $1,794 at tax time, means forgoing a 9 percent increase in monthly income. Whether the smoother income pattern enabled by the advance credit raises family utility is a question of theoretical concern. We turn to that now.

Household Consumption Theory

Discussions of optimal spending often implicitly invoke an economic model of savings, specifically the life-cycle or permanent income hypothesis. Is this the most appropriate conceptualization? Theoretical explanations of households' consumption uses of the EITC must take into account the answers to two questions:

- Which delivery mechanism—the advance payment option or the lump sum— gives the greater utility?
- What types of purchase are made with the respective payment forms?

Taken from economic theory, the life-cycle hypothesis of savings and consumption provides a useful starting point for understanding the relation between a household's income, current consumption, and savings.[1] This theory holds that current consumption is a function of the present value of projected lifetime earnings. Anticipated future income is factored into current consumption decisions. Under common assumptions, an increase in future income raises both current and future consumption.

In the life-cycle hypothesis, a wage earner who knows that he or she will get a large tax credit will consume with that credit in mind. In the absence of credit constraints or interest charges, the timing of the income is neutral. A $120 payment today is equal to $120 a year from now, or $10 a month for a year.[2]

There can be situations in which the life-cycle hypothesis holds for households, yet they still do not claim the advance payment. For instance, persons who do not know about the advance cannot claim it. Attempts to claim it might also be stymied by an employer who either does not know about the credit or actively discourages workers from taking advantage of it.[3] In these situations, claiming the advance payment would raise the family's utility, as theory predicts, but is not feasible owing to other constraints.

A second explanation for the low reported claim rates is that this economic theory does not adequately predict household behavior. Citing the life-cycle theory's mixed empirical success in a number of different areas, Richard Thaler and Hersh Shefrin (1981) propose an augmented version of the hypothesis that incorporates psychological concerns: the behavioral life-cycle model.

The behavioral life-cycle model incorporates three aspects of human behavior: self-control, mental accounting, and framing. In this model, self-control has a cost, and persons are willing to pay a price to avoid having to exercise a certain level of discipline in their spending.[4] Consumers act as if they have separate funds within their accounting system by separating income into current income and wealth. Finally, the marginal propensity to consume from different income sources (for example, salary versus bonus) varies, even if the action that resulted in the income (work) is the same. People are more likely to build assets or savings with money they view, or "frame," as wealth, relative to money they view as current income. An emerging collection of theoretical and empirical work builds on this model (see, for example, Zimmerman et al. 1999; O'Donoghue and Rabin 1999; Souleles 1999), particularly in the area of saving for retirement (Bernheim et al. 1997; Lusardi 1999; Levin 1998).

In the case of the EITC, the behavioral life-cycle model has different predictions and prescriptions concerning the decision of when and how the credit will be spent. The theory is no longer neutral with respect to timing and form. The cost of spending discipline suggests that persons might prefer the lump-sum payment over the advance form, particularly if they have "lumpy" consumption needs, such as a down payment on a home or two months' rent in advance. Mental accounting and framing suggest that a lump sum is seen as different from additional income received in a paycheck. Specifically, the marginal propensity to save from a lump-sum payment is greater. Unlike the life-cycle model, the behavioral life-cycle hypothesis does not suggest that the advance form of the credit necessarily enables a household to reach greater utility.

An examination of these predictions requires data on household income and consumption streams. In this chapter, we draw on ethnographic data to provide a detailed description of low-income families' spending over time. Our design precludes explicit hypothesis testing and cannot reject one theory in favor of another. Rather, we aim to describe and analyze household behavior surrounding the EITC. In doing so, we raise questions about household consumption theory.

DATA AND ANALYSIS

The ethnographic data used in this analysis come from a much larger study, integrating multiple research perspectives and methods. For context, we briefly describe the larger study. Our sample is a subset of 1,357 households that volunteered for the New Hope project, a community-initiated antipoverty program in Milwaukee, Wisconsin. New Hope enrollees participated in a program evaluation by the Manpower Demonstration Research Corporation (MDRC). (Interested readers may consult Brock et al. 1997 and Bos et al. 1999 for additional information on the New Hope program and study. Also see chapter 10, this volume.)

The Ethnographic Sample

A subset of sixty families was randomly drawn from families with young children and assigned to field-workers.[5] Families that agreed to take part were paid fifty dollars for each quarter they remained in contact with the researchers and participated in interviews and field visits. Excluding cases outside of the Milwaukee-Chicago metropolitan areas, the ethnographic sample included 87 percent of those families contacted. The analysis presented here draws on forty-two families with whom field-workers completed at least three visits as of April 15, 1999.

In most cases, the primary contact within the family was a woman. Four-fifths were between twenty-five and forty-five years old; the average age at the two-year follow-up was slightly over thirty-two. About half were African American. One-third was Hispanic, a category comprising Puerto Ricans, Mexican Americans, and immigrants from other Latin American countries.

Family structure, particularly number of children, is an important indicator of the amount of EITC credit that a family receives. Most families in our survey had more than one child. In fact, most had two or more, and about half had three or more children, hence qualifying for the maximum Wisconsin EITC credit. About one-eighth were married and living with a spouse; slightly fewer reported living with a partner. A significant number also lived in households with other adult relatives. Members of our sample were less likely to be married than the average federal EITC recipient (that proportion was one-third in 1994; see General Accounting Office 1996).[6]

Between signing up for the New Hope project and completing the two-year follow-up survey, 92.9 percent of respondents worked in a job in which earnings were reported to the Unemployment Insurance Administration. Among those who worked, average earnings were between $8,000 and $9,000 per year, which placed them within the phase-in or early plateau portion of the credit for families with children. They also reported working more than 1,400 hours a year, on average. (Working forty hours for fifty weeks is 2,000 hours.) The respondent's earnings were not the only source of income. Many households had other wage earners or received transfer payments such as W-2 (Wisconsin Works, the Wisconsin TANF program) or Supplemental Security Income (SSI). On average, less than two-thirds of household income came from earnings. This partial reliance on transfer income further illustrates economic disadvantage.

This was not a nationally representative sample and cannot be generalized as such. However, it was a good sample for addressing questions concerning the EITC and low-income families. The sample was drawn from Milwaukee, a unique and interesting site for research on income tax credits and workers at the lower end of the earnings distribution. Owing to the relatively generous state EITC, Wisconsin residents were eligible for a larger total EITC than persons from other states. Wisconsin was also among the first states to receive a waiver to reform the AFDC system; it initiated its statewide reform two years before Congress passed the Personal Responsibility and Work Opportunity Reconciliation Act (PRWORA).

Ethnographic Analysis

Several techniques were used to gather the data on the families and children in the program and on the control groups. Field-workers used focused, semistructured interviews and participant observations in homes and community settings. Interviews focused on work, child care, budgets and incomes, health care, social supports, family history, children's schooling, and a common list of related topics. Field-workers also prepared questions on specific topics. These questions were circulated to other field-workers, answered by field-workers following visits with their families, and posted on a project website. This was the approach used to gather information on the EITC and related family budget data. Common topics and questions regarding the EITC, budgets, and related topics were explained to the field-workers, and preliminary findings were discussed during meetings.

The product of all these field visits was field notes, which were organized according to common topics and then used in analysis. Analysis of qualitative data is an iterative process. We started by reading through the complete field notes to identify themes and patterns. Notes were then coded and tallied according to these preliminary findings. Narrative summaries that included all relevant information were written for each case. Summaries were double-checked by a research assistant and by each case's field-worker. New hypotheses emerged in the course of analysis, prompting notes to be recoded and summaries to be revised.

The use of ethnographic data distinguishes this analysis from most other work on the EITC. The strengths of our ethnographic data lie in their longitudinal and personal nature. We followed families over time, both hearing plans and observing behavior. Collecting data by means of an ongoing relationship in which one field-worker visited a family every four to eight weeks also encouraged honest responses on touchy subjects such as tax noncompliance and purposeful misreporting. However, field-workers did not ask the exact questions of every family. Due to the idiosyncrasies of individual households, the depth and thoroughness of data on any given topic varied. Our goal in presenting data from intensive qualitative work with a small number of households is to provide a complement to other types of analysis.

FINDINGS: FAMILY FINANCES AND TAX TIME

We here present findings on how people view and use the EITC, first presenting an overview of some families' financial situations, both generally and as they related to tax time. Several findings suggest that the behavioral life-cycle theory accurately describes the choices about their use of the lump-sum EITC.

Household Finances

Thoughts and decisions about taxes and credits are one element of a family's total financial picture. Overall, our data show that making ends meet was a difficult and time-consuming task for these families. This is congruent with the findings of Kathryn Edin and Laura Lein (1997), who interviewed more than 350 low-income, single, welfare-reliant, working women in the late 1980s and early 1990s. They document the careful accounting that goes into managing a low-income household. Mothers know the sources of all their income and where it all goes. Although our sample included married households and allowed for slightly higher household income, the same financial acumen was present.

Like the wage-dependent women in Edin and Lein's sample, the working mothers and fathers in our sample had many conflicting demands on their time and money. Problems that all working parents face—arranging day care, finding time to spend with children, completing housework—were exacerbated by parents' reliance on undependable transportation to get to work, their evening and weekend work shifts, and the lack of adequate services, such as grocery stores and doctors, in their home neighborhoods.

Although most families in the sample supported themselves primarily through their jobs, few had predictable work lives. Most held several jobs over the two years of the study. Only eight (19 percent) worked at the same job during that time. Those who worked held an average of just over two jobs during the two years after they signed up for New Hope. In addition, over one-quarter (eleven) held formal or informal second jobs at some point.

Income varied, but bills remained constant. Seventeen families (40 percent) had debts other than mortgages. Among families with which we discussed outstanding debt, one-third owed more than $400. Estimated total debt ranged from $200 to $10,000, with the median between $1,000 and $3,000. This debt included cars, credit cards, and furniture payments as well as bills that the families were not currently paying. Back utility bills were the most common form of outstanding debt, followed by medical bills.

Money-related stress varied among families. Up to 40 percent felt comfortable with their financial situation. Respondents from these families often cited their ability to budget their limited money. One woman described herself as a "penny pincher"; another said she would rather cut back on consumption than go into debt. A significant number—24 percent—felt the opposite, so bills were constantly overwhelming them. Parents said that they could not "get ahead" or were constantly short on money. The remaining 36 percent fell somewhere in the middle, surviving but always having financial problems. One woman commented, "As long as things were going okay, then [I] could make it." Another women felt stressed by bills and the costs of helping a sick relative, yet said, "I believe it will work out. . . . It's tight now, but we got a roof over our head, we got food. You know we don't have a lot of little splurging or anything." Against this financial background—less-than-stable work and constant budgeting, with varying degrees of success—families made their decisions about how to receive and use their EITC.

Tax Time

Not all families were eligible for the EITC. Two held two jobs and clearly earned too much; several others were close to the total phaseout limit of the credit. Two were wholly self-employed in cash businesses and did not file income taxes.[7] Another four had no earned income, three relied on welfare, and one received SSI disability payments. This left thirty-four of the forty-two (81 percent) potentially eligible for the credit. This is higher than the administrative estimate of the actual percentage of recipients reported in table 11.1[8]

TABLE 11.1 / Knowledge and Use of the Earned Income Tax Credit

Source	Data
New Hope survey	
Have heard of the earned income tax credit.	90 percent
If so, in the last year have used it on federal or state tax return.	72 percent
Administrative Records, 1996	
Those filing	76 percent
Those eligible	45 percent
Amount (among those who received the credit)	
Wisconsin	$481
Federal	$1,036
Total	$2,772

Note: Data comes from New Hope two-year survey (1996 to 1997) and tax administrative data, which used survey data on the forty families of the current ethnographic sample that were contacted for the survey. Administrative records show estimated figures for all forty-two families. The research group requested and received tax filing information from the IRS and the Wisconsin Department of Revenue. To preserve anonymity, individual tax records were not provided. However, group-level data for subgroups of approximately fifteen families stratified by experimental status, income level, and family structure allow us to consistently describe the mean filing rate and level of EITC credit received by sample members.

Not all of these working families received their income tax refund. Six households (14 percent) had their tax refunds and EITC garnisheed automatically in one or both years due to outstanding debts incurred in government-administered programs. Three owed student loans, the most common reason for garnishment; the others owed back taxes, had received unemployment insurance overpayments, or had been convicted of welfare fraud.

Among respondents who discussed how they prepared their tax forms, 10 percent completed the forms themselves, 60 percent used commercial services, 15 percent relied on nonprofit community agencies or the free tax assistance offered by the government, and another 15 percent relied on a friend or relative. Informal tax preparers (relatives and acquaintances) frequently charged a small sum (fifteen or twenty dollars). Most respondents who used a commercial service did so because they could get their refund and EITC check more quickly: participants used terms featured in commercial tax preparation firms' advertising, most notably H&R Block's "rapid refund" (Olson and Davis 1994).

Among those who filed, most began to think about tax time long before their W-2 forms arrived, planning what they would do with the money. One respondent exclaimed, "I tell people, 'I can't wait for January,' and when they ask why, I tell them, 'It's so I can file my taxes.'" Generally, people viewed tax time as a time when they could catch up on their bills and feel a little ahead for a while. Field notes describe the thoughts of one woman, who was counting on a $4,000 combined refund and credit: "She can pay off all her [back] bills, be caught up with all her bills and not feel stressed . . . all she has to do is keep working until December. Then in January she can turn in her tax form so she can get that money."

Up to this point, we lump tax money together with the EITC. This reflects the views of our sample members. The delivery mechanism that links the EITC with the income tax system was reflected in people's views of the credit.

EITC Awareness

Most respondents had heard of the EITC. In 1997 only three (8 percent of filers) had never heard of it. By 1998 only two were unaware of it. Without tax records, we have no way of knowing whether these families claimed the EITC, although the dollar amounts of their combined federal and state tax checks ($2,900 and $4,000) suggest that they received the credit. An additional one-fifth of the respondents recognized the EITC with slight prompting. Participants often noted that they heard about the credit through New Hope (if they were in the New Hope sample group), another community agency, family members, or friends.

Although most families (53 percent of 1998 filers) were aware of the credit, they could not give an exact breakdown of how much they received from the EITC and how much from their tax refund. Field notes describe a typical response from October 1998: "Although [she] could not recall if the money she got at tax time was EITC money or not, she does recall how much she got and what she has done with it. Last year [she] said she got about $4,000."

About 10 percent recognized that a portion of their tax check came from the EITC program and could give a dollar breakdown of the amounts. The field notes on a working mother with four children is typical for this group (notes translated from Spanish): "[She] knows pretty well what EITC is, she showed me her tax forms and explained to me what EITC was. According to the tax form that she showed me, last year she got $1,350 thanks to the EITC. In the end she got almost $3,000 refunded from her income taxes."

Marginal Incentives

How sophisticated is this understanding? The EITC credit falls as families move beyond the upper end of the plateau into the phaseout structure. Economists' concerns about the work disincentives of the phaseout portion of the credit are not reflected in the descriptions most of our families gave of the relation between how much they worked and how much credit they got. With an average income of less than $9,000, most of the families in our sample were in or below the plateau area. This limited experience drove their understanding of the credit.

Among participants who discussed the relation between the amount they worked and the amount of the check, one-third could be described as holding a "more work, more money" view, which is accurate for those in the phase-in part of the credit. One woman described her thoughts on the issue to a field-worker: "[She] said that sometimes when she thinks about whether she is going to work overtime, she does think that if she works more, her tax check will be bigger, but that thought really doesn't sway her to work too much more."

The perception of marginal incentives may be related to work experience. Recent welfare reforms and a very strong labor market in Milwaukee had drawn many of our sample members into full-time work (see Romich and Weisner 2000 for a more detailed description of labor supply adjustment, strategic use, and noncompliance).

The Use of the Advance

Consistent with general perceptions (and with General Accounting Office 1992), most of the families in our sample received their credit in a lump sum. Four of the taxpayers chose the advance payment in 1997; three continued to claim the advance payment in 1998. One of them chose the advance as a way of preventing her EITC from being garnisheed for outstanding welfare overpayments. Another worked for a community not-for-profit agency and was encouraged by her employer to take the "W-5 plan." The woman who discontinued the advance ended up owing money in 1997 and switching employers at the end of the year. She did not file a W-5 with the new employer. A sample member who had received the advance at a previous job was told the option was not available through her current employer.

Among sample members who did not claim the advance, most did not know much about it. When asked generally about the EITC, six mentioned that they got their credit in a lump sum or that they did not take the advance. Others did not volunteer knowledge about the advance payment option. Field-workers told some of the families about the option, but most of them continued to express a preference for the lump sum, generally saying that they wanted to get all the money at once. On learning of the advance payment option, no one said they would prefer it to the lump sum. (These findings are consistent with the more systematic analysis in Olson and Davis 1994.)

This description of families' generally stressed financial state, their awareness of the EITC, and their eagerness to get their tax checks makes their preference for the lump sum over the advance payment puzzling. If some families were constantly struggling to make ends meet, and if most knew that the EITC could be a steady source of income, why did so few choose the advance option?

FINDINGS: THE BEHAVIORAL LIFE-CYCLE HYPOTHESIS

Several pieces of evidence support the use of the behavioral life-cycle hypothesis as an explanation for household behavior. We find (like Thaler and Shefrin 1981) that a need for spending discipline drives spending and saving patterns and find support for Thaler and Shefrin's assertion that people keep money in separate mental accounts. We argue against the assumption that people do not use the advance merely because they do not know about it. The uses of the lump-sum credit are consistent with the predictions of the behavioral life-cycle theory, and delivery of the EITC through a lump sum actually maximizes some families' utility.

Spending Discipline

Some families in our sample said it was difficult to exercise spending discipline. Among families whose budget decision we observed or discussed, more than half (58 percent) had trouble budgeting money. One woman wished she could set money aside, but said, "The majority of money when I do get paid is going to bills." Savings accounts get whittled down easily. This led to different coping mechanisms. From field notes:

> [She] had to take money out of the bank that she had been trying to save, "not to get things that I want, but to get things that I need. It's like, Uh! Sometimes you can't win for losing." She explained that she purposely opened a bank account far away so she wouldn't take her money out so often.

Another mother tried to work out a payment plan with her day care provider that meshed with her pay schedule: "She said that she has tried to make an arrangement in which she pays a lump sum every two weeks when she gets her check, because if she waits she won't have any money left on the week she doesn't get paid."

In light of strained resources, those in our sample use various spending discipline mechanisms.

Mental Accounts: Tax Time and the EITC

Applying Thaler and Shefrin's (1981) behavioral adaptations to the life-cycle consumption theory results in distinct predictions about how people viewed and used their EITC. According to this theory, households act as if they explicitly divide money into mental accounts. Separating money this way allows for greater spending discipline over the money viewed as wealth.

People in our sample viewed tax time as a unique season of the year, when they could catch up or even get ahead financially. They talked about money from tax credits in different terms than those they used to describe paycheck money. Often they would discuss tax time in a ritualistic manner: "I always buy furniture with my tax money," or "When I get my check I buy a car." People would splurge during tax time in ways they normally would not. One family went out to dinner, "to all the places they could never normally afford."

Consistent with the behavioral life-cycle assertion of mental accounts, people saw tax money as different from periodic income. However, they generally did not distinguish the EITC from the rest of their refund. This lack of a distinction between the two sources raises a question about the relation between knowledge of and use of the lump sum. Are people not claiming the advance payment because they do not know about it? Recall that this would be consistent with the low reported use rate and the life-cycle hypothesis.

Information and Use

There are two possible interpretations of the relation between not knowing about and not claiming the advance credit. The most common argument, consistent with the life-cycle hypothesis, is that people do not claim the advance credit because they do not know about it. With sufficient information and education, people would claim and benefit from the advance. (Olson and Davis 1994 argue for increased education about the advance option.)

Although we agree that increased education will do no harm and may very well inform people who could benefit from the program, we argue for a second interpretation of the lack of information. People do not know about the advance payment option because it is not useful knowledge.

It is interesting to compare knowledge of the advance with knowledge of another tax-based benefit available to the members of our sample. The Wisconsin State Homestead Credit provides a tax credit for low-income households with earned income who own or rent homes or apartments. This credit was not originally a topic in the ethnographic template; hence field-workers did not ask about it. However, respondents mentioned the Homestead Credit voluntarily when talking about taxes. Field notes from an early visit show one woman educating a field-worker.

> L_____ is looking into something called the Homestead Program (which I had never heard of, so if this sounds fuzzy, it is probably due to my lack of understanding; L_____ seemed to have a pretty good grasp of what it was). This is a program that is offered to low-income families whereby they will pay you back for up to half of your rent. You don't qualify if you are getting subsidized housing. L_____ thought that, for example, if you were paying $500 a month, that the Homestead Program would pay you up to $250.

This participant's understanding is basically correct for her family income. In 1999 a family with two children and an annual income of $15,000 that pays $500 a month for a heated apartment would qualify for $290 from the Homestead Credit program (author calculations using Wisconsin Department of Revenue 1998c). Other sample members displayed similar knowledge of this credit. This included familiarity with the process needed to claim the credit, namely, saving rent receipts and having a landlord fill out a rent certificate to attach to the state income tax. Widespread knowledge of the Homestead Credit—a program with clear financial benefits— contrasts with the scant knowledge of the EITC advance payment option.

The life-cycle hypothesis would hold if information had no cost. However, that is not true; people have limited time to pass on and absorb information. The most useful information gets passed on first, and people may choose not to pass on useless information. This suggests a different interpretation of the lack of knowledge of the advance: the option arguably does not represent a valuable benefit for low-income working families. To understand why the advance might not be a benefit, we turn to the marginal consumption patterns enabled by the credit.

Post-Check Consumption

Not only does the behavioral life-cycle theory suggest that people think about tax money differently from the way they think about paycheck income, it also predicts that they spend it on different things. Following the prediction of Thaler and Shefrin (1981), we should expect more savings and large-ticket purchases from the EITC money than from normal income.

We concentrate our discussion on two aspects of family well-being: expenditures on children and asset accumulation. The former confirms the policy intention that the program benefit children. The latter shows support for the behavioral life-cycle hypothesis. We find that families' plans for and uses of tax checks generally paralleled the findings of Timothy Smeeding, Katherin Ross Phillips, and Michael O'Connor (2000).

Two-thirds of the parents in our ethnographic sample who received the EITC or a substantial tax refund cited expenditures on children as a priority use of the check. Among the eight families that did not specifically mention buying items for children, four used the check as a lump-sum down payment on a house or car (two instances each). Clothes were the most commonly cited child-specific purchase. The mother of a preschool-age child and a kindergarten-age child explained,

> When my taxes come . . . then I'll take the kids shopping because my kids really need to go shopping, especially [my older son]. He has no clothes. He needs clothes. . . . I can't send my son to school like this. I need to go shopping for him really bad. Once I get the money, you know send in all the papers—my W2 thing—I [am] most definitely going shopping for my son. Go to Wal-Mart and Kmart and just stock up.

The lump-sum payment enabled purchase of a child's whole wardrobe—socks, underwear, and school uniforms—rather than only a few items at a time.

Other child-specific uses of the credit were to pay private school tuition (three instances) and to establish savings accounts in a child's name (two instances). People also took joy in being able to give their kids money to spend or to take the family out for a special treat—some of the credit was used for "fun money" or to "fool with." Most child-oriented expenditures were nondurable consumption, but durable good purchases were a more visible part of postcheck consumption.

Whenever taxes were discussed during interviews, family members often pointed to some item that had been purchased after the prior tax time: furniture, a car, appliances, a house. Furniture is the most common purchase. Among the families that received tax checks, 60 percent bought couches, tables, beds, or other furniture. Appliances were also purchased. Inexpensive Milwaukee apartments generally rent without stoves, refrigerators, washers, or dryers. The first two are crucial; the latter two are important time-savers for working families (Edin 1998). Our respondents used their tax checks to buy washers, dryers, refrigerators, and a deep freeze. Entertainment equipment, such as TVs, VCRs, and videos, was another popular purchase (29 percent reported such purchases).

Transportation and housing were the next two most common uses of the refund and credit check. Just over one-quarter of our sample used or planned to use their credit on a car, including making repairs on a car, buying a car outright, and making a substantial down payment on a car. One person's only planned use of her refund was personal transportation: "I said I don't care what I get back as long as it's enough to get me a car . . . get me a car that can take me around for . . . at least a year or two."

Nine members of our sample (21 percent) owned a home, with three having used their tax refund–EITC for a down payment. Five more were house shopping in 1999, including two who planned to use their 1998 tax check as part of a down payment. These asset-building uses of the lump-sum credit are consistent with the behavioral life-cycle theory.

Many families hoped to save a portion of their tax check; some were able to. Among the twenty-eight families that received a net positive EITC-refund and whose subsequent spending we tracked, nineteen (68 percent) did not have cash savings left from their most recent check after two months. As one woman lamented, "With bills and seven kids, the money didn't last long enough. Now it's back to week-to-week." Three of these rapid spenders arguably used the money for savings-like purposes—one paid for a land contract on her house, another made a loan to a friend. The third, a woman from a close-knit extended family, gave money to family members as an insurance payment, knowing that they would help her if needed. Three others paid several months' rent in advance.

Nine families (32 percent) had money in the bank more than two months after receiving their checks. These families either had large savings goals, such as saving for a down payment on a house, or kept the money in the bank for emergencies. Of these nine, four families admitted to generally having problems saving money.

SPENDING DISCIPLINE REVISITED: EXPANDING THE TOTAL RESOURCE PIE

The use of the lump-sum tax refund and EITC check as a spending discipline mechanism to enable big-ticket purchases and savings follows the predictions of the behavioral life-cycle model. Ethnographic data give insight into a secondary, interesting, and less conventionally visible aspect of this phenomenon. Following a family over time helped us determine how it made ends meet in the eleven months of the year when it did not receive a large refund.

We found that both formal and informal labor supply increased to cover budget shortfalls or to cover special expenditures. One woman paid for holiday gifts by working more hours: "[In] October and November [she] had extra time to spend at work. On certain days she worked twelve hours a day, but it wasn't so bad because her job keeps her active and it is not boring. The money she made was used for Christmas gifts."

A more subtle form of increased labor supply happened informally—the extra labor of tightening the belt when finances were very short. Often, pinching pennies makes for extra work. Field notes describe how one woman dealt with an unexpected shortage: "[She] said that she had to go down to the food pantry to get food for the kids to eat for the week. . . . She hadn't been to the food pantry in a long time, but she had no choice."

Other nonmarket strategies include cooking inexpensive meals at home (49.6 percent of the survey sample reported having "enough food, but not always the kinds of food we want to eat"), being more vigorous about collecting child support from noncustodial parents, borrowing from relatives, and being frugal with utility use. These nonmarket methods of providing parallel many of those documented by Edin and Lein (1997).

All of these practices require extra labor, which is obvious when talking with the women in our sample. Given their very low incomes, the general lack of benefits associated with their jobs, and their high rate of job turnover, struggling to make ends meet drives such informal work much of the year. In effect, the lump-sum format of the EITC creates an informal, unseen labor incentive for nearly all of the year. A family's income constraint is expanded as people cope with shortfalls that would be covered by the advance.

SUMMARY AND DISCUSSION

This study offers insight into use of the EITC, the largest income transfer program targeting American families with children. Our Milwaukee sample is not nationally representative, but our findings may arguably foreshadow trends in other regions as more states add EITCs and take other measures to move from an entitlement welfare system to work-based supports.

The extreme low-income members of our sample generally knew about the EITC and other specific programs, yet they did not know much about or choose to use the advance credit. Evidence suggests that this is rational optimizing behavior, given a behavioral life-cycle description of household income and consumption. People viewed the combined income tax–EITC check differently from the way they viewed paycheck income. In particular, they were more likely to buy durable goods and make large purchases. Also, in the short run, they put their EITC money into savings. Finally, the use of the EITC as a spending discipline mechanism served to increase the total amount of consumption available to the families, as they substituted market and nonmarket labor during months when they did not receive a credit payment.

The preference for the lump-sum delivery is puzzling in the context of the life-cycle model. Our study design is not a rigorous test of household consumption theories, but findings imply that many aspects of the way families view and use the EITC align with the predictions of the behavioral life-cycle theory proposed by Thaler and Shefrin (1981). It also aligns with recent quantitative empirical work (Bernheim et al. 1997; Lusardi 1999; Levin 1998; Souleles 1999). Although our study focuses on low-income families, the tenets of the behavioral life-cycle model apply at all income levels, as reflected in other current work.

Our research suggests that, relative to a periodic supplement, a lump-sum EITC can help very low-income families manage larger purchases such as furniture, cars, and homes, a finding congruent with that of Lisa Barrow and Leslie McGranahan (2000) in their analysis of national expenditure data. Many parents also devote a portion of their tax check to current consumption, almost invariably making their children a high priority in their spending.

Current and possible future variation among state EITCs could allow more conclusive investigation of some of the hypotheses suggested by this research. One currently testable hypothesis involves the savings level of low-income working families. If a large lump-sum refund and EITC are more likely to be saved than paycheck income, we would expect low-income households in states with more progressive EITC and income tax packages to hold more assets and have larger savings accounts than families with the same net income in less progressive states.

If the EITC does indeed allow families to save and build assets, another link must be made between these behaviors and family well-being. Some recent attention centers on asset accumulation as a way of promoting well-being (Sherraden 1991; Oliver 1997; Edin 1998; Canedy 1998). However, further specification of how assets contribute to functioning, and eventual well-being, is necessary to inform policy trade-offs. Are assets a better buffer than more monthly cash income for children in low-income families? What is the developmental trade-off between a more stressed-out parent during the year and a mattress to sleep on or a home in a safer neighborhood? Given that income is not timing-neutral for low-income families, steps to identify the parameters of an optimal mixture of regular and lump-sum income must include specifics of how money translates into family welfare.

Perhaps a hybrid of the advance and lump-sum payments would raise family well-being by allowing greater flexibility in timing. We propose a lump-sum advance, perhaps available quarterly. For a family that earns a $2,000 EITC, being able to claim $600 in one sum halfway through the year could provide the benefits of the advance payment while maintaining a family's spending discipline. Some states provide loans or lump-sum grants to people making the transition from welfare to work. Allowing families to claim the advance on an as-needed basis can have some of the same benefits of helping people to buy cars or make deposits on new apartments.

Understanding how American families use the EITC is key to understanding what the effects are of the overall package of welfare reforms on family life and children. For the families in our sample, the combination of periodic wage income and lump-sum EITC checks would help with both daily living expenses and purchase of durable goods and assets.

NOTES

1. Modigliani and Brumberg (1955) receive credit for developing this theory. Friedman's (1957) permanent income hypothesis mirrors the life-cycle hypothesis (Frank 1997). We refer only to the life-cycle hypothesis for the sake of simplicity.

2. Life-cycle theory is often augmented to reflect credit constraints (Thaler and Shefrin 1981). With the plausible assumption that a low-income family faces high interest rates for borrowing or credit constraints, timing is no longer neutral. Now a monthly payment is superior to the year-end lump sum. Hence the life-cycle hypothesis makes a prescriptive statement about timing of payment: the advance form of the EITC is superior to the year-end lump sum. Another way to conceptualize the difference is to calculate the interest earned on the money if it were invested. The actual forgone interest is modest. A household that qualifies for the maximum advance of $115.58 a month and faces a 10 percent interest rate loses $89.60 in net future value by choosing a pure lump sum delivery rather than the advance payment.

3. See U.S. General Accounting Office (1992) or Smeeding, Phillips, and O'Connor (2000) for additional discussion of employer-level explanations of low uptake rates of the advance payment option.

4. Throughout the rest of this work, we use the term *spending discipline* where Thaler and Shefrin use *self-control*. The term *self-control* is used in economic work that seeks to explain inconsistent and present-biased consumption patterns, a phenomenon that spans all income levels. See O'Donoghue and Rabin (1999) for a review of how economic theory specifies the concept. We use the more specific term *spending discipline* to convey to a general audience that our concern is not with a global personality characteristic but rather with specific budgeting considerations. We owe thanks to Diane Scott-Jones and John Modell for advice on this issue.

5. The sample was stratified by experimental status, ethnicity, number of parents in household, and date of program entry. Ethnicity was recorded as African American, Latino, white, and other. A Spanish-speaking field-worker was assigned to families in which Spanish was the primary language in the home. Many of the "other" group were Asian, mostly recent Hmong refugees resettled in Milwaukee. Because of the complexity of Hmong culture and language and the need for a specialized study of this group, Hmong were excluded from the ethnographic subsample.

6. When applicable, we compared our sample to the comprehensive national distribution of all 1994 EITC recipients, as described by the U.S. General Accounting Office (1996). Although the GAO report predates our study, this comparison with publicly available data illustrates that our sample is a policy-relevant subgroup of possible EITC recipients rather than a nationally representative group. Overall, our sample seems to be more persistently economically disadvantaged than average federal EITC recipients, likely reflecting the persistent poverty that characterizes the particular Milwaukee neighborhoods targeted by the project.

7. Of these, one acknowledged that she was noncompliant and feared an audit.

8. This likely represents the difference in timing between administrative and ethnographic data. Many sample members were not working in 1996 but joined the formal labor market

by the time of our study. In addition, part of this discrepancy is due to sample members who, legally or illegally, did not file taxes.

REFERENCES

Barrow, Lisa, and Leslie McGranahan. 2000. "The Effects of the Earned Income Tax Credit on the Seasonality of Household Expenditures." *National Tax Journal* 53: 1211–43.

Bernheim, B. Douglas, Jonathan Skinner, and Steven Weinberg. 1997. "What Accounts for the Variation in Retirement Wealth Among U.S. Households?" NBER working paper 6227. Cambridge, Mass.: National Bureau of Economic Research.

Blank, Rebecca. 1999. "What Public Policy Research Should We Be Doing?" Lecture presented at the Institute for Policy Research at Northwestern University, Evanston, Ill. (February 1999).

Bos, Johannes, Aletha Huston, Robert Granger, Greg Duncan, Thomas Brock, and Vonnie McLloyd. 1999. *New Hope for People with Low Incomes: Two-year Results of a Program to Reduce Poverty and Reform Welfare.* New York: Manpower Demonstration Research Corporation.

Brock, Thomas, Fred Doolittle, Veronica Fellerath, and Michael Wiseman. 1997. *Creating New Hope: Implementation of a Program to Reduce Poverty and Reform Welfare.* New York: Manpower Demonstration Research Corporation.

Canedy, Dana. 1998. "Down Payment on a Dream." Ford Foundation, New York. Available at: *http://www.fordfound.org/QR.29.1/down/index.html*.

Center on Budget and Policy Priorities. 1998. "Earned Income Tax Credit Outreach Campaign Kit." Center on Budget and Policy Priorities, Washington, D.C.

Clinton, William J. 1998. "Remarks by the President at Income Tax Credit Event." (December 4, 1998). Available at: *www.whitehouse.gov/WH/New/html/19981204-27859.html*.

Council of Economic Advisers. 1998. "Good News for Low-Income Families: Expansions in the Earned Income Tax Credit and the Minimum Wage." Washington: Council of Economic Advisers.

Edin, Kathryn. 1998. "The Role of Assets in the Lives of Low-Income Single Mothers and Non-Custodial Fathers." Philadelphia: Department of Sociology, University of Pennsylvania.

Edin, Kathryn, and Laura Lein. 1997. *Making Ends Meet: How Single Mothers Survive Welfare and Low-Wage Work.* New York: Russell Sage Foundation.

Eissa, Nada, and Hillary W. Hoynes. 1998. "The Earned Income Tax Credit and Labor Supply: Married Couples." Working paper. Berkeley: University of California.

Ellwood, David. 2000. "The Impact of the Earned Income Tax Credit and Social Policy Reforms on Work, Marriage, and Living Arrangements." *National Tax Journal* 53: 1063–1105.

Frank, Robert H. 1997. *Microeconomics and Behavior.* 3d ed. New York: McGraw-Hill.

Friedman, Milton. 1957. *A Theory of the Consumption Function.* Princeton, N.J.: Princeton University Press.

General Accounting Office. 1992. *Earned Income Tax Credit: Advance Payment Option Is Not Well Known or Understood by the Public.* GAO/GGD-93-145. Washington: General Accounting Office.

———. 1996. *Earned Income Tax Credit: Profile of Tax Year 1994 Credit Recipients*. GAO/GGD-96-122BR. Washington: General Accounting Office.

Greenstein, Robert, and Isaac Shapiro. 1998. *New Findings on the Effects of the EITC*. Washington, D.C.: Center on Budget and Policy Priorities.

Internal Revenue Service. 1999a. *The Earned Income Tax Credit (EITC)*. Washington: Department of the Treasury. Available at: *www.irs.gov/prod/ind_info/eitc4.html*.

———. 1999b. Form W-5: Earned Income Advance Payment Certificate. Washington: Department of the Treasury.

———. 1999c. 1999 1040 Instructions. Washington: Department of the Treasury.

Levin, Laurence. 1998. "Are Assets Fungible? Testing the Behavioral Theory of Life-Cycle Savings." *Journal of Economic Behavior and Organization* 36(1): 59–83.

Lusardi, Annamaria. 1999. "Explaining Why Households Do Not Save." Working paper. Joint Center for Poverty Research, Chicago.

McCubbin, Janet. 2000. "EITC Noncompliance: The Determinants of the Misreporting of Children." *National Tax Journal* 53: 1135–64.

Meyer, Bruce D., and Daniel T. Rosenbaum. 2000. "Making Single Mothers Work: Recent Tax and Welfare Policy and Its Effects." *National Tax Journal* 53: 1027–61.

Modigliani, Franco, and Richard Brumberg. 1955. "Utility Analysis and the Consumption Function: An Interpretation of Cross-section Data." In *Post Keynesian Economics*, edited by K. Kurihara. London: Allen and Unwin.

O'Donoghue, Ted, and Matthew Rabin. 1999. "Doing It Now or Later." *American Economic Review* 89(1): 103–24.

Oliver, Melvin L. 1997. "Building Assets: Another Way to Fight Poverty." *New York: Ford Foundation, 1997*. Available at: *www.fordfound.org/QR.28.1/QR2814.html*.

Olson, Lynn M., and Audrey Davis. 1994. "The Earned Income Tax Credit: Views from the Street Level." Working paper. Evanston, Ill.: Institute for Policy Research, Northwestern University.

Romich, Jennifer, and Thomas Weisner. 2000. "How Families View and Use the EITC: Advance Payment versus Lump Sum Delivery." *National Tax Journal* 53: 1245–65.

Sherraden, Michael. 1991. *Assets and the Poor: A New American Welfare Policy*. Armonk, N.Y.: M. E. Sharpe.

Smeeding, Timothy, Katherin Ross Phillips, and Michael O'Connor. 2000. "The EITC: Expectation, Knowledge, Use, and Economic and Social Mobility." *National Tax Journal* 53: 1187–64.

Souleles, Nicholas S. 1999. "The Response of Household Consumption to Income Tax Refunds." *American Economic Review* 89(4): 947–58.

Thaler, Richard H., and Hersh M. Shefrin. 1981. "An Economic Theory of Self Control." *Journal of Political Economy* 89(2): 392–406.

U.S. House of Representatives. 1998. *1998 Green Book: Background Material and Data on Programs Within the Jurisdiction of the Committee on Ways and Means*. Washington: U.S. Government Printing Office.

Weiner, Tim. 1999. "Criticism Appears to Doom Republican Budget Tactic." *New York Times,* October 1, 1999, A20.

Wisconsin Department of Revenue. 1998a. Form 1A and WI-Z Instructions. Madison: State of Wisconsin.

———. 1998b. Wisconsin Tax Bulletin 111. Madison: State of Wisconsin (October). Available at: *badger.state.wi.us/agencies/dor/ise/111.*

———. 1998c. Wisconsin Homestead Credit Schedule H and Schedule H Instructions. Madison: State of Wisconsin.

Zimmerman, Raymond A., Patricia Eason, and Mary Gowan. 1999. "Taxpayer Preference Between Income Tax and Consumption Tax: Behavioral Life-Cycle Effects." *Behavioral Research in Accounting* 11: 111–42.

Chapter 12

Welfare Waivers and Nonmarital Childbearing

Ann E. Horvath-Rose and H. Elizabeth Peters

Nonmarital childbearing increased dramatically in the second half of the twentieth century, from 3.8 percent of births in 1940 to more than 32.0 percent of births in 1996.[1] A large body of research shows that unmarried mothers have lower education level and lower earnings and are more likely to experience other negative life outcomes than married mothers. Similarly, the children of these mothers are also more likely to have worse outcomes compared to children born within marriage (Annie E. Casey Foundation 1998; Baldwin and Cain 1980; Bane and Ellwood 1986; Blank 1993, 1997a; Card 1981; Duncan and Hoffman 1990a, 1990b; Foster et al. 1998; Furstenberg et al. 1987; Goerge and Lee 1997; Geronimus and Korenman 1992, 1993; Grogger 1997; Haveman et al. 1997; Hoffman and Foster 1997; Hoffman et al. 1993; Kahn and Anderson 1992; Maynard 1997; McLanahan and Sandefur 1994; Moore et al. 1997; National Governors' Association 1996; Wolfe and Hill 1993).

Whether (and how much of) these negative outcomes are actually caused by nonmarital childbearing is a subject of scholarly debate. Specifically, the observed associations could instead be related to some third characteristic that is the cause of both nonmarital childbearing and, for example, lower education and earnings. In addition, there is little consensus about the causes of nonmarital childbearing. Conservatives tend to blame the welfare system itself for perpetuating a culture of dependency and subsidizing nonmarital childbearing (see, for example, Murray 1993), while liberals stress the importance of economic opportunities in reducing incentives for nonmarital childbearing. Nonetheless, both sides agree that the high rate of out-of-wedlock births deserves attention (see chapter 2, this volume).

In part as a result of increasing welfare caseloads and the federal welfare system's lack of success in reducing poverty, states began applying to the U.S. Department of Health and Human Services in the late 1980s for waivers granting them permission to implement other state-level welfare policies. One of the explicit goals of state policymakers when drafting the waivers was to influence unmarried women's fertility decisions by altering the incentives in welfare programs. This experimentation by states with welfare reforms led to the comprehensive overhaul of federal welfare policy in August 1996, known as the Personal Responsibility and

Work Opportunity Reconciliation Act (PRWORA). Two of the goals of PRWORA are similar to the goals of the individual states' welfare experiments: to prevent and reduce out-of-wedlock pregnancies and to encourage the formation and maintenance of two-parent families.

Since 1994 welfare caseloads have been cut in half. In many states, the incidence of nonmarital births has fallen as well, although this decline is much less dramatic than for caseloads. Policymakers have taken credit for both declines. There is, however, a debate about how much of the declines stem from changes in policy and how much from changes in economic and demographic variables or other unmeasured social phenomena. Several studies estimate the relative effects of economic factors and policy change (Blank 1997a; Council of Economic Advisers 1997; Figlio and Ziliak 1998). We use a similar approach here to examine nonmarital childbearing. Specifically, we estimate the effect of the changes in policy on nonmarital birth ratios—births to unmarried women as a proportion of all births—separately by race and age. We also measure the relative importance of economic, demographic, and policy variables.

Findings from the analysis show that the family cap policy (a policy that discourages women from having additional children while receiving welfare by not considering those children in the total cash benefit) lowers nonmarital birth ratios for each age and race group studied. We also find that allowing more two-parent families to receive welfare benefits decreases teen nonmarital birth ratios but has little effect on post-teen ratios. Other types of waiver provision, however, either have insignificant effects or effects contrary to policymakers' intentions.

Overall, our analysis shows that demonstration projects had the desired effect on nonmarital birth ratios. However, we also find evidence that some of the declines in nonmarital childbearing occurred before the implementation of the waiver. The latter finding suggests that the rhetoric surrounding the adoption of these policies or something else about the environments in the states that implemented welfare waivers was partly responsible for the declines. Measurable changes in policy, economic, and demographic variables explain only a small part of the overall change in nonmarital birth ratios. It is clear, therefore, that although policy variables have some effect, other variables such as social norms and unmeasured aspects of the socioeconomic variables included in our model play a larger role in affecting nonmarital childbearing.

TRENDS IN NONMARITAL FERTILITY

Between 1984 and 1996, the period examined here, U.S. nonmarital birth ratios increased steadily until 1994, at which point there was a slight decrease. Both the race and age composition of these mothers changed substantially over time. For example, the percentage of all nonmarital births to white women increased from 51 percent in 1984 to 63 percent in 1996, while the share of white women in the total population declined. The percentage of nonmarital births to teens fell during this period, from 34 to 30 percent. Within both teen and post-teen age groups, the share of nonmarital births to white women increased, while the share to black women decreased.

Also over this time, nonmarital birth ratios increased in all states, although many states recorded a leveling off or a decline near the end of the period. Washington, D.C., consistently had the highest teen and post-teen nonmarital birth ratios each year. However, that city also had the smallest increase in both teen and post-teen nonmarital birth ratios over the period. The greatest increase in nonmarital birth ratios occurred in Nevada, where the teen ratio increased by 84 percent and the post-teen ratio by 270 percent between 1984 and 1996.

THEORIES OF NONMARITAL FERTILITY

Research suggests a number of explanations for nonmarital childbearing. These explanations include both motivations for childbearing and motivations for not marrying, two events necessary for a nonmarital birth to occur. Economic demography models focus on the role of the opportunity cost of fertility. That is, women who have children out of wedlock do so because the cost, in terms of alternatives given up, is low (Acs 1994; An, Haveman, and Wolfe 1993; Anderson 1989; Billy and Moore 1992; Duncan and Hoffman 1990a, 1990b; Hogan and Kitagawa 1985; Wilson 1987). The costs often discussed are lost labor market work and, especially for teens, forgone education.

It has also been argued that a low-income, single woman may choose to have a nonmarital birth because welfare makes this option economically more attractive. A woman chooses between the perceived benefits—both monetary, in the form of welfare payments, and nonmonetary, in the form of utility—and the perceived costs (An et al. 1993; Duncan and Hoffman 1990a, 1990b; Lundberg and Plotnick 1990; Rosenzweig 1995). Others (Moore et al. 1995) point out that it is not the absolute size of welfare benefits that is important but these benefits relative to the other income-making alternatives available to the woman. Welfare benefits may affect both fertility decisions and marital decisions because welfare benefits are more readily available to single mothers than to married mothers. However, although theoretically appealing, the empirical evidence of a positive link between welfare and nonmarital fertility is mixed (see Moffitt 1995 for a review of this literature).

Another body of research explores the disincentives for marriage that exist when male earning potential is low (Brewster 1994; Lichter 1995; South and Lloyd 1992; Wilson 1987). William Julius Wilson (1987) contends that young black women in particular are "facing a shrinking pool" of employed, single, young black men. Thus, he argues, women are more likely to rear a child on their own.

A teen's desire for the constant and unconditional love of a baby is often cited as a reason for intentional teen pregnancy (Elster et al. 1980; Moore et al. 1995). Pregnancy and birth may also offer the young mother the attention and respect from the community that she cannot elicit in other ways (Acs 1994; Duncan and Hoffman 1990a, 1990b). In fact, childbearing is seen in many communities as a symbolic passage into adulthood, whether or not it is done out of wedlock (Anderson 1989; Hayward et al. 1992; Hogan and Kitagawa 1985; South and Lloyd 1992). The lessened stigma associated with nonmarital births is also noted as a factor in their rise (Duncan 1995; Lichter 1995; Plotnick 1990). Particularly in poor black communities, the social pressure against abortion remains strong (Anderson 1989).

It is clear that a combination of factors creates the environment for a nonmarital birth to occur. The perceived opportunity costs and the possible economic benefits from welfare payments join with a myriad of noneconomic benefits to explain why an unmarried woman may choose to become pregnant and why she may choose not to have an abortion. A poor marriage market explains why she may not marry before the birth. These explanations shaped our selection of economic and demographic controls used in the multivariate analysis.

WELFARE WAIVERS

Since 1962 state governments have had the option of applying to the U.S. Department of Health and Human Services (DHHS) for waivers granting permission to implement state-level welfare reforms. States began applying for waivers in substantial numbers at end of the first Bush administration, and waivers were used extensively during the Clinton administration. A combination of waivers was called a *demonstration project*.

Between January 1987 and August 1996 (when PRWORA was passed into law) forty-six states (including Washington, D.C.) received approval to implement at least one demonstration project to amend their Aid to Families with Dependent Children (AFDC) and Job Opportunities and Basic Skills (JOBS) training programs.[2] Of the states that received approval, thirty-nine implemented the waivers before the new law of August 1996.[3]

In this study we classify waivers into eight categories:

- The family cap
- The minor parent provision
- Time limits on welfare receipt
- Modified work requirements
- Strengthened child support
- Expanded eligibility for the AFDC–Unemployed Parent (AFDC-UP) program for two-parent families
- Expanded income disregard and asset limits
- School attendance and performance requirements.[4]

The two waivers that most directly target nonmarital fertility are the family cap and the minor parent provision. The family cap reduces or eliminates the incremental increase in AFDC benefits for mothers who have a child while on welfare.[5] Several studies indirectly estimate the potential effect of the family cap by exploring the relation between the number of children born to a woman on welfare and the variation by state in the incremental increase in benefits for additional children (Acs 1994, 1996; Averett et al. 2000; Fairlie and London 1997). Of these studies, only one (Averett et al. 2000) finds some evidence that the family cap may lower nonmarital childbearing. A study based solely on the New Jersey family cap (O'Neill 1994) finds that the policy seems to discourage single mothers from having an additional child. Two later studies of the New Jersey family cap (Camasso et al. 1998; Rutgers University 1998) similarly conclude that women subject to the family cap waiver have a lower nonmarital birth rate than those not subject to the cap.

The minor parent provision requires an unmarried teen mother to stay in school and live at home or in another supervised setting in order to receive welfare benefits. It has been argued that the existence of AFDC may allow a teenager in a bad home situation to have a child in order to move out and set up an AFDC household (An et al. 1993; Sklar and Berkov 1974). By no longer allowing teens to move out on their own after having a baby, policymakers expected this waiver to discourage teen nonmarital births. Teen mothers made up less than 10 percent of welfare recipients over the 1984 through 1996 period, but research shows that more than 75 percent of teen mothers go on welfare in the first five years after the birth of their first child (Congressional Budget Office 1990).

Although the other waivers were not designed to directly alter nonmarital childbearing, they have the potential to alter incentives in such a way as to indirectly affect nonmarital fertility. For example, time limits for welfare and work requirements are assumed to lower nonmarital childbearing. When the amount of time a woman can spend on welfare is finite, she may be more reluctant to have a baby, because this support will be available for a shorter period of time. Furthermore, if a woman on welfare is forced to work or to participate in a JOBS training program, she will have to pay for child care. The direct negative effect on her budget from the loss of welfare payments and the increase in child care payments could serve as a disincentive to having another child.

Several waivers attempt to strengthen child support. Some require mothers to cooperate with state efforts to establish paternity as a way to increase child support from nonresidential fathers. It is shown that states with better child support enforcement have lower nonmarital birth rates because the costs of childbearing are shifted to men (Garfinkel et al. 1999). Therefore, it is possible that child support waivers could lower nonmarital fertility rates. Another type of child support waiver increases the amount of child support "passed through" to the family.[6] These waivers increase the resources available to the mother and child without increasing the father's obligations or costs. The effect of this type of waiver may be to increase nonmarital childbearing. Finally, some states have implemented a waiver that expands eligibility for the JOBS training program to noncustodial parents in an attempt to increase the ability of fathers to pay child support. Taken together, the expected effect of the child support waivers is ambiguous.[7]

Waivers that expand the AFDC-UP program make it easier for two-parent families to receive welfare benefits. This may decrease nonmarital fertility by increasing the incentive to marry. The magnitude of any effect is likely to be small, however, because participation in the AFDC-UP program is low; over the 1984 through 1996 period, families with an unemployed parent made up less than 10 percent of all AFDC families.

The effect of the (combined) expanded income disregard and asset limit waivers is ambiguous. On the one hand, both waivers increase eligibility for welfare and thus may increase nonmarital fertility. On the other hand, because a recipient is allowed to earn more money—that is, to work more hours without affecting the level of welfare payment received—the waiver may increase the opportunity cost of bearing subsequent children while on welfare. Thus arguments can be made to support both a positive and a negative effect.

Finally, some states experimented with educational mandates for children of welfare recipients. The school attendance and performance requirement may serve to increase interest in school for teens from welfare families, thus improving their grades and perhaps preparing them for a college education. Several studies show that high levels of school engagement are associated with decreased teen pregnancy (Manlove 1998; National Governors' Association 1996; Ohannessian and Crockett 1993). Thus in the long run, school attendance and performance waivers might lower nonmarital fertility rates among teens from welfare families.

MODELS AND DATA

Our analysis is based on state-level panel data, spanning the years 1984 through 1996. The sample was broken into two age groups, teen women (fifteen through nineteen years of age) and post-teen women (twenty through forty-nine years of age). It was broken into three racial groups: all women (including white, black, Hispanic, Asian, and all other races), white women (including white Hispanic), and black women (including black Hispanic).[8] The dependent variables for each model are state-, race-, and age-specific log odds ratios of nonmarital birth ratios.[9]

The regressions for each race and age group include independent variables measured at the state level that control for opportunity costs, marriage market opportunities, abortion costs and availability, welfare generosity, and other relevant demographic and economic characteristics of the state.[10] State and time dummies were also included to account for unobserved heterogeneity across states and time. (For the means and standard deviations for the variables used in the analysis for the six age-race groups, see appendix table 12A.1; for data sources for each independent variable, see appendix table 12A.2.)

We constructed three separate independent variables that indicate if any welfare waiver was requested, approved, or implemented in a given state in a specific year. The request date is when the state sent the proposed demonstration project to the DHHS for approval. The approval date is when the DHHS notified the state that the demonstration project was approved and could be implemented. The implementation date is, to the best knowledge of the DHHS, the date when the waivers were instituted statewide or in the entire area intended by the demonstration project. We also measured the above-noted eight individual waiver variables. The minor parent provision and school attendance and performance requirement waivers were included only in the teen regressions, because theory suggests that their effect should be limited to teen fertility. The scope of each waiver and the time frame of request, approval, and implementation were taken into account in the coding.[11]

If the constraints imposed by the program are what matter for behavior, we would expect only implementation dates to have a significant effect on nonmarital fertility. However, the announcement of and discussion about the intended policy changes heighten public awareness and may have resulted in a response to the proposed policies before actual implementation (henceforth termed *advertising effect*). It has also been suggested that waivers may be endogenous. In other words, the policies do not necessarily change public actions and opinions; rather, the change in the public mood sets the stage for the waivers to be requested. In either case, one could expect the request or approval dates to be correlated with the dependent variable.[12]

RESULTS

In table 12.1, we report the results of a model in which the independent variables were measured in the same year as the dependent variable (current model). However, to check for robustness of our results, we ran a number of additional specifications. These include models with lagged independent variables and dynamic models that include a lagged dependent variable.[13] We indicate in the text when the results reported in table 12.1 are not robust with respect to the different model specifications.

Economic and Demographic Variables

As discussed, many economic and demographic variables can affect a woman's decision to have a nonmarital birth. The variables are intended to capture the opportunity cost of having a child, of marrying, and of carrying the baby to term. Several important results emerge from the analysis.

First, we find that higher female wages reduce nonmarital childbearing for post-teen women. This result supports the notion that an unmarried woman's fertility decision is affected by the opportunity cost of having children. Specifically, our result suggests that increased wages decrease nonmarital fertility by a greater percentage than increased wages decrease marital fertility.

The role of sexual behavior in nonmarital childbearing is captured by the negative coefficient on AIDS prevalence rates. This result suggests than an increase in the cost of sexual activity will reduce nonmarital childbearing. Social contagion theory predicts that the behavior of the minority population becomes more like that of the majority. Consistent with this theory, we find that nonmarital childbearing among black teens is reduced when they are a smaller proportion of the total population in a state.

TABLE 12.1 / Effects of Economic, Demographic and Waiver Variables on Age- and Race-Specific Nonmarital Birth Ratios

	Ages Fifteen Through Nineteen			Ages Twenty Through Forty-Nine		
Variable	All	White	Black	All	White	Black
Socioeconomic characteristics and other state controls						
Twenty-five percent increase in mean poverty rate	0.03 (0.09)	0.18 (0.51)	0.11 (0.33)	0.03 (0.26)	-0.06 (-0.54)	-0.05 (-0.21)
One dollar increase in race-specific mean female wage	0.3 (0.53)	0.002 (0.00)	-0.1 (-0.91)	-0.8** (-3.38)	-0.6** (-3.18)	-0.4** (-2.65)
One dollar increase in race-specific mean male wage	-0.1 (-0.15)	0.5 (1.18)	-0.03 (-0.74)	0.003 (0.02)	0.1 (1.03)	-0.02 (-0.66)
Twenty-five percent increase in race-specific mean female unemployment rate	0.48* (1.65)	0.10 (0.38)	-0.50** (-3.02)	-0.04 (-0.43)	-0.08 (-1.12)	-0.60** (-5.11)
$100 increase in mean real maximum AFDC and food stamp guarantee	-1.0 (-1.29)	-0.5 (-0.51)	0.1 (0.08)	-0.6* (-1.84)	-0.2 (-0.58)	-0.7 (-0.94)
Twenty-five percent increase in mean AIDS rate	-0.16** (-2.55)	-0.04 (-0.56)	-0.03 (-0.51)	-0.07** (-2.47)	-0.03 (-1.03)	-0.10** (-1.98)
Twenty-five percent increase in mean ratio of whites to blacks	-0.28** (-2.02)	-0.07 (-0.45)	-0.40* (-1.73)	-0.09 (-1.40)	0.04 (0.78)	-0.25 (-0.91)
Twenty-five percent increase in mean high school completion rate	-1.17 (-0.94)	-1.75 (-1.18)	-0.68 (-0.51)	-0.45 (-0.85)	-0.67 (-1.42)	-0.68 (-0.64)
Twenty-five percent increase in mean race- and age-specific eligible men per single woman	2.15** (3.49)	1.64** (2.23)	0.27** (2.03)	0.16 (0.55)	-0.47** (-2.07)	0.04 (0.35)
Twenty-five percent increase in mean proportion growing up in a teen-parent or single- parent household	3.61** (4.42)	2.96** (3.15)	1.53** (2.70)	0.97 (1.57)	-0.19 (-0.34)	3.20** (2.65)

(Table continues on p. 230.)

TABLE 12.1 / Continued

Variable	Ages Fifteen Through Nineteen			Ages Twenty Through Forty-Nine		
	All	White	Black	All	White	Black
Twenty-five percent increase in mean paternity establishment rate, lagged one year	-0.36** (-4.10)	-0.42** (-4.21)	-0.25** (-2.55)	-0.05 (-1.30)	-0.09** (-2.82)	0.04 (0.50)
Twenty-five percent increase in mean abortion providers per 1,000 women of childbearing age	-0.22 (-0.68)	0.25 (0.67)	-0.32 (-0.96)	-0.51** (-4.01)	-0.23** (-2.06)	-0.34 (-1.26)
Family cap waiver	-6.1** (-6.30)	-5.4** (-4.76)	-4.4** (-3.86)	-2.5** (-6.47)	-1.4** (-4.15)	-3.3** (-3.89)
Minor parent provision waiver	7.0** (5.79)	8.0** (5.73)	4.9** (3.56)			
Time limit waiver	-0.2 (-0.17)	0.1 (0.09)	0.5 (0.30)	1.0** (2.23)	0.9** (2.22)	-0.2 (-0.19)
Work requirement waivers	1.1 (1.06)	0.02 (0.01)	1.4 (1.14)	0.2 (0.53)	-0.1 (-0.22)	0.4 (0.48)
AFDC-UP waivers	-5.1** (-4.30)	-4.7** (-3.35)	-2.6** (-1.97)	-0.03 (-0.06)	0.2 (0.60)	0.02 (0.03)
Child support waivers	3.5** (3.33)	3.4** (2.74)	2.5** (1.95)	0.9** (1.94)	0.4 (1.13)	1.8** (1.92)
Expanded income disregard and asset limit waivers	-1.3 (-1.12)	-1.3 (-0.91)	-1.5 (-1.01)	-0.5 (-1.03)	-0.7* (-1.77)	-1.1 (-1.13)
School attendance and performance requirement waiver	1.4 (1.55)	0.7 (0.71)	-0.7 (-0.71)			
R^2	95.01	95.63	87.39	96.47	95.65	94.41

Source: Author's estimation results and calculations based on data from sources summarized in table 12A.1.
Note: The effects represent percentage point changes in nonmarital birth ratios. Independent variables are measured in the same year as the dependent variable. Regressions are weighted to account for heteroscedasticity using $N_i P_i (1-P_i)^{1/2}$. State and time fixed effects are included in each regression. Marginal coefficients are calculated as $Bp_{mn}(1-p_{mn})$ from the logit $\ln(P/1-p) = XB + e$. t-statistic in parentheses.
* Significant at 10 percent. ** Significant at 5 percent.

A woman's decision to have a nonmarital birth is, in theory, linked to the availability of abortion services in her state. We find that an increase in abortion providers reduces nonmarital childbearing by reducing the likelihood that a pregnant woman will carry the baby to term.

Our results also suggest the importance of intergenerational effects. We find a positive relation between teen nonmarital childbearing and the probability that the teen was born to a teen mother. This finding is consistent with the theory that early or nonmarital childbearing in one generation (or the circumstances that lead to it) may increase the likelihood of early or nonmarital childbearing in the next generation.

Several researchers show the importance of marriage market opportunities on nonmarital fertility (Brewster 1994; South and Lloyd 1992; South 1993, 1996; Wilson 1987). Our results show an unexpected positive relation between marriage market opportunities and nonmarital birth ratios for teens; the more marriageable men, the higher the nonmarital birth ratio. This is contrary to the theory (Wilson 1987) that fewer eligible men mean more nonmarital births because fewer women marry. On the other hand, some authors argue that greater mate availability increases the risk of nonmarital fertility because there are more potential partners for each woman (Billy et al. 1994; Billy and Moore 1992; South 1996).

Finally, although much of the discussion about nonmarital fertility revolves around decisions made by women, it is important to acknowledge that nonmarital fertility can also be affected by men's decisions. We find that increases in paternity establishment rates, which make fathers financially responsible for their nonmarital children, reduce nonmarital childbearing (also see Garfinkel et al. 1999).

Waiver Variables

The results of the current model with all eight waivers included as separate variables are reported in table 12.1.[14]

FAMILY CAP The family cap waiver is the policy hypothesized to most directly influence teen and post-teen nonmarital childbearing decisions (for second- and higher-order births). The results support this hypothesis and are robust to model specification. The coefficient on family cap is consistently negative and highly significant for all race and age groups. The family cap is associated with a 9 percent decrease in nonmarital birth ratios for all teen and white teen women, and a 5 percent decrease in the black mean ratio for teens.[15] For post-teens, the family cap is associated with decreases of 12 percent, 10 percent, and 6 percent in the all, white, and black mean nonmarital birth ratios, respectively.

Another way to illustrate the effect of the family cap is to use the regression coefficients to predict nonmarital birth ratios among women living in a state without a family cap and among similar group living in a state with a family cap; the regression includes each age and race group for representative women with mean sample characteristics. The results of this exercise are shown in figure 12.1. The bar chart shows that for each race and age group the percentage of nonmarital births are larger in the state with no family cap.

MINOR PARENT PROVISION   Although the minor parent provision waiver might be expected to reduce teenage nonmarital fertility, it, surprisingly, has the opposite effect: it is consistently positive and significant for each race group and is robust across model specifications. The provision increases the mean ratios of teen nonmarital childbearing by 10 percent for all teens, 14 percent for white teens, and 6 percent for black teens. This was certainly unintended by policymakers. A plausible explanation for this positive relation is that the waiver actually puts the teen in a better bargaining position. Parents who care about their daughters are less likely to force them out of the house for getting pregnant when the means of support offered by welfare benefits is limited. Thus the threat of having to leave the family home because of a nonmarital pregnancy loses much of its credibility. In fact, if the teenager has the child and stays home, she may be more likely to receive her parents' help in caring for her child.

AFDC-UP   The waiver expanding AFDC-UP is associated with decreases in mean nonmarital birth ratios for all teens by 7.5 percent, for white teens by 8 percent, and for black teens by 3 percent. This result is consistent with the hypothesis that increasing welfare eligibility for two-parent families increases incentives for marriage. The fact that the effect is limited to teens can be explained by the changes in eligibility requirements for AFDC-UP that are more salient for teens. Before the waiver, eligibility for AFDC-UP required the principal earner to demonstrate previous labor force attachment. Because teens have not been in the workforce as long as post-teens, this constraint was more binding for them. Note,

FIGURE 12.1   /   Effect of Family Cap on Race- and Age-Specific Nonmarital Birth Ratios, Current Model

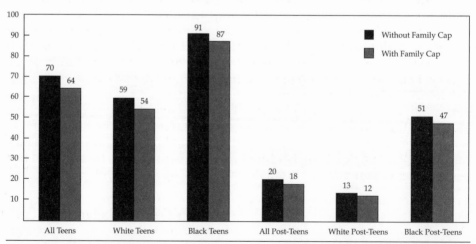

Source: Author's estimation results and calculations based on data from sources summarized in table 12A.1.

however, that our AFDC-UP result is sensitive to the different specifications of our model.

Despite the occasional significant coefficients reported in table 12.1, none of the other waivers has consistent results across race or age. Nor are the other waivers robust to the other model specifications.

Although each waiver provision on its own may have a positive or negative effect on nonmarital fertility, it is interesting to measure the overall effect of adopting waivers. Table 12.2 reports the marginal effects of any waiver requested, any waiver approved, and any waiver implemented on nonmarital childbearing ratios. Each waiver coefficient is from a different regression controlling for socioeconomic variables (current model) and for state and time fixed effects. The results show that each separate stage of the process, from request for the waiver to its implementation, is negatively correlated with nonmarital birth ratios. For example, for black teens "any waiver implemented" is associated with a 1.7 percentage point decrease in the nonmarital birth ratio, and "any waiver requested" is associated with a 1.3 percentage point decrease.

There is an interesting evolution of the effect of requested, approved, and implemented waivers. In particular, the magnitude of the effect increases from "any waiver requested" to "any waiver implemented." The fact that the "any waiver requested" variable is significant suggests some pre-implementation effect of the waiver, perhaps owing to the advertising effect or to the endogeneity of the policies. That is, some part of the effect on nonmarital childbearing may be a result not of the actual implementation of the waivers but rather of the rhetoric surrounding their adoption or certain characteristics of the states that implemented them.

For both teens and post-teens, the largest effects occur for nonmarital birth ratios among blacks. However, because the means of the nonmarital birth ratios differ widely across ages and races, it is more informative to calculate the impact of the policy in terms of percentage change relative to the mean. Implementation of a demonstration project is associated with 2 to 3 percent decreases in mean nonmarital birth ratios among teens and 3 to 4 percent decreases in mean nonmarital birth ratios for older women.

Changes in Nonmarital Birth Ratios

Figure 12.2 shows the results of attributing the change in nonmarital birth ratios over the 1987 through 1996 period to demographic and economic variables, welfare waiver variables, and the time effect. The base year was chosen as 1987 because it was the first year of waiver implementation. Over this period there was an increase in the ratio for women in each race and age group, ranging from 5 percent for black teens to 60 percent for white post-teens. Changes in demographic and economic variables alone would have predicted decreases in nonmarital birth ratios for several groups (all teens, white teens, black teens, and white post-teens) but increases for all post-teens and black post-teens. Changes in the waiver variables

TABLE 12.2 / Marginal Effect of Waivers Requested, Approved, and Implemented

Variable	Ages Fifteen Through Nineteen			Ages Twenty Through Forty-Nine		
	All	White	Black	All	White	Black
Any waiver requested	−0.8	−0.9	−1.3**	−0.6**	−0.3*	−1.1**
	(−1.40)	(−1.44)	(−2.23)	(−2.73)	(−1.77)	(−2.49)
Any waiver approved	−1.2**	−1.5**	−1.5**	−0.8**	−0.6**	−1.4**
	(−2.16)	(−2.49)	(−2.73)	(−4.10)	(−3.47)	(−3.43)
Any waiver implemented	−1.4**	−1.6**	−1.7**	−0.8**	−0.6**	−1.6**
	(−2.56)	(−2.60)	(−3.00)	(−3.98)	(−3.25)	(−3.87)

Source: Author's estimation results and calculations based on data from sources summarized in table 12A.1.
Note: The effects represent percentage point changes in nonmarital birth ratios. Each coefficient is from a different regression in which controls for socioeconomic variables and state and time fixed effects are included along with the waiver variables. t-statistic in parentheses.
* Significant at 10 percent. ** Significant at 5 percent.

FIGURE 12.2 / Change in Nonmarital Birth Ratios, 1987 to 1996 (Percentage)

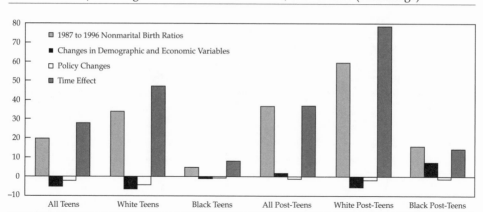

Source: Author's estimation results and calculations based on data from sources summarized in table 12A.1.

alone would have predicted decreases in the ratios over the period for each age and race group. The actual increase in the predicted ratio, however, is attributable primarily to the unobserved time effect.[16]

Even when policy variables have a statistically significant effect, they may not explain differences over time or across states. Our breakdown shows that, in the case of nonmarital childbearing, changes in variables such as social stigma, expectations, and unmeasured aspects of the socioeconomic variables included in our models play a much larger role than do changes in welfare policy.

CONCLUSION

An explicit goal of state-level welfare reforms implemented in the late 1980s and 1990s was to decrease the incidence of nonmarital births. Changes in the number of nonmarital births can be caused by three factors:

- Socioeconomic and demographic changes that affect opportunity costs, marriage decisions, and pregnancy resolution decisions
- Policy changes
- Unexplained state variation and time trends.

We find a number of socioeconomic and demographic variables to be important determinants of nonmarital birth ratios. Wage rates, prevalence of AIDS, number of abortion providers, and paternity establishment rates all lower nonmarital birth ratios, while the probability of growing up in a teen or single-parent home and (unexpectedly) marriage market opportunities are associated with increased ratios. Other economic and demographic variables such as the poverty rate, male wages, teen unemployment, and high school completion do not have a significant effect on nonmarital births.

Policy changes include both changes in welfare generosity and the implementation of welfare waivers. Our results show little relation between welfare generosity and nonmarital fertility. Welfare waivers are responsible for a small downward pressure on nonmarital birth ratios, but some of this observed effect may be caused by the rhetoric surrounding the policy changes or by a relation between a strong state commitment to lowering nonmarital fertility and state adoption of these types of policy.

Although the overall effect of the waivers is small, some have consistently significant statistical effects on nonmarital birth ratios. Our results offer evidence that the family cap decreases nonmarital fertility ratios. We also find that the waiver aimed most directly at reducing teen nonmarital fertility—the minor parent provision—seems to have the opposite effect. This calls into question the use of this policy tool for reducing nonmarital teen fertility. Finally, there is some evidence that the AFDC-UP waiver, which makes it easier for two-parent families to receive benefits, lowers teen nonmarital fertility; there is no evidence that expanding the AFDC-UP program has an effect on post-teen nonmarital fertility. Time limits and work requirements—the two waivers most central to welfare reform—have surprisingly little effect on nonmarital fertility, even though theory predicts a negative effect. Because unexplained time trends have the largest effect on changes in nonmarital birth ratios, the relation between policy and social norms and attitudes is ripe for further investigation.

APPENDIX

TABLE 12A.1 / Means and Standard Deviations for Variables, Six Age-Race Groups

Variable	Ages Fifteen Through Nineteen			Ages Twenty Through Forty-Nine		
	All	White	Black	All	White	Black
Ratio of nonmarital births[a]	0.68	0.58	0.87	0.21	0.14	0.51
	(0.13)	(0.15)	(0.14)	(0.08)	(0.05)	(0.15)
Poverty rate (percentage)[b]	13.6	13.6	13.6	13.6	13.6	13.6
	(4.3)	(4.3)	(4.3)	(4.3)	(4.3)	(4.3)
Race-specific female hourly wage (dollars)[c]	8.34	8.56	7.40	8.34	8.56	7.40
	(1.22)	(1.41)	(2.23)	(1.22)	(1.41)	(2.23)
Race-specific male hourly wage	11.68	12.13	9.42	11.68	12.13	9.42
	(1.53)	(1.63)	(4.40)	(1.53)	(1.63)	(4.40)
Race-specific female unemployment rate (percentage)[c]	6.1	5.2	10.7	6.1	5.2	10.7
	(1.8)	(1.6)	(5.1)	(1.8)	(1.6)	(5.1)
Unemployment rate among sixteen-through-nineteen-year-olds (percentage)[c]	17.1	14.4	17.1			
	(5.1)	(4.2)	(5.1)			

TABLE 12A.1 / *Continued*

Variable	Ages Fifteen Through Nineteen			Ages Twenty Through Forty-Nine		
	All	White	Black	All	White	Black
Maximum AFDC and food stamp guarantee (percentage)[b]	614.3 (133.9)	614.3 (133.9)	614.3 (133.9)	614.3 (133.9)	614.3 (133.9)	614.3 (133.9)
Number of AIDS cases per 1,000 state population[b]	0.13 (0.23)	0.13 (0.23)	0.13 (0.23)	0.13 (0.23)	0.13 (0.23)	0.13 (0.23)
Ratio of whites to blacks[b,e]	43.1 (73.0)	43.1 (73.0)	43.1 (73.0)	43.1 (73.0)	43.1 (73.0)	43.1 (73.0)
High school completion rate among eighteen-through-twenty-four-year-olds (percentage)[b]	84.7 (5.7)	84.7 (5.7)	84.7 (5.7)	84.7 (5.7)	84.7 (5.7)	84.7 (5.7)
Race- and age-specific eligible men per single women[a]	1.10 (0.20)	1.15 (0.27)	1.21 (0.78)	0.53 (0.07)	0.57 (0.06)	0.50 (0.06)
Proportion growing up in a teen-parent or single-parent household[d]	0.18 (0.04)	0.16 (0.04)	0.29 (0.07)	0.16 (0.05)	0.16 (0.05)	0.16 (0.05)
Paternity establishment rate, lagged one year[b]	0.36 (0.24)	0.36 (0.24)	0.36 (0.24)	0.36 (0.24)	0.36 (0.24)	0.36 (0.24)
Abortion providers per 1,000 women of childbearing age[b]	0.04 (0.03)	0.04 (0.03)	0.04 (0.03)	0.04 (0.03)	0.04 (0.03)	0.04 (0.03)
Dummy for parental consent required for an abortion[b]	0.34 (0.47)	0.34 (0.47)	0.34 (0.47)			
Dummy for sexual education and sexually transmitted disease education required in schools[b]	0.52 (0.50)	0.52 (0.50)	0.52 (0.50)	0.52 (0.50)	0.52 (0.50)	0.52 (0.50)

Source: Author's compilation.
Note: Standard deviations are in parentheses.
[a] These variables are race and age specific.
[b] These variables are not race and age specific.
[c] These variables are race specific and not age specific.
[d] This variable is age specific; it is race specific only for teens.
[e] The mean ratio of whites to blacks is large because it is an unweighted national mean calculated from state means.

TABLE 12A.2 / Data Dictionary

Variable	Description and Sources
Ratio of nonmarital births	Data for numerator and denominator from: National Center for Health Statistics. *Vital Statistics of the United States 1984–1992,* Volume 1, Natality. US Department of Health and Human Services. 1993–1996 data from Stephanie Ventura.
Number of AIDS cases weighted by the state population	Center for Disease Control and Prevention. 1984–1996. Morbidity and Mortality Weekly Report, Summary of Notifiable Diseases. USDHHS. State populations from Census Bureau.
Poverty rate	*www.census.gov/hhes/poverty/histpov/ hstpov21.html*
Female unemployment (all, white, and black)	Bureau of Labor Statistics. 1985–1998. Geographic Profile of Employment and Unemployment.
Unemployment sixteen to nineteen-year-olds (all and white)	Bureau of Labor Statistics. 1985, 1986, 1987, 1988, 1989, 1990, 1991, 1992, 1993, 1994, 1995, 1997, 1998. Geographic Profile of Employment and Unemployment.
Ratio of whites to blacks	Calculated using: *www.census.gov/population/ estimates/state/stintasr* and *www.census.gov/population/ estimates/state/sasrh*
High school completion among eighteen to twenty-four-year-olds, three yr. moving average	1984–1989 from: Oct. CPS; 1990–1996 from: US Department of Education. National Center for Education Statistics. *Dropout Rates in the US.*
Proportion of children under eighteen living with one parent, lagged twenty-four years	Calculated using data from: *US Census of the Population*: 1960, 1970 and 1980. Volume 1, Characteristics of the Population, Part 1 US Summary.
Proportion of teen births to all births, lagged seventeen yrs. (all, white and black)	Calculated as number of births to teens/all births from Vital Statistics
Real maximum AFDC payment + cash value of food stamps for family of three	Green Book and CPI
Parental consent required and enforced	NARAL. 1989–1998. *Who Decides? A State by State Review of Abortion Rights in America.* and Merz, J., C. Jackson and J. Klerman. "A Review of Abortion Policy: Legality, Medicaid Funding, and Parental Involvement, 1967–1994." RAND/RP-565.

TABLE 12A.2 / *Continued*

Variable	Description and Sources
Number of abortion providers/ 1,000 females ages fifteen to forty-four in each state	Data provided by Stanley Henshaw, AGI, from AGI publications. Population data from Census Bureau.
Marriage market opportunities	[SjPjaMj]/(Fa); where Pja is the probability that a woman in age group "a" will marry a man in age group "j"; Mj is the number of single employed men in age group "j" (assumed to be the marriageable pool); and Fa is the number of single women in age group "a." This variable is race specific as data shows that there is still only a small percent of racial intermarriages. Proportion single to total men and women from March CPS applied to census population projections; weight for proportion of men in each age group which women in age group marry from Vital Stats, Marriage & Divorce, 1987.
Sexuality and sexually transmitted disease education required in school	Kenney, Asta. 1989. *Sex Education and AIDS Education in the Schools.* AGI; NARAL. 1995. *Sexuality Education in America: A State-by-State Review*; NARAL. 1998. *Fact Sheet: "State Sexuality and STD/HIV Education Regulations."*
Median real wage: female (all, white and black)	Calculated as three-year moving average from March CPS
Median real wage: male (all, white and black)	Calculated as three-year moving average from March CPS
Paternity establishment rate	Number of paternities established divided by number of non-marital births data from Green Book and Vital Statistics
Waiver information	From published and unpublished USDHHS sources; various welfare related websites; and unpublished data collected directly from states.

Source: Authors' compilation.

NOTES

1. The increase in nonmarital births in the 1980s and early 1990s may be due, in part, to an increase in births to unmarried couples living together. According to one estimate, among unmarried births between 1990 and 1994, 41 percent occurred to cohabiting parents, up from 29 percent ten years earlier (Bumpass and Lu 1998).

2. States that either did not apply for approval or did not receive approval of their application are Alaska, Kentucky, Nevada, New Mexico, and Rhode Island.

3. States that did not implement the waivers before August 1996 are Washington, D.C., Idaho, Kansas, Louisiana, Maine, South Carolina, and Tennessee. These states then either implemented them under the new TANF laws or rewrote them.

4. Because many of the waivers were implemented together in demonstration projects, there is a high degree of collinearity among some waivers. The waivers that states most often implemented together were the work requirement, expansion of the AFDC–Unemployed Parent (AFDC-UP) program, and the expansion of income disregard and asset limits. The implementation of the family cap waiver is not as systematically associated with the implementation of other waivers.

5. The incremental increase for each additional child varies across states, time, and number of children.

6. Similarly, some states increase the child support disregard so that less of the child support payment counts toward reducing AFDC payments. Twelve states requested waivers that increase the child support pass-through or disregard. Only three states (Hawaii, Maryland, and North Dakota) requested a decrease in the pass-through, but none of those waivers was implemented before August 1996.

7. Most states with child support waivers combined policies that might be expected to raise the cost of nonmarital childbearing with policies that might have the opposite effect. Thus it is impossible to separate the positive and negative aspects of child support policies, and our results can only be interpreted as the effect of all child support waivers taken together.

8. The proportion of "all" that is nonwhite and nonblack is very small, and thus it was impossible to model this left-out group separately.

9. The log-odds ratio dependent variable results in a heteroscedastic disturbance term. Therefore, the regressions are weighted to account for states with smaller populations that have greater variance in nonmarital birth ratios across time. The weight is based on the inverse of the error variance of the unweighted regressions: $[N_i P_i (1 - P_i)]^{1/2}$.

10. In this model, we included the number of abortion providers in the state per thousand women of childbearing age. We also estimated models including abortion cost and availability of public funding for abortions and got similar results.

11. For example, if the waiver was implemented in the middle of the year and in one-fourth of the state, the variable would be coded $(.5 \times .25) = .125$ the first year; the next year, when it was in place for the entire year but still in only one-fourth of the state, it would be coded $(1 \times .25) = .25$. Finally, if the waiver became statewide in the middle of the following year, this would be coded $[(.5 \times .25) + (.5 \times 1)] = .625$.

12. One analysis of welfare caseload changes (Blank 1997a) finds that recipients begin to respond to waivers before the approval dates.

13. Due to the expected collinearity among waivers, each of the race- and age-specific regressions were also estimated, including only one welfare waiver policy at a time. Results reported are only those consistent in terms of sign, significance, and magnitude when the waiver, alone, was included as well as when the seven other waivers were included. There is some evidence that the models suffer from autocorrelated errors. When the models are corrected for autocorrelation, the main points highlighted in this chapter still remain.

14. The fact that states tended to implement several different waiver policies in one package makes it difficult to estimate precisely the effect of each waiver individually when there is little independent variation. We also estimated models in which each waiver was included in a separate regression. Although these models are misspecified owing to omitted variables, consistency between these results and models in which the eight waiver policies are included in the same regression could strengthen our conclusions.

15. In general the results of the lagged model are of larger magnitude, and the results of the dynamic model are of smaller magnitude.

16. We also did the decomposition in two other ways. One, we divided the time into two periods: 1987 through 1994 (when ratios were increasing) and 1994 through 1996 (when ratios leveled off). And two, we included a maximum AFDC and Food Stamp guarantee as a policy variable along with the waiver variables. In each case, the results were consistent with the results we present here.

REFERENCES

Acs, Gregory. 1994. "The Impact of AFDC on Young Women's Childbearing Decisions." Unpublished paper. Urban Institute, Washington, D.C.

———. 1996. "The Impact of Welfare on Young Mothers' Subsequent Childbearing Decisions." *Journal of Human Resources* 31(4): 898–915.

An, Chong-Bum, Robert Haveman, and Barbara Wolfe. 1993. "Teen Out-of-Wedlock Births and Welfare Receipt: The Role of Childhood Events and Economic Circumstances." *Review of Economics and Statistics* 75(2): 195–8.

Anderson, Elijah. 1989. "Sex Codes and Family Life Among Poor Inner-city Youths." *Annals of the American Academy of Political and Social Science* 501: 59–78.

Annie E. Casey Foundation. 1998. *When Teens Have Sex: Issues and Trends*. Kids Count Special Report. Washington, D.C.: Annie E. Casey Foundation.

Averett, Susan, Laura Argys, and Daniel Rees. 2000. "Welfare Generosity, Pregnancies, and Abortions Among Unmarried AFDC Recipients." *Journal of Population Economics* 13(4): 569–94.

Baldwin, Wendy, and Virginia Cain. 1980. "The Children of Teenage Parents." *Family Planning Perspectives* 12: 34–40.

Bane, Mary Jo, and David Ellwood. 1986. "Slipping Into and Out of Poverty: The Dynamic of Spells." *Journal of Human Resources* 21(1): 1–23.

Billy, John, Karin Brewster, and William Grady. 1994. "Contextual Effects on the Sexual Behavior of Adolescent Women." *Journal of Marriage and Family* 56(2): 387–405.

Billy, John, and David Moore. 1992. "A Multilevel Analysis of Marital and Nonmarital Fertility in the U.S." *Social Forces* 70: 977–1011.

Blank, Rebecca. 1993. "Why Were Poverty Rates So High in the 1980s?" In *Poverty and Prosperity in the USA in the Late Twentieth Century*, edited by D. Papadimitriou and E. Wolff. New York: St. Martin's Press.

———. 1997a. "What Causes Public Assistance Caseloads to Grow?" NBER working paper 6343. Available at: *www.nber.org/papers/w6343*.

———. 1997b. *It Takes a Nation: A New Agenda for Fighting Poverty*. Princeton, N.J.: Princeton University Press.

Brewster, Karin. 1994. "Neighborhood Context and the Transition to Sexual Activity Among Young Black Women." *Demography* 31(4): 603–14.

Bumpass, Larry, and Lu Hsein-Hen. 1998. "Trend in Cohabitation and Implications for Children's Family Contests." Working paper 98-15. Center for Demography and Ecology, University of Wisconsin.

Camasso, Harvey, Radha Jagannathan, and Mark Killingsworth. 1998. "New Jersey's Family Development Program, Results on Program Impacts, Experimental-Control Group Analysis." Rutgers University, New Brunswick, N.J.

Card, Josefina. 1981. "Long-term Consequences for Children of Teenage Parents." *Demography* 18(2): 137–56.

Congressional Budget Office. 1990. "Sources of Support for Adolescent Mothers." Unpublished paper. Congressional Budget Office, Washington, D.C.

Council of Economic Advisers. 1997. "Explaining the Decline in Welfare Receipt, 1993–1996." Washington: Council of Economic Advisers.

Duncan, Greg. 1995. "How Nonmarital Childbearing Is Affected by Neighborhoods, Marital Opportunities, and Labor-Market Conditions." In *Report to Congress on Out-of-Wedlock Childbearing*. PHS 95-1257. Washington: Public Health Service, U.S. Department of Health and Human Services.

Duncan, Greg, and Saul Hoffman. 1990a. "Welfare Benefits, Economic Opportunities, and Out-of-Wedlock Births Among Black Teenage Girls." *Demography* 27(4): 519–35.

———. 1990b. "Welfare Receipt and Subsequent Dependence Among Black Adolescent Mothers." *Family Planning Perspectives* 22(1): 16–20.

Elster, Arthur, Susan Panzarine, and Elizabeth McAnarney. 1980. "Causes of Adolescent Pregnancy." *Medical Aspects of Human Sexuality* 14: 83–7.

Fairlie, Robert W., and Rebecca A. London. 1997. "The Effect of Incremental Benefits Levels on Births to AFDC Recipients." *Journal of Policy Analysis and Management* 16(4): 575–97.

Figlio, David, and James Ziliak. 1998. "Welfare Reform, the Business Cycle, and the Decline in AFDC Caseloads." Paper prepared for Joint Center for Poverty Research Conference on Welfare Reform and the Macroeconomy. Washington, D.C. (November 19–20, 1998).

Foster, E. Michael, Damon Jones, and Saul Hoffman. 1998. "The Economic Impacts of Nonmarital Childbearing: How Are Older, Single Mothers Faring?" *Journal of Marriage and the Family* 60(1): 163–74.

Furstenberg, Frank, Jr., Jeanne Brooks-Gunn, and S. Morgan. 1987. *Adolescent Mothers in Later Life*. New York: Cambridge University Press.

Garfinkel, Irwin, Daniel Gaylin, Sara McLanahan, and Chien Huang. 1999. "Will Child Support Enforcement Reduce Nonmarital Childbearing?" Unpublished paper. Columbia University, New York.

Geronimus, Arline, and Sanders Korenman. 1992. "The Socioeconomic Consequences of Teen Childbearing Reconsidered." *Quarterly Journal of Economics* 107: 1187–1214.

———. 1993. "The Socioeconomic Costs of Teenage Childbearing: Evidence and Interpretation." *Demography* 30(2): 281–95.

Goerge, Robert, and Bong Joo Lee. 1997. "Abuse and Neglect of the Children." In *Kids Having Kids: Economic Costs and Social Consequences of Teen Pregnancy*, edited by Rebecca Maynard. New York: Urban Institute.

Grogger, Jeff. 1997. "Incarceration-Related Costs of Early Childbearing." In *Kids Having Kids: Economic Costs and Social Consequences of Teen Pregnancy*, edited by Rebecca Maynard. New York: Urban Institute.

Haveman, Robert H., Barbara Wolfe, and Elaine Peterson. 1997. "Children of Early Childbearers as Young Adults." In *Kids Having Kids: Economic Costs and Social Consequences of Teen Pregnancy*, edited by Rebecca Maynard. New York: Urban Institute.

Hayward, Mark D., William R. Grady, and John O. G. Billy. 1992. "The Influence of Socioeconomic Status on Adolescent Pregnancy." *Social Science Quarterly* 73: 750–72.

Hoffman, Saul, and E. Michael Foster. 1997. "Economic Correlates of Nonmarital Childbearing Among Adult Women." *Family Planning Perspectives* 29(3): 137–40.

Hoffman, Saul, E. Michael Foster, and Frank Furstenberg Jr. 1993. "Re-evaluating the Costs of Teenage Childbearing." *Demography* 30(1): 1–14.

Hogan, Dennis P., and Evelyn M. Kitagawa. 1985. "The Impact of Social Status, Family Structure, and Neighborhood on the Fertility of Black Adolescents." *American Journal of Sociology* 90: 825–52.

Horvath-Rose, Ann, and H. Elizabeth Peters. 1999. "Welfare Waivers and Nonmarital Childbearing." Working paper. Joint Center for Poverty Research, Chicago.

Kahn, Joan R., and Kay E. Anderson. 1992. "Intergenerational Patterns of Teenage Fertility." *Demography* 29: 39–57.

Lichter, Daniel. 1995. "The Retreat from Marriage and the Rise in Nonmarital Fertility." In *Report to Congress on Out-of-Wedlock Childbearing*. PHS 95-1257. Washington: Public Health Service, U.S. Department of Health and Human Services.

Lundberg, Shelly, and Robert Plotnick. 1990. "Effects of State Welfare, Abortion, and Family Planning Policies on Premarital Childbearing Among White Adolescents." *Family Planning Perspectives* 22(6): 246–51.

Manlove, Jennifer. 1998. "The Influence of High School Dropout and School Disengagement on the Risk of School-Age Pregnancy." *Journal of Research on Adolescence* 8(2): 187–220.

Maynard, Rebecca, ed. 1997. *Kids Having Kids: Economic Costs and Social Consequences of Teen Pregnancy*. New York: Urban Institute.

McLanahan, Sara, and Gary Sandefur. 1994. *Growing Up with a Single Parent: What Hurts, What Helps*. Cambridge, Mass.: Harvard University Press.

Moffitt, Robert. 1995. "The Effect of the Welfare System on Nonmarital Childbearing." In *Report to Congress on Out-of-Wedlock Childbearing*. National Center for Health Statistics. Washington: U.S. Government Printing Office.

Moore, Kristin, Donna Morrison, and Dana Glei. 1995. "Welfare and Adolescent Sex: The Effects of Family History, Benefit Levels, and Community Context." *Journal of Family and Economic Issues* 16(2/3): 207–37.

Moore, Kristin A., Donna R. Morrison, and Angela D. Greene. 1997. "Effects in the Children Born to Adolescent Mothers." In *Kids Having Kids: Economic Costs and Social Consequences of Teen Pregnancy,* edited by Rebecca Maynard. New York: Urban Institute.

Murray, Charles. 1984. *Losing Ground: American Social Policy, 1950–1980.* New York: Basic Books.

———. 1993. "Welfare and the Family: The U.S. Experience." *Journal of Labor Economics* 11 (part 2): S224–62.

National Governors' Association. 1996. "Issue Brief: Preventing Teen Pregnancies: Key Issues and Promising State Efforts." Washington, D.C.: National Governors' Association.

Ohannessian, Christine, and Lisa Crockett. 1993. "A Longitudinal Investigation of the Relationship Between Educational Investment and Adolescent Sexual Activity." *Journal of Adolescent Research* 8(2): 167–82.

O'Neill, June. 1994. "Report Concerning New Jersey's Family Development Program." Unpublished paper. Department of Economics, Baruch College, CUNY.

Plotnick, Robert. 1990. "Welfare and Out-of-Wedlock Childbearing: Evidence from the 1980s." *Journal of Marriage and the Family* 52: 735–46.

Rosenzweig, Mark. 1995. "Welfare, Marital Prospects, and Nonmarital Childbearing." Unpublished paper. University of Pennsylvania, Philadelphia.

Rutgers University. 1998. *A Final Report on the Impact of New Jersey's Family Development Program: Results from a Pre-Post Analysis of AFDC Case Heads, 1990–1996.* New Brunswick, N.J.: Rutgers University.

Sklar, June, and Beth Berkov. 1974. "Teenage Family Formation in Post-War America." *Family Planning Perspectives* 6(2): 80–90.

South, Scott J. 1993. "Racial and Ethnic Differences in the Desire to Marry." *Journal of Marriage and the Family* 55: 357–70.

———. 1996. "Mate Availability and the Transition to Unwed Motherhood: A Paradox of Population Structure." *Journal of Marriage and the Family* 58: 265–79.

South, Scott J., and Kim M. Lloyd. 1992. "Marriage Opportunities and Family Formation: Further Implications of Imbalanced Sex Ratios." *Journal of Marriage and the Family* 54: 440–51.

Wilson, William Julius. 1987. *The Truly Disadvantaged: The Inner City, the Underclass, and Public Policy.* Chicago: University of Chicago Press.

Wolfe, Barbara, and Steven Hill. 1993. "The Health, Earnings Capacity, and Poverty of Single-Mother Families." In *Poverty and Prosperity in the USA in the Late Twentieth Century,* edited by D. Papadimitriou and E. Wolff. New York: St. Martin's Press.

Part IV

Policy Approaches and Options for the Future

Chapter 13

Reducing Child Poverty by Improving the Work-Based Safety Net

Wendell Primus and Kristina Daugirdas

several changes in poverty policy, most notably welfare reform in 1996, were intended to promote work effort among the poor. However, when families with children earn low wages, even if they are working full time and year-round, it is unlikely that they will escape poverty through their wages alone. Government benefits in the form of refundable tax credits, food stamps, child care subsidies, health insurance, and cash assistance play a crucial role in supplementing earnings from low-paying jobs and in lifting children from poverty.

Because eligibility for these government benefits depends on income, as income increases, eligibility for various benefits decreases. Assessing how well work is supported requires calculating the increases in income from all government programs as earnings increase. To "make work pay," government benefits must be structured in a way that ensures that when families become employed and increase their earnings, they are economically better off. Research shows that too often low-income, single parents increase their work effort from part-time to full-time employment but see little increase in their disposable income. We make a number of suggestions in this chapter to reduce child poverty by supporting work and ensuring that families' disposable incomes increase as their work effort increases.

POLICY EMPHASIS ON WORK

The three recent policy changes that most strongly reflect a focus on increasing work effort among the poor are the 1996 welfare reforms, the dramatic expansion of the Earned Income Tax Credit (EITC), which provides a refundable tax credit to low-income, working families, and doubling the child tax credit and making it partially refundable. The 1996 welfare reforms, which replaced Aid to Families with Dependent Children (AFDC) with Temporary Assistance for Needy Families (TANF), placed a federal five-year lifetime limit on the receipt of cash assistance for most families, gave state and local governments substantial flexibility through the block grant financing structure, and removed the legal entitlement to benefits. States that fail to meet work participation requirements (aided by a caseload reduction credit) face financial penalties from the federal government. Individuals who do not comply with work participation face sanctions that reduce or eliminate the amount of cash assistance they receive. Earned income disregards—which allow welfare recipients to keep a portion of their earnings when they work while remaining on welfare—also increased the incentive to work. To a large extent, the emphasis on work was also at the heart of most of the state waivers that were approved by the Clinton administration before the enactment of the 1996 federal legislation.

In his first State of the Union address in 1993, President Bill Clinton stated that a family whose parent works full time throughout the year should not have to live in poverty. This goal shaped the administration's historic EITC expansion of 1993. The EITC was enacted in 1975 and had been expanded previously in 1986 and 1990. To increase the financial rewards of low-wage work, the 1993 expansion of the EITC increased the maximum credit by more than $1,000—to $2,528 for low-income, working families with two or more children. By tax year 2000, the maximum benefit for a family with two or more children reached $3,888. For a worker earning about $10,000 a year, this credit represents a 40 percent increase in income, or the equivalent of almost a $2 per hour raise.

A third policy change, enacted as part of George W. Bush's tax cut, would eventually double the child tax credit from $500 to $1,000 and add a refundable feature that would benefit families with children that earn more than $10,000 per year. The credit is phased in at 10 percent (eventually 15 percent) for income above $10,000 (Greenstein 2001).

A fourth policy change, which has been gradually implemented since the late 1980s and which has had significant implications for making work pay, is the "delinking" of TANF and Medicaid.[1] Under current law, eligibility for Medicaid is based on income. In contrast, eligibility for Medicaid has historically depended on (was "linked" to) receiving cash assistance. This policy discouraged welfare recipients from working because, by becoming employed, they were forced to give up Medicaid coverage and risked being unable to pay medical bills and going without needed medical treatment for their children (Yelowitz 1995; Moffitt and Wolfe 1993). This meant that, too often, poor, nonworking families on welfare had better health coverage than did poor, working families.

A fifth policy change embedded in the 1996 welfare reform legislation is that states are provided a significant amount of additional resources to help families meet their child care needs. The 1996 law consolidated funding streams, increased available funding, and increased state flexibility and subsidy design. States also were allowed to transfer up to 30 percent of their TANF funding to the child care and development block grant, and to use TANF funds directly to pay for child care. As a result, more families and children are receiving child care assistance, although many eligible families are still not receiving assistance.

These policies (except for the recent changes to the child tax credit), in combination with an extraordinarily strong economy, a low unemployment rate, and real wage gains among low-skilled workers, contributed to a significant increase in work effort among poor families, especially single mothers with children. In 1992, 44 percent of single mothers with children with income under 200 percent of the poverty line were employed. By 1999 this figure was 59 percent. Among all single mothers who received cash assistance in the previous year, 19 percent were employed in 1992, while in 1999, 33 percent were employed (U.S. Department of Health and Human Services 2000, table 4.1).

However, as work effort increases, fewer families are receiving the benefits for which they are eligible. Caseload declines in both the TANF and Food Stamp programs since 1995 greatly exceeded declines in poverty. In 1999 only 38 percent of poor children received TANF cash assistance, down from 57 percent in 1995. The ratio of the number of children receiving cash assistance to the total number of poor children was substantially lower in 1999 than in any year since 1970. Likewise, between 1995 and 1999 the number of children receiving food stamps dropped 34 percent, while the number of poor children fell by only 18 percent (Center on Budget and Policy Priorities 2000).

The erosion in the receipt of means-tested benefits has had an effect on overall child poverty during the last several years. The child poverty gap, which measures the total amount by which the incomes of all children who are poor fall below the poverty line, failed to improve significantly between 1995 and 1999, despite the improvement of the economy. The reason that the child poverty gap changed so little during this time is that, on average, the children who remained poor became poorer (Center on Budget and Policy Priorities 2000; Porter and Primus 1999). This finding coincides with recent evidence that the poorest single-mother families with children experienced declines in disposable income between 1995 and 1999, in contrast to significant income gains between 1993 and 1995 (Center on Budget and Policy Priorities 2000; Primus et al. 1999).[2]

LIFTING CHILDREN FROM POVERTY BY MAKING WORK PAY

At the beginning of the Clinton administration in 1993, projected non–Social Security budget deficits totaled about $5 trillion over the next ten years. Prior to the enactment of President George W. Bush's tax cut, those same projections yielded surpluses of about $3 trillion.[3] This fiscal situation represented an unparalleled opportunity to build on the successes of welfare reform, to ensure that the working poor have a livable income, to reduce child poverty, and to provide health insurance to a greater proportion of low-income, working parents and their children. Unless the tax cut is partially rescinded for higher-income families, this opportunity may be lost.

A substantial number of children can be lifted out of poverty by enhancing these work support systems. Our analysis of the Census Bureau's March supplement to the *Current Population Survey* indicates that using the expanded definition of poverty that includes taxes and transfers, about one-third of all poor children in 1999 lived in families with incomes within $3,000 of the poverty line. Half of all poor children lived in families with incomes within $5,000 of the poverty line.

The poorest 40 percent of single-mother families increased their earnings by about $2,300 per family, on average, between 1995 and 1999, after adjusting for inflation. However, their disposable income increased, on average, only by $292, after adjusting for inflation. Many of these families are not receiving the benefits that could move them closer to, or even above, the poverty line. Most families with incomes below the poverty line are eligible for food stamps. However, between 35 and 55 percent of poor children, depending on family structure and distance from the poverty line, do not receive food stamps.

Furthermore, the child support program is not doing enough for children in low-income, single-parent families. Among this group, 75 to 85 percent do not receive support from the noncustodial parent. When child support is paid, any government cash assistance is, in many states, reduced dollar for dollar, leaving the family no better off financially.

Thus it is important to assess the overall picture of work supports and benefits targeted at low-income families and to understand what happens as each support phases out with increasing income. The effective marginal tax rate tells us how much work "pays" as income increases. We define the effective marginal tax rate as the percentage of each additional $1,000 in earnings that a hypothetical family or individual would lose in the form of taxes or benefits. For example, a family that loses $600 in benefits when income increases by $1,000 faces a 60 percent marginal tax rate. When marginal tax rates are high, families are penalized significantly for each extra dollar they earn. In these cases, work is not rewarded adequately and does not leave the families much better off.

We present the effective marginal tax rates faced in 1998 by a single mother, living in Maryland, with one school-age child and one preschool child enrolled in a day care center that is subsidized by the state on a sliding scale (see table 13.1). As the mother entered the labor force and earned $10,000, continued to receive food stamps, and began to receive child care subsidies, the income gains were substantiated. However, as the mother's earnings increased from $10,000 to $20,000, the family's disposable income rose by only $1,203 owing to lost benefits. But if the mother entered the labor force and earned $10,000, but did not receive food stamps or child care subsidies after going to work, despite (in most cases) continued eligibility, the family would be left worse off in terms of disposable income than when the family had no earnings. This example highlights the importance of families receiving the work support benefits for which they are eligible.

Some state organizations have completed similar analyses of the impact of marginal tax rates on the working poor. For example, an analysis by the Public Policy Forum (1999) in Wisconsin examines tax rates on low-income families in several states and finds the same pattern of high marginal tax rates, especially for families with children in roughly the same earnings range. To maintain an incentive to work and to increase earnings, we believe that effective marginal tax rates on earnings generally should not exceed 50 percent, or about the same marginal tax rate on income for the highest income earners in the federal and state tax codes. For some families that have housing subsidies or higher child care costs because of additional children, the marginal rate may need to be higher because of cost implications.

TABLE 13.1 / Effect of Increased Earnings on Disposable Income, Single Mother with
Two Children, Maryland, 1998 (Dollars)

Example	Earnings	TANF and Food Stamps	Taxes and Work Expenses[a]	Child Care Expenses[b]	Total Income
Family receives food	0	8,367	0	0	8,367
stamps and child	10,000	2,160	3,178	(192)	15,146
care assistance	15,000	1,514	1,855	(2,040)	16,329
	20,000	0	69	(3,720)	16,349
Family does not receive	0	8,367	0	0	8,367
food stamps or child	10,000	0	3,206	(4,500)	8,706
care assistance once	15,000	0	1,872	(4,500)	12,372
employed	20,000	0	69	(4,500)	15,569

As earnings increase	Food stamps and child care	No food stamps or child care
0 to 10,000	6,779	339
10,000 to 20,000	1,203	6,863
0 to 20,000	7,982	7,202

Source: Author's calculations based upon policies in Maryland.
Note: Parentheses indicate a cost, other numbers indicate a credit.
[a] Includes federal and state income taxes and payroll taxes. Work expenses are assumed to be 5 percent of income up to a maximum of $750.
[b] Child care expenses in first example are based on copay amounts for center-based care for one child, Baltimore.

PROPOSALS

We propose the following options to "make work pay" and to reduce poverty among children, taking advantage of the unparalleled opportunity created by the current federal budget surplus.

- Increasing the participation rate in the Food Stamp program and enhancing benefits for the working poor
- Increasing access to and the financing of child care services
- Increasing the minimum wage and indexing it to inflation
- Increasing the health insurance coverage of low-income, working parents
- Providing economic incentives for the payment of child support
- Strengthening the EITC
- Ensuring that more of the child tax credit goes to lower-income families by making it more refundable.

Policies That Would Help the Food Stamp Program Promote Work

The Food Stamp program is a critical resource for low-income families. However, unless low-income, working families receive the benefits to which they are entitled, they will be unlikely to escape poverty on their wages alone, even when combined with the EITC. For example, in 1999 the poverty line for a family of four was estimated to be $17,072. Combined income from full-time, minimum-wage work, the EITC, and food stamps brought a family of four close to the poverty line. This achievement—bringing these families nearly out of poverty—would be secured, however, only if low-income, working families received food stamps. Indeed, food stamps are nearly as significant to such families as the EITC. In tax year 1999 a family with full-time, minimum-wage earnings qualified for $3,816 from the EITC; their food stamps for 1999 would have totaled approximately $3,650.

Despite its high value, participation in the Food Stamp program by low-income, working families is low. Some working poor families are ineligible for food stamps for reasons such as the rules governing the value of their car. For some of these families, a modest car needed to commute to work disqualifies them from the Food Stamp program. Many other working, poor families are eligible for food stamps but are not enrolled, in part because of complexities in the application process and other procedural barriers that make it harder for working than for nonworking families to participate in the program or that discourage them from participating.

It appears likely that another significant factor in the low rate of participation among working families is state practices designed to reduce food stamp error rates among working families in response to pressures from the U.S. Department of Agriculture (USDA), which administers the Food Stamp program at the federal level.[4] Until new regulations were issued at the end of 2000, the federal policy made it difficult for states to serve working poor households and households receiving child support without risking errors (since those households' incomes fluctuated). Many states seeking to reduce their error rates have instituted increasingly burdensome procedures for the working poor, apparently causing some to either drop out of or not apply for the program. For example, states increasingly require working poor households to visit the Food Stamp office every three months to reapply, forcing some to miss time from their jobs.

Poor families must weigh the benefits of the program against lost wages from time taken off work, fear of irritating their employer, the difficulty of applying, and the cost of getting to and from the Food Stamp office. Many may elect to leave the program or not to enter it in the first place because of these costs. Studies in the late 1980s found that when the administrative hurdles required to receive food stamps became more burdensome, working poor families were more likely to judge food stamps as not worth pursuing. More recent studies show continued problems with barriers in the program.

Barriers to participation are not limited to repeated, often lengthy, office visits. For example, on a case-by-case basis, some states have begun to call a worker's employer every three months to verify the family's earnings when information from the household is considered inadequate. Low-wage workers concerned that this may alienate their employers may not wish to continue in the program. Data are unavailable to measure the effects of these additional efforts, but certainly changes should be made to lower the transaction cost of obtaining food stamps, such as

- Simplifying reporting requirements
- Making error rate measurements and sanctions more realistic insofar as they relate to working, poor families
- Creating incentives for states that enroll the highest percentages of working, poor families
- Ensuring that more working, poor families know about eligibility for food stamps
- Making it easier for working, poor families that are not on welfare to apply jointly for Medicaid and food stamps by encouraging states to develop one simple application for both Medicaid and food stamps that is available at places other than the welfare office and during evenings and weekends.

In addition to these efforts, several changes in eligibility for food stamps should be considered. For example, the asset rules about cars should be simplified and liberalized. New regulations published by the USDA contain a provision to stop counting the market value of vehicles in which a household has less than $1,500 in equity toward the asset limits of the program. Legislation enacted in fall 2000 effectively gives states the option to completely exclude vehicles from the resource calculations for the program. These are important steps in the right direction; it makes little sense to force poor households to sell their cars, which may be necessary to keep their jobs, to qualify for food stamps. In addition, benefits could be raised to equal the current value of the thrifty food plan. Benefits are now often below the cost of purchasing the thrifty food plan at present food prices.

Increase Access to and Financing of Child Care Services

The cost of child care is another major work-related expense for low-income families, especially single-parent families leaving cash assistance rolls and entering the workforce. The most recent data on child care costs are from 1995, when it was estimated that the average child care expenditure was $59 a week for families below the poverty level, an amount that equaled 36 percent of income for these families (U.S. House of Representatives 2000). For parents earning low wages, child care costs can significantly lower their disposable income and reduce financial incentives to work. Some families try to avoid this expense by making informal child care arrangements, although these arrangements tend to be less stable than formal arrangements. Government support in the form of child care subsidies is a critical component in making work pay for low-income families. Access to and financing of child care services should be increased.

Although significant federal funding for child care subsidies is available, a relatively small proportion of families leaving welfare actually receives child care subsidies. A study by the Urban Institute finds that, in the first three months after leaving cash welfare assistance, only 20 percent of these families were receiving government-funded child care (Loprest 1999). State studies of families leaving the cash assistance program reinforce that finding. A review of state studies finds that, in most states, less than a third of the families that left welfare and were working were receiving child care assistance (Schumacher and Greenberg 1999). Several steps can be made to remedy this situation:

- Greater efforts need to be made to ensure that low-income, working families know that child care assistance is available, especially when they are transitioning off welfare.

- Child care should be reimbursed appropriately for all child care arrangements. The adequacy of reimbursement rates should be evaluated given the growing inability of child care providers to hire and retain staff at the compensation rates they are able to pay (Schumacher and Greenberg 1999).

- Application processes and eligibility requirements for child care assistance must be simplified.

- States should evaluate need and develop more child care supply as necessary for infants and toddlers, for families that work outside of regular business hours (evenings, nights, and weekends), for sick and disabled children, and for low-income areas.

Expanding access to child care will require additional funding, although it is not clear by what mechanism funding should increase. There are two basic options. One is providing additional dollars in the child care development block grant. The second option is providing reimbursement for child care expenses by expanding tax credits related to child care expenses. Increased block grant funding has at least two advantages over new or expanded child care tax credits: the funds are available on a monthly instead of an annual basis and child care quality can be monitored. The disadvantage is that, because they must be appropriated annually at the federal level, block grants are more susceptible to change than subsidies provided through the tax code.

Increasing and Indexing the Minimum Wage

Discussion in Congress is under way over whether to increase the federal minimum wage from its current level of $5.15 to $6.65 over three years. If the minimum wage were increased to $6.65 today, 11.9 million workers, or 9.9 percent of the workforce, would benefit (Rasell et al. 2001). Opponents of minimum wage increases frequently argue that increasing the minimum wage will price low-wage workers out of the labor market, forcing employers to lay them off after the increase takes effect. This claim has been carefully studied by labor economists interested in testing the actual effect of increases in the minimum wage on low-wage workers. Research generally finds the job-loss effect to be either small or nonexistent and the benefits to low-wage workers of increasing the minimum wage substantially exceeding the costs (Card and Krueger, 1994, 1998).

Steps also should be taken to maintain the real value of the minimum wage over time by indexing it either to overall inflation, to maintain its purchasing power over time, or to some wage index, to keep the minimum wage trend in line with overall wage trends. If the minimum wage remains at $5.15 in 2001, its purchasing power will be approximately 9 percent lower than it was in late 1997, when the $5.15 minimum wage level was implemented. If the minimum wage is indexed, it will in effect be frozen at its indexed value. The real value of today's minimum wage is 30 percent below its peak in 1968 and 24 percent below its level in 1979 (Rasell et al. 2001).

Health Insurance for Low-Income, Working Parents

Providing health care coverage to all low-income children and their parents, including noncustodial parents who pay child support, would both reduce marriage penalties (because families would no longer fear losing coverage if they were to marry) and improve the well-being of children in low-income families. In the typical (or median) state, a parent in a family of three loses Medicaid eligibility when her income surpasses 67 percent of the poverty line. Research shows that expanding state Medicaid programs to provide coverage for parents also increases the number of low-income children protected by health insurance (Ku and Broaddus 2000). We should expand funding for the State Children's Health Insurance program (SCHIP) and allow states to use the funds to extend coverage (either through Medicaid or through separate state health insurance programs) to low-income, working parents (including noncustodial parents who pay child support) and their children.

Securing health care coverage improves the well-being of low-income children and adults: recent studies in Tennessee and Oregon demonstrate that newly covered people make greater use of preventive health services, have fewer unmet medical needs, and have better continuity of medical care than do similar individuals who lack medical coverage (Ku and Broaddus 2000).

Improving Child Support Policies

The child support system is another important source of income for low-income, single parents. Strong child support enforcement also reduces entrances into and hastens exits out of welfare by increasing the economic security of mothers outside welfare, by complementing work, and by increasing the costs of welfare by requiring mothers to cooperate in identifying and locating the fathers of their children (Garfinkel 2001). However, nationally, in 1996 only 22 percent of poor children with a noncustodial parent both had a child support order and received some financial assistance from their noncustodial parent (Sorensen and Zibman 2000).[5]

The child support system is problematic for many low-income families for several reasons. In some states, low-income, noncustodial parents face child support orders that are high relative to their current income, even though the orders fall short of what it costs to rear a child. These orders are difficult to modify when they do not match current noncustodial parent income. These factors contribute to the substantial arrearages that many low-income, noncustodial parents accumulate by falling behind on their current child support orders. The combination of these arrearages and high current support orders may cause some low-income, noncustodial parents to work exclusively in the underground economy to avoid detection by child support enforcement. For most noncustodial parents whose children receive cash assistance, another perceived difficulty with the current system is that none of the child support that the parent pays makes their children financially better off; instead, the money reimburses the state for its cash assistance.

The following policy options should improve the operation of the child support program significantly for low-income families:

- Pass through and disregard child support when custodial families are receiving welfare.[6]

- Subsidize the payment of child support.

In most states, child support policies create large disincentives for low-income, noncustodial parents to pay child support when their children reside in families that receive welfare. The 1996 federal welfare law repealed a requirement that states pass through and disregard the first fifty dollars per month in child support payments to custodial parents and their children. This requirement meant that, rather than retaining the full amount of paid child support as a reimbursement for cash assistance, states forwarded the first fifty dollars per month in child support payments to the custodial parent and did not decrease the size of her TANF benefit on account of the payment. More than half of the states responded to this change in federal law by eliminating the pass-through and the disregard completely. In those states, child support payments are counted dollar for dollar against TANF benefits, effectively resulting in a 100 percent tax rate on those payments.[7] Under these circumstances, fathers have no economic incentive to pay child support: regardless of how much they pay, their children do not end up better off financially.

Noncustodial parents who pay child support should know that their children are better off because of that support. States can encourage such payments by reinstating or expanding child support pass-throughs and disregards so that a larger portion, or all, of the child support payments goes directly to custodial families. One option is to treat child support payments in the same manner as earned income when calculating welfare benefits. For example, a state that allows custodial families on welfare to keep 50 percent of their earnings (without offsetting reductions in welfare benefits) also could pass through half of all child support payments. This shift in policy would restore incentives for payment of child support to custodial families receiving welfare and would ensure that the contributions made by noncustodial parents would improve their children's well-being.

Steps beyond improved pass-throughs and disregards also should be considered by states and local communities for two reasons. First, the low earnings of many noncustodial parents prevent them from providing financial support at a level commensurate with their children's needs. Second, expanding child support disregards improves the well-being of children in welfare households but has no effect on the income available to support low-income children living in nonwelfare households.

Matching or supplementing the child support payments made by low-income, noncustodial parents can alleviate these limitations. If society believes that such parents should pay child support, then these policies should reflect that value, and child support payments, rather than being discouraged by high effective tax rates, should instead be subsidized. Child support incentive payments made to custodial families can encourage noncustodial parents to pay child support in much the same way that earned income tax credits reward work effort. Typically, noncustodial parents are ineligible for an earnings subsidy through the EITC. Expanding the EITC to this group is not politically feasible if these parents are not paying child support. Essentially, this proposal would provide an earnings subsidy through the matching of child support payments (Primus and Daugirdas 2000).

The basic elements of such an approach would include a structure of matching payments to be made by the state to the custodial family for every dollar of child support paid by the low-income, noncustodial parent. The matching rate would decline as the income of the noncustodial parent income increased. The payment would phase out completely when the income of the noncustodial parent rose to a specified level. This would create an economic incentive for the payment of child support, because each dollar of child support paid by the low-income, noncustodial parent would make the custodial family better off by more than a dollar.

These incentive programs could be structured in many ways. The key aspect is that the program should reward child support payments. Issues that states would need to address in establishing this structure are

- The maximum rate at which matching payments will be provided

- The range of the noncustodial parent's income over which this maximum rate will be applied

- The phaseout rate, or how quickly the matching rate will be reduced as the income of the noncustodial parent increases.

To provide an incentive for the noncustodial parent to pay child support, the phaseout rate should be low. As the child support order increases, the total amount received by the family (order plus subsidy) should increase as well. These parameters will then determine the income level beyond which the noncustodial parent will no longer qualify for matching payments.

The benefit level under this alternative would be determined in much the same manner as the current federal EITC. As the income of the noncustodial parent rises from zero to a level approaching that generated by full-time work at the minimum wage, the matching rate would remain constant. Within this range, however, the amount of matching payments to the custodial family would typically rise, because the child support order would increase as the noncustodial parent's income grew. Beyond this income range, the matching rate as well as the amount of matching payments would decline and eventually phase out.

Table 13.2 illustrates one possible version of such a child support subsidy program for a custodial family with two children. The matching rate is a function of the non-custodial parent's gross annual income. For incomes of $8,000 and lower, child support payments would be matched at 150 percent, reaching a maximum subsidy of $1,500. This maximum subsidy would apply for noncustodial parents with incomes up to $12,000. At the end of this plateau, the subsidy would phase out at an approximately 12 percent rate, reaching zero when the noncustodial parent's income slightly exceeds $24,000. Under this scenario, if a noncustodial parent with $10,000 in annual earnings had a child support order of $1,500 and he or she paid that amount, the child support payment would be matched by a $1,500 child support incentive payment (CSIP) subsidy, for a total of $3,000.

This strategy for subsidizing child support payments would supplement, not replace, vigorous and effective child support enforcement efforts that hold non-custodial parents legally responsible for the financial support of their children. The strategy is likely to be most successful if accompanied by an employment program for low-income, noncustodial parents. Employment services (including publicly funded transitional jobs) should be provided to bolster the earnings of low-income, noncustodial fathers. Additional services to be considered include a broader range

TABLE 13.2 / Child Support Incentive Plan, Custodial Family with Two Children (Dollars, Except as Indicated)

Gross Income of Noncustodial Parent	Child Support Order	CSIP Matching Rate (Percentage)	CSIP Subsidy	Order plus CSIP
6,000	500	150	750	1,250
8,000	1,000	150	1,500	2,500
10,000	1,500	100	1,500	3,000
12,000	2,200	68	1,500	3,700
14,000	2,900	43	1,255	4,155
16,000	3,600	28	1,010	4,610
18,000	4,300	18	765	5,065
20,000	5,000	10	520	5,520
22,000	5,700	5	275	5,975
24,000	6,400	1	30	6,430
26,000	7,100	0	0	7,100

Source: Author's calculations based upon illustrative CSIP parameters and child support orders.

of counseling, peer group support, parenting, case management, and mediation services to promote noncustodial parents' involvement in the lives of their children. In addition, child support enforcement offices must address issues of child support arrearages, the size of child support orders, and the modification of those orders when appropriate for low-income parents.

A similar outcome could be achieved by making changes in federal or state tax codes. This approach may be politically more practical than the CSIP proposal. Low-income, noncustodial parents would receive a refundable tax credit much like the EITC, which would phase out as earnings increased. To ensure that noncustodial parents who were behind on child support did not benefit from this credit, it could be conditional on compliance with child support payment. In other words, if noncustodial parents did not pay the entire, current child support order during the tax year, they would be ineligible for this credit. Alternatively, the tax credit could be structured so that noncustodial parents would be eligible for a partial credit if their child support payment was above a given threshold (for example, 75 percent of the current order). Administratively, this would require that child support agencies issue an information form (similar to the 1099) to noncustodial parents and to state or federal tax authorities that indicated how much child support was owed and paid in a given year.

Strengthening the Earned Income Tax Credit

The EITC not only substantially increases the proportion of single mothers who work, it also has a powerful effect in reducing poverty.[8] Analysis of census data shows that in 1998 the EITC lifted 4.8 million people out of poverty, including 2.6 million children; in other words, the EITC lifts more children out of poverty than any other program or category of programs (Center on Budget and Policy Priorities 2000). However, the EITC could be even more effective in reducing both child poverty and the high effective marginal tax rates described earlier.

Under its current structure, the EITC is available to all families with children whose income qualifies them to receive the credit. For families with one child, the EITC in tax year 2000 was equal to 34 percent of income for earnings up to $6,920. Families with one child and incomes between $6,920 and $12,690 were eligible for the maximum credit of $2,353. With earnings above $12,690, the credit phases out at a 16 percent rate, reaching zero percent at $27,413. For families with two or more children, the structure is the same but the credit amount is higher. The credit rate is 40 percent for incomes up to $9,720; the credit amount plateaus at $3,888 for incomes between $9,720 and $12,690 and then phases out at a 21 percent rate, reaching the cutoff point at $31,152. Workers without children are eligible for a small EITC with a maximum benefit of $353.

The structure of the EITC could be altered somewhat to reduce marginal tax rates on increases in income between $12,690 and $20,000. This could be accomplished in a variety of ways. One option would be to extend the range of income at which the maximum benefit applies to all families with children. This income range for married couples filing jointly could also be extended by several thousand dollars more than it is extended for single-parent families.[9] In addition to, or in lieu of, extending the eligible income range for the maximum subsidy, marginal tax rates on the working poor could be reduced by decreasing the phaseout rate below its current 21 percent level for families with two or more children.

Both of these changes would reduce the marginal tax rate by reducing the overlap of the phaseout between the EITC and other benefit programs, such as food stamps. Under these proposals, as income increases, families with incomes in the $12,000 to $20,000 range would not lose as much of the EITC while their food stamps and other benefits were phasing out.

In addition to changing the structure of the EITC to reduce marginal tax rates, we advise establishing an additional EITC tier with higher benefit levels for families with three or more children. Large families are much more likely than small families to live below the poverty line and therefore need an earnings subsidy. As former welfare recipients struggle to replace welfare benefits (which were adjusted by family size) with earnings (which do not vary by family size), adding a third tier to the EITC takes on greater importance. The third tier could be established by extending the 40 percent phasein rate to an earnings level that increases the maximum EITC for families with three or more children. A preferable option would increase both the phasein rate (to approximately 45 percent) and the earnings level at which the maximum benefit was reached. Both actions would increase the EITC for larger families.

Improving the Child Tax Credit

The child tax credit was doubled and made partially refundable for families earning above $10,000 annually. It could be improved further for low-income, working families if the threshold for receiving it was lowered from $10,000 to $5,000 or even to zero. This would ensure that all working families would receive some benefit from the child tax credit.

THE EFFECTIVENESS OF THESE POLICIES IN REDUCING CHILD POVERTY

Our proposed policy changes, especially if enacted together, hold promise for significantly lowering child poverty. They also would enhance efforts to continue to "make work pay" by alleviating some of the disincentives to work. Although these proposals have a significant price tag, they represent only a small percentage of the tax cut received by higher-income families.

These policy changes would enhance the work-based safety net and significantly reduce poverty among children. Under an expanded definition of poverty, about half of poor children are within $5,000 of the poverty threshold. If our proposals—to further improve the EITC, to make the child tax credit more refundable, to better enforce and also to subsidize the payment of child support, to enhance the Food Stamp program for the working poor and increase participation in it, to raise the minimum wage, and to expand access to child care assistance and Medicaid for low-income, working families—many of these children would no longer be poor. Furthermore, many others would be less poor, and their parents would have stronger financial incentives to work, to increase their earnings, and to pay child support.

NOTES

1. Legislators enacted the Transitional Medical Assistance program to provide temporary medical coverage to families leaving welfare in 1988 as part of the Family Support Act.

2. Supplemented by additional analysis by Wendell Primus, incorporating census data from the March 1999 *Supplement to the Current Population Survey.*

3. The portion of the surplus that was available for tax cuts, program initiatives, and funds to improve Medicare and Social Security solvency is considerably smaller—about $2 trillion over ten years—because of the costs of maintaining current policy in various areas (for example, renewing the expiring tax credits, maintaining payments to farmers) and the likelihood that the Medicare portion of the surplus will be set aside (see Greenstein and Kogan 2001).

4. Under the Food Stamp Act, states are charged with an error when an incorrect amount of food stamps is issued, without regard to whether the state originally made a proper benefit determination and was unaware of a subsequent change in a household's circumstances. Thus when a family's source of income is not fixed (for example, when the family is employed or receives child support), states worry that the family will not understand the need to report quickly changes in its circumstances, such as a few additional hours of work. New procedures unveiled by the USDA in July 1999 may ameliorate these problems to some degree.

5. Of the estimated 11.9 million single-parent families with children under the age of eighteen in 1998, about 9.8 million (82 percent) were maintained by the mother and roughly 2.1 million (18 percent) were maintained by the father (U.S. House of Representatives 2000). Since the majority of noncustodial parents are men and the majority of custodial parents are women, we use the terms *noncustodial parent* and *noncustodial father* interchangeably. However, we recognize that there are a number of male custodial parents and female noncustodial parents. The policies we propose would apply to these families as well.

6. *Pass-through* and *disregard* are two related but different concepts in the child support enforcement community. Pass-through means that the child support office receives a child support payment from a noncustodial parent and gives (passes through) 100 percent of that payment to the custodial parent. If the custodial family is receiving cash assistance, there is a second policy issue of how much of this payment should be disregarded (not counted) in determining the TANF cash benefit. In most states today, when a family is receiving TANF cash assistance, the child support check is retained (not passed through) by the child support office, and the family receives the same TANF check regardless of whether a child support payment was received by the child support office. In this case, none of the child payment is disregarded in calculating the TANF benefit, and the family essentially receives no benefit from the payment of child support.

7. Normally, a tax rate is defined as the percentage of earnings or income that must be paid to the government. In this case, the effective tax rate refers to the percentage of child support that is claimed by the government as opposed to being available to the child.

8. Variations of the three proposals described here were included in President Bill Clinton's budget for fiscal year 2001. These include adding a third tier to the EITC for families with three or more children, increasing the plateau (or range of income over which families are eligible for the maximum EITC benefit) for married filers, and reducing the phaseout rate for families with two or more children (see Greenstein 2000).

9. To reduce the marriage penalty, the Bush tax cut would increase the eligible income range for married-couple families by $1,000 in 2002 and by $3,000 in 2008 (Greenstein 2001).

REFERENCES

Card, David, and Alan Krueger. 1994. "Minimum Wage and Employment: A Case Study of the Fast Food Industry in New Jersey and Pennsylvania." *American Economic Review* 84: 772-84.

———. 1998. *A Reanalysis of the Effect of the New Jersey Minimum Wage Increase on the Fast Food Industry with Representative Payroll Data.* Princeton, N.J.: Princeton University Press.

Casper, Lynne M. 1995. *What Does It Cost to Mind Our Preschoolers?* Current Population Reports. Washington: U.S. Census Bureau (September).

Center on Budget and Policy Priorities. 2000. Tabulations of Census Data from March 1999 Current Population Survey. Unpublished. Center on Budget and Policy Priorities, Washington, D.C.

Garfinkel, Irwin. 2001. "Assuring Child Support in the New World of Welfare." Paper presented to Conference on the New World of Welfare: Shaping a Post-TANF Agenda for Policy, Washington D.C. (February 1–2).

Greenstein, Robert. 2000. *Should EITC Benefits Be Enlarged for Families with Three or More Children?* Washington, D.C.: Center on Budget and Policy Priorities.

———. 2001. *The Changes the New Tax Law Makes in Refundable Tax Credits for Low-Income Working Families.* Washington, D.C.: Center on Budget and Policy Priorities.

Greenstein, Robert, and Richard Kogan. 2001. *What the New CBO Projections Mean.* Washington, D.C.: Center on Budget and Policy Priorities.

Ku, Leighton, and Matthew Broaddus. 2000. *The Importance of Family-Based Insurance Expansions: New Research Findings About State Health Reforms.* Washington, D.C.: Center on Budget and Policy Priorities.

Lav, Iris J. June 1999. *Extending Marriage Penalty Relief to Working Poor and Near Poor Families.* Washington, D.C.: Center on Budget and Policy Priorities.

Loprest, Pamela. 1999. *Families Who Left Welfare: Who Are They and How Are They Doing?* Washington, D.C.: Urban Institute.

Moffitt, Robert, and Barbara Wolfe. 1993. "Medicaid, Welfare Dependency, and Work: Is There a Causal Link?" *Health Care Financing Review* 15: 123–33.

Porter, Kathryn, and Wendell Primus. 1999. *Changes Since 1995 in the Safety Net's Impact on Child Poverty*. Washington D.C.: Center on Budget and Policy Priorities.

Primus, Wendell, and Kristina Daugirdas. 2000. *Improving Child Well-being by Focusing on Low-Income Noncustodial Parents in Maryland*. Baltimore: Abell Foundation.

Primus, Wendell, Lynette Rawlings, Kathy Larin, and Kathryn Porter. 1999. *Initial Impacts of Welfare Reform on the Incomes of Single-Mother Families*. Washington, D.C.: Center on Budget and Policy Priorities.

Public Policy Forum. 1999. *Making Work Pay in Wisconsin: An Evaluation of Tax-Based Work Incentives and Their Impact on Welfare Reform and the Working Poor*. Milwaukee: Public Policy Forum.

Rasell, Edith, Jared Bernstein, and Heather Boushey. 2001. *Step Up, Not Out: The Case for Raising the Federal Minimum Wage for Workers in Every State*. Washington D.C.: Economic Policy Institute.

Schumacher, Rachel, and Mark Greenberg. 1999. *Child Care After Leaving Welfare: Early Evidence from State Studies*. Washington, D.C.: Center for Law and Social Policy.

Sorensen, Elaine, and Chava Zibman. January 2000. *To What Extent Do Children Benefit from Child Support*. New York: Urban Institute.

U.S. Department of Health and Human Services. 2000. *Temporary Assistance to Needy Families (TANF) Program: Third Annual Report to Congress*. Washington: U.S. Department of Health and Human Services.

U.S. House of Representatives. 2000. *2000 Green Book: Background Material and Data on Programs Within the Jurisdiction of the Committee on Ways and Means*. Washington: U.S. Government Printing Office.

Yelowitz, Aaron S. 1995. "The Medicaid Notch, Labor Supply, and Welfare Participation: Evidence from Eligibility Expansions." *Quarterly Journal of Economics* 110(November): 909–39.

Chapter 14

Effects of Welfare Reform at Four Years

Ron Haskins

In recent years, the nation has experienced two social policy changes that, taken together, constitute a revolution in American domestic policy. The welfare reform law of 1996, which codified and extended a reform movement that had been growing in the states for several years, made unprecedented changes in the federal statutes that govern cash and other welfare benefits for able-bodied adults with children. In effect, the welfare reform law of 1996 renegotiated the nation's social contract with the poor. The second revolution, which began in the mid-1980s and may still be happening today, aimed to use federal dollars to make work pay. If the welfare reform revolution encouraged and, when necessary, forced welfare recipients to work, the work support revolution made it possible for families to work at low-wage jobs and still provide a decent if somewhat spartan life for their children. In this chapter I briefly review the nature of these two vital developments in American social policy, examine evidence on their effects, and discuss policies for improving and strengthening their effects.

More scholarly and cautious observers may disagree, but I believe history will show that the welfare reform law of 1996 represents a discontinuity with previous welfare policy and that the new policy has already dramatically changed the way politicians, scholars, reporters, public intellectuals, and the American people think about welfare. An unusual constellation of forces created the background support necessary for the remarkable welfare reform legislation of 1996. These forces were seized by a determined Republican majority following the 1994 congressional elections—a majority that knew in detail how it wanted to change welfare. The new majority came prepared with a legislative proposal and a core group of members of Congress who supported the proposal and who had created a set of arguments to defend their policy against criticisms from both Democrats and the press. At every crucial moment in the debate, Capitol Hill Republicans were joined by Republican governors in defense of their far-reaching proposals.

THE NEW WELFARE SYSTEM

The 1996 reforms replaced the Aid to Families with Dependent Children (AFDC) program with the Temporary Assistance for Needy Families (TANF) block grant.

The major features of the reform—ending the individual entitlement to benefits, creating a block grant with fixed funding, imposing rigid work requirements on individuals and states, imposing financial sanctions on individuals and states that fail to meet the work requirements, and imposing a five-year time limit—are summarized in chapter 2 of this volume. These five features had been developed by House Republicans over a period of years and enjoyed almost universal support among House and Senate Republicans and among the thirty Republican governors who played a key role during the congressional debate. These features were also strongly opposed by a majority of Democrats and elicited howls of protest and charges of Republican extremism and cruelty.

Taken together, these five provisions of the new TANF program constituted one of the most substantial changes ever made in a major American social program. Because the AFDC program was, in many respects, the lynchpin of entitlement welfare policy for the able-bodied, these reforms were designed to have a major impact not just on the AFDC program but also on the host of programs that contribute to the entitlement mentality that Republicans argued had proved so destructive to many young Americans and to scores of inner-city communities (Kaus 1992; Mead 1986; Murray 1984).

DEVELOPING THE WORK SUPPORT SYSTEM

Although the welfare reforms of 1996 have enjoyed extensive coverage in the media, a more subtle set of changes in means-tested programs for poor and low-income workers had been taking place since the mid-1980s. To fully understand the choices confronting welfare applicants and recipients, and to comprehend the financial incentives put in place to assist adults deciding whether to avoid or leave welfare, it is essential to understand this work support system in greater detail. The system can be defined as a set of means-tested programs that provide public benefits to supplement the income of working families. For our purposes, the work system has five major and several minor components. The major components are the Earned Income Tax Credit (EITC), Medicaid, child care, food stamps, and child support enforcement. The other components include housing, transportation, school lunches, Head Start, the Workforce Investment Act, and a growing set of state-supplied benefits.

The Earned Income Tax Credit

The heart of the work support system is the EITC (U.S. House of Representatives 2000, 808–13). The EITC is essentially a reverse income tax that supplements the incomes of low-wage workers. When enacted in 1975 the credit was a mere 10 percent of income up to $4,000, yielding a maximum credit of $400. Since then, Congress has expanded the initially modest credit on several occasions. The credit received a nice boost, first proposed by that famous liberal Ronald Reagan, in the major tax overhaul of 1986. Another substantial boost was provided by the bipartisan child care reform legislation, supported by the Bush administration in 1990. Finally, the biggest boost of all was proposed by President Bill Clinton and enacted in 1993. After all of these reforms, the EITC now provides a refundable credit of 34 percent applied to incomes up to about $7,000 for workers with one dependent child, and 40 percent applied to incomes up to about $9,800 for workers with two or more children in 2000. Thus low-income working mothers with two children can now receive a cash wage supplement of nearly $4,000 from taxpayers.

Medicaid

The Medicaid program pays for health services provided to eligible low-income families with children as well as to the aged, the blind, and the disabled. In the case of children, Medicaid provides access to preventive health care through early and periodic screening, diagnosis, and treatment; well-child care; physician and hospital services for acute care; prescription drugs; vision and dental care; and long-term care for children with disabilities.

With minor exceptions, until the 1980s only those enrolled in either the AFDC program or the Supplemental Security Income (SSI) program could gain access to Medicaid benefits. However, beginning in the mid-1980s, Congress embarked on a series of largely bipartisan reforms that had the effect of allowing many more children, including children not enrolled in either the AFDC or SSI programs, to be eligible for Medicaid. These reforms can be boiled down to three types of coverage that operate outside the cash welfare programs. First, by the year 2000, states had to cover all children under age sixteen in families with incomes below the federal poverty level (about $14,150 for a family of three in 2000). When it was enacted, this provision required states to cover only children under the age of five. However, the legislation mandated states to annually raise by one year the age groups receiving coverage, until in 2003 all children under the age of nineteen would receive coverage. Second, states had to cover all children younger than age six living in families with incomes below 133 percent of the federal poverty line (about $18,800 for a family of three in 2000). Third, states have the option of covering children under age one and pregnant women in families with incomes up to 185 percent of the federal poverty level (about $26,200 for a family of three in 2000).

If these provisions opened the door to Medicaid coverage to those outside the welfare programs, then the 1996 welfare reform law blew the door off its hinges. Both Republicans and Democrats were determined to ensure that children would not lose Medicaid as a result of the new emphasis on work. The revised Medicaid statute breaks the link between Medicaid and welfare and requires states to cover any family that meets the income, resource, and family composition guidelines in place for AFDC eligibility on July 16, 1996, before the enactment of welfare reform. The welfare reform law also added two mandatory coverage requirements for families leaving welfare. Specifically, welfare leavers with employment were given six months of Medicaid and, if family income remained below 185 percent of the federal poverty level ($26,200 in 2000) at the end of the first six months, an additional six months of coverage was mandated.

Thus by the time the welfare reform law was signed by President Clinton in August 1996, Medicaid had been transformed from a program tied almost exclusively to participation in cash welfare programs to one that provided a host of ways to qualify for coverage. A year later, in the Balanced Budget Act of 1997, Congress provided still more health insurance coverage for children by enacting the $20 billion (over five years) State Children's Health Insurance Program (SCHIP). This program was intended to help states provide health insurance to children from families with incomes above the Medicaid cutoff but, in most cases, below 200 percent of the federal poverty level ($28,300 in 2000). Combining the expanded Medicaid coverage with the new SCHIP program, there is no question that there are now more children eligible for government health coverage than ever before. The upshot of these various expansions is that mothers can leave welfare and retain Medicaid coverage for their children and, often, for themselves.

Child Care

The major conflict in federal child care policy over the past several decades has been a struggle between those who want to simply provide federal subsidies for routine market care while poor and low-income parents work and those who want to provide high-quality "developmental" child care so that preschool children receive the stimulation they need to achieve proper development. Since the 1970s federal child care policymaking, especially among Democrats, has followed two strategies to achieve the goal of providing more developmental care.

The first strategy is to directly provide federal funds to create developmental care. Nearly everyone, Republicans and Democrats alike, agrees that preparing poor children for school is a worthy goal and that it is appropriate for the federal government, in its role of helping the poor, to spend money and set general policy directions in this area. Head Start, which grows almost every year and now spends more than $5 billion a year, is the quintessential child care program promoting the development of poor children.

The second policy pursued by Democrats to ensure increased availability of developmental care is the regulatory route. Now almost forgotten, for two decades and more there was a serious struggle at the federal level over the federal interagency day care requirements (FIDCR) (Nelson 1982; Steiner 1976). The goal of the FIDCR was to create federal regulations on quality child care, including staff-child ratios, teacher training, physical resources, curriculum, and a host of other requirements that had to be met by any facility receiving federal funds. If Head Start represents the direct federal creation and virtual federal ownership of developmental child care, FIDCR represents the indirect creation of developmental care by imposing quality guidelines on hundreds of thousands of child care facilities in both the private and public sectors throughout the country.

As the drive to help mothers leave welfare increased, it became clear that inexpensive child care was a key for any policy aimed at helping mothers escape welfare dependency (Steiner 1971; Haskins 1992). If welfare reform were to reduce the welfare caseload by half, and if half of these families had a preschool child, the cost to the federal government of providing a Head Start–like program full time, year-round, would be, at a conservative cost estimate of $9,000 a year per child, more than $11 billion per year. Rather than try to finance such an expenditure, federal policymakers have continued to make moderate increases in the budget for Head Start, have resisted federal regulations (including FIDCR), and have provided states with more money to purchase routine care for poor and low-income working mothers, especially those leaving welfare. Because everyone agreed that much more child care would be needed once the welfare reform law was enacted, the final bill included an additional $4.5 billion in child care funds to be used over six years. The federal government spent about $16 billion in 2000 for all the major tax and spending programs that subsidize child care.

Food Stamps

The Food Stamp program is viewed by both Republicans and Democrats as an important link in the work support system. Every individual and family that meets the program's income and resource standards and submits an application receives coupons or an electronic benefit transfer card redeemable at millions of facilities that sell food. The gross income test is 130 percent of the federal poverty level, or around $18,400 for a family of three in 2000. If this test is met, a series of calculations is applied to earnings to determine the benefit amount.

Although there were numerous changes in the program in the 1996 welfare reform law, most of these changes had modest effects on welfare recipients. In most cases, if a mother goes to work, she faces nearly the same maximum benefit and the same phaseout rate that she would have faced before welfare reform was enacted. The program, however, remains an important part of the work support system, because most mothers leaving welfare for work at low wages are eligible for at least $1,500 in food stamps.

Child Support Enforcement

Signed into law by President Gerald Ford in 1975, the child support enforcement program is designed to encourage and, when necessary, force noncustodial parents to support their children even though they no longer live with them. The most important changes in child support enforcement included in the 1996 welfare reforms were extensive automated data processing requirements, a state and national directory of basic information on all new employees hired in the United States, a state and federal registry of all child support orders in the country, an emphasis on providing more child support payments to mothers and children rather than government, a set of strong requirements for paternity establishment, and mandatory state enforcement mechanisms such as revocation of fishing and drivers' licenses, searches of financial institutions to discover additional or hidden resources, and periodic matches of new-hire data with case registry data to promote rapid collections. Taken together, the 1996 reforms are generally agreed to be the most thorough and far-reaching reforms of child support in the history of the program. The Congressional Budget Office (1996) estimated savings of approximately $320 million a year through increased collections among welfare cases when the reforms were fully implemented (although the associated administrative costs would absorb most or all of the savings).

Other Benefits

Low-income working families are eligible for a number of additional benefits, including school lunches, the women, infant, and children (WIC) special supplemental nutrition program, housing, and a host of education and training programs. In fact, according to the Congressional Research Service about eighty programs provide benefits to those with limited income, twenty-eight of which had a funding level of at least $1 billion in 1996 (Burke 1997). Unfortunately, I know of no analysis that attempts to identify the portion of this spending that helps working families. The amount, however, must be substantial; probably at least $20 billion in addition to the amount spent under the primary entitlement programs. Moreover, many states conduct their own benefit programs to help working families. The point is simply that our nation has made a substantial commitment to low-income families that work.

ASSESSING THE WORK SUPPORT SYSTEM

Table 14.1 shows how changes in the AFDC-TANF cash welfare programs conducted by states, coupled with the growth of the work support system since 1986, have combined to greatly increase work incentives for mothers receiving welfare in a typical state (Pennsylvania) that provides median benefits. On the one hand, even in 1986, mothers receiving welfare had a financial incentive to work because they could increase their income by nearly $3,600. On the other hand, by increasing their incomes, they would lose all Medicaid coverage for themselves and their children. Given such a system, it is not difficult to imagine a mother making a rational decision to stay on welfare. By 1998, however, the financial incentive to work had increased to well over $9,000, both the mother and her children were eligible to receive Medicaid for at least a year after leaving welfare, and most children would retain Medicaid coverage for as long as the mother's income was less than the poverty level and often well above the poverty level.

In addition to Medicaid coverage, the three major sources of added work incentives depicted in table 14.1 are a decline in welfare benefits of about $900 for nonworking mothers, an increase of more than $1,600 in the amount of welfare a mother can retain when she goes to work, and an increase of about $3,000 in the EITC. The first change can be attributed primarily to states allowing inflation to erode the value of the AFDC-TANF benefit. The second can be attributed to generous changes in

TABLE 14.1 / Returns to Work and Welfare, 1986 and 1998 (Dollars)

Year	Earnings	Federal Taxes	AFDC-TANF and Food Stamps	Earned Income Tax Credit	Total Income	Medicaid Coverage
1986						
Welfare	0	0	8,747	0	8,747	Yes
Work	10,000	-956	2,584	728	12,356	No
Difference	10,000	-956	-6,163	728	3,609	No
1998						
Welfare	0	0	7,870	0	7,870	Yes
Work	10,000	-765	4,240	3,756	17,231	Yes
Difference	10,000	-765	-3,630	3,756	9,361	Less adult coverage

Source: U.S. House of Representatives 1986; U.S. House of Representatives 1998.
Note: Estimated 1986 numbers are based on a Pennsylvania worker with $7,000 in earnings. Taxes and benefits adjusted for inflation from January 1986 to July 1998. Calculations for 1986 assume no 33 percent deduction but do assume the standard deduction of $75, the $30 deduction, and a $160 child care deduction. Federal taxes are income taxes and FICA taxes. Calculations made by the Congressional Research Service.

state income disregard rules for reducing the TANF benefits of mothers who go to work. The third change can be attributed to the large increases in the federal EITC. Clearly, both states and the federal government have made policy changes in the last decade that, taken together, greatly increase the returns to low-wage work for mothers leaving welfare.

Figure 14.1 reveals the magnitude of the federal changes. In 1998 the Congressional Budget Office (Congressional Budget Office 1998) estimated how much the federal government would spend in entitlement dollars on the work support programs (child care, SCHIP, the child tax credit, Medicaid, and the EITC) that had been expanded or created by Congress since the mid-1980s. As shown in the left bar graph, if Congress had not expanded these work support programs, the federal government would have spent less than $6 billion to subsidize the incomes of low-income, working families in 1999. However, with the expansions, the federal government was expected to spend nearly $52 billion in 1999. The difference between $6 billion and $52 billion in entitlement funding represents a dramatic growth in the federal commitment to working families. The federal commitment is even more impressive than these figures suggest: the analysis was based only on entitlement

FIGURE 14.1   /   Support for Working Families Increases Between 1984 and 1999 (Billions of 1999 Dollars)

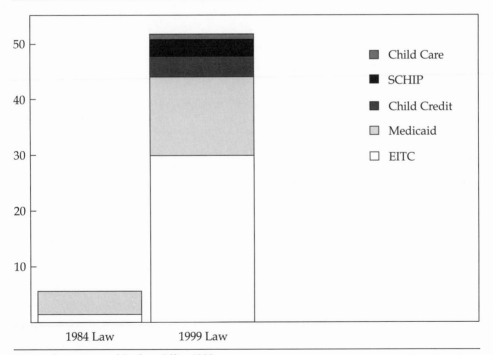

Source: Congressional Budget Office 1998.

spending and on programs that had changed substantially since 1984. Thus food stamps, housing benefits, school lunches, and a host of other, primarily nonentitlement, benefits were excluded from the analysis. If these programs were included, it is likely that the federal government spent at least $65 billion on benefits for poor and low-income working families in 1999.

There can be no question that the federal government has committed itself to a new approach to policy for poor and low-income families. Although it is certainly true that welfare reform greatly strengthened the likelihood that mothers would work or leave welfare, under duress if necessary, it is also true that the nation has developed a very generous work support system that helps former welfare mothers, as well as other low-income working families, and their children.

THE EFFECTS OF THE 1996 WELFARE REFORM LAW

It has been seven years since more than half of the states implemented their own welfare-to-work programs under waivers and five years since passage of the federal welfare reform law itself in 1996. Few pieces of legislation have stimulated as much study and research as the 1996 reform law. As a result, we have abundant information on the effects of the law. This information permits us to make informed judgments about the joint effects of the welfare reform legislation and the expansions of the work support system. Although many observers claim that we must wait for additional studies, enough is now known to conclude that the immediate effects of welfare reform are positive. To be sure, there are issues and questions that require further attention, but enough is known to draw at least tentative conclusions about the effects of the 1996 law.

At the most general level, there seems to be widespread agreement that

- There has been no race to the bottom by states; indeed, many states have increased benefits.

- There is little evidence that states have simply dumped people from the welfare rolls.

- Many poor families formerly on welfare have shown that they are capable of supporting themselves once they leave the rolls, in part because of the work support system for working families.

- There is little evidence of an increase in homelessness or increased hunger related to welfare reform.

- There is little or no evidence of an unusual increase in state foster care caseloads.

The implementation of welfare reform has raised other issues and problems, but the widely predicted disasters have not materialized.

By contrast, there is solid evidence of a host of positive effects on welfare offices around the country; on caseload sizes in every state; on federal money available per family distributed to states to conduct their benefit and work programs; on employment of mothers, especially never-married mothers; on income in single-mother families; and on poverty. There are problems, and I examine the most important ones, but overall, the news is good.

Caseload Reductions

Consideration of the effects of welfare reform properly begins with caseload reductions (figure 14.2). Between spring 1994 and spring 2000, the most recent period for which we have data, the number of families on welfare fell 56 percent, with six consecutive years of decline. This caseload decline is without precedent in the history of welfare programs. In fact, declines in just two consecutive years are almost unprecedented.

Two additional points provide perspective on these caseload declines. First, many people seem to think that welfare rolls move up and down in rough correlation with the economy: when the economy is good and employment is high, the rolls decline; when the economy is bad and employment is declining, the rolls increase. Almost every media story about the recent caseload decline contains the claim that a primary cause of the decline is the nation's booming economy. This view is questionable, however. Over the course of the economic recovery in the 1980s, during which the economy produced a net increase of approximately 20 million jobs, the welfare rolls increased by more than 12 percent. Similarly, during the initial three years of the recovery in the 1990s, as the economy was adding approximately 3 million jobs, the welfare caseload experienced a period of rapid growth, increasing from 4.4 million to 5.1 million families. It was not until spring 1994, at which time more than half of the states had mounted their own welfare reform programs by obtaining waivers from federal requirements, that the caseload began to decline. The

FIGURE 14.2 / AFDC-TANF Caseload, 1959 Through 1999 (Millions of Families)

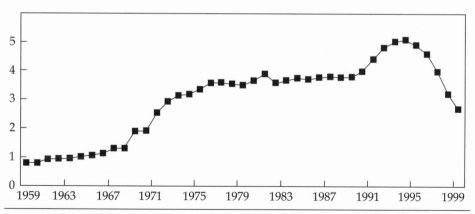

Source: Author's configuration based on data from U.S. Department of Health and Human Services, available at: *www.acf.dhhs.gov/news/stats.*

decline was modest until 1996, when federal reform was enacted. Since then, the rolls have been in free fall. The President's Council of Economic Advisers (Council of Economic Advisers 1999, 119) claims that only one-fifth of the caseload decline can be attributed to the economy.

A second interesting point about caseload declines is that, as remarkable as a national 50 percent decline might be, many states have had substantially greater declines. Fourteen states have seen declines between 50 to 59 percent, and fifteen states have experienced drop-offs of more than 60 percent. Three of these states—Idaho, Wyoming, and Wisconsin—have experienced declines exceeding 80 percent.

Money Available to States

Because caseloads have plummeted, the average number of federal TANF and child care block grant dollars that states have to spend per family has increased substantially. Whereas the average state had federal funds averaging $3,522 per family under the old AFDC and child care programs, by 2000 states had an average of more than $9,000 per family. This impressive increase is the mathematical result of the fixed funding feature of the TANF block grant, scheduled increases in the child care block grant, and the precipitous drop in caseloads.

Although many experts predicted a race to the bottom if states were given full responsibility for cash welfare, this has not happened. States have used their money to maintain and even expand benefits, primarily by making their income disregard rules more generous so that working mothers can retain more of their cash welfare benefit once they begin working. Moreover, many states are investing in child care, transportation, postsecondary training, education, wage supplements, and a host of other welfare-to-work services and benefits designed to help poor mothers and fathers join the workforce. Thus the financial landscape five years after the welfare law was enacted is exceptionally positive.

Work Rates

A fundamental expectation of the Republicans who insisted on strong work requirements was that most people who left welfare would work. Although Democrats argued that the poor must have entitlement benefits or they would be unable to support their families, Republicans responded that most of the poor were capable of supporting themselves but did not do so because they had been trapped by the entitlement-based welfare system. We now have two major sources of empirical information on whether mothers who leave welfare are working. The first source is national data sets of representative samples of the U.S. population; the second is studies by states that locate and interview former welfare recipients. Both sources reveal a dramatic increase in work.

To begin with the national picture, figure 14.3 summarizes data from the Current Population Survey (CPS) on annual changes in the percentage of married, single,

FIGURE 14.3 / Married, Single, and Never-Married Mothers Working,
1985 Through 1999 (Percentage)

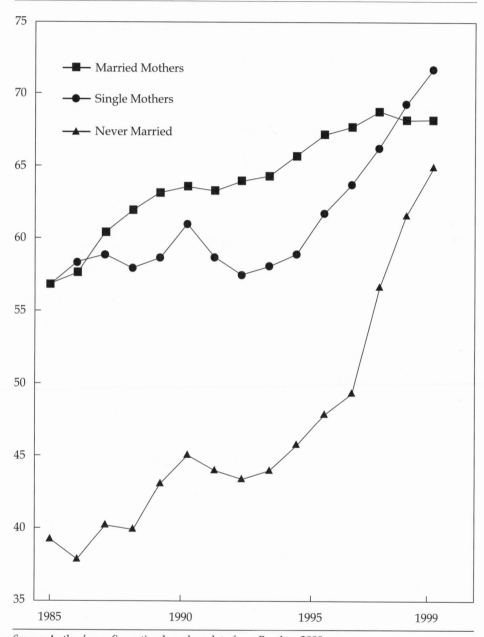

Source: Author's configuration based on data from Burtless 2000.

and never-married mothers who were employed in March of each year between 1985 and 1999 (Burtless 2000). The trend for married mothers shows a slow and steady rise until the last two years, at which time the trend stabilized. The percentage working grew from 57 to 68, or by nearly 20 percent over the entire period.

The trend for all single mothers contrasts sharply with the slow, steady rise for married mothers. Between 1986 and 1994 the percentage of working single mothers was almost flat. In 1986 it was 58.3 percent; eight years later, in 1994, it was still only 58.8 percent. The effect of the upward trend for married mothers, combined with the flat trend for single mothers, meant that a higher percentage of married mothers worked during the period 1986 through 1994. Most important for our purposes, the trend for single mothers changed abruptly after 1994 and began a sharp rise, which by 1998 carried the percentage of working single mothers above the percentage of working married mothers. In the five years after 1994, the percentage of single mothers working rose almost 22 percent, a greater percentage rise than for married mothers over the entire fourteen-year period.

Even more remarkable than the rise in work among all single mothers was the rise in work among the never-married subgroup of single mothers. For our purposes, this is the most interesting group because never-married mothers are the ones who have the least education and who historically have worked the least. They are also the most likely to be on welfare and to stay on welfare for long periods (Adams and Williams 1990; U.S. House of Representatives 1998, 532–41). Thus the fact that the percentage of never-married mothers who worked exploded after 1993 is extremely important. Compared with a mere 6 percent increase among married mothers and nearly a 25 percent increase among all single mothers, the percentage of never-married mothers working increased by almost half over the six years between 1993 and 1999.

The second source of data on the effects of welfare reform on employment is state surveys of mothers who have left welfare. In an early review of state studies, the General Accounting Office (1999b) determined that seven state studies (Indiana, Maryland, Oklahoma, South Carolina, Tennessee, Washington, Wisconsin) were of sufficient quality that reliable conclusions could be drawn from the results. These states located and interviewed welfare leavers who had been off the rolls between two and eighteen months. Two findings from these seven states are pertinent here. First, of the six states reporting the percentage of welfare leavers employed at the time of the interview, all found at least 60 percent of them employed. Second, in all but one state, at least 80 percent had been employed at some time since leaving welfare. A more recent review of more than forty state leaver studies produced conclusions similar to those of General Accounting Office (Devere, Falk, and Burke 2000).

These increases in labor force participation are precisely what Congress and the president hoped to achieve with welfare reform. Now at least 1.5 million additional mothers, including many who were very disadvantaged, are working rather than languishing on welfare.

Income and Spending

There are now more than 2.8 million fewer families receiving cash assistance than in 1994. Some adults were on welfare but left. However, because others did not begin receiving welfare (when, before 1994, they most likely would have), studying only those who leave welfare would present a biased picture. Thus the best method to make judgments about the effects of welfare reform on income is to examine population data.

A number of studies of changes in income for poor and low-income mothers using such data are now beginning to appear (see Bavier 2000; Haskins 2001; Primus 1999; Schoeni and Blank 2000); these studies use national samples either from the March CPS, from panels in the Study of Income and Program Participation (SIPP), or from the Consumer Expenditure Survey.

These studies agree that the income of single mothers in the bottom fifth (or quintile; incomes under approximately $11,800 in 1999) of the income distribution of mothers heading families was greater in 1999, the most recent year for which data are available, than in 1993, the year before a majority of states had undertaken reform under welfare waivers. In the CPS, for example, income for this quintile rose from $6,711 to $7,606, an increase of about 13 percent (all figures in constant 1999 dollars). Income rose rapidly—by nearly $1,000—in both 1994 and 1995 but then lost about half of that gain in 1996 and 1997 before holding even in 1998 and increasing again in 1999. The study of the 1996 SIPP panel (Bavier 2000) finds that the number of mothers who left welfare in 1996 grew as a proportion of mothers in the bottom quintile and that their trends in income were slightly downward during the year following exit.

The pattern of changes in sources of income is strikingly consistent across CPS studies: earnings and EITC income increase substantially, but income from cash welfare and food stamps falls. Even during 1996 and 1997, the years of falling income in the bottom quintile, earnings and the EITC continued to increase while cash assistance and food stamps fell more, resulting in a net loss of income.

According to the SIPP data, more than two-thirds of mothers who leave welfare have income that puts them in the second income quintile ($11,800 to $17,250 in 1999 in the CPS) or higher. During the 1993-through-1999 period, average CPS income for mothers in the second quintile increased every year except 1996. Over the entire period, income increased from $13,201 to $16,019, a rise of more than 21 percent. Interestingly, the pattern of changes in sources of income is the same as that for the bottom quintile: increases in earnings and EITC, declines in cash welfare and food stamps. In the second quintile, however, the combined increase in earnings and the EITC was nearly four times greater than the gain in income from earnings and the EITC in the bottom quintile.

Finally, according to data from the Consumer Expenditure Survey, spending by mothers in both the bottom and second quintiles generally increased from 1993 to 1999 (Haskins 2001). In the bottom quintile, not only did spending exceed income by at least $1,000 every year, and more than $2,000 in some years, but also increased by around $1,000, or 12 percent, over the period. Although the explanation of how mothers consistently spent more than their income is unclear, it probably involved borrowing, use of savings, gifts from household members or relatives, and under-reporting of income. Whatever the explanation, the picture of the bottom quintile that emerges from spending data is more positive than the one suggested by income data. Both income and spending data for the second quintile are unambiguously positive.

These data on income and spending justify at least two conclusions. First, most mothers who leave welfare (and especially if two-thirds of leavers enter the second income quintile, as shown in the SIPP data) appear to have more money than they did when they depended on welfare. Second, there is a group of mothers at the bottom of the distribution who are worse off as a result of welfare reform. Although available data will not allow a good estimate of the number of these mothers, there is no question that a relatively small group is not flourishing under welfare reform.

Poverty

Figure 14.4 shows the percentage declines in the welfare caseload, the child poverty rate, and the poverty rate among black children from 1995 through 1999 (the last year for which poverty data are available). Both the welfare caseload and child poverty declined in every year, most notably in 1997, the first full year of federal welfare reform implementation. During that year, welfare rolls declined by almost 20 percent, more than in any previous year. Yet during that year, overall child poverty declined by around 3 percent, and poverty among black children declined by nearly 7 percent, the biggest single-year decline ever for black children up to that time. However, the decline in poverty among black children in 1999 was even greater. By then poverty among all children was at its lowest level since 1979, and poverty among black children was the lowest ever.

The official measure of poverty is flawed because it ignores many benefits, including those that comprise the work support system. The data in figure 14.5 present children's poverty rates under a broader Census Bureau definition, which takes into account additional benefits such as the EITC and food stamps. The bar graphs on the far left show the rate of child poverty during the year before and the last year in which poverty declined during the economic expansion of the 1980s. The second set of bar graphs shows the rate of child poverty during comparable years of the economic expansion of the 1990s. The last set of bar graphs shows the percentage decline in child poverty during the 1980s and during the 1990s. There is not much doubt which decade saw the most rapid and deepest decline in child poverty.

The explanation for the more rapid progress against poverty in the 1990s seems straightforward. First, as the CPS data on employment show (see figure 14.3), single and never-married mothers were much more likely to work during the 1990s. It is likely that many of these mothers would still have been on welfare if the demanding reforms of 1996 had not been enacted. With more mothers working,

FIGURE 14.4   /   Welfare Caseload and Child Poverty Simultaneous Decline,
                  1995 Through 1999

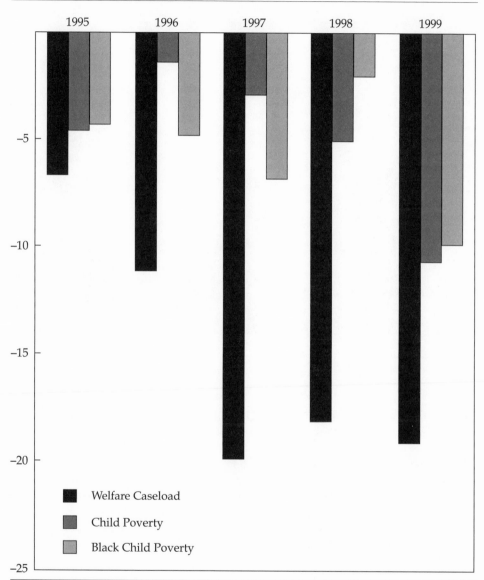

Source: Caseload data from U.S. Department of Health and Human Services; poverty data from U.S. Census Bureau 2000.

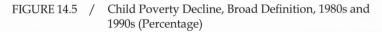

FIGURE 14.5   /   Child Poverty Decline, Broad Definition, 1980s and
1990s (Percentage)

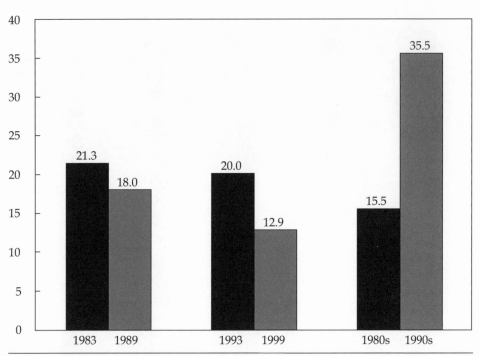

Source: U.S. Census Bureau 2000.

and with more mothers receiving the EITC, the economic expansion actually had an impact on poverty because, for the first time, mothers who normally stayed on welfare were now working. In short, the combination of more work and more work support explains the rapid decline in poverty during the 1990s.

In summary, poverty has fallen during each year of welfare reform, has fallen among minority children by an unprecedented amount, is even lower if we use a poverty measure that includes benefits from the work support system, and fell more in the 1990s than in the 1980s. That our nation has been able to achieve historic declines in welfare caseloads simultaneously with substantial declines in poverty is a solid achievement.

THE NEW WORLD OF WORK

Five years into the nation's experiment of replacing welfare with work, two broad conclusions are justified. First, the combination of strict welfare rules, which encourage or force families into self-support, and the work support system, designed to help low-income working families, has produced substantial success. Nevertheless, there is much left to do. In examining where welfare policy is now and where it should be headed, it is useful to recall that under the old welfare system, progress against child poverty was virtually impossible to achieve. The nation tried for thirty years to decrease it by wrapping families in entitlement benefits. Just giving poor people more money turned out to have both political flaws and unintended consequences for family and community life. Thus even though the nation increased means-tested spending by nearly a factor of nine in constant dollars between 1965 and 1995 (Burke 1997; Rector and Lauber 1995), child poverty did not fall.

Currently, public opinion, much of the media, and most politicians now send or reflect the clear message that adults, including single mothers of young children, must work. Given the welfare reforms of 1996 and nearly two decades of expanding government support for low-income working families, the work message is now backed by pressure to leave welfare to enter or stay in the labor force. As the review of evidence demonstrates, early indications are that this new approach will reduce poverty and increase income for most (though not all) families at the bottom of the income distribution. Mothers who in the past would have been on welfare are now working, and their earnings, combined with income from the greatly improved work support system, are improving their economic status.

The best way to ensure both political support for the new system and continued progress in reducing poverty and increasing incomes is to study the defects in the new system and fix them. My own version of this approach produces an agenda of four items, all of which could and should receive bipartisan attention and support. These are to fix Medicaid, fix food stamps, help floundering families, and build a permanent employment system.

Fix Medicaid

Why is it that when the nation has enough entitlement money to provide health insurance for nearly all children in families earning less than $28,000 for families of three or $34,000 for families of four, Medicaid enrollment is declining? Since its inception in 1965, Medicaid has achieved almost continuous increases in children's enrollment. Between 1991 and 1996, for example, children's enrollment increased from 16 million to more than 20 million, an increase of nearly 30 percent. In 1997, however, the very year in which the SCHIP program was enacted, child enrollment in Medicaid dropped by more than 840,000, or 4 percent. Between 1995 and 1998, Medicaid enrollment declined 12 percent in California, 18 percent in Florida, and 29 percent in Wisconsin, despite the fact that all three states had broadened their coverage (M. Ellwood 1999).

Fortunately, good studies of the causes of declining Medicaid coverage are beginning to appear (M. Ellwood 1999; Lyons 1999; Smith et al. 1998). These studies are based on careful reviews of the Medicaid program in one or more states, on interviews with the state personnel responsible for administering the program, on reviews of the computer system in place to facilitate enrollment and send notices, and on close inspection of state written policies and procedures. My reading of these studies is that a great deal can be done fairly quickly to improve coverage.

The first problem is in the federal statutes. It is certainly a good thing that new mandatory and optional coverage is now part of federal law, but the price has been complexity. One solution to this complexity is increased state flexibility in the use of federal funds. Both the Bush I and the Clinton administrations allowed state demonstrations under Section 1115 of the Social Security Act, but much more flexibility is needed. The logical extension of state flexibility is a block grant. Four or five states should be allowed complete flexibility with their Medicaid and SCHIP money as long as they provide at least minimum coverage to all children living in families earning under 200 percent of the poverty level. The amount of federal money that states receive each year would be negotiated before the demonstrations begin. Converting the entire Medicaid program into a block grant has no political prospects of succeeding, but given the right contractual guarantees by both the federal and state governments, it should be possible to allow a limited number of states to experiment with a block grant, especially if they agree to thorough third-party evaluation of their program and its effects.

Another important factor in the decline of Medicaid enrollment is that both state administrators and parents have a difficult time understanding eligibility. In most states TANF caseworkers continue to play a major role in educating families about Medicaid eligibility (M. Ellwood 1999). But TANF workers, logically enough, often see themselves as responsible primarily for TANF, with Medicaid an unwelcome secondary responsibility. This fact, combined with the immense complexity of Medicaid eligibility rules, further undermines the role that these caseworkers should be playing in guaranteeing Medicaid coverage.

Researchers also find several administrative problems with Medicaid's eligibility determination procedures, which also contribute to reduced coverage. These problems include the automated systems for determining eligibility, which do not work well; complex and lengthy application forms, which both caseworkers and parents have trouble following; burdensome office visits for continuing eligibility; and notices that are sometimes sent improperly and that are often difficult for parents to understand, sometimes because of language barriers.

Thus states should carefully evaluate their programs and then take action to achieve administrative simplification, better computer capability, and better staff training at the state and local levels. Aggressive state action can significantly reduce the number of eligible children who are not receiving Medicaid coverage.

Fix Food Stamps

Like the Medicaid program, the Food Stamp program has experienced large declines in enrollment. In 1994, at the outset of state-initiated welfare reform, 27.5 million people were receiving food stamps (at any given moment, roughly half of the people receiving food stamps are children). By May 1999, 18 million people were receiving food stamps, a decline of 35 percent in just over four years. Although there were some changes in food stamp eligibility in the 1996 welfare reform bill, this decline is much greater than the one predicted by the Congressional Budget Office in 1996. The decline is also much greater than in previous economic recoveries.

Even more compelling, the National Survey of America's Families being conducted by the Urban Institute (Zedlewski 1999) reveals that families leaving welfare are less likely than families that never received cash welfare to be receiving food stamps. Averaged across all income levels up to the program's gross limit of 130 percent of poverty, 62 percent of families never on welfare are receiving food stamps, compared with only 46 percent of families leaving welfare. The General Accounting Office (1999a) finds that in fiscal year 1997, while the number of children living in poverty dropped by 350,000, or 3 percent, the number of children participating in the Food Stamp program declined by 1.3 million, or 10 percent. Thus the percentage of children living in poverty who received food stamps probably dropped during 1997.

Not all of the decline in program participation is bad. Some families leaving welfare now earn too much to qualify for food stamps. In addition, there are undoubtedly families that regard food stamps as welfare and therefore do not want them. This group of families raises the difficult issue of stigma. Some observers believe stigma is bad; if people qualify for benefits, they should receive them, and others should not think less of them for needing such income supplements. At least in my view, however, this argument is naive. All of us are motivated to some extent by the expectations, and especially the condemnation, of family members, friends, peers, and even the abstract "they." Family and community norms and expectations are a powerful influence on human behavior. As demonstrated by recent studies of welfare recipients (Burton et al. 1998; Quint et al. 1999), those receiving benefits believe that adults should try to support themselves. I believe a majority of Americans agree with this sentiment and are highly respectful of families that reject food stamps because they do not want to carry the stigma of welfare. Stigma is a powerful and usually positive force; it should be maintained and respected.

Even so, few Americans are likely to begrudge a thousand dollars or so in food stamps to a working single mother with an annual income (from earnings and EITC) of $15,000 or less. For my part, I would be satisfied to let the mother make her own decision. Yet to make the decision, she must be fully informed about her eligibility and about the size of the benefit for which she is eligible. Thus states have an obligation to ensure that families are fully informed about their continuing eligibility status for food stamps once they begin working.

In this regard, part of the problem of ensuring continued food stamp eligibility is identical to the problem of ensuring continued Medicaid eligibility. Once families leave welfare, they are more difficult to follow. Some may not even know that they are eligible, or if they have a general belief that they may be eligible, they may not know the size of the benefit for which they remain eligible and what they must do to get it. As with Medicaid, there is much administrative work that states must complete so as to keep clients informed of eligibility and to make application and continuing eligibility determinations as easy as possible, including the use of mail-in continuing eligibility forms, better computer-generated notices, and better staff training.

Another cause of reduced food stamp enrollment is the program's quality control system. States are required to pay financial penalties to the federal government if they make too many errors in determining eligibility. Unfortunately, the cases most likely to result in errors are the households in which someone works. Thus TANF encourages or requires adults to work, which in turn raises the state's error rate, which in turn results in financial penalties. Although some type of quality control is necessary, there is a clear tension between the TANF goal of work and the federal goal of reducing errors in the Food Stamp program.

Given these many and diverse issues, the major burden is on states to revise their computer systems, to simplify their application and redetermination processes, and in general to make every effort to be certain that eligible families know they are eligible and find it easy to apply for and maintain their food stamp benefits. However, as long as there is such a vast difference in philosophy between the Food Stamp program and TANF, there will be problems with the administration of the Food Stamp program. One approach to determining whether this program and TANF could be reconciled would be to conduct a demonstration project in which states are given complete control over their food stamp money. With proper oversight and evaluation, such a demonstration would allow Congress to discover whether the Food Stamp and TANF programs can operate together in a more effective and efficient fashion.

Help Floundering Families

The review of income data shows that there are problems at the bottom of the income scale. Some critics argue that a substantial group of mothers are worse off as a result of welfare reform (Primus 1999; Children's Defense Fund 1998). That some mothers are worse off is not surprising. Mothers receiving welfare are now required to participate in work or work preparation activities. If they fail to comply with requirements, they are sanctioned by having their welfare checks reduced. Up to 30 percent of recipient families are sanctioned in some states, and thirty-seven states have full-check sanctions, meaning that the state can terminate all TANF benefits to families that violate work rules (Rector and Youssef 1999, table 1; General Accounting Office 2000; also see chapter 6, this volume). Thus whereas incompetent adults could remain on the rolls year after year under the old AFDC program, now adults who cannot or do not comply with requirements can lose their benefits and as a result have very low incomes.

Few policies do not make at least some people worse off. On balance, the research shows that more people are better off than worse off as a result of welfare reform. Even so, because some people are worse off, every effort should be made to help these families.

At least three actions should be taken. First, income data from the bottom quintile makes it clear that the decline in income in 1996 and 1997 was caused primarily by a drop in welfare income, especially cash welfare and food stamps (earnings and EITC actually increased). Although food stamp income did drop, it seems apparent that the average family was eligible for more food stamps than the family received. On average, these families received about $1,000 in food stamps in 1999 based on earnings of approximately $2,400. In most cases, a family of three with earnings of $2,400 is eligible for nearly $4,000 in food stamps. Thus ensuring that these families participate in the program and receive their full benefits could make a big difference in the income of these families.

Second, as research suggests (Herr and Wagner 1998), much can be done to help these floundering families stay in or get back into the labor force. A host of techniques have been developed for helping multiple-problem families, most of which involve direct contact with the family, use of small steps to move them toward work, and much hand-holding following failure (Herr and Wagner 1998). Conservatives can be convinced that this type of intervention is justified, especially given that this is precisely the kind of work at which they believe churches and other faith-based organizations excel. However, it must also be acknowledged that much of this work with multiple-problem families will take place while they are still receiving welfare. States have enough TANF money to keep these families on welfare as long as it takes to help them achieve self-sufficiency. Moreover, the 20 percent exemption from the time limit, plus the leeway states have to use state programs funded by state maintenance-of-effort dollars to provide welfare for these families, offer the flexibility needed to keep them on welfare provided they are meeting work requirements. At some point, when families fail to cooperate completely with work requirements, government responsibility is greatly diminished.

Third—and here there are serious partisan issues—marriage among poor and low-income young adults should be pursued vigorously by the states. There is now extensive research showing that marriage has substantial advantages for both men and women (Gallagher 1999; Waite 1995; Waite and Gallagher 2000). These advantages include positive effects on health and economic status, frequency of and satisfaction with sex, and happiness. Moreover, since publication of Sara McLanahan and Gary Sandefur's *Growing Up with a Single Parent* in 1994, there appears to be nearly universal agreement that two-parent families confer substantial advantages on children.

Based on the overwhelming House passage of bipartisan fatherhood legislation at the end of the 2000 session of Congress (H.R. 4678), it seems likely that Congress will be able to pass legislation promoting marriage, better parenting, and fathers' employment within the next several years. In addition, there appears to be bipartisan support for a tax code provision that would reduce the marriage penalty inherent in the structure of the EITC (D. Ellwood 1999). Indeed, this provision, which would lengthen the phaseout range of the EITC for married couples, was included in the tax bill enacted by Congress in both 1999 and 2000. Although President Clinton vetoed the congressional tax bill, if there is bipartisan tax legislation within the next few years, the EITC provision will have an excellent chance of being included. Clearly, Congress has been taking action to make both work and marriage pay, and can be expected to continue enacting similar policies in the future.

Build a Permanent Employment System

As the economy moves toward an increasing number of small employers and an increasing number of job changes (and even career changes) for most workers, there will be even more churning of employees and employers than there is now, bringing new meaning to Schumpeter's aphorism that capitalism is "creative destruction." In short, many Americans, not just the poor, will be playing musical jobs. Rather than trying to stop the music, the role of government should be to help people join the dance (Good 1998).

Focusing exclusively on policy for poor and low-income workers, I believe we should develop a chain of government centers that blanket the nation to render four services: to help clients find jobs, to help them retain their jobs, to help them find new jobs when they are facing transitions, and to help them improve their education and training (either directly or through brokered arrangements) to qualify for new and better jobs. None of these services is new; most even have a fairly substantial research base. Furthermore, there are now a few centers around the country that perform at least three of these four functions. These model centers are now demonstrating what can be accomplished by containing interagency rivalries, coordinating federal and state funds, emphasizing staff training, and insisting on good customer service.

Although these centers would probably have unique funding structures, TANF, the U.S. Employment Service, and the Workforce Investment Act would underwrite the basic funding for most of them. If these centers are to provide the range of services outlined above, they would need access to funding that provides great local flexibility. TANF already meets this requirement, but future legislation will need to build additional flexibility into funding of the Employment Service and the Workforce Investment Act. The goal of these changes should be to provide state and local officials with maximum control and flexibility over funding so they could spend money for any of the four services and for any of the clients that they judge to be in need of the services.

A FINAL WORD

My final word concerns—what else?—money. The states are now fortunate to have sufficient money to help poor and low-income families find and keep work. Indeed, the Congressional Budget Office estimates that the states will have saved about $11 billion in TANF funds by the end of 2002. Although some of this money is being saved by states as a rainy-day fund against future recessions, states should spend some of these savings on the activities recommended in this chapter. Above all, however, states must not use TANF funds to play budget games and supplant other state spending. Although state budget officials may be tempted to use these funds to free up state funds for non-TANF purposes, in the long run, Congress will make states pay a serious price if they misuse the flexibility in the TANF block grant in this fashion. As the nation moves toward a society of full employment for nearly all adults, it would be a shame if state governments were handicapped in helping poor and low-income families keep up because state legislatures and administrative agencies did not use federal resources properly. It would equally be a shame if Congress interpreted accumulated savings or the misdeeds of a few states as a sign that the welfare and work systems were fulfilling their promise and did not need all of the available federal money. Thus the message to states is: Spend TANF money wisely. The message to Congress is: Ensure full TANF funding.

REFERENCES

Adams, Gina, and Roberton C. Williams. 1990. *Sources of Support for Adolescent Mothers.* Washington: Congressional Budget Office.

Bavier, Richard. March 2000. "A Look at Welfare Reform in the Survey of Income and Program Participation." Unpublished manuscript. Office of Management and Budget, Washington, D.C.

Burke, Vee. 1997. *Cash and Noncash Benefits for Persons with Limited Income: Eligibility Rules, Recipient and Expenditure Data, FY1994–FY1996.* 98-226 EPW. Washington, D.C.: Congressional Research Service.

Burtless, Gary. 2000. *Can the Labor Market Absorb Three Million Welfare Recipients?* Washington, D.C.: Brookings (March).

Burton, Linda, Andrew J. Cherlin, Judith Francis, Robin Jarrett, James Quane, Constance Williams, and N. Michelle Stem Cook. June 1998. *What Welfare Recipients and the Fathers of Their Children Are Saying About Welfare Reform.* Baltimore: Department of Sociology, Johns Hopkins University.

Children's Defense Fund. 1998. *Welfare to What? Early Findings on Family Hardship and Well-being.* Washington, D.C.: Children's Defense Fund.

Congressional Budget Office. 1996. *CBO Memorandum: Federal Budgetary Implications of the Personal Responsibility and Work Opportunity Reconciliation Act of 1996.* Washington: Congressional Budget Office.

———. September 1998. *Policy Changes Affecting Mandatory Spending for Low-Income Families Not Receiving Cash Welfare.* Washington: Congressional Budget Office.

Council of Economic Advisers. 1999. *Economic Report of the President.* H. Doc. 106-002. Washington: U.S. Government Printing Office.

Devere, Christine, Gene Falk, and Vee Burke. 2000. *Welfare Reform Research: What Have We Learned Since the Family Support Act of 1988?* RL-30724. Washington, D.C.: Congressional Research Service.

Ellwood, David T. 1999. "The Impact of the Earned Income Tax Credit and Other Social Policy Changes on Work and Marriage in the United States." Kennedy School of Government, Harvard University, Cambridge, Mass.

Ellwood, Marilyn. 1999. *The Medicaid Eligibility Maze: Coverage Expands, but Problems Persist.* MPR 8511-200. Cambridge, Mass.: Mathematica Policy Research.

Gallagher, Maggie. 1999. *The Age of Unwed Mothers: Is Teen Pregnancy the Problem?* New York: Institute for American Values.

General Accounting Office. 1999a. *Food Stamp Program: Various Factors Have Led to Declining Participation*. GAO/RCED-99-185. Washington: General Accounting Office.

———. 1999b. *Welfare Reform: Information on Former Recipients' Status*. GAO/HEHS-99-48. Washington: General Accounting Office.

———. 2000. *Welfare Reform: State Sanction Policies and Number of Families Affected*. GAO/HEHS-00-44. Washington: General Accounting Office.

Good, Larry. 1998. *Never Leaving the Workforce: Creating a New Employment Model*. Ann Arbor, Mich.: Corporation for a Skilled Workforce.

Haskins, Ron. 1992. "Is Anything More Important than Day Care Quality?" In *Child Care in the 1990s: Trends and Consequences*, edited by Alan Booth. Hillsdale, N.J.: Lawrence Erlbaum.

———. 2001. "The Second Most Important Issue: Effects of Welfare Reform on Family Income and Poverty." In *The New World of Welfare*, edited by Rebecca M. Blank and Ron Haskins. Washington, D.C.: Brookings.

Herr, Toby, and Suzanne Wagner. 1998. *Moving from Welfare to Work as Part of a Group: How Pathways Makes Caseload Connections*. Chicago: Project Match, Erikson Institute.

Kaus, Mickey. 1992. *The End of Equality*. New York: Basic Books.

Lyons, Barbara. 1999. *Health Coverage and Access to Care: Key Issues for Low-Income Children and Their Families*. Washington, D.C.: Packard Foundation.

McLanahan, Sara, and Gary Sandefur. 1994. *Growing Up with a Single Parent: What Hurts, What Helps*. Cambridge, Mass.: Harvard University Press.

Mead, Lawrence. 1986. *Beyond Entitlement: The Social Obligations of Citizenship*. New York: Free Press.

Murray, Charles. 1984. *Losing Ground: American Social Policy, 1950–1980*. New York: Basic Books.

Nelson, John R. 1982. "The Politics of Federal Day Care Regulation." In *Day Care: Scientific and Social Policy Issues*, edited by Edward F. Zigler and E. W. Gordon. Boston: Auburn House.

Primus, Wendell. 1999. "The Impact of Welfare Reform on Low-Income Families." Testimony before the Subcommittee on Human Resources, Committee on Ways and Means, U.S. House of Representatives (May 27).

Quint, Janet, Kathryn Edin, Maria Buck, Barbara Fink, Yolanda Padilla, Olis Simmons-Hewitt, and Mary E. Valmont. 1999. *Big Cities and Welfare Reform: Early Implementation and Ethnographic Findings from the Project on Devolution and Urban Change*. New York: Manpower Demonstration Research Corporation.

Rector, Robert, and William F. Lauber. 1995. *America's Failed $5.4 Trillion War on Poverty*. Washington, D.C.: Heritage Foundation.

Rector, Robert, and S. Youssef. 1999. *Welfare Reform and Caseload Decline*. Washington, D.C.: Heritage Foundation.

Schoeni, Robert F., and Rebecca M. Blank. 2000. "What Has Welfare Reform Accomplished? Impacts on Welfare Participation, Employment, Income, Poverty, and Family Structure." Unpublished manuscript. University of Michigan, Ann Arbor.

Smith, Vernon, Robert G. Lovell, Karin A. Peterson, and Mary Jo O'Brien. October 1998. *The Dynamics of Current Medicaid Enrollment Changes*. Lansing, Mich.: Health Management Associates.

Steiner, Gilbert Y. 1971. *The State of Welfare*. Washington, D.C.: Brookings.

———. 1976. *The Children's Cause*. Washington, D.C.: Brookings.

U.S. Census Bureau. 2000. *Poverty in the United States*. Current Population Reports, series P60–210. Washington: U.S. Government Printing Office.

U.S. House of Representatives. 1986. *1986 Green Book: Background Material and Data on Programs Within the Jurisdiction of the Committee on Ways and Means*. Washington: U.S. Government Printing Office.

———. 1998. *1998 Green Book: Background Material and Data on Programs Within the Jurisdiction of the Committee on Ways and Means*. Washington: U.S. Government Printing Office.

———. 2000. *2000 Green Book: Background Material and Data on Programs Within the Jurisdiction of the Committee on Ways and Means*. Washington: U.S. Government Printing Office.

Waite, Linda. 1995. "Does Marriage Matter?" *Demography* 32(4): 483–507.

Waite, Linda, and Maggie Gallagher. 2000. *The Case for Marriage*. New York: Doubleday.

Zedlewski, Sheila R. 1999. "Declines in Food Stamp and Welfare Participation: Is There a Connection?" Testimony before the Subcommittee on Department Operations, Oversight, Nutrition, and Forestry, Committee on Agriculture, U.S. House of Representatives (August 5).

Chapter 15

Reforming the Social Family Contract: Public Support for Child Rearing in the United States

Paula England and Nancy Folbre

Politicians offered a number of reasons for reforming the social welfare system in 1996. The actual wording of the legislation emphasized the importance of reducing out-of-wedlock births.[1] Conservatives pointed to the advantages of giving states more autonomy from the federal government. They also emphasized the importance of reducing the number of families receiving welfare. Another goal, especially among liberal Democrats who supported the bill, was to create a stronger political consensus for reducing poverty among children. By at least one account, President Bill Clinton offered this hope as his rationale for signing the bill (Morris 1998). Since that time, a number of social scientists have speculated that a new "contingent social contract" that enforced mothers' responsibilities to engage in paid employment would reduce opposition to more generous forms of public assistance (see Joint Center for Poverty Research 1999).

Explaining this concept, J. Lawrence Aber of the National Center for Children in Poverty writes,

> The public (and many policymakers) appear to believe that if parents work full-time, no matter the job, their children should not live in poverty. Some commentators see these attitudes as support for a new "contingent social contract": If you work, you and your children should be able to receive an adequate income and set of basic services. (Aber 1999)

One good example of this approach is the successful expansion of the Earned Income Tax Credit (EITC), a program that has done a great deal to help low-wage earners with children.

Overall, however, the contingent social contract that is emerging seems inadequate. Although the number of families receiving public assistance has fallen dramatically, the poverty rate among children has fallen only moderately, remains far higher than in other industrialized countries, and varies greatly across states. Part of the explanation for persistent child poverty lies in the relatively low level of public support. The EITC provides only modest assistance, with a high phaseout rate, which has the same effect as a high marginal tax rate on families as they earn more money and lose eligibility. Real benefit levels provided through Temporary Assistance for Needy Families (TANF), never very high, have declined significantly since 1996.

The principle of offering public assistance in return for work raises the question of how work is defined. Applied in its ordinary use—for instance, in the term *work requirement*—it denotes paid work. Many people, not just critics of the new welfare regime, strongly disagree with the implication that time and effort devoted to the care of family members is not work. Many public policies, including Social Security and federal income tax provisions, offer indirect support for family work, usually in the form of benefits for the spouses and children of participants in paid employment. The level of assistance to affluent families is comparable to that provided to poor families. Yet both work and eligibility for public support seem to be defined quite differently for the poor than for the nonpoor. In short, the contingent social contract seems poorly specified and inconsistent as well as inadequate.

This chapter situates an analysis of public assistance for children within the larger picture of social and family policies in the United States in 1999, which included tax benefits linked to family structure and federal entitlements such as Social Security as well as so-called welfare programs. Other scholars emphasize the need to reconsider our system of public provision and social insurance as a whole (Graetz and Mashaw 1999; Page and Simmons 2000). We hope to further this reconsideration by focusing on the subset of policies that affect families with children, or what we call *the implicit social family contract*. We argue that this contract should be renegotiated for all families, not just for the poor.

CURRENT SOCIAL AND FAMILY POLICIES

Most Northwest European countries offer universal family allowances designed to reward the socially productive work of rearing the next generation of citizens and workers. The United States does not. However, embedded in our tax and welfare policies in 2000 were several programs that represented implicit family allowances, with very different rules depending on family income and composition. Some social programs, such as TANF and the EITC, target families with incomes below the poverty line. Other benefits, such as those embedded in the federal income tax code, tend to increase with family income. Public spending on in-kind benefits such as food stamps, housing, and child care subsidies benefits the poor. In contrast, tax provisions such as the mortgage interest tax deduction and the nontaxability of employer-provided pensions and health insurance tend to benefit the affluent.

Comparisons are seldom made across these programs, in part because they appear in different places in the overall federal budget. Yet the programs are similar in basic respects. All residents of the United States pay taxes and, in return, enjoy eligibility for certain benefits. The three primary sources of federal revenue are income taxes, Social Security taxes, and sales and other excise taxes. The income tax is progressively graduated, imposing higher rates on those with higher income; other taxes are, however, regressive in structure. The overall structure of federal taxation in the United States is roughly proportional (Stiglitz 1988; Page and Simmons 2000).[2] That is, taxpayers at both the bottom and the top of the income distribution pay about the same proportion of their income in federal taxes.

Both public expenditures and tax exemptions or credits cost taxpayers money and increase the disposable income of those who receive them.[3] Although budget accounts for Social Security and Medicare that are labeled *social insurance* are kept separate from those labeled *public assistance,* both programs are financed from tax revenue. Furthermore, a significant portion of Medicare is subsidized by general federal tax revenue rather than by taxes originating from Social Security–Medicare taxes (Graetz and Mashaw 1999, 61). A significant portion of overall social insurance expenditures takes the form of tax exemptions for employer-sponsored pension plans and health insurance.

In other words, what we label *social insurance* is more a matter of history and habit than of underlying principle or funding structure. Therefore, when one asks what kinds of public support is provided to families with children in the United States, one must look beyond TANF, the EITC, and in-kind benefits such as food stamps and Medicaid to examine a wide variety of programs. The results of such an examination are somewhat surprising.

Tax Benefits by Income Category

The EITC is a fully refundable tax credit aimed at low-income families with children. It has become our largest "welfare" program, with total expenditures exceeding those devoted to TANF. The EITC benefit formula was designed, in principle, to allow one full-time, minimum-wage worker to support three dependents at an income above the poverty line. Benefits are closely tied to earnings, and phase out steeply after family income reaches $12,460.

The EITC is sometimes described as a wage subsidy program because a family must have *earned* income to receive it. However, it more closely resembles an income-tested family allowance. Since 1993 low-income taxpayers with no children have been eligible for the EITC, but the maximum they can receive is small, about $330. By contrast, taxpayers with one child could claim a maximum credit in 1999 of $2,312. Taxpayers with two or more children could claim a maximum credit of $3,816. No extra benefits accrue from additional children.

The federal income tax exemption for dependents, set at $2,750 in 1999, had a value equal to the taxes that would have been paid if it had not been exempt from taxation.[4] Exemptions in a progressive tax system such as that in the United States inevitably confer greater benefits to higher income families. For married couples filing a joint return in 1999, benefits amounted to $412 per child for families in the 15 percent tax bracket (with adjusted gross income of $43,050 or less), $770 per child for families in the 28 percent income tax bracket (adjusted gross income between

$43,050 and $104,050), and $852 per child for families in the 31 percent tax bracket (adjusted gross income between $104,050 and $158,550). In higher brackets, these benefits gradually phased out.

Families paying taxes also benefited from the child tax credit, a provision of the tax code implemented in 1998 that offered a credit of $500 for each child under age seventeen. The credit phased out as income exceeded $110,000 ($75,000 if single, head of household, or a qualifying widow or widower). Because it is a credit and not a deduction, its value remained the same across different tax brackets. However, it could be deducted only from taxes due; at lower incomes, it was preempted by the EITC. As a result, families with incomes below approximately $15,000 did not benefit from it.

The complexity of the tax system makes it difficult to offer precise estimates of benefits across all family types and income levels. Stylized comparisons, however, are telling. Adding together the value of the dependent exemption and the child credit, a family with two children in the 31 percent tax bracket enjoyed a subsidy of $2,704. A family with two children in the 15 percent tax bracket enjoyed the considerably lower subsidy of $1,824. A family with two children receiving the EITC could potentially have received the most generous support of all, a maximum benefit of $3,816. David Ellwood and Jeffrey Liebman (2000) describe the resulting U-shaped pattern as the "middle-class parent penalty." One could also term it a "low-income parent penalty," given that many families in the 15 percent bracket have incomes near the poverty level.

As table 15.1, which summarizes these differences, shows, the differences in level of support were greatly accentuated for families with three children, because EITC benefits did not rise for additional children. With three children, a family in the 31 percent bracket received benefits worth $4,056; with four, benefits worth $5,408. More than one-third of all children in this country live in families with

TABLE 15.1 / Tax Benefits for Families Raising Two or More Children, 1999 (Dollars)

Family	Tax Benefit
Family below poverty line	
Earned income tax credit maximum, two or more children	3,816
Family in 15 percent tax bracket	
Dependent exemption plus child credit, two children	1,824
Family in 31 percent tax bracket	
Dependent exemption plus child credit	
Two children	2,704
Three children	4,056
Four children	5,408

Source: Authors' compilation.
Note: For married couples filing jointly, the upper bound for the 15 percent tax bracket in 1999 was an adjusted gross income of $43,050; the 31 percent tax bracket applied to those with adjusted gross income between $104,050 and $158,550. These benefit estimates omit the value of the dependent exemption for a stay-at-home spouse, which represents an additional source of support for homemakers who are raising children.

three or more children; in part a result of limited EITC coverage, they are prone to significantly higher poverty rates. In 1988 the official poverty rate for children in families with one or two children was below 14 percent; for families with three or more children, the poverty rate was 28.6 percent (Greenstein 2000). These comparisons have prompted at least some bipartisan support for extending the EITC to families with three or more children.

Stylized comparisons also illustrate the impact of the personal tax exemption for a stay-at-home spouse, a child-related benefit to the extent that it subsidizes a parent who provides child care at home. The ability to claim an additional exemption offered a family in the 31 percent bracket a potential $837 in disposable income. Families receiving the EITC do not receive additional benefits for a stay-at-home spouse but are not penalized for this, either. Unlike TANF, the EITC allows an eligible, married parent to stay home with his or her children. Indeed, the steep phaseout rate imposes a high marginal tax rate on a second earner, which creates a significant marriage penalty in families in which both parents earn income (similar to the penalty imposed by the income tax code on two-earner families in general). Because the EITC, the dependent exemption, and the child credit all represent tax expenditures, it is straightforward to compare their overall costs to taxpayers. The EITC was projected to cost $31 billion in fiscal year 2001, while the combined cost of other child-related subsidies was projected to cost $54 billion (Ellwood and Liebman 2000).

Some argue that eligibility for the EITC should be expanded in such a way that increases public support for child-rearing among near-poor and middle-income families. Ellwood and Liebman of the Kennedy School of Government at Harvard University advocate this approach. Robert Cherry of Brooklyn College at the CUNY Graduate Center and Max Sawicky of the Economic Policy Institute have developed a detailed proposal for a universal unified tax credit, which would combine the dependent exemption, child credit, and the EITC into a single credit. This credit would initially rise along with earnings and then phase down to a minimum benefit of $1,270 per child for all families (Ellwood and Liebman 2000; Cherry and Sawicky 2000). This would be a distinct improvement over existing policies.

Public Assistance Versus Social Insurance

Benefit levels for TANF, like those for its predecessor, Aid to Families with Dependent Children (AFDC), vary considerably by state. In 1998 the average monthly benefit ranged from a low of $139.58 a month in Alabama to a high of $565.70 in Wisconsin (U.S. House of Representatives 2000, table 7.6). The maximum benefit in the median state in 2000 was $421 a month for a family of three, which amounted to $5,052 per year (U.S. House of Representatives 2000, table 7.7).

This amount was low in absolute terms. Even if the income that a mother and two children would receive is attributed entirely to the children, it amounted to $2,526 a year per child. This is substantially less than the cost of foster care, which averaged about $6,000 a year per child on a national level in 1996 (Boots and Green 2000). New welfare rules have encouraged states to give priority to foster caregivers who are related to a child, although states vary in the extent to which they do so and the level at which they remunerate this care. Foster care payments are usually higher than welfare grants in the same state. For instance, in 1996 two children living in Maryland with relatives licensed by the foster care system would have received over $1,000 a month, but if financed by that state's AFDC program, they would have received only $292 a month (Boots and Green 2000).

In part as a result of new rules established in 1996 and in part as a result of a booming economy, AFDC-TANF caseloads fell by almost 50 percent between 1994 and 1999. Average benefit levels did not increase. Indeed, the real value of maximum benefits fell in most states, with an overall decline of about 11 percent in inflation-adjusted value over that time period (U.S. House of Representatives 2000, table 7.6). Average benefits declined even more, as recipients increased their earnings. Indeed, the declining value of benefits is another reason that caseloads have fallen (Council of Economic Advisers 1999).

The new rules include both a work requirement and time limits, with considerable discretion allowed to states. The basic parameters are work (as defined by the state) after a maximum of two years of benefits. The lifetime limit on federally funded aid is five years, with as much as 20 percent of the caseload eligible for exemption owing to hardship. The new rules were accompanied by a significant expansion in funding for child care, but unlike AFDC, TANF provides no child care guarantees for recipients who need it in order to work.

One rationale given for imposing time limits was the observation that staying home with children was a luxury that even middle-income families could no longer afford. By 1998 the labor force participation rate of married mothers of children under age six was quite high by historical standards, at 64 percent (*Statistical Abstract of the United States* 1999, table 660). This measure, however, overlooks differences in the *extent* of married mothers' labor force participation. In the same year, only 35 percent of married mothers of young children worked full time, year-round (Cohen and Bianchi 1999, 26).[5] Given the wage rates that most welfare leavers can command, the goal of self-sufficiency requires full-time, full-year employment, which is considerably more demanding than the norm for married mothers.

Studies show that most mothers leaving TANF have moved into relatively low-paying jobs, which tend not to offer health or retirement benefits (see Page and Simmons 2000, 280). These jobs are also unlikely to offer family benefits that would "enable them to meet the routine health, developmental, and sick day needs of their children."[6] This does not imply that mothers who have moved into paid employment have not gained important labor force experience or the confidence that can come with economic independence. It does, however, help explain why they are probably not better off than they were when receiving TANF, especially when work-related expenses such as child care are taken into account.

Is this simply part of a contingent social contract that requires mothers to work for pay in return for receiving assistance? If so, it is difficult to explain why we provide tax benefits to affluent families with stay-at-home parents. It is even more difficult to explain why we provide a generous range of social insurance benefits to married mothers through Social Security and Medicare, regardless of whether they were ever employed. The current structure of retirement benefits under Social Security offers a married man and his never-employed wife benefits that are 50 percent greater than those of a single man with exactly the same earnings and contribution history. Spouses are also eligible for Medicare benefits that are completely independent of their own history of labor force participation.

An even more direct comparison with TANF emerges from consideration of survivors' benefits provided through Social Security. This program provides substantial benefits to the surviving spouse and children of a deceased wage earner. Eligibility is virtually universal; under a special rule, benefits can be paid if the deceased worked for a year and a half in the three years just before death. In contrast to TANF, surviving spouses are not required to work for pay in return for benefits. Indeed, they are encouraged not to work (because their benefits are reduced if their earnings exceed certain limits) and not to remarry (because, on doing so, they lose their benefits). Far from being time limited, survivor's benefits are paid as long as the surviving parent is caring for a child under age sixteen. Unmarried children receive benefits until they reach age eighteen or until age nineteen if they are in school.

The Social Security program pays more benefits to children (through survivors' benefits) than any other federal program. The reason for this is simple: even though relatively few children receive them, their average levels are quite high. They are set at 75 percent of the deceased's basic Social Security retirement benefit. In 1999 the monthly benefit for survivors of workers with yearly earnings equal to the average wage amounted to $1,917 a month, or $23,004 a year for a widowed mother or father and two children (U.S. House of Representatives 2000). This was more than three times what a comparable family on TANF would have received.

It is often argued that this comparison is misleading because one program is "insurance" and the other is "welfare." It is true that eligibility for survivors' benefits is contingent on the spouse of the surviving parent having worked and paid into Social Security for at least a year and a half. However, neither program requires a voluntary decision to pay an explicit insurance premium, and both survivors' benefits and TANF are designed to insure children against poverty that is due, in part, to lack of support from a parent—in one case due to death, in the other case due to economic desertion.

One could argue that the reason the benefits that insure children against parental desertion are set so much lower than those that insure children against parental death is that the former is more likely to create what economists call a "moral hazard," or an incentive to bad behavior. A parent may be more likely to financially abandon a child if he or she knows the state will fully compensate. By contrast, taking risks that lead to fatal illness or accident are unlikely to be strongly influenced by knowing one's child would be covered by Social Security survivors' benefits. However, the moral hazard of desertion could be reduced by more stringent child support enforcement as well as by stronger guarantees of the visitation rights of noncustodial parents.

The risk of financial desertion is far more serious than the risk of death, and it negatively affects a large percentage of children. Most Northern European countries provide the equivalent of child support insurance precisely because failure to obtain such support poses a serious risk of poverty. Child support enforcement efforts in the United States have improved in recent years, but success rates remain quite uneven across states, especially for women who are not on the TANF rolls (Turetsky 1998). The bottom line is that we insure children against some risks much better than others. Further, because these risks differ systematically by race, ethnicity, and income group, we insure some children far more generously than others. Table 15.2 summarizes differences across programs that remain largely unchanged today.

The restrictions on EITC eligibility, the low level of TANF benefits, and the low wages in jobs typically held by women moving from welfare to work help explain why poverty rates among children have fallen only slightly during the economic boom of the last several years, from about 21 percent for individuals under age eighteen in 1996 to about 17 percent in 1999 (U.S. Bureau of the Census 1999). Low take-up rates and eligibility levels are also relevant: the Census Bureau estimates that fewer than 30 percent of children in poverty resided in a family that received cash public assistance in 1998 (Kids Count 2000). Variation in state policy accounts for a significant portion of the variation in child poverty across states (Meyers et al. forthcoming). In 1998 the child poverty rate in the District of Columbia was 45 percent, more than five times greater than in the neighboring state of Maryland (National Center for Children in Poverty 2000). Clearly, public policies in the United States offer children very unequal protection against the risks of poverty.

In-Kind Benefits

In-kind transfers such as food stamps and Medicaid are an additional source of public support for poor families with children, even though the presence of children is not a requirement for receiving them. It is worrisome that use of these programs is falling among the eligible population, which may be confused or discouraged by new TANF rules (Steinhauer 2000; Ku and Bruen 1999; Zedlewski and Brauner 1999). Expenditures on these programs remain significant. They are, however, counterbalanced by tax expenditures that primarily benefit the nonpoor. Tax expenditures are defined as deviations from normal tax policy that are functionally equivalent to spending programs. In fiscal year 1996 total federal tax expenditures

TABLE 15.2 / Social Insurance for Children 1996 (Dollars)

Social Insurance	Benefit
Temporary Assistance for Needy Families	
Maximum benefit in median state in 1996, one parent and two children	4,548
Foster care	
Average cost in 1996, foster care for two children	12,000
Social Security Survivors' Insurance	
Average benefit in 1996, one surviving spouse and two children	18,288

Source: Authors' compilation.

came to approximately $455 billion, almost two-and-one-half times more than was spent on all means-tested direct spending programs (Citizens for Tax Justice 1999, 3). For example, the cost of the tax exemption offered to employer-paid health insurance, and not available to most minimum-wage earners, amounted to $57 billion in 1996, while the cost of the mortgage interest tax deduction, available only to homeowners, was $43 billion. The sum of costs of these two programs was roughly equivalent to Medicaid expenditures limited to poor families, which amounted to about $92 billion (Citizens for Tax Justice 1999, 2; U.S. House of Representatives 1998). Public subsidies for health care of the elderly are expensive and not currently means tested.

Federal support for child care, like public support for parental care, takes two very different forms. Tax benefits are of primary relevance to nonpoor families. In 1999, the child care tax credit amounted to between 20 and 30 percent of child care expenses (depending on family income level), up to $2,400 for one child under age thirteen and up to $4,800 for two or more children, if these expenses were incurred as a result of parental work for pay. Thus the credit could offer as much as $720 per child, although the average amount paid was considerably lower, and most families were reimbursed at only 20 percent (although many other business and work-related expenses were 100 percent deductible). Because this credit was not refundable, it offered no tax benefit for most families with incomes below $15,000. No upper-income limit was imposed on this credit, and because affluent families were more likely to spend the maximum amount, they were the more likely to benefit.

A less well-known, but more generous, subsidy is the dependent care pretax account, which allows working parents with child care expenses to set aside up to $5,000 a year in an employer-sponsored account that is exempt from income and payroll taxes. Employers have an incentive to set up such accounts because their payroll taxes are reduced. Here, again, the value depends on the tax rate, but a family in the top federal income tax bracket could garner a subsidy in 1999 amounting to $1,980, not counting the effect of payroll taxes. In sum, the range of tax subsidies generated reimbursements ranging from $480 a year (20 percent of $2,400 for those least eligible for the child care credit) to a high of almost $2,000 (the benefit to a family in the highest tax bracket of a fully used dependent care tax account).

In the early 1990s the cost of these tax expenditures far exceeded federal expenditures on programs serving low-income families. In 1993 the cost of the child and dependent care tax credit alone was $2.5 billion, compared with $1.7 billion spent on child care for AFDC recipients, transitional child care, at-risk child care, and the child care and development block grant (National Academy of Science 1996). Since that year, child care funding targeted at low-income families has been significantly increased, and program delivery has been reorganized as part of the changes to the larger welfare system legislated in 1996. Still, the amount of total entitlement expenditures authorized for 1999, $2.2 billion, remained slightly below the overall cost of the child and dependent care tax credit (U.S. House of Representatives 1998, 684).

Most recent administrative effort has focused on providing child care for recipients of TANF as a way of encouraging transitions to paid employment. As a result, many of the working poor have found it difficult to find subsidized slots; families with an income above the poverty line but less than $40,000 a year remain the group least likely to receive assistance with child care costs (Hofferth 1995). Here again, benefits seem to follow a U-shaped curve, lowest for the lower-middle part of the income distribution. As one expert puts it, "Concerns about the potential costs of that increased level of demand, along with concerns about the implications of future economic downturns, have made some states hesitant to expand their child care programs much beyond the welfare population" (Long 1999, 3). Even states that allocate additional state funds, such as Massachusetts and New York, had long waiting lists for low-income families in 2000.

More detailed analysis of the impact of in-kind support policies by income level and family structure is needed. State-level investments in services, such as child care, could play an increasingly important role in years to come. In general, public subsidies of in-kind services—such as health, housing, and child care—benefit not only the poor but also the population as a whole.

DIRECTIONS FOR CHANGE

The peculiar combination of tax benefits, public assistance, and social insurance currently represents the basic features of an implicit social family contract: benefits that families enjoy partly in return for rearing children. Several factors explain why many of its provisions seem inconsistent. The programs were developed at different times for different purposes. They emerged in an ad hoc way, reflecting the political power of interest groups grappling with specific economic problems, such as the Great Depression and the rapid inflation of the 1970s. Furthermore, most social and family policies were put into place during an era of marital stability, with a clear division of labor between male breadwinners and female homemakers. These conditions no longer hold.

Once a social contract is established, it is difficult to alter the expectations it creates. This helps explain why welfare reform generated so much controversy and why proposals to modify the Social Security system elicit such fierce debate. On the other hand, the changing structure of U.S. families, communities, and the economy pushes the country to adapt. The increasing size of the elderly population relative to the working-age population requires serious reconsideration of intergenerational commitments. By taxing the younger generation to support the older one, we have "socialized" many of the benefits of rearing children but have done far less to socialize the costs (Folbre 1994a, 1994b). We need to update our social contract (see Graetz and Mashaw 1999; Penner 2000).

A consideration of the ways that the aspects of our social contract that concern children might be reformed raises a number of difficult conceptual and political issues. At least three steps toward a better system for poor families follow directly from this discussion. In the long run, however, the larger question of how to support and organize child rearing in an increasingly competitive market economy must be addressed.

Three Steps Forward

In considering possibilities for reforming the way child rearing is supported, it is useful to begin with one of the hopes that smoothed the way for welfare reform: more generous support for the poor who engage in paid employment. The American people have long combined their disapproval of specific welfare policies with a strong commitment to the principle of helping poor families (Gilens 1999). In a classic example, a 1985 national poll found that, although only 9 percent of respondents agreed that the country was not spending enough on welfare, 63 percent believed we were not spending enough on "assistance to the poor" (Solomon 1996). Likewise, most Americans today approve of the work requirements implemented by welfare reform but worry that the country has made little progress in reducing poverty (Public Agenda Online 1998).

Furthermore, Americans say they are willing to put their money where their mouth is. In a 1998 Harris poll, respondents were asked to respond to the following:

> Many government programs cost a lot of money. Some are designed to help children, or old people, or people with disabilities, or poor people, and so on. In general would you say that the federal, state, and local governments spend too much, or too little, or about the right amount on programs which provide money or services for poor people?

More than half of respondents said "too little."

Polling evidence suggests that voters support more generous assistance for poor families in return for a commitment to engage in paid employment. In a 1998 survey 77 percent of respondents agreed that, "When parents on welfare find jobs, government should provide help if their jobs do not pay enough to financially support their children." An even higher percentage, 81 percent, agreed that, "When parents on welfare find jobs, government should provide help if their jobs do not provide affordable health insurance" (Public Agenda Online 1998).

A first step in addressing the problems described here would be to expand eligibility for the EITC (so that it benefits near-poor and lower middle-income families) and to raise benefit levels for TANF. A second step would be to ensure access to paid employment no matter what stage of the business cycle the U.S. economy is in. Otherwise, an increase in the general unemployment rate could render it impossible for poor families to fulfill their obligations. A third step would be to improve the quantity and quality of child care available to parents who are obliged to work for pay in order to support their children. Beyond these three steps, however, reform of our system of public assistance for families intersects with the larger question of public support for all families. We close with a brief consideration of this question.

Children as Public Goods

Policymakers should move beyond debates over which families "deserve" assistance and which ones do not and directly ask, How should the costs and risks of rearing children be distributed? The economists Robert Haveman and Barbara Wolfe (1995, 1831) calculate that, in 1992, government spending (including education and transfers to families with children) covered about one-third of total expenditures on children. This is likely an overestimate of public contributions. Furthermore, the proportion of public support varies considerably by income group (Bainbridge and Garfinkel 1999). This estimate nevertheless testifies to the fact that, though small by international standards, public support for child rearing is significant. What is needed is more explicit discussion of levels of public support as well as ways in which it is distributed.

The primary economic argument for public support is that children represent public goods. That is, the optimal development of their capabilities benefits society as a whole, not merely parents and children themselves. Children are not consumer goods in the same sense that, say, dogs and cats are. When parents devote time and money to the development of children's capabilities, they are engaged in socially productive work, which yields benefits to others (Folbre 1994b). Some of these benefits are intangible, such as our collective sense of pride in a new generation of citizens. Other benefits are tangible, such as the taxes that today's children will pay when they grow up and enter the workforce, repaying our national debt and supporting our Social Security system. All citizens of this country implicitly enjoy a claim on the earnings of the younger generation, whether they have helped to rear them or not. Social Security provides benefits based on paid work history or marital status by taxing the current working-age population. The time, energy, and effort devoted to producing these workers are not adequately rewarded.

Conventional economic reasoning supports the claim that those without children should assume a share of the costs of children, reflecting the benefits they derive from them. In developing this claim, however, it is important to specify that society wants to reward the effort of parenting, not the fact of biological parenthood. Providing the genetic material is the least costly aspect of child rearing. Parenthood is a dichotomy: either someone has produced biological offspring or not. Parenting is not confined, however, to biological kin, and it falls on a continuum, in which some parents contribute far more than others. Therefore, if parenting is to be a criterion for public support, differences in effort and commitment must be acknowledged. We favor direct recognition of the value of time and effort devoted to the care of family members as well as more indirect programs such as public provision of child care and health care.

Gender Inequality and the Costs of Children

On average, mothers assume a larger share of the costs and risks of rearing children than do fathers (Folbre 1994a; Joshi et al. 1999). Some argue that they also derive a disproportionate share of the psychological benefits and that mothering must, by definition, be its own reward (Fuchs 1988). There is no meaningful way to ascertain whether this is the case; one could argue that mothers are, in a sense, prisoners of love. In any case, whatever the distribution of emotional benefits, it is clear that mothers pay a high economic price for their commitment to caring for children and other dependents. Specialization in family work lowers their market earnings. Unless they have been married for at least ten years to a covered worker, full-time mothers or homemakers without an employment history of their own are ineligible for Social Security retirement benefits.

About 28 percent of all children in this country are living in single-parent households, more than 85 percent of which are headed by women. Fewer than half of these households receive adequate and reliable child support payments. Recent efforts to improve child support enforcement focus on the low-income population as a way of reducing public expenditures. Little increase is evident in transfers to separated or divorced mothers (Sorensen and Halpern 1999). Even mothers in intact families who enjoy generous support from the fathers of their children must face the risks of divorce, separation, and widowhood, all of which are considerable.

The traditional ideal of extreme specialization in child rearing is weakening. Sometimes economic stresses lead to a rearrangement of the division of labor, as when parents adopt shift work to minimize the cost of purchasing child care (Presser 1994). Husbands who take on child care while their wives are at work spend far more time with their children than most fathers. Their numbers are small but significant. In 1993 about 19 percent of the 14.8 million U.S. husbands with preschool children and wives working outside the home were primary care providers for their children; an additional 25 percent of these husbands provided some care (Casper 1994).

Many fathers are taking on more direct child care responsibilities, even in the absence of such external pressures. A spate of recent books emphasizes the benefits of shared parenting (Deutsch 1999; Coltrane 1996; Mahoney 1995; Peters 1998). Many voices in the emergent men's movement encourage fathers to play a more active role in child rearing (Hewlett and West 1998; Popenoe 1996). Many current economic policies, such as significantly lower hourly pay and benefits for part-time than for full-time work, reinforce undue specialization between breadwinner and homemaker. Even a recent *Business Week* article included the headline, "Men face greater expectations at home. But work isn't giving them the slack they need" (Hammonds 1998, 56).

Public policies must address this problem directly. We argue for public support for parenting on the grounds that parents provide a public good. Increasing public support for parenting, however, could also reduce gender inequality. Men earn more and pay slightly more in taxes than women do and are also less likely to devote money and time to children. As a result, public expenditures on child care and other forms of support for child rearing redistribute resources from men to women. Furthermore, empirical evidence suggests that provision of subsidized child care makes it easier for fathers and mothers to equally share child care responsibilities (Juster and Stafford 1991).

CONCLUSION

Contrary to the received wisdom, current family support policies are only slightly redistributive; they do relatively little to compensate for significant inequalities in child opportunity and well-being. Furthermore, these policies reflect a double standard that imposes more restrictions on transfers to poor than to affluent families. This double standard suggests the need for broader public discussion of basic principles of support for family work. The increased labor force participation of women, along with major changes in family structure, has rendered many existing policies and conventional ways of thinking about them obsolete.

Would Americans support a new social family contract that provides genuine insurance against poverty and more generous support for all families with children? Because the current system of support for children is both inadequate and inconsistent, a simple but sweeping reform that combines public assistance and social insurance with the expansion of in-kind services, such as child care, could mobilize more support than piecemeal changes. Universal programs have generally proved more successful and politically resilient than those aimed exclusively at the poor (Skocpol and Leone 2000).

The United Nations Convention on the Rights of the Child, ratified by all nations of the world except for Somalia and the United States, stipulates that "parents have joint primary responsibility for raising the child, and the nation shall support them in this. The nation shall provide appropriate assistance to parents in child-raising." Perhaps it is time for the United States to sign on. More consistent and generous policies of support for families would not only improve the welfare of parents and children. They would also help move this country toward the realization of one of its most precious political ideals: equal opportunity for all.

NOTES

1. See especially section 101, Findings, H.R. 3734, Personal Responsibility and Work Opportunity Reconciliation Act of 1996.

2. This reflects both the published rates and the actual incidence of different federal taxes and is not significantly affected by the deductions and exemptions described in this chapter.

3. Note also that both expenditures and tax benefits have incentive effects, which make calculation of actual incidence of the benefits difficult to calculate.

4. The value of this exemption has declined considerably over time. Between 1948 and 1960 it almost completely offset income tax liability for families with children. After 1960, however, its real value was undermined by inflation. The economist Eugene Steuerle estimates that the tax rate on families with two children increased 43 percent over this period, while the average tax rate for families without children remained essentially unchanged (Children's Defense Fund—Minnesota 1999, 1; Whittington 1992). If the exemption had remained at the same percentage of median family income at which it was originally set in the 1940s, it would have amounted to $6,500 in 1996 (Hewlett and West 1998, 263).

5. Cohen and Bianchi follow the Bureau of Labor Statistics convention of defining full-time work as thirty-five hours or more a week. They point out that most estimates of labor force participation are based on a reference period of the preceding week but that data are also collected using a reference period of one year. As they emphasize, a reference period of one year is a more accurate standard of comparison when constructing hypothetical annual budgets for single mothers.

6. Heymann and Earle (1999) find that, compared with mothers who have never received welfare, mothers leaving welfare for work are significantly less likely than other working mothers to have sick leave for the entire time they worked (20 percent, versus 36 percent) or flexible schedules (18 percent, versus 30 percent). These inequalities are compounded by the fact that mothers who left welfare to work are more likely to be caring for at least one child with a chronic condition (37 percent, versus 21 percent).

REFERENCES

Aber, J. Lawrence. 1999. *Welfare Reform at Three: Is a New Consensus Emerging*? New York: National Center for Children in Poverty. Available at: *cpmcnet.columbia.edu/dept/nccp/news/win00/1win00.html*.

Bainbridge, J., and Irwin Garfinkel. 1999. "The Cost of Children in the U.S." Unpublished manuscript. Columbia University, New York.

Boots, Shelly Waters, and Rob Green. 2000. "Family Care or Foster Care? How State Policies Affect Kinship Caregivers." Washington, D.C.: Urban Institute.

Casper, Lynne M. 1994. *"My Daddy Takes Care of Me!" Fathers as Care Providers.* Current Population Report P70-59. Washington: U.S. Bureau of the Census.

Cherry, Robert, and Max Sawicky. 2000. "Giving Tax Credit Where Credit Is Due," Briefing paper. Washington, D.C.: Economic Policy Institute (April). Available at: *www.epinet.org/briefingpapers/eitc.html*.

Children's Defense Fund—Minnesota. 1999. "Family Tax Policies." Available at: *www.cdf-mn.org/family.htm* (November 19, 1999).

Citizens for Tax Justice. 1999. *The Hidden Entitlements*. Available at: *www.ctj.org/hig_ent/part-1.htm* (November 18, 1999).

Cohen, Philip N., and Suzanne M. Bianchi. 1999. "Marriage, Children, and Women's Employment: What Do We Know?" *Monthly Labor Review* (December): 22–31.

Coltrane, Scott. 1996. *Family Man*. New York: Oxford University Press.

Council of Economic Advisers. 1999. *The Effects of Welfare Policy and the Economic Expansion of Welfare Caseloads: An Update*. Washington: Council of Economic Advisers.

Deutsch, Francine M. 1999. *Halving It All: How Equally Shared Parenting Works*. Cambridge, Mass.: Harvard University Press.

Ellwood, David T., and Jeffrey B. Liebman. 2000. "The Middle Class Parent Penalty: Child Benefits in the U.S. Tax Code." Unpublished paper. John F. Kennedy School of Government, Harvard University.

Folbre, Nancy. 1994a. Who Pays for the Kids? Gender and the Structures of Constraint. New York: Routledge.

———. 1994b. "Children as Public Goods." *American Economic Review* 84(2): 86–90.

Fuchs, Victor. 1988. *Women's Quest for Economic Equality*. Cambridge, Mass.: Harvard University Press.

Gilens, Martin. 1999. *Why Americans Hate Welfare: Race, Media and the Politics of Antipoverty*. Chicago: University of Chicago Press.

Graetz, Michael J., and Jerry L. Mashaw. 1999. *True Security: Rethinking American Social Insurance*. New Haven, Conn.: Yale University Press.

Greenstein, Robert. 2000. "Should EITC Benefits Be Enlarged for Families with Three or More Children?" Washington, D.C.: Center on Budget and Policy Priorities. Available at: *www.cbpp.org/3-14-tax.htm*.

Hammonds, K. 1998. "The Daddy Trap." *Business Week,* September 21, 1998, 56–64.

Haveman, Robert, and Barbara Wolfe. 1995. "The Determinants of Children's Attainments: A Review of Methods and Findings." *Journal of Economic Literature* 33: 1829–78.

Hewlett, Sylvia Ann, and Cornel West. 1998. *The War Against Parents*. New York: Houghton Mifflin.

Heymann, S. Jody, and Alison Earle. 1999. "The Impact of Welfare Reform on Parents' Ability to Care for their Children's Health." *American Journal of Public Health* (April): 502–5.

Hofferth, Sandra. 1995. "Caring for Children at the Poverty Line." *Children and Youth Services Review* 12(1/2): 1–31.

Joshi, Heather, Pierella Paci, and Jane Waldfogel. 1999. "The Wages of Motherhood: Better or Worse." *Cambridge Journal of Economics* 23(5): 543–64.

Joint Center for Poverty Research. 1999. "CPR Commissioned Research Conference." *Joint Center for Poverty Research News* 3(1). Chicago: Joint Center for Poverty Research.

Juster, F. Thomas, and Frank Stafford. 1991. "The Allocation of Time: Empirical Findings, Behavioral Models, and Problems of Measurement." *Journal of Economic Literature* 29: 471–522.

Kids Count. 2000. 2000 Kids Count Data Online. Available at: *www.aecf.org/kidscount/kc2000/sum_11.htm*.

Ku, Leighton, and Brian Bruen. 1999. "The Continuing Decline in Medicaid Coverage." Report A-37. Washington, D.C.: Urban Institute.

Long, Sharon K. 1999. "Child Care Assistance Under Welfare Reform: Early Responses by the States." Testimony Before the Subcommittee on Human Resources, Committee on Ways and Means, U.S. House of Representatives, March 16, 1999. Available at: *www.urban.org/TESTIMON/long3-16-99.html*.

Mahoney, Rhona. 1995. *Kidding Ourselves: Breadwinning, Babies, and Bargaining Power*. New York: Basic Books.

Meyers, Marcia, Janet Gornick, and Laura Peck. Forthcoming. "Packaging Support for Low-Income Families: Policy Variation Across the U.S. States," *Journal of Policy Analysis and Management*.

Morris, Dick. 1998. *Behind the Oval Office: Getting Reelected Against All the Odds*. New York: Renaissance Books.

National Academy of Science. 1996. *Child Care for Low-Income Families*. Washington, D.C.: National Academy of Science. Available at: *www.nap.edu/readingroom/books/child care*.

National Center for Children in Poverty. 2000. "Childhood Poverty." Research brief 9. New York: National Center for Children in Poverty.

Page, Benjamin I., and James R. Simmons. 2000. *What Government Can Do: Dealing with Poverty and Inequality*. Chicago: University of Chicago Press.

Penner, Rudolph. 2000. "A New Agenda for the Radical Middle." Interview. Available at: *www.urgan.org/news/events/social_contract/penner_int.html*.

Peters, Joan K. 1998. *When Mothers Work: Loving Our Children Without Sacrificing Our Selves*. Reading, Mass.: Addison-Wesley.

Popenoe, David. 1996. *Life Without Father*. New York: Free Press.

Presser, Harriet B. 1994. "Employment Schedules Among Dual-Earner Spouses and the Division of Labor by Gender." *American Sociological Review* 59: 348–69.

Public Agenda Online. 1998. Available at: *www.publicagenda.org/issues/angles.cfm?issue_type =welfare*.

Public Agenda Online. 1998. Harris Telephone Interview. April 22–27.

Skocpol, Theda, and Richard C. Leone. 2000. *The Missing Middle: Working Families and the Future of American Social Policy*. New York: W. W. Norton.

Social Security Administration. 1998. *Annual Statistical Supplement*. Bulletin. Washington: Social Security Administration.

———. 1999. *Social Security Survivors Benefits*. Publication 05-10084. Washington: Social Security Administration (July). Available at: *www.ssa.gov/pubs/10084.html*.

Solomon, Norman. 1996. "Media Beat." May 17. Available at: *www.fair.org/media-bet/ 960517.html*.

Sorensen, Elaine, and Ariel Halpern. 1999. "Child Support Is Working Better Than We Think." Report A-31. Washington, D.C.: Urban Institute. Available at: *www.urban.org*.

Statistical Abstract of the United States, 1999. Washington: U.S. Bureau of the Census.

Steinhauer, Jennifer. 2000. "States Proved Unpredictable in Aiding Uninsured Children." *New York Times*, September 28.

Stiglitz, Joseph E. 1988. *Economics of the Public Sector*. New York: W. W. Norton.

Turetsky, Vicki. 1998. "You Get What You Pay For: How Federal and State Investment Decisions Affect Child Support Enforcement." Washington, D.C.: Center for Law and Social Policy.

U.S. Bureau of the Census. 1999. *Money Income and Poverty in the United States, 1999*. Current Population Report. Washington: U.S. Bureau of the Census.

U.S. House of Representatives. 1998. *1998 Green Book: Background Material and Data on Programs Within the Jurisdiction of the Committee on Ways and Means*. Washington: U.S. Government Printing Office.

———. 2000. *2000 Green Book: Background Material and Data on Programs Within the Jurisdiction of the Committee on Ways and Means*. Washington: U.S. Government Printing Office.

Whittington, Leslie A. 1992. "Taxes and the Family: The Impact of the Tax Exemption for Dependents on Marital Fertility." *Demography* 29(2): 215–26.

Zedlewski, Sheila, and Sarah Brauner. 1999. "Are the Steep Declines in Food Stamp Participation Linked to Falling Welfare Caseloads?" Report B-3. Washington, D.C.: Urban Institute.

Chapter 16

Lessons Learned

P. Lindsay Chase-Lansdale and Greg J. Duncan

W elfare reform in the 1990s—as instituted by state waivers and then as federal law—came about as a sweeping effort to reduce the dependency of
the poor on government. Taken together, it has ushered in a new "work-
contingent social contract," which holds that every healthy family, regardless of
income level or child-rearing responsibility, should seek employment before or, in
some cases, in conjunction with turning to the state for support. No longer does this
nation guarantee that children living in poverty will receive some cash assistance
from the state for basic survival needs. Instead, the prevailing assumption is that children are better off if their parents are working than if their parents are receiving cash
transfers from government. Most of the focus of welfare reform, however, is on adult
behavior and not on children. We have lost sight of the health and development of
children in the wake of the success in cutting welfare caseloads in half.

Our purpose in compiling this volume was to understand how welfare reform
affects the well-being and healthy development of children. Leading policy-oriented
academic researchers summarize theoretical insights from their respective disci-
plines; leaders of large, national, and multistate evaluations of welfare summarize
early returns from their qualitative and quantitative studies; and policy specialists
spell out their recommendations for further reforms. In this chapter, we pull together
lessons gleaned from these authors by addressing three questions:

- How do reformers and state policymakers link new policies to family and child
well-being?

- How are families and children faring to date?

- What policy changes enhance child well-being?

HOW DO REFORMERS AND STATE POLICYMAKERS LINK
NEW POLICIES TO FAMILY AND CHILD WELL-BEING?

Maternal employment, family income, and family structure emerge as key pathways through which reformers, advocates, and states expect that children may be
helped or, in some cases, hurt by welfare reforms. Maternal employment dominated

the early reform agendas of states as well as the rhetoric about how children are likely to be affected by the reforms. The chapters in this volume reveal that both the rhetoric surrounding the welfare reform debate and state policymakers' comments reflect the view that maternal employment is key to enhancing children's well-being. Cathy Johnson and Thomas Gais, in chapter 3, term this the "family environmental theory." It posits that children benefit from the enhanced self-esteem parents gain from work as well as from the discipline and structure that work routines, rather than welfare dependence, impose on family life (Haskins 1995; Wilson 1987). In this view, children's developmental needs are addressed indirectly, but effectively, by promoting a mother's transition from welfare to work.

Concerns are raised by some that forcing mothers to commute and to work long hours devalues their parenting role, reduces their ability to monitor their children's behavior, and may increase their already high levels of stress. As Kristin Moore, in chapter 4, reports, however, the positive impact of maternal employment was uppermost in the minds of state policymakers as they considered how reforms might affect children's well-being.

Less rhetoric and attention has been focused on a "family resource theory" of children's well-being, which sees changes in family income as the key ways in which welfare reform helps or hurts children. Policies to make work pay, for example by increasing the generosity of the Earned Income Tax Credit (EITC) and the minimum wage, have received their share of attention; however, these policies have been viewed primarily as incentives for maternal employment rather than as a way to reduce child poverty. Although the 1996 Personal Responsibility and Work Opportunity Reconciliation Act (PRWORA) penalizes states that allow poverty rates to increase, the overall reductions in poverty fueled by a booming economy have masked whatever differing effects state policies have had on children's economic well-being.

One reason that relatively little attention has been paid to the postreform economic status of children is the nature of the data available for tracking welfare reforms. Counts of Temporary Assistance for Needy Families (TANF) cases are compiled monthly by the state agencies that administer these programs. The dramatic caseload reductions since the mid-1990s can be tracked in timely ways and easily compared across states. The task of tracking children's economic well-being is much more difficult, with data from different sources sometimes telling different stories. The economic story is further complicated by the fact that average income changes reveal much less about the effect on children than does the distribution of those changes. Because welfare reform is likely to both increase the economic well-being of some children (for example, through successful welfare-to-work transitions) and reduce it for others (for example, through sanctions and time limits), the story of economic effects is subtle and easily muddled by the rhetoric of advocates, who use the data to tell only one side.

More important than data problems in the lack of attention to children is the fact that promoting children's well-being by increasing family income costs states money. This is most obvious when family income is enhanced with cash payments or tax credits. It is also apparent, however, in states' efforts to fashion the comprehensive packages of work-based supports (for example, earnings supplements, child care subsidies, and health insurance) that might cover low-income families regardless of whether or not they receive TANF cash benefits. Alan Weil, in chapter 5, finds great diversity in states' efforts to extend some of these supports to working-poor or near-poor families. His typology of states classified by their generosity of support and nature of work requirements defies the regional stereotypes applied to the old Aid to Families with Dependent Children (AFDC) policy regimes.

The family structure theory of how welfare reform might promote children's well-being has spawned more rhetoric than serious implementation. The preamble to the 1996 PRWORA legislation identifies marriage as "an essential institution of a successful society which promotes the interests of children," posits that "responsible fatherhood and motherhood are integral to successful child rearing and the well-being of children," and declares that the "prevention of out-of-wedlock pregnancy and reduction in out-of-wedlock birth are very important Government interests." State policymakers have echoed concerns that children's well-being suffers from living in a single-parent family or being born to a teen mother. A few policies directed at family structure have been widely implemented. Family caps—the reduction or elimination of the incremental increase in TANF benefits for mothers who have additional children while on welfare—are relatively easy to administer, and they save, rather than cost, states money. They have been adopted by nearly half of all states. Similarly, all states require that teen parents live with an adult if they are to receive benefits for themselves and their children. Reform advocates have long argued that mandated time limits on cash assistance send a powerful message to teens contemplating childbearing. More direct attempts by states to promote marriage or prevent teen pregnancy have been spotty and underfunded.

HOW ARE FAMILIES AND CHILDREN FARING TO DATE?

To answer the question posed here, we look at maternal employment, the family income, and the family structure.

Maternal Employment

Federal law requires that welfare recipients participate in work activities within twenty-four months of receiving TANF, and many states have implemented a stricter work requirement. Most states sanction families that do not meet the work requirements by cutting (either partially or fully) benefits until compliance occurs, although there is enormous variability in how states implement sanctions. In addition, all states must implement the sixty-month federal time limit on receipt of benefits, but they have the discretion to shorten or, by using state funds, to extend the time period. In light of these requirements, it is hardly surprising that states shortening the time period have restructured their rules, incentives, and local-office operations to promote employment transitions and, in some cases, to discourage would-be recipients as a way to reduce their welfare caseloads.

Ron Haskins in chapter 14 illustrates the sizable increase in mothers' employment over time. This increase is particularly steep for never-married mothers, especially since 1997, when federal reform was implemented. Employment among this group rose from a little over 45 percent in 1996 to about 65 percent in 1999. Other reports also indicate the high work response to welfare reform (Danziger et al., forthcoming; Rolston 1999), even when the effect on unemployment of the booming economy is taken into account (Wallace and Blank 1999). Studies of various states show that approximately two-thirds of "leavers" (mothers who have left the welfare rolls) are employed at some point (Brauner and Loprest 1999). Jack Tweedie, in chapter 6, shows that roughly 40 percent of sanctioned families are working.

What are the implications for children? Does evidence support reformers' beliefs that employed mothers are better role models for their children than are mothers on welfare and that the experience per se of a market job raises mothers' self-esteem and sense of self-respect, reduces the likelihood of her suffering depression, and brings predictability, order, and routine into her family's life? The developmental literature shows that employed mothers are more likely to have better mental health, but much of the data for these studies comes from middle-class samples, and the causal direction for these associations may run as much from maternal mental health to maternal employment as vice versa (Hoffman and Youngblade 1999).

Interviews with eighty welfare-reliant mothers in Cleveland and Philadelphia, summarized in chapter 8 by Ellen Scott and coauthors, are consistent with the hypothesis that employment may improve maternal mental health. Mothers in this in-depth, qualitative component of the Urban Change Study undertaken by the Manpower Demonstration Research Corporation repeatedly talked about how their future employment would improve their financial condition and bring them self-respect and a sense of pride in their accomplishments. They were also eloquent on the topic of how much more their children would respect them if they held a market job, rather than staying at home. Moreover, they believed that having a job would provide them with more credibility as they exhort their children to work hard in school, stay in school, and strive for success now and in the future.

Chapter 8 adds to the growing literature indicating that the work ethic, self-sufficiency, and high expectations for children's futures are widely held values across all income levels (Furstenberg et al. 1987; Newman 1999; Wilson 1987, 1996). These qualitative data indicate that women on welfare also value work enormously. A recent report from the Three-City Study on Welfare Reform (Cherlin et al. 2000) shows that women on welfare are knowledgeable about work requirements, and this may be due to the importance they place on work.

However, caution is in order. The qualitative interviews in chapter 8 were conducted in 1997 and 1998, when the women were still at home, receiving welfare, and anticipating how they would deal with the new work requirements. It is important to learn what they might say now, after welfare reform has been in force for several years. Moreover, the study's design provides no data on whether the children were affected by the greater optimism of their mothers.

The optimism of the mothers in chapter 8 is not matched in quantitative studies comparing welfare-reliant and low-socioeconomic-status, working, single mothers. Greg Duncan and coauthors (chapter 7) use data from the 1980s and early 1990s to compare these two groups of mothers along several dimensions of mental health, including depression, self-esteem, self-mastery, and future orientation. They find no significant effect of employment, despite the fact that unmeasured differences between the two groups likely lead to an overstatement of employment's role in promoting beneficial mental health differences.

Moreover, other studies provide little evidence that employment-based interventions have a significant effect on maternal mental health. For example, the employment-supportive treatments in the New Hope project produced employment gains but no noticeable differences between program families and control families in depression, self-esteem, or efficacy of the mothers (Huston et al., forthcoming). (In chapter 10 in this volume, Rashmita Mistry and coauthors report on the New Hope project's effects on children.) The combination of training and parenting services in New Chance (a separate program), if anything, increased maternal depression (Quint et al. 1997). It appears that one needs more than welfare-to-work changes to produce the kinds of mental health changes envisioned by welfare reformers.

Fragmentary evidence does not support the hypothesis that maternal employment improves household order, predictability, and routine. The employment-enhancing New Hope treatment had no effect on the regularity of family routines (Huston et al., forthcoming). Duncan and coauthors (chapter 7) report that, compared with welfare-reliant families, families with employed single mothers ate fewer meals together and that children did not contribute any more to housework than before their mothers went to work. The Three-City Study (Winston et al. 1999) will provide more comprehensive data for testing these hypotheses.

Critics of welfare reform believe that requiring welfare mothers to find jobs will increase maternal stress and negative effects on children, as these women balance child rearing with low-paying, tedious jobs, irregular work hours, or difficult shifts. The New Hope experiment provides virtually no support for these ideas. Ariel Kalil and coauthors (chapter 9) draw on longitudinal data from the Women's Employment Study to examine the effect of mothers' welfare-to-work transition on children's mental health. The work and welfare histories of mothers in Michigan, a state whose welfare waiver requires employment, were measured over two years, with mothers interviewed in both years. At the time of the first interview, all were receiving welfare. Importantly, the study controls for children's mental health at the first interview in addition to an impressive array of maternal background factors (race-ethnicity, family structure, and mothers' education) and potential barriers to employment, including mothers' mental health, domestic violence, and physical health problems of mothers or children. The study finds little evidence that moving from welfare to work leads to more behavior problems in children.

The Kalil chapter is important for its ability to investigate the effect of welfare-to-work transitions on children's well-being, and it supports the view that children are not harmed by most of the employment transitions occasioned by welfare reform. This finding is not, however, without qualification. Child outcome measures are derived from mothers' reports, and it is well known that mothers' mental health can color how they perceive their children's behavior. In addition, there is little information on other domains of child development, such as physical health, cognitive functioning, and school achievement.

Emerging evidence from studies released too late to be included in this volume confirms that children's development is rarely hurt by mandated maternal employment. Moreover, these same studies show that children's achievement can be promoted by welfare reforms, provided that they go beyond mere work mandates and provide financial supports for work. These conclusions are based on the New Hope experiment (summarized in chapter 10) and several other experiments that began in the early 1990s, as states implemented various packages of welfare reform (Morris et al. 2001). Some of these experiments augmented family economic resources; others did not. In all cases, evaluations tracked family process and child well-being, and participants were randomly assigned to a treatment group that received the welfare reform package or to a control group that continued to abide by the prior AFDC rules.

The evidence (compiled by Morris et al. 2001) comes from four experiments other than New Hope: the National Evaluation of Welfare-to-Work Strategies (NEWWS), which evaluated the effects of both labor force attachment and human capital development on children in Atlanta, Georgia, Grand Rapids, Michigan, and Riverside, California (Hamilton 2000; McGroder et al. 2000); the Minnesota Family Investment program, which combines participation mandates, make-work-pay incentives, and services in a way that constitutes a somewhat more generous version of Minnesota's current TANF program (Gennetian and Miller 2000); the Canadian Self-sufficiency project, which, by offering a generous but temporary (three-year) earnings supplement for full-time work, is a pure make-work-pay approach (Morris and Michalopolous 2000); and Florida's Family Transition program, which offers a small earnings supplement, a participation mandate, and fairly intensive case management.

Comparable analyses of these data (Morris et al. 2001) reveal that welfare reforms that both increase work and provide financial supports for working families promote achievement and positive behavior among elementary school children. In contrast, welfare reforms that mandate work but do not support it have few effects, positive or negative, on children. No discernible patterns of effects emerge from the data on these types of programs. Also of interest is the lack of effects on a range of parenting practices (such as warmth and monitoring) across all types of programs.

Further, the effect of reforms depends on the ages of the children. Elementary school children were helped by the reforms that increased family resources and, for the most part, not harmed by unsupportive reforms. For adolescents, limited evidence suggests that even generous reforms that promote maternal employment may cause detrimental increases in school problems and risky behavior.

Many questions remain about the employment requirements of welfare reform and their effects on children. How will sanctions imposed when parents fail to meet work requirements affect children? Are sanctions worse than time limits? Tweedie (chapter 6) points to the limited data available on the states that are implementing sanctions and on the characteristics of families that are sanctioned. Early reports indicate that a sizable proportion of sanctioned mothers are employed, but they are earning less than others who left the welfare rolls. Again, almost nothing is known about their children's well-being, and we urge the collection of relevant data.

Similarly, we know next to nothing about time limits and their impact on children and families. Tweedie makes the important point that sanctioned families and families reaching the time limits may be very vulnerable. They may include families that do not have the capacity to meet work requirements as well as those who continue to need assistance but have used up their sixty-month allotment. This is another significant topic for future research.

Family Income

Critics of welfare reform argued that the end of a federal entitlement to public assistance, combined with time limits and sanctions, would push more children into poverty as families lost essential cash support. Proponents of welfare reform claimed that participation in the labor market would be the most reliable pathway out of poverty for these families.

What has in fact occurred? As both Ron Haskins (chapter 14) and Wendell Primus and Kristina Daugirdas (chapter 13) point out, child poverty has fallen during the period of welfare reform. Approximately two-thirds of adults who have left welfare are employed, but many (and their families) remain in poverty (Brauner and Loprest 1999). Although most would agree that the goal of reducing welfare rolls and ending "widespread dependency on government" has been broadly achieved in the short term, the long-term outcomes of welfare reform remain unknown. In the meantime, the nation's child poverty rate remains quite high (16.3 percent in 1999), higher, in fact, than that of any other industrialized nation (Atkinson et al. 1995). Similarly, the percentage of children in poverty whose families receive cash assistance declined from 64 percent in 1995 to 47 percent in 1998 (Greenberg and Laracy 2000).

Primus and Daugirdas as well as Haskins show an important pattern of increased average income for poor families since the early 1990s, resulting from a combination of earnings, federal programs designed to make work pay (most notably the expansion of the EITC and child care assistance), and federal programs that counteract poverty (such as food stamps, Medicaid). This is a noteworthy accomplishment. However, Primus and Daugirdas show that averages can be deceptive. Single-parent families in the bottom 40 percent of the income distribution experienced virtually no change in disposable income between 1995 and 1999, with increases in earning offset nearly dollar for dollar by reductions in government transfers.

These chapters focus on this vulnerable group, which Haskins characterizes as worse off as a result of welfare reform. Both chapters emphasize the importance of supporting work with government programs so that employed families can get out of poverty. According to Ron Haskins, "We shouldn't think welfare reform is a success because we've been able to move a mom with two kids off welfare into a $12,000-a-year job. That may be great, but it's not enough" (cited in Greenberg and Laracy 2000, 12).

What do these findings mean for children? Apart from statistics on the number of children in poverty, children's health and development are not the focus of any of these studies. An extensive research literature shows that poverty has real detrimental effects on children's development (Chase-Lansdale 1999; Brooks-Gunn and Duncan 1997; Duncan and Brooks-Gunn 1997, 2000), although the effects appear larger for some domains of child well-being (such as achievement) than others (such as behavior and health). Furthermore, the effects of poverty are not as large as the simple poor versus nonpoor differences in mortality, morbidity, cognitive development, school achievement, mental health problems, nonmarital births, child abuse, and neglect would indicate.

Based as they are on a randomized experiment, the large and favorable effects of the New Hope package of work supports on boys' achievement and behavior are the most persuasive and hopeful evidence about child well-being revealed in this volume. New Hope provided a set of work supports to low-income families randomized into the treatment group, which could then be compared with control families. Supports for individuals who were employed for thirty or more hours a week included an earnings supplement, child care and health care subsidies, and in-depth case management. Relative to controls, New Hope's incentives increased the employment and earnings of treatment families, who worked little when they first entered the program. We caution, however, that the New Hope experimental treatment was generous and does not represent the full range of reforms implemented by states.

Is the favorable effect on boys a maternal employment effect or a family income effect? The positive effects appear to be linked to boys' increased participation in structured after-school programs, made possible by program subsidies and mothers' higher earnings, which suggest more of an effect of resources than employment per se. The authors suggest that boys are more vulnerable than girls (indeed, the girls outperformed boys on all indexes in both experimental and control groups) and that parents are keenly aware of the dangers facing boys, such as deviant peers and gang involvement.

The more general look taken by Paula Morris et al. (2001) across five experiments reinforces the conclusion that enhancing family resources is the key to promoting child well-being, although they do not replicate New Hope's pattern of gender-specific effects. Taken together, these evaluations show that a work-related intervention for parents can indeed improve children's well-being. They also show what the nation could accomplish if it viewed as unacceptable that people would work full time and still remain in poverty. The work supports tried in New Hope and some of the other experiments are within reach of states' capabilities; specifically, states could expand the EITC, provide child care assistance and health insurance, and offer more effective case management.

Family Structure

A third goal of welfare reform was to reduce the number of out-of-wedlock births in this country and to promote marriage. This volume focuses on the former. By the time PRWORA was passed in 1996, fully one-third of all births in the United States occurred outside of marriage (Ventura et al. 1995). Proponents of welfare reform believed that the new policies of time limits and work requirements would send a message that rearing children as a single, unmarried woman would not be as feasible as it was under AFDC. In addition, welfare reform also allowed states to impose family caps, under which benefits would no longer increase when an additional child was born to a woman already receiving assistance. Finally, teenage mothers were required to live with parents or guardians and stay in school in order to receive benefits. This minor-parent provision was proposed because of evidence that higher levels of welfare benefits encouraged young mothers to move away from their families and set up separate households (Ellwood and Bane 1985).

In chapter 12, Ann Horvath-Rose and Elizabeth Peters summarize results from the first study to use national data to examine the effect of the family cap and the minor-parent provision on nonmarital childbearing. They find that family cap waivers were related to a 9 percentage point decrease in white teen nonmarital birth ratios and a 5 percentage point decrease among African Americans. Somewhat smaller effects were estimated for nonmarital births among older women. Surprisingly, the minor-parent provision was associated with increases in teen nonmarital childbearing ratios. The Horvath-Rose and Peters study will serve as an important benchmark for the next generation of research on this important topic.

WHAT POLICY CHANGES ENHANCE CHILD WELL-BEING?

Most promising about welfare reform is its possibility of bipartisan support for new, comprehensive supports for low-income working families. Several chapters focus on whether individuals from diverse perspectives—liberal, conservative, and feminist political orientations—can agree on a package of supports and benefits to low-income families that promotes the positive development of children.

Given the diverse abilities and situations of low-income families, we framed our challenge to the authors of policy chapters in the form of two questions. First, what more should be done to support families willing and able to secure employment? And second, what programs should be directed toward families that, despite favorable labor markets, are unable to secure employment? Recommendations include the following:

- Fix existing programs that support low-income working families no longer relying on cash benefits.

- Expand services to help low-wage workers find more secure and higher paying employment.

- Consider intensive programs to address the needs of problem families unable to secure employment.

To this list we add our own recommendations, based on the need to design programs that address the developmental needs of low-income families and children.

Fix Existing Programs

Both the Haskins and the Primus and Daugirdas chapters identify as problematic the declining take-up rates among those eligible for Medicaid and food stamps, two key programs designed to support low-income families that no longer receive TANF benefits. Paula England and Nancy Folbre, chapter 15, issue a more general call for promoting children's economic interests through health insurance, food assistance, and other programs.

Haskins and Primus and Daugirdas propose solutions focused on addressing state-based administrative problems but also including federal legislative changes that would ease the administrative burdens on both states and potential recipients. The Primus and Daugirdas agenda is more expansive than Haskins's, but they agree on the need to

- Address problems of low take-up in the Medicaid and Food Stamp programs by helping states ensure that eligible families—both working and not working—secure the medical and food assistance benefits to which they are entitled.

Jennifer Romich and Thomas Weisner, chapter 11, review the mounting evidence that the EITC has promoted many transitions into paid employment and assists families in budgeting for important household expenditures. All of the policy chapters support expansions of the EITC, although they differ in the details. Haskins worries about the EITC's marriage penalty and supports extending the phaseout range for married couples. Primus and Daugirdas propose several changes that would lower the tax credit's implicit tax on earnings and also support bolstering the credit's antipoverty potential by adding a third tier of benefits for families with three or more children. Romich and Weisner propose steps to assist families in using their EITC payments to make beneficial lump-sum purchases. England and Folbre endorse the EITC's role in reducing poverty and promoting economic security among children. Thus, though all authors do not agree on the details, they do agree on the need to

- Optimize the role of the Earned Income Tax Credit in attaining such goals as increasing adult employment, reducing poverty among children, promoting marriage, and facilitating family budgeting.

More selective support is provided for expanding other programs. Primus and Daugirdas and England and Folbre emphasize the need to expand support for child care, while England and Folbre also support universal prekindergarten education programs. Primus and Daugirdas support increasing the minimum wage and indexing it to the rate of inflation. They also propose a number of ways in which child support policies might be improved. England and Folbre would reduce the cost of paid employment with more generous and mandatory parental leave policies and with supports for part-time employment.

No doubt the cost of this collection of proposals is far more than the current political climate will bear. England and Folbre argue that women's, and especially low-income women's, child-rearing role is seriously undervalued in American society, and they push for changes in the political climate that would expand and rationalize government-funded supports for parenting and children. Haskins, however, cautions that further changes must be consistent with the powerful public consensus that produced the welfare reform legislation.

Expand Services to Help Low-Wage Workers

When the economic boom that began in the 1990s diminishes, states will likely find their TANF rolls growing rather than falling. A consensus forecast based on historical evidence (Danziger 1999) indicates that a recession that increases the unemployment rate by 4 percentage points (rising, say, from 5 to 9 percent) would increase TANF caseloads by 20 to 25 percent. The unexpectedly large drops in TANF caseloads in the late 1990s call into question the precision of these historically based estimates but not the likelihood that a recession will reverse recent caseload trends.

Haskins proposes ways in which states can create job centers to facilitate job finding, job retention, and job training. Although many states provide at least some of these services, they tend to be dispersed among myriad bureaucracies and funded separately. Haskins proposes ways to encourage states to consolidate these services to promote more permanent transitions into the labor force and higher paying jobs.

Programs for Families Unable to Secure Employment

With plunging caseloads capturing most of the publicity about welfare reform, states have paid relatively little attention to families facing difficult barriers to employment. Kalil and coauthors (chapter 9) document the prevalence of some of these barriers, which include maternal depression, physical disabilities, domestic violence, low skill levels, or the care of family members who are disabled or ill. Although the magnitude of caseload declines has shown that earlier estimates overstated the number of families unable to make at least temporary transitions from welfare to work, there is no doubt that significant numbers of families need more help than is available through existing programs.

Two kinds of help are discussed in the policy chapters. First are in-kind support programs such as Medicaid and food stamps, which are available to families regardless of their eligibility for TANF. All of the authors support efforts to ensure that all eligible families receive the benefits to which they are entitled. Haskins in chapter

14 points to the efforts of Toby Herr and her colleagues in developing intensive programs that help families in the step-by-step process of developing the skills and confidence that may eventually lead to paid employment. It is unfortunate that states have not seized on the opportunities provided by TANF funding and the booming economy to experiment with such programs and develop models that work in the context of their own circumstances.

Even with intensive, developmentally oriented programs, the severe problems faced by some families preclude the possibility of employment-based independence from cash assistance. For them, programs are needed to provide a safety net and to establish sensible eligibility criteria that neither include truly ineligible families nor exclude truly eligible ones. Thus

- States should develop effective programs that address the needs of multiple-barrier families.

Design Programs That Address the Developmental Needs of Low-Income Families and Children

Although endorsing these recommendations, we would add others, based on the developmental needs of children and families. We are disturbed by the fact that both children and families are treated as homogeneous entities in the rhetoric and by many policies, when in fact families have extremely diverse abilities and needs and, as every parent knows, infants differ from adolescents.

Research on the effects of economic deprivation on child development suggests that children's cognitive development and achievement is more sensitive to spells of poverty occurring in the first few years of life than later (Duncan and Brooks-Gunn 1997). This makes sense, given that children develop at a dizzying rate very early in life and that the family (as opposed to the school or the neighborhood) dominates the lives of preschoolers.

These facts suggest that indicators of and policies on child poverty should differentiate between children of different ages and focus most on situations involving deep and persistent poverty occurring early in childhood. In terms of indicators:

- It is crucial to track rates of poverty among children—especially deep poverty occurring early in childhood—to inform policy discussions regarding children's well-being.

In terms of welfare reform, policies must be considered in light of their differing effects on children of different ages. For example, if poverty during early childhood is crucial, then time limits may prove to be less worrisome than sanctions and categorical restrictions, especially in states that opt for the full five-year time limits or extend time limits with state funds. Unless additional children are born during the period of receipt, mothers accumulating five years of welfare receipt are not likely to have young children in their households. In contrast, sanctions and many of the categorical provisions are much more likely to deny benefits to families with very young children. Not only do young children appear to be most vulnerable to the consequences of deep poverty, but mothers with very young children are also least able to support themselves through work in the labor market. In short,

- Reform policies should be considered in light of their effects on the economic well-being of young children.

An obvious recommendation is that states consider exempting families with very young children from the adverse effects of time limits, sanctions, and categorical restrictions. Only about half of the states exempt mothers of very young children from various provisions of their welfare reform, but in almost no case does the exemption extend beyond the child's first birthday, and in some cases it holds only until the child is three months old. States without exemptions for the first year should consider granting them. It is also useful to consider gearing benefit levels for more universal programs, such as the EITC and child deductions, to children's ages. Budget-conscious policymakers and advocates should note that programs and policies targeted at children's ages cost much less than universal programs targeted at all children.

The development of older children, especially adolescents, appears less sensitive to family economic resources and more strongly influenced by the affection, supervision, role modeling, and mentoring of the adults in their lives. On the positive side, maternal employment and welfare independence may offer positive role models for these older children. On the negative side, maternal employment reduces the amount of parental time available for supervision and mentoring. A striking result from the New Hope experiment is that program parents used the extra resources to secure after-school care and community-based activities for their school-aged boys. In interviews, mothers worried about the temptations of gangs and the drug trade for their boys and did what they could to counter them. Recent evidence (Morris et al. 2001) shows modest increases in adolescent problem behavior related to programs that promote maternal work, regardless of how much these programs support that work financially. More generally,

- Greater maternal employment creates a need for policies that provide supervision and mentoring for older children.

Several of the chapters urge that families be conceived broadly to include the larger kin network within which a nuclear family is embedded. Such a broad conception of families raises important issues for welfare reform policies. The most obvious considerations concern nonresident biological fathers. Interviews with new unmarried parents as part of the Fragile Families study (Garfinkel et al. 1999) reveal surprisingly strong ties between father and mother, with the vast majority of unmarried couples romantically involved and many planning marriage. What happens during the first few years of parenthood that causes so many of these couples to break up and fathers to disengage from their fatherhood role?

Many policies alter the incentives for fathers to reside with or provide explicit financial support for their children. Key to the healthy development of children is both financial and time inputs from parents. In their zeal to ensure that fathers meet their obligations to provide financial support for children,

- Policies should not discourage fathers from residing with, or in other ways spending time with, their children.

Lost in concerns about meeting the needs of low-income families with children is the question of whether welfare reform will, as reformers ardently hope, reduce the number of such families in the first place. Policies that postpone births from the teen to early adult years will reduce child poverty and may increase the amount of time children live with both of their biological parents. One of the most remarkable empirical results in our chapters is the Horvath-Rose and Peters analysis showing nonmarital childbearing in the early 1990s to be responsive to the provisions of the welfare waivers instituted by most states (see chapter 12). If further research indeed confirms that family caps reduce nonmarital childbearing, while provisions calling for teen mothers to live with their parents increase childbearing, then these and similar policies deserve close attention.

For Better and for Worse

We close with two pleas for policymakers, advocates, and policy analysts. First, do not assume that meeting children's developmental needs depends only on whether their mothers make successful transitions from welfare to paid employment. Although this may sound obvious, it has been extremely difficult to focus people's attention on child-based needs and issues. The public discourse needs to be broadened beyond caseloads and maternal employment to address the larger issues of children's poverty and to the very differing developmental needs of children of different ages.

Second, abandon the search for the one answer to the question of how welfare reforms are affecting children's well-being and realize that reforms simultaneously help some children and hurt others. Rather, ask these questions: Which families and children will adjust to welfare reform? And why? Which parents will adapt only if additional work supports are provided? And which children will be at high risk? Only a collection of diverse programs, addressing the equally diverse needs of children of different ages and in different family circumstances, can determine whether welfare reform will accomplish its lofty goals.

REFERENCES

Atkinson, Anthony B., Lee Rainwater, and Timothy Smeeding. 1995. *Income Distribution in OECD Countries: Evidence from the Luxembourg Income Study.* Paris: Organization for Economic Cooperation and Development.

Brauner, Sarah, and Pamela Loprest. 1999. *Where Are They Now? What States' Studies of People Who Left Welfare Tell Us.* Washington, D.C.: Urban Institute.

Brooks-Gunn, Jeanne, and Greg J. Duncan. 1997. "The Effects of Poverty on Children and Youth." *Future of Children* 7: 55–71.

Chase-Lansdale, P. Lindsay. 1999. "How Developmental Psychologists Think About Family Processes and Child Development in Low-Income Families." Working paper 82. Chicago: Joint Center for Poverty Research.

Cherlin, Andrew J., Pamela Winston, Ronald J. Angel, Linda M. Burton, P. Lindsay Chase-Lansdale, Robert A. Moffitt, and William Julius Wilson. 2000. "The New Welfare Rules: Recipients' Knowledge, Attitudes, and Reported Behavior." Policy brief 00-1. Welfare, Children, and Families Study, Johns Hopkins University, Baltimore.

Danziger, Sandra, Mary Corcoran, Sheldon Danziger, and Colleen M. Heflin. Forthcoming. "Work, Income, and Material Hardship After Welfare Reform." *Journal of Consumer Affairs*.

Danziger, Sheldon H., ed. 1999. *Economic Conditions and Welfare Reform*. Kalamazoo, Mich: W. E. Upjohn Institute for Employment Research.

Duncan, Greg J., and Jeanne Brooks-Gunn. 1997. *Consequences of Growing Up Poor*. New York: Russell Sage Foundation.

———. 2000. "Family Poverty, Welfare Reform, and Child Development." *Child Development* 71: 188–96.

Ellwood, David T., and Mary Jo Bane. 1985. "The Impact of AFDC on Family Structure and Living Arrangements" In *Research in Labor Economics,* vol. 7, edited by Ron G. Ehrenberg. Greenwich, Conn.: JAI Press.

Furstenberg, Frank F., Jr., Jeanne Brooks-Gunn, and S. Philip Morgan. 1987. "Adolescent Mothers and Their Children in Later Life." *Family Planning Perspectives* 19:142–51.

Garfinkel, Irwin, Sara McLanahan, and Kristen Harknett. 1999. "Fragile Families and Welfare Reform." Working paper. Office of Population Research, Princeton University.

Gennetian, Lisa, and Cynthia Miller. 2000. *Reforming Welfare and Rewarding Work: Final Report on the Minnesota Family Investment Program*. New York: Manpower Demonstration and Research Corporation.

Greenberg, Mark, and Michael C. Laracy. 2000. "Welfare Reform, Next Steps Offer New Opportunities: A Role for Philanthropy in Preparing for the Reauthorization of TANF in 2002." Washington, D.C.: Neighborhood Funders Group. Available at: *www.nfg.org/publications/welfare.htm*.

Hamilton, Gayle. 2000. *Do Mandatory Welfare-to-Work Programs Affect the Well-being of Children? A Synthesis of Child Research Conducted as Part of the National Evaluation of Welfare-to-Work Strategies*. Washington: Office of the Secretary for Planning and Evaluation, Administration for Children and Families, U.S. Department of Health and Human Services; and Office of the Undersecretary and Office of Vocational and Adult Education, U.S. Department of Education.

Haskins, Ron. 1995. "Losing Ground or Moving Ahead? Welfare Reform and Children." In *Escape from Poverty: What Makes a Difference for Children?* edited by P. Lindsay Chase-Lansdale and Jeanne Brooks-Gunn. Cambridge: Cambridge University Press.

Hoffman, Lois W., and Lisa M. Youngblade, 1999. *Mothers at Work: Effects on Children's Well-being*. New York: Cambridge University Press.

Huston, Aletha C., Greg J. Duncan, Robert Granger, Johannes Bos, Vonnie McLoyd, Rashmita Mistry, Danielle Crosby, Christina Gibson, Katherine Magnuson, Jennifer Romich, and

A. Ventura. Forthcoming. "Work-Based Antipoverty Programs for Parents Can Enhance the School Performance and Social Behavior of Children." *Child Development*.

McGroder, Shannon M., Martha J. Zaslow, Kristin A. Moore, and Suzanne M. LeMenestrel, 2000. *National Evaluation of Welfare-to-Work Strategies' Impacts on Young Children and Their Families Two Years After Enrollment: Findings from the Child Outcomes Study*. Washington: Administration for Children and Families, Office of the Assistant Secretary for Planning and Evaluation, U.S. Department of Health and Human Services.

Morris, Pamela and Charles Michalopoulos. 2000. *"The Self-sufficiency Project at Thirty-six Months: Effects on Children of a Program That Increased Parental Employment and Income (Executive Summary)."* New York: Social Research and Demonstration Corporation.

Morris, Paula, Aletha Huston, Greg Duncan, Danielle Crosby, and Johannes Bos. 2001. *How Welfare and Work Policies Affect Children: A Synthesis of Research*. New York: Manpower Demonstration Research Corporation.

Newman, Katherine S. 1999. *No Shame in My Game: The Working Poor in the Inner City*. New York: Knopf and Russell Sage Foundation.

Quint, Janet, Johannes Bos, and Denise Polit. 1997. *New Chance: Final Report on a Comprehensive Program for Young Mothers in Poverty and Their Children*. New York: Manpower Demonstration Research Corporation.

Rolston, Howard. 1999. "Effects of Changes to the Welfare System." Testimony Before the Subcommittee on Human Resources of the House Committee on Ways and Means (June 2). Available at: *www.house.gov/ways_means/humres/106cong/5-27-95/5-27rols.htm*.

Ventura, Stephanie J., Christine A. Bachrach, Laura Hill, Kelleen Kaye, Pamela Holcomb, and Elisa Koff. 1995. "The Demography of Out-of-Wedlock Childbearing." In *Report to Congress on Out-of-Wedlock Childbearing*. Washington: U.S. Government Printing Office.

Wallace, Geoffrey, and Rebecca M. Blank. 1999. "What Goes Up Must Come Down?" In *Economic Conditions and Welfare Reform*, edited by Sheldon H. Danziger. Kalamazoo, Mich.: W. E. Upjohn Institute for Employment Research.

Wilson, William J. 1987. *The Truly Disadvantaged: The Inner City, the Underclass, and Public Policy*. Chicago: University of Chicago Press.

———. 1996. *When Work Disappears: The World of the New Urban Poor*. New York: Knopf.

Winston, Pamela, Ronald J. Angel, Linda M. Burton, P. Lindsay Chase-Lansdale, Andrew J. Cherlin, Robert A. Moffitt, and William Julius Wilson. 1999. "Welfare, Children, and Families: A Three-City Study, Overview and Design." Johns Hopkins University, Baltimore.

Index

Boldface numbers refer to figures and tables.

Index

Internal Revenue Service (IRS), 203
Iowa, sanctions analysis, 84–86. *See also* state analysis

Jencks, C., 20, 23, 105
job centers, 286, 317
Job Opportunities and Basic Skills (JOBS), 18, 182
job retention, 286, 317
job search, 16–17, 286, 317
job training, 286, 317
job transitions, 160, 165, 166, 169, 174–75

Kaus, M., 20–21
Klawitter, M., 108

labor force participation, 201, 274–76, 295
Lein, L., 207, 216
Lewis, O., 106
Li, J., 50*n*7
liberal agenda, 10–12, 12–21. *See also* Democrats
Liebman, J., 293, 294
life-cycle hypothesis of savings and consumption, 204, 218*n*2
long-term poor, 284–85, 317–18
Losing Ground (Murray), 16, 106
Lovell, B., 58
low-SES working families: defined, 112–13; family process and time usage, 114–17; psychological characteristics, 120, **121–22**; social capital connections, 117–20; spending of, 120; vs. welfare-dependent families, 104–5, 126–28

mandatory work programs: and definition of work, 291; devolution analysis, 74–76; and nonmarital childbearing, 225, 226, 236; Republican vs. Democratic view of, 274; and school achievement, 158; welfare recipients' knowledge of, 310; welfare reform debate, 16–17,

20, 21, **26,** 28; and well-being, 40–42, 58–60, 132–33
Manpower Demonstration Research Corporation (MDRC), 16–17, 40, 54, 134, 205
marginal tax rates, of income growth, 250–51, 260
marriage: and family structure theory of child well-being, 38–40; nonmarital childbearing analysis, 224, 226, 231, 235, **239**; promotion of, 285; State-Level Child Outcomes Project, 59; welfare-reliant women's post-TANF views of, 144–48
marriage penalty, 255, 262*n*9, 285, 294
married mothers, labor force participation of, 274–76, 295
Maryland, sanctions analysis, 90. *See also* state analysis
Massachusetts, time limits analysis, 92–93. *See also* state analysis
McGranahan, L., 217
McLanahan, S., 285
Mead, L., 16
Medicaid: access to, 45–48, 281–82, 316; administrative issues, 282; eligibility, 248, 255, 269, 282; enrollment, 281; establishment of, 11; federal funding, 271, 282, 297–98; state analysis of sanctioned and time-limited cases, 85, 86, 89, 91, 92–93, 98; for working poor, 266–67
medical care, state analysis of sanctioned and time-limited cases, 89
Medicare, 10–11, 261*n*3, 295–96
Memoir on Pauperism (Tocqueville), 12
mental health: maternal work and children's behavior, 162, 166, 310, 311–12; of welfare recipients, 104–5, 108
minimum wage, 254–55, 316–17
Minnesota Family Investment Program (MFIP), 158, 183, 312

minor parent provision, of state waivers, 225, 226, 232, 236, 315
mobility analysis. *See* intergenerational analysis
Modigliani, F., 218*n*1
"Moving Ahead: How America Can Reduce Poverty Through Work" (Shaw, Johnson, and Grandy), 22–23
The Moynihan Report and the Politics of Controversy, 106
Murray, C., 14–15, 16, 30, 106, 108

Nathan Deal bill, **26,** 27
National Evaluation of Welfare-to-Work Strategies (NEWWS), 157–58, 182, 312
National Institute of Child Health and Human Development (NICHD), 53, 54
National Research Council, 133
National Survey of America's Families, 283
National Survey of Families and Households (NSFH), 112, 113
New Chance program, 182–83
New Hope project: earnings and public assistance benefits, 43; EITC analysis, 205, 206; evaluation of, 183–95, 312, 314; purpose of, 180; school performance and behavior, 158
New Republic, 21
NEWWS (National Evaluation of Welfare-to-Work Strategies), 157–58, 182, 312
Next Generation study, 192
NICHD (National Institute of Child Health and Human Development), 53, 54
noncitizens, comparison of welfare reform bills, **26**
noncustodial fathers, 259, 261*n*5
nonmarital childbearing: causes of, 222; economic and demographic variables, 228–31, 235–36; and family structure theory of